Leigh Hunt

The Wishing-Cap Papers

Leigh Hunt

The Wishing-Cap Papers

ISBN/EAN: 9783337217747

Printed in Europe, USA, Canada, Australia, Japan

Cover: Foto ©Thomas Meinert / pixelio.de

More available books at **www.hansebooks.com**

THE WISHING-CAP PAPERS

Mr. Hunt is a man of the most indisputably superior worth; a *Man of Genius* in a very strict sense of that word, and in all senses which it bears or implies; of brilliant, varied gifts; of graceful fertility; of clearness, lovingness, truthfulness; of childlike, open character; also of most pure and even exemplary private deportment; a man who can be other than *loved* only by those who have not seen him, or seen him from a distance through a false medium.

THOMAS CARLYLE.

THE

WISHING-CAP PAPERS

BY

LEIGH HUNT

NOW FIRST COLLECTED

Though I cannot promise as much entertainment, or as much elegance
as others have done, yet the reader may be assured he shall have as much
of both as I can. He shall, at least, find me alive while I study his
entertainment ; for I solemnly assure him I was never yet possessed of the
secret at once of writing and sleeping

GOLDSMITH

BOSTON 1888
LEE AND SHEPARD PUBLISHERS
10 MILK STREET NEXT " THE OLD SOUTH MEETING HOUSE "

CHARLES T. DILLINGHAM
NEW YORK 718 AND 720 BROADWAY

TO THE READER.

Not only those who, like Lord Macaulay, "have a kindness for Mr. Leigh Hunt," but all lovers of the pleasant art of essay writing, should find much to amuse and interest them in this volume, which contains articles, hitherto uncollected, on an agreeable variety of subjects, from the Indicator, Examiner, Literary Examiner, Companion, Tatler, London Journal, Monthly Repository, New Monthly Magazine, and Edinburgh Review.

Most of the Wishing-Cap Papers are written in Leigh Hunt's happiest manner, and abound in rich and felicitous descriptions of nature, in loving comments on favorite authors and books, and in thoughtful and good-natured speculations on human life. Indeed, some of the essays in the collection are, it seems to me, more terse in style, more vigorous in thought, and more masculine in tone, than even the best papers in the Indicator * or the

---

* Not the original edition of the Indicator, but a selection from that work made by the author himself.

Seer; they show, moreover, that the genial essayist had "true capabilities of wrath," and could battle·
bravely for the right, as the hacks of the Tory press
learned to their cost. If, as M. Taine asserts, wit is
"the art of stating things in a pleasant way," this is
a very witty book, and Leigh Hunt is a great wit, for
almost all his sentences are charming examples of
the brilliant Frenchman's definition of wit.

Through the courtesy of Mr. James T. Fields, I
have had the opportunity of consulting Leigh Hunt's
own copies of the Tatler and the Literary Examiner, containing some marginal emendations in the
author's own handwriting, to which the readers
of the Wishing-Cap Papers are indebted for sundry
valuable corrections, and for a few little characteristic
touches added to several of the chapters.

J. E. B.

MELROSE, December 4, 1872.

THE WISHING-CAP.

9

"At Maiano I wrote the articles which appeared in the *Examiner*, under the title of the *Wishing-Cap*. Probably the reader knows nothing about them; but they contained some germs of a book he may not be unacquainted with, called *The Town*, as well as some articles since approved of in the volume entitled *Men, Women, and Books*.

"The title was very genuine. When I put on my cap, and pitched myself in imagination into the thick of Covent Garden, the pleasure I received was so vivid — I turned the corner of a street so much in the ordinary course of things, and was so tangib'y present to the pavement, the shop windows, the people, and a thousand agreeable recollections which looked me naturally in the face, that sometimes when I walk there now, the impression seems hardly more real. I used to feel as if I actually pitched my soul there, and that spiritual eyes might have seen it shot over from Tuscany, into York Street, like a rocket. It is much pleasanter, however, on waking up, to find soul and body together in one's native land: yes, even than among thy olives and vines, Boccaccio!" — *The Autobiography of* LEIGH HUNT.

[Of course none of the *Wishing-Caps* which the author collected and published in *Men, Women, and Books*, are included in this volume. We have, however, inserted the articles on different parts of London. It is true, most of the persons and places mentioned in these graceful and characteristic little papers are more fully described in *The Town*. But "the first sprightly runnings" are in the earlier sketches, which have also more gusto, and are richer in personal reminiscences than the chapters on the same localities in that book. — ED.]

THE WISHING-CAP.

—◦◦—

No. I.

INTRODUCTION.

I have cut through the air like a falcon. I would have it seem strange to you. But 'tis true. I would not have you believe it neither. But 'tis miraculous and true. Desire to see you brought me. — DECKER's *Old Fortunatus.*

AS when a traveller, long expected, and yet but half expected from abroad, suddenly enters a room full of his old friends, instantly all the room is in motion towards him, mouths are opened, hands are stretched forward, card tables deserted, and old ladies left in a state of inveteracy: he, with all his feelings on tiptoe, and happy to be torn in pieces, grasps as many hands as he can at once, turns to this friend, makes half an answer to that, cuts short the questions of soft lips, and revels in all the rewards of the meritoriousness of absence ; thus, I trust, my old friends of the Examiner will feel with me, when they see the hand at the bottom of this paper.*

* Leigh Hunt's well-known signature — 🖘. ED.

After a thousand questions are asked on both sides, delightful memories brought up, and others that will not bear touching upon spared, I hear the most good-natured person in the company exclaim, " Bless me ! you are not at all changed." I do bless thee, thou handsomest of thy sex. Between you and me, I should not care how dilapidated I looked with some persons in a private meeting, — and for a short time. I could make a merit of the silver hairs that come amongst my black ones, and expect a double tenderness of look for my sunken cheeks. But after all, one does not like to grow old. Man is in no haste to be venerable. The fact is, I am not old, nor do I wish anybody to believe that I am. But at forty there is a pleasure in affecting age on purpose to be disbelieved. (I say forty, because I am only nine and thirty.) We talk of " declining into the vale of years," that people may say, " You decline into the vale of years ! " and that we may be complimented on the youthfulness of our appearance. The provocation lies in saying we are middle-aged. It is a malignant benediction of the poets, —

"God bless your middle-ageish face ! "

I believe there are many persons abroad who regret the not having returned to their native country in time, but who would rather be shut up for life in a German fortress, than appear again in a public place in England. Thirty and forty years ago they were Adonises, and cannot, for the life of them, take to being reverend. Being at a distance from home, and not having contemporary faces to compare with, they try to think that everybody grows old but themselves.

They would fancy that the shore moves, and not they. I own to this weakness, though I never was an Adonis, nor ever shall be, which is more.

But I can conceive no circumstances but one, that at any time of life would conquer in me the desire to be among my old scenes and friends. I used to think that with all my love of particular places, I should not care where I went, provided I could take my friends with me. But I find it otherwise. The fine buildings in Genoa made me long to take a walk down a London alley. The vineyards and olives of Tuscany gave me a calenture for my old green fields. Walking about under the galleries and government offices of Florence, I yearned infinitely to be at the Examiner office in Covent Garden; *and so here I am.*

But it will be asked whether I am really here; whether I am arrived in *propria persona,* — come home, — seated visibly in the Examiner office. Doubtless I am. I have just poked the fire, and am toasting a foot upon each hob, with the Morning Chronicle in my hand. Yesterday I was in all parts of the town. If my presence is doubted, and the gentleman I run against yesterday in Fleet Street has any manliness in him, he will come forward and state that I nearly knocked the breath out of his body in turning the corner of Shoe Lane.

I am as surely here in London as I shall be in Madrid, in Athens, in North or South America, when I inform the reader to that effect: perhaps I shall be in one of these places to-morrow. Incredulous readers may smile, especially when I inform them, that

so far from condescending in general to travel on foot,
I fly. But they would be hard put to it to prove the
contrary. Let them first account for the power of
the human mind to fancy itself in Arabia, and then
they may undertake to prove it impossible for me, by
dint of a thought, actually to be there. Cogitation
has been held by some to be nothing but local motion. Their motion was a vulgar one, being as different from mine as that of a telegraph is from lightning; but I desire to know how an uninitiated person is to pronounce these travels of mine impossible;
how he is to prove, and be assured that when I fancy
myself in Arabia, I, that is, my personal consciousness, the best part of me, the *anima* of my *mundus*,
the true immaterial life and soul, of which my body
is but a vulgar symbol, is not, at that moment, to all
intents and purposes, in Arabia. " I pause for a reply," as a man says, when he expects none. " I
think, therefore I am," said the French philosopher:
now I think I am in Arabia, therefore I am there. I
beg to know the difference between these two propositions.

I pitch myself wherever I please, like a rocket or
a falling star.

In short, let those who doubt my reasoning look at
my Cap. With them, anything that is visible puts
an end to mystery. This is an age of mechanism and
manufacture and, therefore, they say, there can be
no longer anything fanciful. *Ecce signum.* This
Cap is one out of several now existing, and by no
means the most extraordinary of its kind. It is not
the famous Wishing-Cap of Fortunatus, but a poor

relation. Sir Walter Scott has that, and the Purse
into the bargain. He is in the habit of going to
court in it, to refresh his good opinion of mankind.
The two finest Wishing-Caps are in possession of
Mr. Wordsworth and Mr. Coleridge. The one belonging to the latter is a great curiosity, and carried
him into those dreadful seas where he saw the Ancient Mariner. I look upon it with more reverence
than all the curiosities in the Museum. Mr. Southey
has one, with which he has taken some pretty long
flights into the East. I wish he would relate his travels in prose instead of verse.

I do not know to what class to refer the Cap of my
friend Elia, of the London Magazine; certainly not
to a modern one, with bells to it, much in use at
courts, though it has a considerable resemblance to
one of the same cut, worn by a retainer to the famous
King Lear, and also to that other belonging to the
celebrated Yorick. I mean Hamlet's Yorick. Nobody who hears him in it will say, " Where be your
gibes now? Your flashes of merriment that were
wont to set the table in a roar?" Nobody who sees
well into the stuff of it, will take it for any other than
a Cap fit for the wisest head in England, provided the
rain is to rain every day. Having less thought, but
stouter muscles, I, for my part, must still endeavor,
till I die, to push the world a little farther into the
sunshine. It is for this reason I am in all parts of it;
one of hundreds of beings who are trying to furnish
philosophers with a lever.

But the reader must know that this Cap of mine
not only carries me where I please, like that of For-

tunatus, and introduces me to the invisible world, like the Caps of the mountain spirits. It makes as little of time as it does of space. It pitches me back into ages. I make love very often a hundred years ago, and may dine to-morrow at the table of Anacreon. My tea I am fond of taking with Pope and the Miss Blounts. A person in Tuscany often rouses me out of the club, at the Mermaid in Cornhill, where I am listening to Beaumont and Ben Jonson. I make nothing of being in Arcady at twelve o'clock, and with Horace between two and three. I meet old King Ban " on the top of Fiesole." And this is as real as all the rest. It was thought a modest request in the two lovers to say, —

> " Ye gods, annihilate but space and time,
> And make two lovers happy." *

But let the reader peruse only two or three metaphysical treatises (one of them being on time), and then say if it is not easy to annihilate both. It is a vulgar supposition, that one man of forty and another man of forty are of the same age; and that if two

---

* Readers of Carlyle will remember Herr Teufelsdröckh's philosophical speculations upon space and time in one of the most stupendous chapters of Sartor Resartus. " Fortunatus had a wishing-hat," says the learned Professor, "which when he put on, and wished himself anywhere, behold he was there. By this means had Fortunatus triumphed over space, he had annihilated space; for him there was no Where, but all was Here. Were a hatter to establish himself in the Wahngasse of Weissnichtwo, and make felts of this sort for all mankind, what a world we should have of it ! Still stranger, should, on the opposite side of the street, another hatter establish himself ; and, as his fellow-craftsman made space annihilating hats, make time-annihilating ! Of both would I purchase, were it with my last groschen ; but chiefly of this latter. To clap on your felt, and, simply by wishing that you were Any*where*, straightway to be *there* ! Next to clap on your other felt, and, simply by wishing that you were any*when*, straightway to be *then* !" — ED.

persons set out at four o'clock to dinner, and arrive
at the same place at the hour commonly called five,
they have both taken the same time to arrive in. Notions of boys and stockjobbers! We have no idea
of time but that of space. In thinking of the hour
between one and two, we measure a distance on our
watches. Now, as in the same space of measure-
ment may be crammed many particles, and in the
same journey one road may be straight and another
crooked, so in the same space of time (the common phrase), we may include many different masses
of duration and varieties of experience. One man's
time is so much tin, another's lead, another's gold.
The link on which he tells his thoughts is his clock;
and the more he tells the longer he lives. The hour
of the many-thoughted man contains many hours.
His metal is heavy and full of matter.

" Time, then," some of my readers may say, " is first
nothing, and then it is something. It is easy to be
annihilated, and yet is heavy as lead or gold." I do
not assert that it is nothing, though it is easy of anni-
hilation. I find it to be much : and yet how shall not .
this much be altered or melted away. How shall not
this lead be turned into gold by the sunshine of love
and kindness! How shall not this gold, by the force
of imagination, be beaten out into endless ·contact
with ages !

Perhaps with no man living has time been a heavier
or a lighter thing than with me. My metal resembles
quicksilver, except that it is more malleable to
warmth than cold; though cold also renders it very
grave and solid. Like quicksilver, it is not precious

2

and weighty as gold; and yet it easily unites with it, and helps gold itself to gild a variety of common things. Furthermore, it is subject to change of the barometer. But I am running my metallic simile too far for a spirit. A spirit I certainly am, by universal acknowledgment; though what sort of one has been much contested. "Time," as the philosopher says, "will show." Certainly I am not a malignant spirit, though I trifle now and then with a Caliban. Neither am I the devil on two sticks, confined to my bottle; nor the spirit, that according to the Italian poet, dwelt in the smoke of roast meat. But like certain spirits in poetry and romance, I have seen a good deal of the world, visible and invisible. Like them, I see knowledge. Like them I am fond of music, of the air, of the trees and flowers, and of liberty. In some things, I am not unlike the Sylph Husband of Marmontel. Like a spirit, I can dilate myself, till mountains become mole-hills; or shrink into such diminutive compass, as to stand by the side of a brook, and live in imagination on the banks of it, with the little insects, as if it were some mighty river. Millions of times have I ridden on the bat's back, and gone to sleep in a buttercup. But my tears inform me that I am human, to say nothing of my frailties. It is not for me to think of the drowning,* and to doubt whether or no I feel

> "All as sharply,
> Passioned as they."

I shall take up, in this paper, any subject to which I feel an impulse, politics not excepted. It would be

---

* Of Shelley. — Ed.

idle to expect that a periodical paper, however un-
political, would go into any quarters but those of
the Reformers, when published in a reforming journal.
My first intention was to render it a sort of with-
drawing-room, or retirement from the more public
part of the Examiner; but I thought it better, upon
consideration, to take the opportunity of giving myself
full scope, political as well as otherwise. It is a foolish reproach to men of letters, that they meddle with
politics. Who is to do so if they do not? And how
is a man of any warmth of sympathy (unless he is
hopeless of all change) to see what is going on in the
world, and be able honestly to repress his blame and
his praise? The necessity becomes stronger if he has
been accustomed to do so. Politics, however, will
occupy but a small part of my lucubrations.*

I am a spirit, not without hands or feet; but my
strength lies in my power of flight, — in my Wishing-Cap. The greatest distinction (talents apart) between me and other spirits that have manifested themselves to these latter times, is not in age or bodily

---

* Most of Leigh Hunt's literary contemporaries meddled with politics. Sir
Walter Scott dabbled in them. Southey contributed political essays to the Quarterly Review, and Coleridge wrote political articles for the Morning Post and
the Morning Chronicle. Wordsworth was the author of a political pamphlet on
the peace of Cintra, and Moore dashed off many a witty political squib. Wilson was a rash and bitter political writer; and Hazlitt published a volume
of Political Essays. Sydney Smith wrote political pamphlets, and published
political articles in the newspapers. Even "the gentle Elia" wrote political
squibs and epigrams for the Examiner and the New Times. Politics, to those
who are desirous of becoming acquainted with anything that concerns mankind, are, as Hunt says elsewhere, "a part of humane literature; and they who
can be taught to like them in common with wit and philosophy, insensibly do
an infinite deal of good by mingling them with the common talk of life, and helping to render the stream of public opinion irresistible." — ED.

appearance (for those, as I said before, are notions) ; but in my being a very truth-telling spirit. I tell nothing of myself or others, which is not pure matter-of-fact, or, at least, which appears to me to be such ; a verity, which I would have the reader bear in mind. He will easily distinguish between the things which I talk of in a mere spirit of fancy (as the world calls it), and what I lay before them in the grosser shapes of truth.

With regard to speaking of myself and my experiences (which I shall do very freely whenever inclined), I have several reasons for it. In the first place, it is impossible for me to sustain a fictitious character, like that of Bickerstaff and others, in the great periodical works. Secondly, authors sometimes, as well as kings, "lack subjects." Thirdly, it is advisable that authors should write only upon subjects with which they are acquainted. Fourthly, people are often much better acquainted with themselves than the old adage implies ; though many, for that reason, take care never to show it. Fifthly, I am much alone, and have been in the habit of speculating upon my feelings and adventures. I believe that if the first person we meet in the street were to put down upon paper the experiences he has had in life, his school-days, journeys, &c., they would be found interesting. I have been perplexed whether to speak of myself in the singular or the plural number, — whether to subject myself to the impatience of people vainer, by saying I ; or to hamper my verisimilitudes and my euphonics, with saying, *We were*, *We would*, and *We once.*

The last reason, or apology, which I have to lay
before him for talking of myself, I shall repeat in the
words of a great master of human nature : —

" The most sovereign remedy for self-love is to do
quite contrary to what these people direct, who in for-
bidding others to speak of themselves, do consequently
at the same time interdict thinking of themselves too.
Pride dwells in the thought : the tongue can have but
a very little share in it. They fancy, that to think of
one's self is to be delighted with one's self; to frequent and converse with a man's self, to be over indulgent. But this excess springs only in those who only
take of themselves a superficial view, and dedicate their
main inspection to their affairs ; that call meditation,
raving and idleness, looking upon themselves as a
third person only, and a stranger. No particular quality can make any man proud, that will at the same time
put so many other weak and imperfect ones, as he has
in him in the other scale." — *Montaigne's Essays*,
book ii. chap. 6.

1824.

No. II.

A WALK IN COVENT GARDEN.

Ante oculos errant domus, urbs, et forma locorum,
Succeduntque suis singula facta locis. — OVID.

Streets, houses, city, glide before my face,
With all that's done in each successive place.

THERE are three things that give a pleasant
look to the most ordinary commonplaces:
health, imagination, and coming from abroad.
I have been flying from place to place in London
for the last week, and have made my Cap as dingy
as a city swallow. At one time I dipped about Covent Garden; now I was at the West End; and then
again I was at St. Paul's. I turn about the streets, as
if I had never seen them before. To the list of
human pleasures I have to add the satisfaction which
arises from traversing a dirty lane.

There is Maiden Lane here in the neighborhood.
I do not care for it because the Examiner office was
once there, or because the Royal Academy there held
its infant sittings; much less on account of the cider-
cellar; but, in the first place, I have traversed it a thousand times; secondly, here are some poor book-stalls
and picture-shops; and thirdly, when Voltaire lived
here "at the sign of the White Peruke," I guess that
he did so to be in the neighborhood of Congreve and
other wits, who had their lodgings in Southampton
Street and Bow Street. My head is filled with them
all. I imagine the thin Frenchman picking his way
towards his abode in a lank peruke. I fancy that it

was not far off that he astonished the mob, who
pelted him, with haranguing them in our language,
producing as lively a movement in his favor as if they
were all turned into Parisians. He got on the step
of a doorway, and appealed " to the nobleness of the
national character," complimenting them on their in-
stitutions and love of liberty. I believe they proposed
to carry him home on their shoulders.

I like everything about Covent Garden. It pleases
me even that the ground belongs to the Russells, a
liberal and lettered family. I like the green market
in the middle, the noble portico (not to be thought
less of, after visiting Italy), the Grecian-built church,
the spacious streets, the narrower ones with their
book-stalls, the neighborhood of the theatres. Other
associations I have mentioned elsewhere.* Though
I am fond of going to the play, I do not care in general for play books; but I delight to see whole shops
of them here. They are in harmony with the place.
It is moving and alive with the best times of English
comedy, and one of the pleasantest of English Society
and verse. There, at Will's Coffee-House,† used to
sit Dryden in his arm-chair, encouraging a young author with a pinch out of his snuff-box. Addison is
keeping it up over the way at Button's, with Steele,
Garth, Congreve, and Colonel Brett (who married
Savage's mother, and bought Cibber's wig). ‡ Here
come, to attend a rehearsal, Mrs. Barry, who acted

---

* In the Pleasant Memories Connected with the Various Parts of the Metropolis, in The Indicator. — ED.

† It was on the north side of Russell Street, near Bow Street. In Malone's
time was numbered 23, and occupied by a perfumer.

‡ The reader will find a lively account of the purchase in the eleventh chapter of Cibber's Apology. — ED.

such fine love-parts with her husband; Mrs. Bracegirdle, Congreve's mistress, and Mrs. Oldfield, the
Flavia of the Tatler, who gave Savage a pension.*   I
cannot help thinking with Dr. Young, that it was a
pity Congreve did not leave his money " to poor Mrs.
Bracegirdle," instead of a duchess who bought diamond necklaces with it.   But the insinuation implied
on the part of Young (a preferment-hunter, who wrote
like a hermit) may be regarded with suspicion.   In
Spence's Anecdotes, Congreve has the praise of all
who knew him as an honest, good-natured man : we
know not what he may have otherwise given Mrs.
Bracegirdle, nor how much regard for him was mixed
up with the singularities of the Duchess of Marlborough, who had an image of him seated with her at table after his death.   To be sure, there seems a vanity in
those bequests to people of rank ; and Johnson says
the money was wanted by his relations.   Let us hope
that those who were most intimate with him knew
him best.   The story of his reception of Voltaire
(perhaps in Southampton Street, when he lived near
Mrs. Bracegirdle) is not in his favor.   I will take this
opportunity of repeating an anecdote of Wycherley,
which is ill told in Spence's book.   Pope is made to
inform us, that one day as Wycherley passed the
Duchess of Cleveland's carriage in the ring, " she
leaned out of the window, and cried out, loud enough
to be heard distinctly by him, ' Sir, you're a rascal ;
you're a villain.' "   Spence's memory appears to have
deceived him.   The other account says, that she

---

* See Tatler, No. 212. [In The Town, however, Hunt doubts if Mrs. Oldfield was Flavia, and conjectures that the lady immortalized under that name
was a Miss Osborne, who married the Bishop of Atterbury. — ED.]

accosted him in a much coarser manner than this. Wycherley next day waited on her, and begged to know the reason. " Why, sir," said she, " in one of your plays you say that the appellation I gave you belongs to all men of wit; so I thought it fairly bestowed." The compliment was not ill turned, such as it was: but " her grace " must have been a very disagreeable woman. Wycherley, however, was not nicer than his master.

It is with difficulty that I call to mind Inigo Jones, as the architect of Covent Garden. Even Donne, in the mansion of his father-in-law, Sir Thomas Drury, in Drury Lane, with all his graver wit and his romantic passion, is thrust out of my mind by the crowd of beaux and comedians. I can sooner find a pleasure in recollecting that Rowe frequented a tavern in Long Acre, and that in the same quarter dwelt Prior's Chloe. Who she was, I do not stop to inquire. Suffice it for me, that I know her in his verses. The character of all this neighborhood is essentially gay and social, scented with snuff-boxes, and rustling with hoop petticoats. The tragedy of those times does not interfere with it. Tragedy herself wore a hoop petticoat then, and was a very courtly personage. I confess, that in latter times, Mr. Kemble carried the old school of Booth and Quin to a pitch of the didactic which disturbs my associations. Booth was a kind of sublimated player at a fair; and Quin a bonvivant.* But Munden and Drury Lane redeem all.

---

* There is a pleasant bit concerning Quin, in Fielding's too little read Voyage to Lisbon. " The only fish," he says, speaking of a great purchase thereof for a " small spill of money," "the only fish which bore any price was a John Dory, as it is called. I bought one of at least four pounds weight, for as many shillings. It resembles a turbot in shape, but exceeds it in firmness and flavor.

I should add Sheridan, but he touches too nearly on grave times and melancholy recollections.   Yet surely he, and Drury Lane, and comedy, and carelessness, were all made for each other.

Those melancholy exits of the gay are vile things. Poor Mrs. Jordan ! did nobody feel for thee in thy sad and mysterious exile, but those who could do nothing to help it?   Her honest-hearted laugh rings at this moment in my ears !

I forget whether it was myself, or whether somebody told me it was he, who saw Jack Bannister (I had almost said Mr. Jack Bannister) standing one day, leaning on his stick, and looking up in a melancholy manner at Old Drury.   Old Drury is new Drury in face, but it is old in situation and fame ; and he had helped to carry all the old spirit into the new house.   A plague on those real old ages that belong to nothing but men !   And Elliston too : — I read in the papers, that he plays his old parts with all the spirit of his former days.   That can hardly be, considering that he did not take care to remain thin like Lewis.   Lewis's old age, after all, was an imposition, though he died of it.   But Elliston is one of those, too, who will never be old, in some senses of the

---

The price had the appearance of being considerable when opposed to the extraordinary cheapness of others of value, but was, in truth, so very reasonable when estimated by its goodness, that it left me under no other surprise than how the gentlemen of this county (Devonshire), not greatly eminent for the delicacy of their taste, had discovered the preference of the Dory to all other fish: but I was informed that Mr. Quin, whose distinguishing tooth hath been so justly celebrated, had lately visited Plymouth, and had done those honors to the Dory which are so justly due to it from that sect of modern philosophers, who, with Sir Epicure Mammon, or Sir Epicure Quin, their head, seem more to delight in a fish-pond than a garden, as the old Epicureans are said to have done." -- Ed

word. I wish with all my heart he was as young as
he was twenty years ago, and I with him, and that
we knew as much then as we do now. I do not
think either of us would be a bit the worse or less
young for it. I would have praised him as much as
I did then for his comedy, and for his making love
better than any man on the stage; but he would not
have acted tragedy so often, nor would I have written
those fierce criticisms on the living dramatists, whose
taking to farce instead of comedy was not their fault,
but the age's. Good-natured Tom Dibdin, behold at
last your critic repentant!

C. L., why didst thou ever quit Russell Street?
Why didst thou leave the warm crowd of humanity,
which thou lovest so well, to go and shiver on the
side of the New River, enticing thy unwary friends to
walk in? Were friends and sittings up at night too
attractive? And was there no other way to get rid
of them? Reader, we have not waked the night-owl
with a catch, for C. L. is not musical. He will put
up with nothing but snatches of old songs. Mozart
is to him an alien, and Paesiello the Pope of Rome.
But we have drawn three souls out of one card-play-
er; and might have waked all the ghosts in our
neighborhood at Will's and Button's, seeing that
there is no pride in the next world, and some wit left
in this. What would I not give for another Thursday evening? It was humanity's triumph; for whist-
players and no whist-players there for the first time
met together. Talk not to me of great houses in
which such things occur; for there the whist-players
are gamblers, and the no whist-players are nobody at

all. Here, the whist was for its own sake, and yet the non-players were tolerated. But the triumph went further. Here was R., to represent among us the plumpness of office and the solidity of government. My brother reformer, W. H., came to rest his disappointments and his paradoxes. Vain expectation! With him contended A. the most well-bred of musicians, who hates a paradox like an unresolved discord. Another A. was there, the best of neighbors, especially if you happen to be confined to your room. Item, a third A. the most trusting of linen-drapers, who lent a poet a hundred pounds. I do not know whether he has been paid. I hope not; for he deserves to enjoy the interest forever, and in his case it is a rich one. M. B. was one of us, having his hands in his waistcoat pockets like his friend, and talking well upon episodes. And there, M. L., — why have I not the art, like the old writers of dedications, of at once loading thee with panegyric, and saving the shoulders of thy modesty? an art, by the by, which was so conspicuously concealed, that nobody would have suspected them of having it. There also came old Captain B., who had been round the world with Cook, and was the first man who planted a pun in Otaheite. Nevertheless, though I met him fifty times, I never had the courage to address him, he appeared to be so wrapped up in his tranquillity and his whist. He seemed to be taking a long repose from his storms. The jovial face of Colonel P., blooming with a second youth, made me bolder. He had been round the world also, when a boy, and had challenged his lieutenant for not standing closer by his captain. This

illegality completed my confidence. With K. we re-
joiced over his successful plays, and tried to be indifferent over the others. He has humanity enough
to remember with pleasure, that on the latter occasion we mustered up (some of us at least) as great an
appetite at supper as if two plays had succeeded at
once. It is more than we could have looked for, had
a critic written them, instead of a poet. But somehow these poetical observers see farther into niceties
of us than your metaphysical. With regard to myself, the fact was (and I shall do myself no harm to
confess it — very likely he knows it already) that my
appetite was really great and craving. On livelier
occasions, if my lungs have not been well exercised,
I will not swear that I could eat the wing of a chicken.
My heart is up and dancing, and objects to the passage of anything grosser than a pint of wine. *

* Lamb moved from No. 4, Inner Temple Lane, to Russell Street, Covent Garden, in the autumn of 1817. " We have left the Temple," writes Mary Lamb
to Miss Wordsworth. " Our rooms were dirty and out of repair, and the inconveniences of living in chambers became every year more irksome. and so, at last,
we mustered up resolution enough to leave the old place, that so long has shel-
tered us ; and here we are, living at a brazier's shop, No. 20, in Russell Street,
Covent Garden, a place all alive with noise and bustle ; Drury Lane Theatre in
sight from our front, and Covent Garden from our back windows. The hubbub
of the carriages returning from the play does not annoy me in the least ; strange
that it does not, for it is quite tremendous. I quite enjoy looking out of the
window, and listening to the calling up of the carriages, and the squabbles of the
coachmen and link-boys. It is the oddest scene to look down upon." Lamb
himself was equally well pleased with their new abode, declaring that they were
in the individual spot he liked best in all London. Here he wrote the best of
the Essays of Elia. In 1823 he left the city, with its theatres and book-stalls, and
took a cottage in Colebrook Row, Islington. It was George Dyer who walked
into the New River, and thus gave Elia a subject for the fine humorous paper
entit'ed Amicus Redivivus.

Perhaps a word or two on some of the initials in the above reminiscence of
Lamb's Thursday evening suppers will not be wholly superfluous. Of course
C. L. is Charles Lamb, and W. H., William Hazlitt, and Captain B. is Cap-

All that part of the metropolis which may now be
called the centre of it, is classic ground: from Fleet
Street, where Johnson and Goldsmith lived, Gerrard
Street, Soho, which contains the residence of Dryden.*   It includes the chief places of resort, during

tain Burney, and M. B., Martin Burney, whose dirty hands were so provocative
of Lamb's wit. The captain, according to Crabb Robinson, was "a fine, noble
creature, — gentle with a rough exterior, as became the associate of Captain
Cook in his voyages round the world, and the literary historian of all these acts
of circumnavigation." The three A.'s were Thomas Allsop, Thomas Alsager, and
William Ayrton, of the Italian Opera. Lamb said Ayrton was "a wit and
devilish good fellow." K. stands for James Sheridan Knowles, the dramatist,
author of Virginius. R. is John Rickman, clerk of the House of Commons. "His manners," writes Southey of Rickman, "are stoical: they are
like the husk of the cocoa-nut, and his inner nature is like the milk within its
kernel. When I go to London I am always his guest. He gives me but half
his hand, but his whole heart — and there is not that thing in the world which
he thinks would serve or gratify me that he does not do for me, unless it be
something which he thinks I can as well do myself." George Dyer introduced
Lamb to Rickman. Lamb was so delighted with the man that he wrote a long
letter about him to Manning. "He is," says Elia, exultingly, "a most pleasant
hand; a fine, rattling fellow, has gone through life laughing at solemn apes; — himself hugely literate, oppressively full of information in all stuff of conversation,
from matter of fact to Xenophon and Plato — can talk Greek with Porson, politics with Thelwall, conjecture with George Dyer, nonsense with me, and anything
with anybody; a great farmer, somewhat concerned in an agricultural magazine
— reads no poetry but Shakespeare, very intimate with Southey, but never
reads his poetry, relishes George Dyer, thoroughly penetrates into the ridiculous wherever found, understands the *first time* (a great desideratum in common
minds) — you need never twice speak to him: does not want explanations,
translations, limitations, as Professor Godwin does when you make an assertion;
up to anything; *down* to anything; whatever *sapit hominem*. A perfect *man*.
All this farrago, which must perplex you to read, and has put me to a little
trouble to *select*, only proves how impossible it is to describe a *pleasant hand*.
You must see Rickman to know him, for he is a species in one; a new class; an
exotic; any slip of which I am proud to put in my garden pot." A "pleasant
hand" truly: but how different from Southey's stoical-mannered man! Is this
description of Rickman true in all its particulars, or was Lamb hoaxing the
"learned Trismegist"? — Ed.

* It was "the fifth," says Mr. Malone, "in coming from Little Newport
Street, and is now numbered 43. Behind, his apartments looked into the gardens of Leicester House."

[We copy this interesting passage relating to Covent Garden from a curious

the three periods, in which poetry and wit were allied
with familiar life; — Dryden's period, with Etherege,
Wycherley, Rochester, and others; — the time of Steele
and Addison, Garth, Vanbrugh, Congreve, &c., and
that of the two authors above mentioned, who left us
just before the French revolution. In the Strand, opposite Beaufort Buildings, walking at a very quick pace
for a man of his years, I once saw Cumberland, the
last survivor of Retaliation. His appearance was gentlemanly (suited to his old character), and his face
earnest and thoughtful. I would have accosted him,
and thanked him for a criticism he wrote on a performance of mine; but besides carrying a certain habit
of independence at that time to a pitch of martyrdom,
I felt as if it would be an impertinence in so young a
man to bring himself into contact on such an occasion with an associate of Goldsmith and Johnson.
The performance, to say the truth, was very crude
and young, and not worth his praises: nor could I
conceal from myself, that a panegyric bestowed on
him in the course of it had warmed the heart of the
old author. But his criticism was delightful, containing some excellent gossip upon Quin, Garrick, and
others. It appeared in the London Review, a work

---

letter by Thomas Grignion, addressed to Tom Dibdin, and published in a little
volume entitled Fly Leaves, or Scraps and Sketches: —
  "You will see by my plan of 1691, that Covent Garden was then in the empo-
rium of the arts and sciences, and the residence of the chief nobility of the kingdom. My late dear grandfather's cordial friend, the celebrated Barton Booth,
lived in Charles Street, No. 4; Colley Cibber lived in No. 3; and Easty's
Hotel was Mr. Garrick's; Mrs. Oldfield lived in Southampton Street. Wilkes
built the house in Bow Street, next door but one to the theatre; Garrick and
Macklin lodged in it. I thought this information respecting our truly classic
ground might not be uninteresting to you." — ED.]

which did not continue long, probably because the reviewers put their names to it. To be praised by one of the heroes of Retaliation appeared to me a piece of good fortune beyond all others; too good even for my vanity to take without drawback.

· I have spoken of the laugh of Mrs. Jordan. There is a delightful little poem by Clement Marot, *On the Laugh of Madame D'Albret*, which seems to record a similar quintessence of glee, cordiality, and lightness. It reminded me of her the moment I read it.

DU RIS DE MADAME D'ALBRET.

Elle ha tres bien ceste gorge d'albastre,
A doux parler, ce cler tainct, ces beaux jeux ;
Mais, en effect, ce petit ris follastre,
C'est a mon gre, ce qui lui sied le mieux :
Elle en pourroit les chemins et les lieux,
Ou elle passe, a plaisir inciter :
Et si ennuy me venoit contrister,
Tant que par mort fusta ma vie abbatue,
Ill ne faudroit, pour me resusciter,
Que ce ris la, duquel elle me tue.

Yes, that fair neck, too beautiful by half,
    Those eyes, that voice, that bloom, all do her honor;
Yet after all, that little giddy laugh
    Is what, in my mind, sits the best upon her.

Good God! 'twould make the very streets and ways
    Through which she passes, burst into a pleasure !
Did melancholy come to mar my days,
    And kill me in the lap of too much leisure,
No spell were wanting, from the dead to raise me,
But only that sweet laugh, wherewith she slays me.

No. III.

PICCADILLY AND THE WEST END.

Lo ! stately streets; lo ! squares that court the breeze. — THOMSON.

IF I had health, and my friends were all comfortable, and the world as happy as it might
be, and I could transport everybody where I pleased
as well as myself, and books were as plentiful as
blackberries, and a thousand other things (as somebody said) were a thousand other things, the pleasure I should take in writing these papers would
be inconceivable. As it is, it is no mean consolation. The house I generally write in being large,
I contrive to dismiss certain little scholars I have
into a distant play-room, and get an hour to myself
after breakfast, uninterrupted : — the sound of a wood
fire is crackling in my ears ; — and with a fresh pen
and a fair sheet of paper, I begin.*

But I am fancying myself in Italy : and forget I
am in London, at the West End of the town.

By the West End of the town, I understand Piccadilly, the squares, and their neighborhood, as far as
the Regent's Park. The other parks ought to be included : but I must treat of them another time.

---

* In Elia's letter to Southey, Leigh Hunt's "little scholars" are affectionately mentioned. Here is the passage: — "Leigh Hunt is now in Italy; on
his departure to which land with much regret I took my leave of him and of his
little fami'y — seven of them, si:, with their mother — and as kind a set of little
people, as affectionate children, as ever blessed a parent. Had you seen them, sir,
I think you could not have looked upon them as so many little Jonases, but rather
as pledges of the vessel's safety, that was to bear such a freight of love " — ED.

The West End is a very agreeable portion of the
world to me for three reasons : — Imprimis, because I
have lived there ; secondly, because it is the next
part of the town to Hampstead, my other place of
abode ; and thirdly, because it contains the fairest
portion of God's creatures under the sun. If the two
first reasons are thought egotistical, they will be
found to resemble most others given by people for
their preference of places. The only difference between them and me is, that I tell what I feel. As to
the third reason, it is not only what no Englishman
will dispute, but no Frenchman or Italian that has
seen English women. But of this, more hereafter.

The West End may be supposed to commence at
Leicester Square. It is but a mongrel square, a
mixture of house and shop ; but it is green in the
middle, and contains a statue of some prince. There
are people who object to these royal statues, thinking
it a pity that they are not rather those of some great
philosophers, poets, or other public benefactors. But
when they reflect that the faces are too far off to be
seen, and that few persons know who they are, the
objection perhaps will vanish. In Leicester Square,
at the house of Sir Joshua Reynolds (situate, I believe, in the west side, towards the alley from which
you cross into Coventry Street), were many meetings
of Johnson, Goldsmith, and others. Leicester House
(now lost in the large house with shops on the north
side) was the residence of Frederick, Prince of Wales.*

---

* In the diseases and jarring tempers of this prince and his wife, may be discerned the seeds of the unfortunate malady which afflicted the late king, their
son. [George III., who was deprived of reason during the last ten years of his
life. — Ed.]

who affected the love of liberty, and patronized
Thomson.* Whitcomb Street was formerly called
Hedge Lane, no doubt from a lane which ran up
from Charring Cross to the fields about Piccadilly
and Marylebone. Think of lovers having walked
here on a May-morning! In a house opposite Coventry Street lodged an early friend of mine, whom
it is a comfort to me to take even this obscure way
of noticing. He was an intelligent fellow, full of
goodness, and in love with music, and poetry, and
all good things. I once walked with him a hundred
and twelve miles along the coast from Margate to
Brighton, talking, laughing, and singing all the way,
eating breakfasts which made us ashamed to ask for
more, and falling to sleep at night the moment we
laid our heads on the pillow. We did it in four days.
Poor J. R.! He had an overstock of love, which was
not very happily placed. He become sick, unsuccess-
ful, a wanderer; and was at last taken prisoner by
the French, and died during the long detention of
his countrymen by Napoleon. He wrote me a long
letter from Bagneres, where he had been suffered to
go for the benefit of his health; and I delayed, from
day to day, in order to write him as long an answer,
till I delayed for months, and heard of his death.
The letter has been upon my conscience ever since.
It would be a useful task for those who have been
culpable during their lives on the score of delay, and
other petty neglects of duty, to set down upon paper

---

* Leigh Hunt should not have forgotten Hogarth, who lived at the " Painter's
Head," in Leicester Square. — ED.

all the unkind and serious consequences resulting
from it. There are petty as well as great remorses
which people feel, on and off, during the whole of
their lives; and a good many of them amount to a
good large remorse; and with reason, considering
what they do. I have an assortment of my own,
which make me speak. The one in question has
never suffered me to pass by that house, or think of
it, without a pang. I hope it was on a more fanciful
account that Dr. Johnson always avoided going
through Sydney's, or Cranborne Alley, in this neighborhood, I forget which.

In Piccadilly, during the time of Cromwell and the
Stuarts, was a house of entertainment with a bowling-green, where the gentry and members of Parliament used to refresh themselves. Here came the
sprightly wits of the court, and the grave heads that
earned for us our liberties. Parliament at that time
used to meet at eight in the morning. If statesmen
got a little too much wine after dinner, it was in hon-
or of Phyllis and Chloe, and not to put themselves in
a fit state for settling the affairs of the world. They
did their work with clear heads; and if they gambled, gambled in the open air, which is better than
losing one's money and health together in the club-
rooms about St. James's. It is doubtful whether the
Burlington House mentioned in Gray's Trivia was
the one in Piccadilly, or another in the Strand:
most probably the former. I cannot refer to books.
As the passage, however, is metropolitan and pleasant, I will lay it before the reader: —

'Come, Fortescue, sincere, experienced friend,
Thy briefs, thy deeds, and even thy fees, suspend;
Come, let us leave the Temple's silent walls:
Me business to my distant lodging calls:
Through the long Strand together let us stray;
With thee conversing I forget the way.
Behold that narrow street which steep descends,
Whose building to the slimy shore extends:
Here Arundel's famed structure reared its frame,
The street alone retains an empty name.
Where Titian's glowing paint the canvas warmed,
And Raphael's fair design with judgment charmed,
Now hangs the bellman's song, and pasted here
The colored prints of Overton appear.
Where statues breathed, the work of Phidias' hands,
A wooden pump or lonely watch-house stands.
There Essex' stately pile adorned the shore,
There Cecil's, Bedford's, Villiers', now no more.
Yet Burlington's fair palace still remains;
Beauty within, without proportion reigns.
Beneath his eye declaring Art revives,
The wall with animated picture lives.
There Handel strikes the strings, the melting strain
Transports the soul, and thrills through every vein.
There oft I enter (but with cleaner shoes)
For Burlington's beloved by every Muse.''

Hv del and Gay must have found two subjects of mutal interest: music, of which the latter was a judge; and good eating, in which, Congreve tells us, he was a great performer.* Handel set his pretty Serenata of Acis and Galatea to music. I have never been inside Burlington House; but I once witnessed an adventure inside the gates, which Gay might have written upon had he seen it, and Handel have set to music with drums and trumpets. The reader must know I have been a soldier, have had a red coat and

---

* In a letter to Pope. See Spence's Anecdotes. "As the French philosopher," says Congreve, "used to prove his existence by *cogito, ergo sum*, the greatest proof of Gay's existence is *edit ergo est*." Gay's poems abound with allusions to eating and drinking. [Thackeray says Gay was "forever eating and saying good things." — ED.]

great long green feather, and *bivouacked* in Du-
four's Place. I have seen horrid war at Wormwood
Scrubbs, and marched from "Ealing to Acton" in
all the dusty glory of a campaign. Our regiment
had not been long organized, when it was announced
to us that we were to have Lord A. for our colonel,
and that his lordship would make his first appearance among us on a certain morning, on the parade
before Burlington House. We mustered about a
thousand strong at that time, and were all under arms
on the day appointed, anxious and exalted. On a
sudden the great gates are thrown open, the band
strikes up, the regiment presents arms, and his lordship, on a gallant white charger, instead of riding
tenderly in, introduces himself to us by pitching head
foremost over his horse's neck ! The debut was awkward : the sympathy hardly made it better ; but nothing came of the bad omen ; unless it was prophetic
of the prostration which was afterwards required of
the noble lord in China, and which he so naturally
refused to make. The *ko-tou* to the band-major was
certainly enough, once in a man's life.

Golden Square is a vile square, though it was
once among the most fashionable.* You gather this
from the slip-slop novels, which always make a point
of being high-bred. No hero can have an interesting
aspect, and no heroine a becoming wretchedness of
mind, unless the family have an establishment in Port-
man or Grosvenor Square to support it. Soho Square

---

* "I have a grim pleasure in thinking that Golden Square was once the resort
of the aristocracy," says Thackeray, in a delightful digression on the mutations
of fashion, in Philip. — ED.

is much better than Golden, for it has trees.* A
great improvement has been made of late years in this
respect in most of the squares; but the two just
mentioned together certainly bear the palm. They
are all great ornaments to the town, and serve to
keep it healthy. In some parts of Italy they have a
pretty custom of putting inscriptions over the doors
and gateways, both in town and country. I have
often thought that mottoes would be an addition both
agreeable and useful to the doors of our fine houses
at the West End. The spaces over the entrances seem
to invite them. The passengers would be amused;
and the householder who put up the inscription (for
every new possessor should have his own) would feel
it a sort of tie on his character. Devices of all kinds
are useful in this point of view, except hereditary
ones; for those are not a man's own, and remind him
of nothing but the antiquity of his family. Once and
away, they may give him a just pride or as just a
qualm. A curious list of contrasts might be made
out between modern lands and the mottoes to their
arms.

The long streets without shops to them, in this part
of the town, and with brick houses all built in the
same manner, have a strange look to persons who have
resided in Italy. In the cities there, the houses vary
at every step, and are faced with stucco. The advantage is on the side of the London houses in point

* Sir Roger De Coverley lived in Soho Square during his visits to London in
his "fine-gentleman days;" but later in life he preferred humbler quarters
when in town. When he came up to London to get a sight of Prince Eugene,
he lodged in Norfolk Street. — ED.

of snugness, especially on the ground floors, which in
Italy have the windows barred over with iron, which
gives them a prison look. It is impossible also for
an Englishman, at least in winter time, to divest himself of the preference due to the snug curtains and
carpets all over the house inside, things which do not
abound in the south. But in point of architecture
and general appearance, there is no comparison. The
houses in Italy are on a larger scale, the variety interesting, and the proportions very often beautiful and in
high taste. The stucco and marble also suit the blue
sky. You see that the houses belong to a country of
artists. Nevertheless, give me the West End of my
old metropolis with its world of comfort, its firesides,
and its fair faces. I flit from drawing-room to drawing-room, delighted with the endless succession of
wealth, beauty, and elegance, the music, the books,
the graceful sisterhoods, the respectable parents, — in
short, with everything except the climate over their
heads, and the spleen too often in their faces. What
a pity the whole world cannot exchange their advantages with one another!

In Marylebone, Pope went for a short time to
school. There was a house and bowling-green there
in his time, similar to the one in Piccadilly, which I
suppose it succeeded. It was frequented by the best
company, bowls at that time being a game justly
held in estimation. Sheffield, Duke of Buckingham,
was so constant a visitor, that he was said to live
there. Marylebone Gardens afterwards became celebrated for the same entertainments as the modern
Vauxhall. They existed up to a late period. Chat-

terton wrote a cantata for them; a burlesque (if I remember) of the quarrels and amours of the pagan heaven. The Thrales had a house in Hanover Square, where Johnson visited.

The West End of London, for an obvious reason, is of little interest in a classical point of view, compared with other parts of the town. One or two writers like Gibbon do nothing for so great a quarter. Even Covent Garden is not the most inspired ground. The most sacred places are now occupied by the money-changers of Cornhill and the Borough. Of these in my next. But O for the evenings again that I have passed there, especially at a house at the other end of Oxford Street! The N.'s lived there, the most Catholic of Catholics, for their spirit embraced the whole world.* There we should have waked the night-owl with a catch, had an owl been within hearing. The watchman did instead. The solitary passenger who was astonished at our Laughing Trios, was not the less so at the majestic rolling of the organ that would follow it; just emblem of the devotion for all good things which we had in our hearts. There came J. G., a set of airy crotchets in the shape of a man; and H. R. (always ready with his tenor, his joke, and his breathing nod of acquiescence), for whom I shall have another pang in my conscience if I do not write to him (not because he will die, but because he will think my friendship is dead, which it can never be), and C. C., who groaned a hundred times of an evening in the fullness of his satisfaction (I

* The Novellos. See Charles Lamb's letter to Hunt, and the Chapter on E ra in the Essays of Elia. — ED.

hope to hear shortly that benevolent grind of his
'epiglottis) ; and the G.s' pleasant specimens of humanity ; and Kate H., a beauty fit to take coffee with
the party in the Rape of the Lock : —

> " On her white breast a sparkling cross she wore,
> Which Jews might kiss, and infidels adore. "

And it was as Catholic too as that of Belinda.
Kate was tall, had a fine black head of hair, with
eyes to match, and a face made for a portrait. When
she came home from the play, and sat down in her
long scarlet mantle, showing only her throat and fine
curls, and sparkling smiles, you saw how many eyes
had been looking at her from the pit. A husband
carried her off to a distance, and we never saw her
again, which was unfair: I wonder how these hus-
bands reconcile it to their consciences. C. L. came
there sometimes " to wonder at our quaint spirits,"
with a quainter spirit of his own. He would put up
with no anthems but Kent's, and with no songs but
Water parted from the Sea. His sister humbly suggested, at a beautiful passage in Mozart, that she
thought there was some merit in that. He would
not hear of it. What was the consequence? Why,
that he got loved by everybody in spite of his in-
tolerance; which, with him, is apt to have more humanity in it than the liberality of other men.

No. IV.

A WALK IN THE CITY.

Rursus et urbe frui.— Ovid.

Again to enjoy the city.

WHEN I entered the metropolis on my present visit, I lighted with my Wishing-Cap on
St. Paul's Cathedral. Could I have fancied a devil
with me on so sacred a place, I should have taken
myself for Don Cleofas in the novel; for roofs and
walls fly open before me, as easily as I fly over them;
and I saw in an instant the whole neighborhood, with
all that was going on inside the houses. The inhabitants need not be alarmed, as it is not my intention to
pursue the likeness between this paper and the Devil
on Two Sticks any farther at present. I shall content
myself with expressing the agreeable surprise that
seized me on observing a little room, the inhabitant of
which was nursing an abundance of plants and flowers
against the spring. Among them was even an orange
tree. The very spirit of the Flora Domestica seemed
to be there. Surely, thought I, Nature must love those
who have so much love for her. If they have joy,
the joy must be doubled; and though they be full of
sorrow, there must be still room, as in the cup of the
Arabian, for the rose-leaf to swim at top.

At their old place of resort in St. Paul's Church-
yard, I used to meet the survivors of the dinner par-

ties of Mr. Johnson, the respectable bookseller. There was G., buckling himself up, with his arms crossed, for a controversy; and F., like a little old white-headed lion, "full of sound and fury," but by no means "signifying nothing;" and L. E., one of a volatile generation, who have the art of settling themselves into teachers; and good old gaunt Bonnycastle (whom I name openly because he is no more), full of his anecdotes and his Shakespeare, and showing his teeth when he smiled, like a Houyhnhnm condescending to wear a human shape: and last, but not least, that whole body of the magistracy personified, Horace-loving old Kinnaird, a romantic aristocrat, to whom God save the King was a requiem, and a bow from a court officer a beatific vision. His frame, poor fellow! was like a square mile of dropsy; but he had a large sparkling black eye, like a boy; and he quoted his Horace, and told his anecdote of "my lud North" to the last. For all his excess of loyalty, he was humane to us Jacobins, his adoration of rank being mainly connected with a notion of its high breeding. To give him quotation for quotation, — to answer, when he said, —

"Persicos odi, puer, apparatus," —

"Ah, Mr. Kinnaird, and that the elegant invitation to Mæcenas, —

'Tyrrhena regum progenies,' " —

was a bond of union with him forever.

I take a melancholy satisfaction (being an author) in walking down Paternoster Row. The booksellers hereabouts and eastwards do not make their shop windows so lively as those of the Strand and West

End. Mr. Hunter, in St. Paul's Churchyard, humane-
ly shows us a portrait of Mr. Edgeworth or Mr. Day,
to qualify the dryness of his divinity; * but the mere
warehouse look of the shops of Messrs. Longman
and others is a satire on the trade.

The City and the Borough contain the most classical ground in the metropolis. In the former, besides
Pope and Gray, were born three out of the four great
English poets, — Chaucer, Spenser, and Milton : the
literary clubs and tavern-meetings of the age of Shakespeare were held in Fleet Street and Cornhill ; and
Shakespeare's theatre was over the water by the
Borough. Another stood near the present Apothe-
caries' Hall, in Blackfriars. From the Borough Chaucer set out on the journey to Canterbury with his
Pilgrims. I have touched upon these matters before ;
but·I repeat them here, partly for the pleasure of
doing so, and partly to remark how the celebrity arising from authorship survives every other. Old city
palaces, the dwellings of a proud nobility, have fallen
one after the other: you must now dig for their memorials in dusty books. Political tumults have shaken perhaps every street in London : you must search
for them in old chronicles, which are not read by one
person in a million. But in the living productions

* Richard Lovell Edgeworth, father of Maria Edgeworth. "Mr. Edgeworth," says Sydney Smith, in a review of the essay on Irish Bulls, "seems
to possess the sentiments of an accomplished gentleman, the information of a
scholar, and the vivacity of a first-rate harlequin. He is fuddled with animal
spirits, giddy with constitutional joy; in such a state he must have written on,
or burst. A discharge of ink was an evacuation absolutely necessary to avoid
fatal and plethoric congestion." Mr. Day is the good and eccentric Thomas
Day, author of Sandford and Merton. — ED.

of genius survive at once the rare individuals born, and the places that gave them birth. A petty incident in the life of one of these men shall be repeated a hundred times to do honor to a particular spot. It is said to be on record, that Chaucer was fined a shilling for beating a friar in Fleet Street, — a circumstance that hardly seems compatible with the character of the gentle poet, who describes himself as shy in his manners, and going along with his eyes bent on the ground. But if the reader has been in the south, and seen what sturdy vagabonds there are among reverend persons, trudging along with their hard, sneering faces, their staves, and their dirty drugget cloaks, the provocation seems far from unlikely ; especially when it is considered that our poet, for all his gentleness, was somewhat of an uproarious reformer.

It must be confessed that it is not easy to walk about London and indulge in retrospective meditation. The noise being great, as Cowley would say, is little. It might serve to deafen itself, like the Falls of Niagara ; but to be shouldered out of one's reverie is not so pleasant. It seems as impossible for anybody but a hypochondriac to think in Cheapside as for a fish in the Channel to be at rest. Yet I prefer a hundred times making my way in the most crowded streets to walking along a suburban city street, which is neither town nor country, — neither City nor West End. In the City, shops and a certain bustle are fitting. Everything ought to be alive, — the pavement, the windows, the prospect. A genuine piece of quiet is good, but this must be in some old street or corner. Bread

Street has a right to be tranquil, both because it is
ancient and because Milton was born there. To go
through Christ-Hospital,* when my old school-fellows
are at their books, is a pleasant transition from the
bustle of grown life to the dreams of boyhood. Any
spot, where you meet with a piece of antique building, a Gothic archway, or an old tottering house with
a coat of arms upon it, is a happy variety. I have a
particular respect for Austin Friars, for a reason
which I shall give presently. But rather than walk
in one of your " respectable " new streets, such as the
"genteel" ramifications out of Blackfriars Road or
the City Road, I would take my stroll through all
the old alleys, from Pudding Lane to Pie Corner. I
must have either antiquity to remind me of the past
generations, or something busy and going on to warm
my heart with the present. A new monotonous brick
street, full, perhaps, of government dependants, who
pass their lives between " the desk's dead wood " and
a vegetation in those long lines of pots from the brick-
kiln, — if I were one of them, I would sooner live in
a brick-field itself, provided there were a single tree
to look at from my window. It is true they walk out
of an evening in the dusty roads. O, charitable Surrey Theatre, and Sadler's Wells, and thou Bagnigge
(who ought to be in being, if thou art not), wrongly
are ye despised by the independent gentlemen who
are fortunate enough to vegetate and be in flower at
the West End ! What the coach-maker and tailor are

---

* This, Hunt maintains, in his Autobiography, is its proper name, and not
Christ's Hospital, as Lamb calls it in his two essays on the old school. — ED.

to them, helping them to their movable pots and their tulip fashions, are ye to the sadder and more thinking generation of the dwellers in by-places. O, half price at the great theatres! much more foul-mouthed are they who cry out against thee, because thou disturbest their polite sympathy at the fourth act, than the throng of money economists, who, re-leased from their long and respectable patience, burst in upon thy expanded doors, time enough to supply themselves with criticism for the next week on Mr. Kean and Mr. Macready, and Mr. Liston in the farce. Besides, what would our worthy London 'prentices do in the absence of their old city sports and tumul-tuous meetings, when the cry of " clubs ! " used to fur-nish them with a proper supply of hard blows and sympathy for one another? To you, gentle sub-urban-ites (not excepting the Cobourg, though its name be modern and its gentility somewhat vociferous), to you they repair " to light their wasted urns," — to rub off the scurf generated by money-getting and hard ser-vice, and fit themselves for becoming creditors, magis-trates, and givers of good dinners. Unfortunately, this intellectual regimen is not so good for digestion as the foot-ball and target-shooting, in which our gallant apprentices excelled of old. Our shopmen partake with others of the sickliness of a lettered generation. They must have their tea to carry off the vapors, and to generate more. " Mighty roast beef" is an enemy not to be encountered with the old impunity ; and gout and peevishness occupy their arm-chairs, amidst a world of provoking comforts, at a time of life when your citizen used only to be reasonably bilious. This is attributed to the progress of civilization, and to "us youth," the authors who grow sickly ourselves in writing against effeminacy. But with the leave of those who at once complain and are proud of the refinement of the age in which they live, our civilization is not so extreme as we pretend. No state of man has arrived at a proper pitch of civilization in which fair play is not attended to between its intellectual and corporal faculties. I confess, "for my own private eating," I would rather have been a citizen of the age of Elizabeth, my checks glowing not only with beef and pudding, but with fresh air and a hundred merry games; but, nevertheless, my content to be a sick author in the nineteenth century "hath a preferment in it." I think, with a modern philosopher, that we must come round again to our gymnastics at last; and, when we do this, having meanwhile got our books and our love of liberty into the bargain, the world will be better off than if London contained the only gallant apprentices going, and the rest of Europe were full of slavery and superstition.

Some drawbacks on the health of our ancient citizens must not be forgotten. Their streets were narrow, which ultimately produced a plague; and, in the time of Henry the Eighth, when Erasmus visited England, it appears that the nation who now pride themselves above all others on the becoming cleanliness of their houses (for Dutch cleanness is dull excess), were, — with humility be it spoken, — one of the filthiest under the sun. I cannot refer to the passage, but I have a vivid recollection of it. He

4

describes our sitting or dining-rooms as incrusted with
a mass of dirt and refuse, ill concealed by the rushes
strewed over it, and never swept away. A sense of
what is due to humanity ultimately increases in every
respect with the progress of knowledge; and this is
what makes me hope that we shall at last find out
the secret of being both healthy and wise.

When Erasmus was in England he lodged in Austin Friars.

Austin Friars, I love thee: and yet it is not for
this. Still less is it for St. Austin and his brethren;
nor yet for thy being so quiet and well-bred a re-
treat. It is because of the feelings with which I used
to turn down thine archway, when a boy, to visit
the family of the T.'s. The T.'s, reader, were among
the most eminent families in the mercantile world,
and remain so still. The princely character of the
English merchant, has perhaps, never been carried
higher than by some of them. But the charm of a
respectable English family is ever to be found in-
doors. The T.'s never forsook the friends they had
known so long, in spite of politics and misfortune.
I used to think sometimes that an East India Director, who visited them, looked rather askance at
dinner-time upon the stuff of my school coats; but
a smile from A. T., or a challenge to a glass of
wine from the father, who used to sit (to my equal
veneration and terror), panting with asthma, at the
head of the table, soon reassured me. As for the
stranger, privately speaking, I thought that my Horace and Demosthenes gave me a right to sit at table
with any man: and I think so still. To this house,

with its music and its kindness, and to another at the other end of the town, where there was a gallery of pictures, I attribute much of the coloring of my after-life, — I mean of my ideas and likings. Both had gardens; the latter of a size as well as tranquillity enough to surprise a visitor in London (at least, it cuts an important figure in my memory), and the Drapers' Gardens abutted on it; so that the imagination, in the very midst of the city, reposed on garden upon garden. But the best thing in the house, even better than the matronly grace and kindness of the mistress of it, was a little apartment, one of two or three which the best-hearted girl upon earth had to herself, and to which I used to hasten up with my mother before dinner, when there was no music practising below. There was a small set of bookshelves in it, containing, among other books, the Turkish Spy, — a work that used to puzzle me exceedingly, and which, I will be bound for it, was as great a puzzle to A. [I long to mention her name, for it is as feminine and handsome a one as can be conceived, and four syllables long to boot; but I fear to startle the unaffected modesty of the bearer with a more public mention than I can help.] This place was a little sanctuary in my eyes. It was a beautiful sight to see the excellent but care-worn person that brought me with her met affectionately at the door with both outstretched hands of a fine girl of eighteen, and served with all the respect and attention that could have waited on a princess. I wonder how I can write about it with dry eyes. Many years afterwards, when the new generation had grown up, and parted different ways, I had the pleasure of seeing A. once again (now no longer T.), and showing her my eldest born, whom I had named after her family. Time had not taken away her smile.* I might have known her, perhaps, still, notwithstanding my politics; and I have a hundred times reproached myself that I did not try.

No. V.

WHITEHALL.

Veterum penetralia regum.— VIRGIL.
The insides of the old abodes of kings.

THE more I loiter about my old places of abode, the more I long to stay. What I relate has no pretensions to the notice of the antiquary. He is acquainted with it already. My antiquities are all out of Pennant, with the exception of what I glean here and there from the wits and poets. The only value of my pictures (if any) is in the coloring, and in the figures occasionally introduced.

Charing Cross was so called from one of the affectionate memorials set up by Edward the First, in honor of places at which his wife's body rested on its way to interment at Westminster. The cross here

---

* Thornton Leigh Hunt, the "dear little T. H." of Elia's Witches and Other Night Fears; and the subject of one of Lamb's poems. We hope the reader is familiar with Leigh Hunt's beautiful lines To T. L. H., Six Years Old, during Sickness. — A. T. is Almeria Thornton, of whom and of her family there is considerable additional information in The Autobiography of Leigh Hunt. — ED.

was the last. Its place is now occupied by the statue
of Charles the First, an unfitting ornament for a free
city. Indeed it can be considered in no other light
than that of an insulting rebuke. Nobody is respon-
sible for the insult now, because it has been of long
standing; but the spirit that has maintained and al
lowed it is not favorable to liberty, nor just to the
true spirit of the constitution. The constant assumption, on the part of this representative of Charles the
First, of a right to beard it thus ostentatiously among
the people, and look in a triumphant manner towards
Whitehall, has its effect, even in stone and brass.
The forms of encroachment make way for the sub-
stance. These are the helps to the gradual introduction of soldiers, that are now suffered to stand sentinel
at museums and theatres, certainly in contradiction to .
the spirit of English liberty. A free people ought
not to be familiarized in this manner with royal dominations and liveries. There is a bust of Charles the
First indecently overlooking the avenue to the House
of Commons.* When the passage was undergoing
repairs some years back, the bust was missed by a late
minister, and eagerly inquired after. The workmen
satisfied the anxiety of the minister, and all went
right. Charles's illegal entrance into the House of
Commons, with the intention of seizing the five mem
bers (the proceeding which afterwards brought him
to the block), rendered his appearance in such a quar
ter still more insulting. It is true, there are statues
in other places, of princes of the house that displaced

---

* This bust does not appear to have been put up in Pennant's time. He
speaks of it as existing, but not in its present situation. It would be curious to
know who put it there

his family. In Russell Square we have even a Whig nobleman and a Whig statesman. But Charles's statue is the most conspicuous and in the most conspicuous and crowded place of any in London; and Charles Fox would not be allowed to confront him in the Parliament Avenue, where he has at least as much right to appear. Even a Whig sovereign is not allowed to see fair play; which is surely unthankful in one quarter, and not eminently unslavish in another. In a thoroughfare behind Whitehall (skulking out of sight, but " insinuated," as it were, " into the boxes ") is a statue of James the Second!

All the noble thoroughfare, now called Whitehall, with the buildings on either side, extended along the river as far as Scotland Yard on one side, and up to the street turning into Spring Gardens on the other, occupies the ground of the immense palace formerly existing under the same name. It was begun by the Earl of Kent in the reign of the third Henry, and became the palace of the Archbishops of York, and the residence of Wolsey. It is the scene of the masquerade in Henry the Eighth. A great masquerade has been played there by Time. Here Wolsey, that magnificent "Jack-priest of the world," displayed his pomps and vanities, grew fat and diseased with debauchery, gave out imperial healths in his gold cups; and at last burst like a bubble. Henry condescended to buy the house, and went swelling both it and himself in his turn, till he became too fat to write his name.* The various exercises which he pursued in

---

* An historical fact. He had a seal made to stamp with instead, and must be imagined moving his body and arm round to achieve the signature, like a porpoise with something stuck in his fin.

this place (for there were a tennis-court, tilting-yard, cock-pit, and bowling-green, and he was fond of robust games) appear to have only been made subservient to the prodigiousness of his appetites. Eating and drinking, gallantry and divinity, he fell to them all with the thirsty self-will and iron nerves of an athlete; only his divinity made him careful to marry before he murdered.*

The pomps and vanities of Elizabeth were better warranted, though she lectured a bishop out of her pew for alluding to them. Her three thousand dresses (for such was the number found in her wardrobe) have almost as many excuses, when we recollect what a noise she made as queen and woman, and what a number of high and gallant tastes were prepared to admire her. It is true, she had "too much sense," was "too great a queen," &c., but in these matters too much sense is very apt not to be enough; nor do we find that women, or even men, of the greatest and gravest sense, are above the little artifices that

---

* Fuller, in his Church History, tells a good story of Henry the Eighth and his fool. "King Henry," says the old divine, "had lately set forth a book against Luther, endeavoring the confutation of his opinions as novel and unsound." None suspect this king's lack of learning (though many his lack of leisure from his pleasures) for such a design: however, it is probable some other GARDENER gathered the flowers (made the collections), though King Henry had the honor to wear the posy, carrying the credit in the title thereof.

To requite his pains the pope honored him and his successors with a specious title, "A Defender of the Faith." . . . There is a tradition, that King Henry's fool (though more truly to be termed by another name), coming into the court, and finding the king transported with an unusual joy, boldly asked of 'im the cause thereof; to whom the king answered, it was because that the pope had honored him with a style more eminent than any of his ancestors. "O, good Harry," quoth the fool, "let thou and I defend one another, and let the faith alone to defend itself." — ED.

help to set off their persons. Age and misfortune
make a difference, but the misfortune must be new
indeed that diminishes the vanity of a throne. In
those times pomp and splendor were thought to
belong as much to the person of the sovereign as
the state ; though nothing, it must be confessed, was
omitted or discontinued that could bring round the
world to a different way of thinking. Here, in the
tilt-yard at Whitehall, did Elizabeth, " in her sixty-
fifth year, wrinkled face, red periwig, little eyes,
hooked nose, skinny lips, and black teeth," preside over the chivalrous exercises, and receive the
homage of her gallant knights, who stormed alle-
gorical forts to get at her " beauty," and died in
all sorts of eloquent despairs if she averted the heav-
en of her looks. It was a set of poetical grown children " making believe," and more grave and self-de-
ceiving than smaller ones. For we must not suppose
that the self-deception was confined to Elizabeth.
Her adoring courtiers would marry secretly against
her will, and occasionally be moved into a prosaical
sense of her age and her skinny lips ; but one charm
stands instead of another, and serves the latter with
its own results. Elizabeth being a great queen, and
able to gratify ever in so many ways the self-love of
her admirers, would remain an attractive woman
long after all pretensions had ceased in any other
station. Wit and good nature have done as much for
women ; and even deformity has been held by some a
fascination ; so much has mere sensation to do in
most extreme cases, beyond any other impulse.

James the First, that slatternly pedant and very ill-

contrived personage, kept up the spectacles of the tilt-
yard, and was the cause of much finery in others.
But the great patron of martial exercises was his son
Henry. After the filial fashion of heirs apparent,
Henry affected a policy quite opposite to that of
his father; and, like all heirs apparent who die
before they come to the throne, was a popular and
hopeful prince. It is to James the First the public are
indebted for the noble banqueting-house built by Inigo
Jones. I have sometimes stood and looked at it till I
thought that, by one of the hidden analogies between
the fine arts, the beautiful proportions of the upper
part of the front affected me like a piece of music.
Let the reader stand and measure with his eye the proportions between the windows and the spaces about
them, and imagine this or that part to be contracted
or enlarged, and he will feel how injurious would be
the alteration. The glory of Whitehall was at its
height in the time of James and Charles the First;
Inigo Jones built for the court, Rubens and Vandyke
painted for it,* and Ben Jonson wrote for it. Royalty had not found out its weak side, nor learnt to become jealous of natural greatness. Genius was
thought only an accessary to " the fair State," and was
allowed to put forth its full lustre. Louis the Fourteenth told Boileau that he had always a quarter of
an hour to spare for his conversation whenever he
chose to visit the court. And this was thought a won-

---

* Holbein was employed at Whitehall under the Tudors. He died there of
the plague, and is supposed to have been buried in the churchyard belonging
to St. Catherine Cree, near the India House. Vandyke also died in England,
and was buried in Old St. Paul's. The Academy should give him a monument
in the New.

derful favor; and so it was, as times went; yet what
was it more than a good bargain made for himself by
a dull gentleman with a man of wit? This, however,
was nothing to poor Racine, who languished like a
lily and died, because the king was displeased with
him. — Painting is still more welcome at court than
poetry. Poets, with all their flattery, have arrogant
ways; assume crowns of laurel, and talk of bestow-
ing immortality. They jostle the sovereign in his
throne with another sovereignty, which is of a suspicious character, and disdains the common fashions
of mortality. But painting takes its place as part of
the show. It offers the most visible and ornamental
display of genius with the least pretensions to it, and
with the greatest flattery to places and persons; and
accordingly has always been welcome. Even an
American and half Republican (the late Mr. West)
was liked at Windsor; though perhaps there was a
particular zest in having an American for a royal
painter. In the time of the Stuarts there was a generosity in the treatment of artists, which argued much
for the intelligence of the patrons.

Rubens (who was employed in negotiations) carried his art with such a high hand, that it seems
doubtful whether he was an ambassador condescending to be an artist, or an artist submitting to be an
ambassador. His pupil Vandyke married the daughter of a British earl. It has been said that architecture was not appreciated, though good architects were
employed. The court had the good fortune to light
on a man of genius; but his pay, they say, shows
what was thought of his art. Now it is true that

Inigo Jones, as Surveyor of the Works, had but eight
and four pence a day, and forty-six pounds per annum
for house rent, a clerk, and extras. But it remains to
be shown how long he was occupied in the business
of his office. Genius deserves all it can get; but it
may be countenanced in a variety of ways; and if it
grow wealthy at last, as Inigo did, nobody can complain. The royal countenance procured him a great
deal of employment, and Ben Jonson accuses him
of thinking himself of so much importance as to aspire
to be made a marquis. The jealous poet, whose
masques he ornamented too well with his machinery,
condescended to write a satire, in which he reproaches
him with commencing life with " forty pounds a year
in pipkins." Jones might have had a large sum of
money given him for every design ; but his profits
would then have become enormous, and beyond all
proportion. There appears to be considerable justice,
upon the whole, in the treatment which genius experiences from the world. Fashion may overdo the
thing one way, and superiority to a man's age be a
drawback another ; but there is fair play in the main.
An architect is obliged to get money, like a builder ;
but he has the honor besides, and more profit. The
painter, though he has workmen also in his pupils,
labors hard himself, and gets profit in the same
manner. Rubens had three thousand pounds for
painting the ceiling of the Banqueting-house. The
poet is apt to get least of all ; but this is owing partly
to the causes before alluded to, and partly to the
greater volatility of his temperament. He is not so
accommodating to others, nor so prudent in himself.

He takes a wider range of thought and imagination, gets more pleasure in that airy circle, and if he gets more sorrows likewise, looks for a more exalted fame, and feels himself to be one of the dictators of posterity. If all this does not make up to him for what he endures, the nature of things renders it necessary that more good should be got out of him than out of any other artist, because all the world can read books and profit by them ; whereas few of us can see fine pictures ; and fine architecture is still rarer, and of less importance. The poet must content himself with the noble fatality of his destiny, and look for reward elsewhere. It is his sympathies with the many that keeps him poor, — the most honorable of all poverties. It is clear, from all history, that great poets might be as rich as any other men of genius ; but they have always some starting-point in them, tangible in some way or other, to the demands of the many, and liable to carry them off from their success. This was the case with Dante, Petrarch, and Milton, with Spenser (though his sympathy took an awkward direction, and must needs subject him to the anger of the Irish), with Chaucer, who got into a four years' imprisonment in his old age for being a Wickliffite, with the patriot Greek poets, and more or less with almost every poet of eminence. Even the best courtiers among them contrive to remain poor. A dramatist has the best chance ; for the wider his sympathy, the greater chance the pit have of liking him ; and it was a theatre that made Shakespeare rich.

The lamentation respecting the little pay to court architects — (I believe there is no such lamentations

now, whoever the architects may be) — has been renewed in speaking of Sir Christopher Wren. The
salary of this excellent person " for building St. Paul's
from the foundation, was not more (as appears from
the public accounts) than two hundred pounds per
annum ; his allowance for building all the parochial
churches of the city of London was about a hundred
per annum, and the same for the repairs of Westminster Abbey ; he was director and chief architect of the
Royal Hospital at Greenwich, *gratis*, and cheerfully
contributed to that work his time, labor, and skill for
several years, without salary, emolument, or reward ;
preferring in this, as in every other passage of his
life, the public service to his own private advantage."
(Seward's Anecdotes, quoted by Dr. Drake in the
notes to his interesting edition of the Tatler, vol. ii.,
p. 13.) This looks formidable enough. It is true
that sovereigns are fond of cheap payments for everybody but themselves ; but still, if the art they countenance is such a one as fashion and private interest
can employ, the artist stands a good chance of becoming rich. Sir Christopher, I believe, did so in
spite of the time he spent in drawing plans for government. He was a member of the House of Commons in two Parliaments.

It is generally supposed that Charles the First went
to the scaffold through one of the front windows of
the Banqueting-house. But he came out at the north
side. Pennant informs us that a passage was broken on purpose. It was remaining in his time, " and
was a door to a small additional building of late
date." Most likely it is still in being. This was the

hour of Charles's life which did him most credit.
Cromwell might have envied it at the close of his
usurpation. Marvell, a lover of liberty, has done it
justice : —

> "He nothing common did, or mean,
>   Upon that memorable scene,
>   But with his keener eye
>   The axe's edge did try :
>   Nor called the gods with vulgar spite
>   To vindicate his helpless right,
>   But bowed his comely head
>   Down as upon a bed."

When will a court-poet write such verses upon a
freeman?

After a "sullen interval" on the part of Cromwell
(who nevertheless got softened by the court air, drank
his wine freely, and had " cunning musicians " to play
and sing to him),* in came " Bacchus and his Revel-
lers," — Rochester's wits and Grammont's maids of
honor. Charles the Second, who somehow or other,
has contrived to be a favorite with some very regular moralists as well as politicians, — Sir Walter
Scott, for instance, and Dr. Johnson, — had in fact
many excuses for his general conduct, setting aside
even the usual indulgence allowed to kings in matters of pleasure. He had gone through a series of
early experiences, very imperious to a sense of the
dignity and hopefulness of human nature. The
sharpness of adversity, joined to his natural acute-
ness, must often have enabled him to see too far

---

* Cromwell took delight in a good voice, and had a church organ, which the
Puritans put down at Oxford, privately set up for his amusement at one of the
palaces.

even into the spirit of-loyalty, which did him such
romantic services. His little court, while in exile,
was a perpetual scene of jealousies and complaints;
and the sudden tide of homage and popularity which
rushed to meet him on the change of his fortune
must have contributed to give no pleasanter turn to
the early furrows cut in his·face by doubt and anxiety. He is called "the merry monarch;" but mirth
in him, as in many others, was set off by a ground
of melancholy. The French vivacity and voluptu-
ousness which he inherited on the mother's side,
had a certain hang-dog contradiction in it derived
from his father. He loved repose still better than
enjoyment. "Sauntering," said one of his companions, "was the true sultana queen he delighted in."
He was often seen in the Park, accompanied by his
dogs, and feeding the ducks he kept there; and he
would chat familiarly with the people, which made
them love him. In Pennant's London is a picture
of the then state of the parade and horse-guards,
with his majesty, attended by his peers and his
puppies.

Most of Charles's mistresses had lodgings within
the precincts of Whitehall. It was one enormous
magazine of princes and their household officers, civil
and military, cooks, wine-cellars, bowling-greens, ten-
nis-grounds, pimps, gamesters, lords and ladies of
all sorts. Dryden, in an epilogue written the year before his death, though he appears always to have retained a liking for his old master and his "fair words,"
does not mend the matter. Speaking of the licentiousness of that time, he says, —

> "The sin was of our native growth, 'tis true;
> The scandal of the sin was wholly new.
> Misses they were, but modestly concealed;
> Whitehall the naked Venus first revealed.
> Who, standing as at Cyprus, in her shrine,
> The strumpet was adored with rites divine."

The scandal drew in its horns in the time of James the Second, who had more of the Jesuit in him; but the time was now approaching when the bustle of Whitehall was to be broken up, and the place no longer to be a seat of royalty. James was obliged to write a letter to his invader, William, inviting him to take up his abode at St. James's. The invitation was accepted, and his majesty in return advised to take his departure from Whitehall. William the Third resided in other palaces; and the only visible part now remaining of the old establishment is the Banqueting-house, which has long been converted into a chapel.

No. VI.

ST. JAMES'S PARK.

" IN the time of King Henry the Eighth," says a note to Dr. King's poems, in Mr. Chalmers's collection, "the park was a wild, wet field; but that prince, on building St. James's Palace, enclosed it, laid it out in walks, and collecting the waters together, gave to the new enclosed ground and new-raised buildings the name of St. James's. It was much enlarged by Charles the Second; who added to it several fields, planted it with rows of lime trees, laid out the mall, formed the canal with a decoy, and other ponds for water-pool. The lime trees, or *tilia*, whose blossoms are uncommonly fragrant, were probably planted in consequence of a suggestion of Mr. Evelyn, in his *Fumifugium*, published in 1661."

Charles the Second was very fond of the Park. His habit of walking there, attended by his dogs, both sad and merry, has been noticed before. His ducks, which he also amused himself with feeding, inhabited a spot called Duck Island, which was erected into a "government," in order to furnish the French exile and wit, St. Evremond, with a pension. Birdcage Walk must not be forgotten, which was an aviary of Charles's raising, and retains its appellation. Waller speaks of the improvements of St. James's Park in the gratuitous style of a poet. The libertines of the court were to sport about the canal, like the harmless wantons of a golden age; while Charles walks among the trees in all the dignity of a Numa, and settles the destinies of the world : —

"Methinks I see the love that shall be made,
The lovers walking in that amorous shade :
The gallants dancing by the river side ;
They bathe in summer, and in winter slide.
Methinks I hear the music in the boats,
And the loud Echo which returns the notes :
While overhead a flock of new-sprung fowl
Hangs in the air, and does the sun control :
Dark'ning the sky, they hover o'er, and shroud
The wanton sailors with a feather'd cloud.
Beneath, a shoal of silver fishes glides,
And plays about the gilded barges' sides :
The ladies angling in the crystal lake,
Feast on the waters with the prey they take :
At once victorious with their lines and eyes,
They make the fishes and the men their prize."

The vigor with which the king plays at mall is then doted on; and the poet proceeds in some striking verses: —

> "Near this, my Muse, what most delights her, sees
> A living gallery of aged trees;
> Bold sons of earth, that thrust their arms so high,
> As if once more they would invade the sky.
> In such green palaces the first kings reigned,
> Slept in their shades, and angels entertained:
> With such old counsellors they did advise,
> And by frequenting sacred groves grew wise.
> Free from the impediments of light and noise,
> Man, thus retir'd, his nobler thoughts employs.
> Here Charles contrives the ordering of his states,
> Here he resolves his neighboring princes' fates:
> What nation shall have peace, where war be made,
> Determined is in this oraculous shade."

Again, in some verses not so good: —

> "Here, like the people's pastor, he does go,
> His flock subjected to his view below:
> On which reflecting in his mighty mind,
> No private passion does indulgence find:
> The pleasures of his youth suspended are,
> And made a sacrifice to public care.
> Here, free from court compliances, he walks,
> And with himself, his best adviser, talks:
> How peaceful olive may his temples shade,
> For mending, and for restoring trade:
> Or, how his brows may be with laurels charg'd,
> For nations conquer'd and our bounds enlarg'd."

Alas, it should have been, —

> "For pensions taken, and for France enlarg'd."

All that his majesty thought of "in this oraculous shade," was how to pass his time and get money for his pleasures.

> "Methinks I see the love that shall be made."

This it was more easy for our grave poet to predicate. The Park is the scene of some of the most libertine

plays of that period. I do not know where the Mul-
berry Garden stood, which gives a title to one of the
comedies of Sedley; perhaps on the site of Spring
Garden, which was a place of entertainment up to a
late period. The milk fresh from the cow, which is
still sold under the trees at the entrance from that
quarter, and which has a pleasing effect on emerging
from the streets, appears to be a remnant of the former traffic.

Marlborough House, now the residence of Prince
Leopold, was one of the national acknowledgments
to the Duke of Marlborough. It was built partly in a
garden belonging to the queen. Her majesty had thus
her defender and her old friend the duchess by her
side; and on the other side, in the palace still called by
his name, lived her old friend and admirer (who, they
say, courted her in his youth,) Sheffield, Duke of
Buckingham. He married her sister, natural child of
James the Second by the daughter of Sir Charles Sedley. Sheffield built the mansion and laid out the
garden. He adorned the four sides of the house with
inscriptions, one of which is much to the purpose:
" Fastidiosus spectator sibi molestus,"— " A fastidious spectator is his own annoyance." This is the
nobleman of whom the Tatler speaks as the " Duke
that lives at Marylebone." A strange story is related
in Pennant, of his giving a dinner to " the most infamous sharpers of the time," who gambled at that
place, and of a toast with which he concluded it:
" May as many of us as remain unhanged next spring,
meet here again." " I remember," says Pennant,
" the facetious Quin telling this story at Bath, within
hearing of the late Lord Chesterfield, when his lord-

ship was surrounded by a crowd of worthies of the same stamp with the above." I cannot help thinking that the company was more suited to the author of the Letters than the writer of the Minor Poems. Sheffield is one of the " twinkling stars " in the Miscellanies, and has a lurking goodness in the midst of his libertinism. He has been accused of pride and arrogance; but they say he was amiable in private. His sharping connections do not look like the man of whom his widow speaks so highly in his Remains; but it is astonishing what strange things come together in high life, and with what accommodating philosophy the great regard their own contradictions. The lie on which their pretensions are founded is the cause of it, and renders it in a certain degree excusable. A man cannot well feel that the world would consent to make distinctions that have no real existence, with impunity.

St. James's Palace was built by Henry the Eighth, on the site of an ancient hospital for lepers. The name was the name of the hospital. The palace was fitted up by William for the Princess Anne and her husband, Prince George of Denmark. She retained it as her residence when queen, and it has since been the headquarters of the British Court. Pennant says, that although the outside is unsightly, it is the most convenient palace for regal parade of any in Europe. There were some interesting pictures there in his time, probably still remaining. One of them was " the diminutive Manhood of Geoffrey Hudson." *

---

* Scott introduced Geoffrey or Jeffrey Hudson into Peveril of the Peak. He also honors the little man with a long note, to which we refer the curious reader — En.

" Here," says Pennant, " is to be seen the famous picture by Mabuse, of Adam and Eve. Mr. Evelyn
justly remarks the absurdity of painting them with
navels and a fountain of rich imagery amidst the
beauteous wilds of Paradise. Raphael and Michael
Angelo made the same mistake of the navel, on which
the learned Sir Thomas Browne wastes a long page
and a half to disprove the possibility." With the
leave of these worthy gentlemen, and of the profound
theosophist, Raphael and Michael Angelo knew more
about these navel affairs than they. The fountain is
not so well; but (not to say anything of what is impossible to Omnipotence), Adam and Eve were
bound to be complete specimens of the human race;
patterns and prototypes, as well as progenitors. As
they anticipated our growth, so they anticipated all
the rest of us : —

> "Adam the goodliest man of men since born
> His sons, the fairest of her daughters Eve." *

The goodliness of the picture desiderated by Mr. Evelyn and Sir Thomas, I leave all people of taste to
imagine.

In books of fifty and a hundred years back, if you
meet with a hungry gentleman who did not know
where to get a dinner, you always find him sitting on
a bench in the Park. Others generally accompany
him, most of whom are politicians. Bickerstaff meets
here his acquaintance the upholsterer, who lets his
affairs run to ruin in his zeal for the King of Swe-

---

* See South's remarkable sermon on The Creation of Man in God's Image
He says that "an *Aristotle* was but the rubbish of an *Adam*." — ED.

den.* People do not appear so patient nowadays
to hunger and thirst, though their politics are more
zealous than ever. In sympathizing with the world
at large, instead of confining themselves to be tragedy
spectators of royalty, they have learned to include
their own rights. They may die by other means,
they may be ruined by a bankruptcy, or be hacked and
hewed by a series of disappointed hopes; but till they
are fairly put an end to, they claim the common privilege of eating their breakfast and dinner. Besides,
others would not let them want a dinner. Revolutions
have produced a tendency to diminish the extent of
royal kitchens, but only that the superflux may be
shaken to the many. Rabelais would delight to see
Gargantua no longer considered as everybody. The
two pilgrims, whom he ate in a salad, would in these
times have at least made considerable objections.

It would appear, from novels, that the Park enjoyed
some privileges from arrest. In Fielding's Amelia,
if I remember, the hero often walks in the Mall,
when he can go nowhere else. During the existence of the old Cathedral of St. Paul's, the inside of
that church was the resort of the hungry; who, in

.* The character of the political upholsterer is by Addison: it is one of the
happiest of his contributions to the Tatler. "We should hope," says Hazlitt,
in the Round Table, "the upholsterer and his companions in the Green Park
stand as fair a chance for immortality as some modern politicians." Beau Tibbs
was fond of sauntering in St. James's Park, now in rags, now in embroidery;
and hither came Miss Hannah (another of Goldsmith's characters), to show l er
finery and criticise the finery of others. It was in St. James's Park that the freeholder saw his friend the Tory fox-hunter feeding the ducks. If the reader is unacquainted with this masterpiece of humorous characterization, he should forthwith
take down his Addison, and read the three little papers on the fox-hunter, in the
Freeholder. — ED.

allusion to a tomb supposed to contain the body of Humphrey, Duke of Gloucester, gave rise to the say-ing of dining with Duke Humphrey.

The Mall is so called from the game of mall to which Waller alludes. Charles the Second transferred it from Pall Mall. It is a great pity that these and similar exercises have been left off. Without canting about the degeneracy of the times, it is a reasonable deduc-tion, from our abandonment of healthy and manly games, that we are an inferior race to our ancestors in point of bodily grace and vigor.

In a house looking into Mr. Bentham's garden, in Bird-cage Walk, lived Milton. The front of it is in York Street, and, without being the ancient one, is in very squalid condition. If it had a new face and an inscription, which it surely deserves, it would turn to better account for all parties. There used to be a bust on the other side, which we believe Mr. Ben-tham put up. But it is not the custom of that emi-nent person to monopolize a good thing, and he ought to let as many people know of the house as possible. It is the privilege of Westminster to exhibit a spirit of liberty proportionate to the encroachments of the other power that lives there.

The Horse-Guards were in poor condition in the time of Charles. The stables looked like the open corridors of an old inn ; and a toy of a building, with staircase outside, appears to have been the Guard House. These conclusions are drawn from the print in Pennant. I thought the design of the present building was by Vanbrugh ; but Pennant says he be-lieves it was the work of an architect of the name of

Vardy. The structure is not older than the reign of
George the Second. There is something fantastic in
the custom of setting two soldiers on horseback to
mount guard in those tenements at the entrance, like
a couple of live statues. But they are fine specimens
of the weight and steadiness of a pair of English
dragoons, and keep a gravity becoming their situations. Some say they have been seen eating pudding and apples; but this is what I will not believe.

The band on parade is worth hearing. They play
some of the best pieces of Mozart and Haydn, which
the wind carries hither and thither in triumph. I
remember taking home to school the air of *Non più
andrai*, long before I knew the name of Mozart.
Here war is to be seen under its most harmless aspect,
with its fringes, its colors, and its gallant sounds. It
is all holiday play and gentle service; a business of
steppings and salutations. The band-major looks
grave and ruling; the blacks toss up their cymbals in
the sun; the little triangle-boys emulate their long
legs; the officers step along, very gentlemanly; the
companies tread solidly at their elbows, like bodies
with their soul beside them; the young ensign is admired in the middle, carrying his colors like a fluttering heart. Anon, the noble instruments give way to
the drum and fife, and the regiment proceeds for the
court-yard in a livelier and more familiar step. During the parade, a trumpet and a stir of cavalry are
heard; and a fine troop of dragoons issue forth on
their long-tailed black horses, the trumpeter on a
white one blowing his trumpet, which mingles with
the instruments of the foot, and makes a gallant con-

fusion. Who would not then be a soldier, and dictate to the world? Certainly if war is a necessary evil, it is pranked up and recommended to us in the best possible manner. Nature will do her utmost to gild her bitterest pills. In one point of view, what can be more silly than those gay and self-satisfied persons, marching away, in the long run, to have their throats cut, and their heads blown to atoms? But in another, what can be more reconciling in its necessity? What more calculated to bring tears of mingled pity and admiration in our eyes? What better way could have been found out to enlist the superfluous part of society into its roughest and most dangerous service? I am no disciple of Mr. Malthus. He either cannot, or, being a clergyman, dare not handle the real question, which I think it requires no great knowledge of economy to see into. But wars have long been a part of the history of mankind, and most have been the necessary result of some modification of its manners. It does not follow that the necessity is to exist forever, or that the alternative is the one he speaks of. The present forms of society must be broken up, and the whole earth properly cultivated, before he has a right to argue that there is not enough for all, much less that *war* is necessary to prevent the redundance of population. See what Mr. Hazlitt has said on the subject at the end of his Political Essays. In the mean time an end is not likely to· be put to war by making mere representations of its misery, however just. God knows they cannot well be exaggerated. See, for one instance, worth a thousand, a note to a certain Ode to Horror, in the works of the Poet Laureate, the Pilgrim to Waterloo. The point is to keep our reasoning faculties on the alert, — our liberties of thinking and speaking; and to enable ourselves to detest sophistry and time-serving. One sound philosophical discovery goes farther towards the alteration of society than millions of complaints. The danger of these is, that the very suffering will be glad to relieve itself, and run into the gayety of despair. It is our business to keep ourselves in heart, as far as a present necessity goes, and in health of mind not to be imposed upon beyond the necessity.

No. VII.

SPRING.

Ah, happy hills! ah, pleasing shade!
Ah, fields, beloved in vain! — GRAY.

HAIL, beautiful season! hail, return of the green leaves! hail, violets, daisies, and buttercups! hail, blue sky; and ye, white little silver clouds, "gay creatures of the elements," the posterity of your turbid sires of winter time!

Hail, moreover, ye evidences of spring, even in cities! Hail, green in the windows, and on the ladies' caps! Hail, coats instead of great-coats! Hail, beaux and other butterflies! Hail, the leaving off of fires; provided, dear fires, among my countrymen, ye are left off! Great encroachers upon sum-

mer time are ye; mighty disputers of the sunshine
with May and June!

There is a tendency all over the temperate part of
Europe to anticipate the beauties of spring, — to
fancy the season more forward than it is, or to complain that it is otherwise. I find this in Italy as well
as in England. Horace Walpole said that it was the
fashion to say there was no winter in Italy. There
is certainly a winter sharp enough to startle foreigners; and the spring in Tuscany is far from premature. I have not found the weather in either season
different from what Horace says of the snows in
winter, and Virgil of the stormy showers in spring.
The *Primavera*, or spring of the Italian poets, dis-
appoints expectation as much as the Aprils and
Mays described by our own. *Primavera* comes in
March, and is properly the first part of the vernal
season, the *ver primum* of the Latins. The blossom
issues forth on the trees, the cranes are seen travelling in the sky, the hedges are lively with violets
and periwinkles; but it is not a season warranting
what the poets say of it, and warming the blood.
Cold winds prevail, as with us; the snows, lingering
on the mountains, embitter them, and the rains are violent. April commences the true poetical spring, and
May is spring confirmed, the real season of the " *no-
velli amori*," the May of the British poets. Whether
the seasons alter from time to time in different parts
of the world is a point contested. Most likely they
do. But, for a long time past, the May of our poets
is rather June, and very often the middle and end of
June rather than the beginning. For many years it

has been common to have fires as late as the old King's birthday, the 4th of June. What we call spring is indeed *spring*, literally speaking; and a very beautiful idea the word gives us. The *ver* of the ancients appears to have meant the rising of the sap. Our Saxon term is more lively and visible. It is not merely the life, but the leaping of the season; the gladness of its pulse. And yet the vivacity belongs rather to nature than to us. We have not got rid enough of our colds and clothings.

If the season is very fine indeed, the true time of enjoyment in England is the one that Thomson has selected for his Bower of Indolence, —

> "A season atween June and May,
> Half prankt with spring, with summer half embrown'd."

When the spring came this year in Tuscany, it was a great pleasure to me to see the corn, wine, and oil, all preparing to flourish together, — for the fields are nothing else. What are meadows and cornfields in England, are orchards full of olives and vines in Tuscany, with the corn growing betwixt them. The green corn running in close stripes among the olive trees, and the preparations for the budding of the vines, — it being the custom here to make trellises of reed-work, really elegant in many parts of the hedges, — furnish a lively spectacle. But spring, as well as winter, made me think of home. I put on my Cap, and pitched myself in those delicious fields, all over daisies and buttercups, which go sloping from Hampstead to West End and Kilburn, — fields, the representatives of thousands of others all over

England, and in which I would rather take a walk
" atween June and May " than in the divinest spot
recorded by the divinest of southern poets. It is
common with persons in love to fancy that everybody
must be happy who lives in the society of the object
of their attachment. In the same manner, when I
am compelled to forego the privileges of my Cap, and
confine myself to wishing without enjoying (which
is sometimes the case), I cannot help envying the
reader for his power to go into the places I write of.
I say to myself, " Now somebody will take it into his
head to go and look at those fields, or he will go and
look at those he is more acquainted with ; or he will,
or he *can*, go into some English field or other, rich
with grass and powdered with flowers. He will see
the hedges ; he will see the elms and oaks (there are
no elms and oaks here). He will, or he may and
can, or might, could, would, should walk in a wood
full of them. Furthermore, he will meet with some
old friends."

Reader, if there is any man who has offended you,
and whom you find it hard to forgive, forgive him, I
entreat you ; for I forgive you, and you are the most
provoking person I have known a long time. I could
knock the paper out of your hand. Don't you sit
giggling there, you other reader, C. L., A. B., or
C., or whatever title pleased thy godfather's ear.
Conscious of your power to take a long walk through
the sun and dust, you take advantage of my weakness
to triumph over me. But, lo ! my Wishing-Cap is on
me in all its glory. The very mention of your name
makes me present. I am with you ; walk with you,

talk with you. It was I who sighed just now while you were reading. — Reader, we are reconciled and together.

Fortunately I am not of a temper to make the worst of any situation I happen to be cast in. And I look upon it as a reward for my love of Nature that I have never been in a situation in which I had not some glimpse of her to console me. Even in prison I had a little garden to myself, and raised my own heart's-ease. It may not be the most grateful thing in the world to think of a jail while strolling about the most classical ground in Tuscany. I confess I think of it very often. But Nature will excuse me, because my dejection is owing to my love. If I had not loved her so much at home, I should not miss, as I do, the old homestead. I do what I can. I think of Petrarch and Boccaccio, of Milton and Galileo, and Fiesole, which I see from my window, and which is a common boundary to my walks. I endeavor to keep the vines and the olive trees new to me. Besides Virgil and the Italy of books, I make the olives remind me of Athens, of Plato, and Homer, and Sophocles, and Socrates, and a still more reverend Name in another country, who went up into a mount of olives to pray. A Dominican convent is a little in my way, with its inscription in honor of the fiery saint, " the destroyer of heretics; " but the friars no longer inhabit it, and I endeavor to consider even the Inquisition as a violent note struck in the ears of mankind to make them attend to the doctrine it contradicted. Philosophy has separated the doctrine from its abuse, and the Inquisition is no more. I think of the gayer sort of abuses, the red side of their cheek, the jollity of a refectory. Pope's picture is before me, of

" Happy convents, buried deep in vines,
Where slumber abbots purple as their wines,"

(A couplet as plump and painted as the subject.) The transition to Horace and Anacreon is a pleasing necessity. I am in the very thick of the vines of Redi, the author of the Bacchus in Tuscany. His Bacchus is as flourishing a god as ever, and sworn by as devoutly, though the saints have displaced his image. Florence, at a little distance, meets the turn of my eye at every opening of the trees. In short, I am in a world of poetry and romance, of vines and olives, and myrtles (which grow wild), of blue mountains and never-ending orchards, with a beautiful city in the middle of it. What signifies? I think of an English field in a sylvan country, a cottage and oaks in the corner, a path and a stile, and a turf full of daisies ; and a child's book with a picture in it becomes more precious to me than all the landscapes of Claude.

I intended to sprinkle this article with some flowers out of the Italian poets ; but positively I will not do it. They are not good. They are not true. The grapes are sour. Commend me to the cockney satisfactions of Chaucer, Spenser, and Milton, who talk of " merry London," of lying whole hours looking at the daisies, and of walking out on Sunday mornings to enjoy the daisies and green fields. There are no daisies here that I can see, except those belonging to the Grand Duke. What is a daisy belonging to a duke ? Nature is not to be put upon a gentleman's establish-

ment. The other fine houses do not impose upon
me. They want comfort and fireplaces, and instead
of parks, and other natural pieces of ground about
them, have vines and olives, vines and olives without
end. The peasants are all vine-dressers and olive-
squeezers. You meet a piece of a cow occasionally
on your table; but a good, handsome, live animal,
with a low, I have not encountered for many months.
You must go to Lombardy for a pasture. There are
goats, very large and bucolic; but goats in England
are poor and small, which is the proper goat, and
renders a kid pathetic. The only one I have a respect for is the companion of our voyage, given us
by a friend, and preserved through various vicissitudes for her sake. A dog belonging to an acquaintance of ours inhospitably bit her ear off, and the
storms at sea frightened away her milk. But she now
reposes for life, like a matron, enjoying herself among
scenes more native to her palate than England itself.

If the sky in England would only mitigate a little
of its clouds and fogs in favor of one of its countrywomen, and of a modest demi-exotic, who loves a
green field better than all the sugar-canes of his ancestors . . . But what signifies talking? Suffice it,
that an Englishman in Italy, who loves Italian poetry,
and is obliged to be grateful to Italian skies, assures
his beloved countrymen (who are not always sensible
of the good things they have about them) that there
is nothing upon earth so fine as a good, rich English
meadow in summer time. That English Frenchman,
La Fontaine, is of the same opinion; for when he
speaks with rapture of a bit of turf, and says there is

nothing to equal it, it must be recollected that such turf is more native to England than to France; and so he would have told us had he come over to England, as he ought to have done, and taken a stroll in our fields with his friend, St. Evremond. Even a Tuscan's idea of a garden is not complete without a piece of turf, though the *podere*, or farm, encroaches everywhere, and pounds and shillings must be planted in the shape of olive trees. A garden in the English taste is a " miracolo " and a " paradiso ; " their poetry rises within them at the sight of it, but they think this is only for princes and grand dukes. Yet Horace could not dispense with his grass and his oak trees; and the valley which I look upon from my window sparkles in the *Decameron* with a perpetual green. Nature inspires great authors, and they repay her by rescuing her very self from oblivion, and keeping her transitory pictures fresh in our hearts. *They*, thank God, as well as the fields, *are* Nature; and so is every great and kindly aspiration we possess.

•

No. VIII.

RAINY-DAY POETRY.

. . . . . . Dicessit ab astris
Humor, et ima petit. — LUCAN.

Humor sets the welkin free,
And condescends with you and me.

CRITICS lament over a number of idle rhymes in the works of Swift, that may come under the above title; and wish, at least, that they had never

6

been published. They designate them as the sweep-
ings of his study, his private weaknesses, unworthy
of so great a genius, and exclaim against his friends
for collecting them.   I really cannot see the humiliation.   If he had written nothing else, there might
be some color of accusation against him; though I
do not see why a dean is bound to be a dull private
gentleman.   But if he had written nothing else, I
think it may be pretty safely pronounced that he
would not have written these trifles.   They bear the
mark of a great hand, trifling as they are.   Their ex-
travagance is that of power, not of weakness; and
the wilder Irish waggery of Dr. Sheridan, slatternly
and muddled, stands rebuked before them.   What
should we have done had we lost Mary the Cook-maid's
Letter, and the Grand Question about the Barracks?
These, to be sure, are excepted by everybody; but I
like, for my part, to hear all that such an exquisite
wag has to say.   I except the coarseness of two or
three pieces, which I never read.   I wish the critics
could say as much.   I have such a disgust of this
kind of writing that there are poems, even in Chaucer,
which I never look at.   But this does not hinder me
from loving all the rest.   Perhaps I carry my dislike
of what I allude to too far.   It is possible that it may
not be without its use in certain stages of society.
But so it is, and I mention it, that I may not be
thought to be confounding or recommending two
different things.

It is our own fault if we take this Rainy-Day
Poetry for more than the author intended it. It is
our loss if we do not take it for as much.   I give

it this title, because we may suppose it written to
while away the tedium of rainy days, or of the feelings that resemble it. There is also Rainy-Day
Prose; of a great deal of which my own writings
are composed, though I was hardly aware of it at
the time. I relish all that Swift has favored us
with, of either kind. The only approach that we
minor humorists can make to such men, is to show
that we understand them in all their moods, — that
nothing is lost on us. The greatest fit of laughter
I ever remember to have had, was in reading the
Commination piece against William Wood, in which
all his enemies are introduced execrating him in
puns. The zest was heightened by the presence of
a deaf old lady, who had desired a friend of mine
and myself to take a book, while waiting to see a
kinsman of hers. Her imperturbable face, the shock-
ing things we said before her, and even the dread
of being thought rude, produced a sort of double
drama in our minds, extreme and irresistible.

A periodical writer derives the same privileges
from necessity which other men do from wit. The
rainy days here in Italy are very rare compared with
those of England; but the damps which the latter
produce within us sometimes make their appearance
when we are away; and a . . . In short, it is not
necessary to inform the reader that periodical writers
produce a great deal of rainy-day poetry, voluntary
or involuntary. If he excuses it, all is well. I shall,
therefore, whenever I am inclined, make use of this
title to pass off rhymes that I have more pleasure in
writing than in publishing. The other day I was

moved to vent my pluviose indignation on the subject of Ferdinand, King of Spain; a personage who
has had the extraordinary fortune (even for a prince)
to become the spectacle of the whole world, precisely
because he is destitute of every quality which deserves their notice.   That my poem might be as
small as my subject, I wrote it in Lilliputian lines
and miniature cantos; but, in consequence of the
variety of feelings that pressed upon me as I proceeded, three out of the four became neither one
thing nor t'other, and are not worth indulgence.
The exordium I lay before the reader, because it
contains an anecdote of his majesty's first appearance on the stage, with which he may not be acquainted.   I had it from a Spanish gentleman now
in England.

> I sing the least of things, —
> To wit, the least of kings.
>
> Imprimis, when the nation
> First raised him to his station,
> And blest him as he rid
> In triumph to Madrid,
> A gentleman who saw him
> (And hugely longed to claw him)
> Said, that he never showed
> One feeling on the road,
> But sat in stupid pride,
> Staring on either side,
> Letting his hand be kissed
> (I think I see the fist).
> As if, where'er they took it,
> They meant to pick his pocket;
> And goggling like an owl, —
> The hideous beaky fool!

The last line is emphatic!   I had not patience to continue in a proper style of burlesque.   Ferdinand has

astonished even those who were never astonished at
kings before. And yet what was to be expected from
this portentous specimen of royalty, — royalty, naked, instinctive, unmitigated, unadorned? What examples he had before him! What an education!
What contempt of decencies, public and private!
What a mother, what a minister, what a father! The
same gentleman who related to me the above anecdote, told me that he had seen the old king dining in
public, and that the spectacle was disgusting beyond
description. Such brutal feeding, such pawing and
grinding, such absorption in the immediate appetite
and will, and contempt of everything else in the .
world, could only be exhibited by one who was accustomed to set up the mere consciousness of royalty
as superior to every other consideration. This is
Ferdinand's principle. He has no other, nor ever
had, even when he petitioned to be made a member
of Bonaparte's family. Bonaparte dazzled him, like
something supernatural, and was an emperor to boot;
but if he had not been one, it would have made no
difference. The royal will, the immediate security,
interest, or even whim, sanctions everything; and
royalty is to come out clear from the furnace upon
the strength of its divine right, let it have gone through
what it may. How much right have we to complain
of it, flattering it as we do, even in the best regulated
monarchies? The frog in the fable swelled herself
to bursting, as it was; but if she had, besides, had all
frogland for spectators, and applauders, if she had
been puffed up with huzzas! and vivas! and been
made a worshipped spectacle wherever she carried

herself, who would have wondered at all her children's bursting themselves, one after the other, in spite
of her example? I pity, for my part (next to suffering nations), every king in existence, except Ferdinand; and will pity him too when he is put out of a
condition to slaughter those who would have made
him an honest man.

Pleasant C. R. I let me recall my happier rhymes
and rainy days by thinking of thee. C. R. is one of
those happy persons whom goodness, imagination,
and a tranquil art conspire to keep in a perpetual
youth. He and his brother once called upon a man
whom I knew, who told me he had seen " the young
gentlemen," and yet this man was not old, and C. R.
was seven-and-thirty if he was a day. C. R. has a
quaint manner with him, which some take for simplicity. It is, but not of the sort which they take it
for. I could hear it talk for an hour together, and
have heard it, delighting all the while at the interest
he can take in a trifle, and the entertainment he can
raise out of it. His simplicity is anything but foolish-
ness, though it is full of *bonhomie.* He is a nice
observer. At the same time he is as romantic as a
sequestered schoolmaster, and will make as grave
Latin quotations. He produces a history out of a
whistle. He will describe to you a steam-engine or
a water-mill, with all the machinery and the noise to
boot, till you die at once with laughter and real interest at the gravity of his enthusiasm. He makes
them appear living things, as the fulling-mills did to
Don Quixote. One day he gave us all an account of
a man he had seen in the Strand, who was standing

with a pole in his hand, at the top of which was a
bladder, and underneath the bladder a bill. He told
us what a mystery this excited in the minds of the
spectators, and how they looked, first at " the man,"
then at " the bill," and then " at the bladder ; " — and
again, said he, they looked at the bladder, then at
the bill, and so on, ringing the changes on these words
till we saw nothing before us in life but a man holding those two phenomena. We begged him to change
the word " man " into " body," that charm of alliteration might be added ; and he complied with a passing laugh, and the greatest good nature conceivable,
entering into the joke, and yet feeling a real gravity in
commenting upon the people's astonishment. This
combination of " bill, body, and bladder " was, after
all, nothing but a man standing with an advertisement of blacking, or an eating-house, or some such
thing. We have been thankful ever since that " such
things are."

I once rode with C. R. from Gainsborough to Don-
caster, making rhymes with him all the way on the
word philosopher. We made a hundred and fifty,
and were only stopped by arriving at our journey's
end. Readers uninitiated in doggerel may be startled
at this ; but nothing is more true. The *words* were
all different, and legitimate doggerel rhymes ; though,
undoubtedly, the *rhymes* themselves must often have
been repeated, that is to say, the same consonants
must have begun them. The following is a rainy-
day production on the same subject, exhausting, we
believe, the real alphabetical quantum of rhymes, with
their combinations. But it is submitted with defer-

ence to the learned.   We dedicate it to our pleasant
friend, heartily wishing we could have such another
ride with him to-morrow.

> You talk of rhyming to the word Philosopher. —
> That jade the Muse! It's doubtless very cross of her
> To stint one even in rhymes, which are the dross of her;
> I can't but think that it's extremely gross of her:
> I told her once how very wrong it was of her:
> If I could help, I'd not ask one, that's poz, of her:
> I would not quote *procumbit humis bos* of her;
> Nor earn a single lettuce yclept Cos of her:
> I would not speak to Valcnaer or to Voss of her;
> Nor Dryden's self, although the Great High Joss of her:
> I would not care for the *divinum os* of her.
> No, though she rhymed me the whole *mos, flos, ros,* of her:
> Walking in woods I wouldn't brush the moss off her:
> Nor in the newest green grown take the gloss of her:
> In winter-time I wouldn't keep the suows off her;
> And yet I don't think either I could go so far:
> Thy anger, certainly, I couldn't show so far:
> I didn't think the hatchet I could throw so far.
> Good heavens! now I reflect, I love the nose of her:
> I could cut off my hair to tie the hose of her:
> The brightest eyes are nothing to the doze of her:
> Love in my heart the smallest keepsake stows of her:
> O, for as many kisses as I chose of her!
> Since I had one there's no sweet air but blows of her:
> There's not a stream but murmurs as it flows of her:
> I could exalt to heav'n the very clothes of her.
> I wonder how a man can speak in prose of her:
> Yet some have e'en said ill (while my blood froze) of her:
> Never again shall any be that crows offer
> To do her harm, or with his *quid pro quos* huff her.
> With pleasure I could every earthly woe suffer
> Rather than see the charmer's little toe suffer:
> 'Tis only gouty Muses that should so suffer.

No. IX.

• EATING AND DRINKING.

Quæ virtus et quanta boni sit vivere parvo,
(Nec meus hic sermo, sed qua præcepit Ofellus,
Rusticus abnormis sapiens, crassaque Minerva)
Discite, non inter lances mensaque nitentes
Cum stupet insanis acies fulgoribus, et cum
Aulinis fa!sis animus meliora recusat :
Vecum hic impransi mecum disquirite. — HORA·.·**.

What, and how great, the virtue and the art
To live on little with a cheerful heart !
(A doctrine sage, but truly none of mine)
Let's talk, my friends, but talk before we dine ;
Not when a gilt buffet's reflected pride
Turns you from sound philosophy aside ;
Not when from plate to plate your eyeballs roll,
And the brain dances to the mantling bowl. — POPE.

S O sang a Roman poet, who describes himself as
having grown as fat as a pig ; and so sang after
him an English one, who is said to have died of eating stewed lampreys. They were judicious in singing before dinner. What is the use, it may be asked,
of repeating maxims so often contradicted, and by the
very persons that broach them? To which it may
be answered, What is the use of any maxims at all?
Why do the world go to school ? Why do they teach
their children ? Why do they pique themselves on their
experience? Is all this useless? The members of a
community that values itself on its good conduct, will
hardly answer no : nor must they answer no on the
present occasion. Poets of the middle order, perhaps

of the greatest, are famous for the warfare they under-
go between their sensibilities and their knowledge.
The stretchers " of the ray to ages yet unborn " play
tricks among their beams of light, that often scorch
their fingers. But the ray is stretched; philosophy
is never so well recommended to the world as by the
radiance they throw upon it. Generally speaking,
the book, rather than the author, is in the reader's
mind ; and where this is not the case, and the danger
of example is apprehended, perhaps the danger is
more than compensated by deduction in favor of charity. Besides, those who do contradict their theories,
would contradict them more, and in worse taste if they
were ignorant of what is good, or in bitter despair of
attaining it. Horace had fits of temperance as well
as luxury. He has said such pretty things of crusts
and salads, that one longs to have eaten them with
him, and laughed at the fume of great dinners.
Pope was a little domestic fowl, brought up tenderly,
and accustomed to be picking. He could not take
stout exercise : his frame would not allow it. " Then
he ought to have eaten little in proportion." True ;
but something is to be allowed to the perpetual wear
and tear occasioned by the exercise of the mind, and
something to the irritability of that very delicacy of
constitution which rendered indulgence perilous. The
moth flies to the candle ; robuster insects avoid it.
Let us thank the butterfly race, notwithstanding, for
reminding us of Nature and the flowers. What numbers of men, of similar constitutions with Pope, have
died of surfeits, and done nothing ! How much more
gracefully might they have lived, how oftener have

varied their pleasures, with temperance, and after all
survived to a pretty good age, considering their creak-
ing bodies (for he lived to be fifty-six), had they possessed his good sense and his elegance of desire !

I like to begin a lecture with a good charitable exordium. In the first place, I have need of it myself;
and secondly, I have observed that advice always does
more harm than good, if it does not see fair play. I
must observe again, then, in behalf of the superfluous
diner, particularly if he is studious and sedentary, that
there may be reasons for his roasting of eggs' beyond
what a commonplace moralist may discern. Study
exhausts the body. Mental excitement demands with
a loud, I do not say always with a lawful voice, the
help of physical nourishment. A poet shall come to
table from a morning's occupation, his nerves shattered, his blood thick and melancholy from over-driv-
ing, his whole soul agitated and confused in his body,
in which it has been at supernatural work. I will
concede, that in this very work he has been sowing
seeds of philosophy, and writing couplets on temperance. Let the future ages who are to benefit from his
inspiration, look back with an eye of tenderness rather
than scorn on the havoc he proceeded to make among
his dishes. Perhaps he will fast to-morrow. At least
they will have the benefit of his remorse. Inspiration, which is nothing but a concentration of the faculties upon the exercise of some natural talent, is a
mighty exhauster of the stomach, a producer of morbid appetites and craving desires for refreshment.
The nerves, trembling from the glowing task, demand
to be set right again; the blood, hot and dragging

with fatigue, calls for an airy lift. He had better go
out into the air, and take exercise : — I exhort him
to do so : — Milton did so : — the greatest of his
brethren have been surely temperate : — he will repent bitterly if he does not. No : the meat and
drink come in, and the deed is done. Let us take
the advice he has left us, and pity him for the dangerous warmth he took in writing it.

It is the same, in proportion, with pleasure and melancholy of all sorts, with any kind of over-fatigue. Fifty things may excuse us in the eye of charity : climate,
anxiety, troublesome tasks, past or to come, bodily
or mental exhaustion, from whatever cause ; nay, the
cheerfulness of our return to one's friends or family.
But melancholy, above all, claims a particular tenderness. It is a hard thing when a man has been in
trouble all the morning, and sees nothing but trouble,
perhaps, before him in the afternoon, to deny him the
pleasure of tickling his palate a little. The loss of a
very little satisfaction is sometimes a great loss in this
world ; the difficulty of foregoing it is in proportion.
Let the abstaining from a particular dish, or the getting up from dinner without a full stomach, be re-
spected accordingly. I confess I had more difficulty
in leaving off butter and cheese (which happen to dis-
agree with my temperament) than in volunteering
some actions, which the world would have thought
less easy. The satisfaction of having one's way, or
of doing what we can to have it, and venting one's
feelings on account of what we think just and honorable, is a mighty and a reasonable help to one's virtue. The pinch comes when our virtue is at war

with our tendencies; when we hold to it through pain
and anxiety, and when we doubt whether we shall be
as well or ill thought of for acting up to our consciences.

Again and again, therefore, I say, let justice be
done to self-denial in matters of beef and port, and
above all, I say, let those consider also the necessity
of the self-denial, who would fain lighten the gathering shadows of age or middle life, and retain as
much health and good temper as they can for themselves and others. They have no alternative between a great deal of it and exercise. The more
they exercise, the more they may indulge; for there
is a business in all things; and citizens must earn
their dinners, as well as the money to purchase them,
if they would not have those other creditors come upon
them, spleen and gout. I do not say that they require
nothing to give them a fillip. Quite the contrary.
I only say that sedentary eating and drinking is not the
best; that the good effects of it are not lasting, and
the bad ones very much so; and that however difficult it may be for a pleasant fellow to deny himself
" t'other plateful " as well as " t'other glass," deny it
he must, or his comfort some day will be grievously
denied to him. He may rub his hands at the sight
of his dishes, he may crow over his wine, he may
throw sayings (as he willingly would the plates) at
the heads of the moral and the musty; but as surely
as he sits there, gay and contemptuous, so surely will
he find the " black ox's foot " come upon his toes under
the table, not to be lightened, to any real purpose,
by all the effects of champagne. Age is always sup-

posed to bring melancholy along with it. I do not
believe it. I believe that many a temperate old man,
who has nevertheless indulged a reasonable appetite,
is as cheerful as the majority of young ones. But age
will have shadows with a vengeance if it has been
intemperate ; and middle life will be plunged in them
before its time. Purple faces and a jovial corpulence
may impose upon the spectator ; but the sick gentleman within knows what his tenement consists of.
A fool may indeed go to his grave pretty comfortably ;
a mere animal, a human prize ox, may swell and
abuse his system for a long time, because he has no
intellect to be hurt by it, and to hurt him in turn ;
but good sense in the head, and a perpetual contradiction of it in the stomach, will never do in the long
run. The head ought to rule ; the stomach will revenge its bad government by sending up its angry
ambassadors of megrims and vapors ; and the anxiety and irritability of the ruler will in time revenge
itself on the stomach.

Are we not then to obey the impulses and benevo-
lences of Nature? Have we palates and appetites for
nothing? Are we to turn hermits and starvelings,
and not enjoy ourselves?

By no means. There is the simple, and eternal,
and benevolent law of Nature: "Earn, and you
may enjoy." Experience adds, Enjoy truly, and you
will know what it is to enjoy with reason. And
Nature adds, Enjoy with reason in general ; and occasionally I will smile and shut my eyes when
friends and festivity call upon you for an amiable delirium. Would you enable yourself to eat heartily,

yet without oppression? Secure a good digestion
with exercise. Would you enable yourself to take
a reasonable portion of wine? Spin your blood first
with exercise, that it may not be roused too abruptly,
and fevered. Would you be free from melancholy, a
strong and cheerful man, an old man free from the
clouds and peevishness of old age? Wash, exercise,
and be temperate, that you may throw off ill humors
at the pores, and not have your soul incrusted with
sordidness of the body. As much, perhaps, ought to
be said about washing as about exercise. It is a
duty not sufficiently attended to in our chill climate.
There is a story of a Scotchwoman, who attempted to
drown herself in a fit of melancholy. She was taken
out of the water in a doubtful state, and underwent
an active rubbing, according to the process of the
Humane Society. She not only returned to life, but
recovered her health and spirits; the physicians pro-
nouncing, that twenty to one her melancholy was
entirely owing to her dirt. There is the same reaction in this respect as in the other. Melancholy people are apt to grow careless of their persons; people
who are careless of their persons grow melancholy.
But cleanliness is the first of virtues; not the first in
rank, but the first in necessity.* The most selfish
people can practise it for their own sakes; the rest

---

* "Cleanliness," observes Charles Lamb, in that little neglected essaying, entitled Saturday Night, "says some sage man, is next to Godliness. It may be:
but how it came to sit so very near, is the marvel. Methinks some of the more
human virtues might have put in for a place before it. Justice — Humanity —
Temperance — are positive qualities; the courtesies, and little civil offices of life,
had I been Master of the Ceremonies to that Court, should have sate above the
salt in preference to a mere negation." —ED.

ought to practise it for themselves and others. With regard to exercise, judge between the two following extremes: A fox-hunter can get drunk every night in the year, and yet live to an old age; but then he is all exercise, and no thought. A sedentary scholar shall not be able to get drunk once in a year with impunity; but then he is all thought, and no exercise. Now the great object is neither to get drunk, nor to be all exercise, nor to be all thought; but to enjoy all our pleasures with a sprightly reason. The four ordinary secrets of health are, early rising, exercise, personal cleanliness, and the rising from table with a stomach unoppressed. There may be sorrows in spite of these; but they will be less with them; and nobody can be truly comfortable without.

There is a great rascal going about town (a traveller to boot in foreign countries, particularly in the East and in the South) who does a world of mischief, under the guise of helping you to a digestion. I am loath to mention him. His very name is beneath the dignity and grace of my Platonic philosophy. But I must. He talks much about the liver. Sometimes he calls himself the Blue Pill, sometimes one thing, sometimes another. He is particularly fond of being denominated " the most innocent thing in the world." Let the sufferer beware of him. He may turn his company to advantage a few times, provided, and *only provided*, he does not anticipate his acquaintance, or let him divert him from his better remedies. Wherever he threatens to become a habit, let the patient *take to his heels*. Nothing but exercise can save him. He is only surfeit in disguise; a perpetual tempter to repletion, under the guise of preventing the consequences. The excess *is* tempted, and the consequences are *not* prevented ; for, at the least, one ill is planted in the constitution instead of another. Disguise the scoundrel as we may, he is only, in a small shape, what an emetic was to Vitellius, or a bath of mud to the drunken barbarian.* Sometimes, with an unblushing foresight and intention, he is even taken before dinner! Imagination escapes from the thought of an abuse so gross. I dart, upon the wings of my Wishing-Cap, out doors, and hail, as I go, those light bodies and animating looks, which are the happy results of EXERCISE.

No. X.

THE VALLEY OF LADIES.

Poichè noi fummo qui, è io desiderato di menarvi in parte assai vicina di questo luogo, dove io non credo che moi alcuna fosse di voi ; e chiamavisi la Valle delle Donne. — DECAMERON.

Since we have been here, I have longed to take you into a spot close by, where none of you, I think, have ever been. It is called the Valley of Ladies.

AS the spring advanced here in Tuscany, and the leaves all came out, and the vines rose like magic, and day after day the green below was contrasted with a blue southern sky overhead, I began, modestly speaking, to be reconciled to the beauties of Italy. I was wrong when I said there were no trees

---

* One of the O'Neales used to inflame himself with drinking, and then stand up to the neck in a bath of mud to cool.

in this neighborhood except olives. We have a few poplars, oaks, and young chestnuts, &c., which make an agreeable variety. They incrust the lanes with a decent quantity of hedge and bower. But the vines make an astonishing difference. In the winter you see nothing of thousands of them ; in the spring out they come, from a bit of a trunk, like so much fairy-work, and grow with a marvellous rapidity: In a few weeks they are up round their standards, and climbing their trees; doubling, as it were, at one blow, the whole prospect of green. Add to this the noble growth of the corn, and the exuberance of everything wild about the hedges, and spring is ten-fold spring here to what it is in the north. The contrast is more striking, because there is no green in winter except dark firs and cypresses and the hazy-looking olive. The beautiful grass, which remains all the year round in England, gives a sort of perpetual summer to the earth, whatever may be the case with the sky ; but the sky in Italy during winter, though it has glorious intervals of blue and warmth, is inclement enough to make the inhabitants chatter with cold, and there is no verdure on the ground. All this being the case, the very green of the vines had in it something of England ; and as the ground is no sooner dry here than it is very dry, I put vigor in my steps, and my Orlando Innamorato in my pocket, and did my best to fancy myself at once abroad and at home in the sunny-bowered Valley of Ladies.

The Valley of Ladies is a spot celebrated in the sixth and seventh books of the Decameron. It lies at the foot of one of the Fiesolan hills, about two miles

from Florence, commencing at the path leading up to
Maiano, and terminating under the Convent of the
Doccia. Doccia signifies a water-spout, a name with
which the convent was christened by a little stream,
the Affrico, which leaps out beneath it and waters the
valley. This stream, and another called the Mensola,
which runs through a neighboring valley, are the
metamorphosed hero and heroine of a poem of Boccaccio's, called the Nimphale of the Fiesole. Upon
the Mensola, about half a mile from the Valley of
Ladies, is the Villa Gherardi, in which Boccaccio laid
the scene of his four first days; and upon the Mu-
gnone, about a mile on the other side of the valley, is
the Villa Palmieri, to which his company retired for
the remainder of their time, on account of the influence of neighbors. Not far from the villa a house is
shown, which is said to have belonged to Dante.
Milton and Galileo give a glory to Fiesole beyond
even its starry antiquity; nor, perhaps, is there a
name eminent in the best annals of Florence to which
some connections cannot be traced with this favorite
spot. When it was full of wood it must have been
eminently beautiful. It is at present, indeed, full of
vines and olives, but this is not wood *woody*, not arbo-
raceous, and properly sylvan. A few poplars and forest trees mark out the course of the Affrico, and the
convent ground contrived to retain a good slice of
evergreens, which make a handsome contrast on the
hillside with its white cloister. But agriculture, quar-
ries, and wood fires have destroyed the rest. Nevertheless, I now found the whole valley beautiful. It is
sprinkled with white cottages ; the cornfields pre-

sented agreeable paths, leading among vines and fig
trees; and I discovered even a meadow, — a positive
English meadow, — with the hay cut, and adorned
with English trees.   In a grassy lane, betwixt the
corn, sat a fair rustic, receiving the homage of three
young fellows of her acquaintance.   In the time of
Boccaccio, the Affrico formed a little crystal lake, in
which (the said lake behaving itself, and being properly sequestered), the ladies of his company, one day,
bathe themselves.   The gentlemen, being informed
of it, follow their éxample in the afternoon; and,
next day, the whole party dine there, take their *siesta*
under the trees, and recount their novels.   This lake
has now disappeared before the husbandman, as if it
were a fairy thing, of which a money-getting age was
unworthy.   Part of the Affrico is also closed up from
the passenger by private grounds, but the rest of it
runs as clearly as it did; and under the convent a
remnant of the woodier part of the valley — a delicious remnant — is still existing.   The stream jumps
into it as if with delight, and goes slipping down
little banks.   It is embowered with olives and young
chestnut trees, and looks up to the long white cloister,
which is a conspicuous object over the country.

A white convent, a woody valley, chestnut trees
intensely green, a sky intensely blue, a stream which
it is a pleasure to stop and drink, — behold a subject
fit for a day in August!   And besides these, there are
stories recounted and ladies bathing.

If the reader objects to the probability of this last
circumstance in a civilized country and so near town,
he must remember that the place in Boccaccio's time

was really sequestered ; that the convent did not exist then (though, of course, monks could have been no objection), and that Florence has always been a walled city, from which you emerge directly into the country. The lake was so little frequented (as, indeed, most beautiful places are apt to be), that Boccaccio represents the male part of his company as unacquainted with it till enlightened by the more inquiring spirit of the ladies. In short, the manners of one time or place argue nothing for the manners of another. I know a lady who has frequently bathed among the rocks of a West India island, as Virginia does in the novel ; and if Thomson does not appear to have hit very nicely the manners of Englishwomen in his episode of Damon and Musidora, he probably copied after Nature as far north as his own country. The two damsels in the Gentle Shepherd bathe in a pool, in one of those pretty landscapes with which that beautiful pastoral abounds. Sir Philip Sydney's heroines, in the Arcadia, do the same. It is true they were princesses, and nobody could enter the place on pain of death ; but an intruder was in it nevertheless. I confess, to my taste, the banks ought to be very rugged and woody, and the bather be able to slip into the water like a fish ; in consideration of which I might allow an agreeable trepidation, and much interesting mixture of modesty and vivacity. But Musidora playing the Venus de' Medici in that open, and at the same time reflecting manner, is what I cannot tolerate, though she begins her answer to her lover's placard in a pretty taste.

This, then, is the " Valle delle Donne." If Boc

caccio's spirit ever visits his native country, here must it repose. It is a place for a knight in romance to take his rest in, his head on his elbow, and the sound of the water in his ear. Why do I say, "if Boccaccio's spirit ever visits"? I have seen him there, such as he looked when he meditated the story of the Falcon. The knight in romance also, — I have seen *him*. He was in dark armor, with a red cross on his shield. He had taken his helmet and gauntlet off to feel the air, and lay, like Lord Herbert of Cherbury in the picture, thinking placidly of achievement.

Being somewhat of a knight-errant myself, I rest in another part of the shade, looking down upon him of the red cross, and, with the help of my book, conjuring up a thousand visions.

How vivid, as you look up, is the green of these young chestnut trees! How blue, indeed, the blue sky! How warm were the paths I came through; how cool is the shade! What a basking, a fertility, a southern richness, a lazy lending and generosity of all that is in earth and air. A smiling slumber of Nature with her hands full, diffuses its influence all over the place! The very bees seem to be at work, that we may lull ourselves to sleep.

I whisk to England in my Wishing-Cap, and fetch the reader to enjoy the place with me.

How do you like it? Is it not a glen most glenicular? a confronting of two leafy banks, with a rivulet between? Shouldn't you like to live in the house over the way, where the doves are? If you walk a little way to the left, through the chestnut trees, you

see Florence. The convent up above us on the right
is the one I spoke of. There is nobody in it now but
a peasant for housekeeper. Look at this lad coming
down the path, with his olive complexion and black
eyes. He is bringing goats. I see them emerging
from the trees; huge creatures, that when they rise
on their hind legs to nibble the boughs almost look
formidable. There is Theocritus for you. And here
is Theocritus or Longus, which you will; for a peasant girl is with him, one of the pleasantest countenances in the world, with a forehead and eyes for a
poetess, as they all have. I wish the fellow were as
neat as his companion, but somehow these goatherds
look of a piece with their goats. They love a ragged
picturesque.

You have only to see the eyes and foreheads in
Tuscany to know that you are among a people capable of great things. And what, indeed, has not this
little region done in the world of art and poetry?
The rest of the face is genial and good-natured, only
to an English eye the features are apt to be too large;
and the higher you rise in society the more advantage
we have in our women. A sophisticated Italian is a
formidable thing, man or woman. All the world
cannot match a room full of young Englishwomen,
delicate and accomplished. And you could sooner
persuade one of them to take up her abode in the
country, and brown her fair face with the sunshine,
than seduce a ready-made Tuscan brunette to live out
of the gates of Florence. Two months in the year,
May and October, — very often only one, — they run
about the villas a little. All the rest of their life is

passed in town; and they are never seen abroad but in their carriages. They are fond of flowers. They have also the grace to visit the Cascine every evening. The Cascine are meadows with trees, where the Grand Duke has an aviary and dairy, a pretty little pastoralized edition of Kensington Gardens, with the Arno on one side and mountains in the distance. But their visitors only come for a drive, and they would not come for that if it were not fashionable. The charm consists in criticising shaped bonnets, and saying, " Ah, there's Tomkins ! " — I beg pardon, — Gian-Battista, I should say ; but these Italian commonplaces sound so finely that they impose on one's ear. The Tomkinses are a numerous race all over the world, " from China to Peru ; " and they abound much more among the upper orders in the south than the lower. If I were a bachelor, and inclined to marry in Italy, I should like to select a peasant girl, of a reasonable age, deepen the depth of her eyes with a little more knowledge, and in five years' time make her my wife. The graces would follow as a matter of course. In her style of language I already defy anybody to discover the difference, except that among the ladies the perpetual recurrence of certain elegancies of no meaning, and phrases of polite deprecation, looks more like the art of Letter-writing made Easy, or the Academy of Compliments.

Let an Englishman, if he is wise and well off, seek his wife among those most respectable of all the re- spectable families on earth, who, in his own native soil, spend a good part of every year in the country, and make everybody happy about them. I have one in my eye now, at C., in Northumberland, the head of which is a second Allworthy. Even the town residence of this family looks upon a noble garden. Never shall I forget how affectionately the mother and daughter (the most unaffected people in the world, and yet they read Latin — hear that, ye Blues and ye anti-Blues !), — never shall I forget how they all came about the object of their love, putting their gentle hands about his neck, and asking him how he fared after his walk. There is not a good of his fellow-creatures which he does not seek, nor a grace to grace it which he does not feel. I sometimes change color when alone to think what regard and gratitude an author may feel towards such men, and how long he may struggle in vain to show it. Why cannot we coin some of the wealth of our imagination into proofs tangible, and pour down our souls upon them in the princely shower? The less they care for it, in one sense, the more desire we have to show them how we care for it in another. And yet, God knows, I grudge no man his generosity. But " these things are a mystery." I look upon it as a blessing in my lot that all the friends I ever was connected with have sympathized with me in preferring a country life. And yet they have liked the town too, and so do I. Luckily, very genuine country may be found near town for those who are not rich enough to go to a distance. Come, let us whisk ourselves back again. There is nothing like it. I pitch myself into one of those old green lanes of which I am so fond, and invite any bachelor that pleases to come and see me. I think there is a cottage in the neighborhood that will suit him.

No. XI.

LOVE AND THE COUNTRY.

Hic gelidi fontes, hic mollia prata, Lycori,
Hic nemus, hic ipso tecum consumere ævo. — Virgil.

A wood, a stream, fair fields, and flowering hedges —
O, love, with thee, here could I live for ages!

IT is a large, low cottage, smoking among the trees, with its back to a couple of green hills that shelter it from the north and east. Everything is neat: Everything is quiet. Listen to the bees! What meadows go down there to the plain! What rich trees are about us, — elms, oaks, and beeches ; not rich in fruit, but rich in verdure and leaves, and food for poetry. By heavens! this is better than Tuscany. The pleasures there are all too tangible and sensual, — all corn, wine, and oil. Here man does not live by olives alone, but by those useful trees also, which, among a number of other calumniated goods, are on the face of them useless. " I love," exclaimed somebody, on passing a moorland, " to see some ground left in God Almighty's hands." So say I. I love to see trees that look as if they were good for nothing but to walk under, and to furnish us with a sentiment. I have a particular regard for those which the carpenter rejects with disdain. I know they do not exist for nothing ; and I take them for what they are, — memorandums of the abundance and poetry of Nature.

At the bottom of the grounds about the cottage, there is a lane by a brook-side, which runs into a cross-country road. But the place, though solitary, is not desolate. There are some farms, and a noble mansion not far off, where a hospitable old gentleman, the possessor, has a fine library. The lanes branch off in all directions, some opening into meadows, others into cornfields, most of them between rich banks of earth ornamented with natural hedges. One of my favorite spots is a bit of heath, looking up to a hill full of trees, out of which peeps a summer-house. Another is a wilderness, where the roots of the old trees issue forth and twist over the ground. But I know scarcely one which I prefer to certain meadows enriched with elm trees. I lie there very often in my Wishing-Cap, when the hay has been cut, and build castles in the air, — I should rather say, cottages in the trees, — for those whom I love.

Is not this a pleasant place to come to of an evening? " What can man more desire ? " when he has been studying all the morning, and is determined to make heavens of his afternoons? Task the most ambitious old bachelor, whether there have not been periods in his life — and the very best of them all — when the idea of such a cottage smoking among the trees, a kettle on the fire, and his arm round a slender waist, has not found the " consummation," of all others, " most devoutly to be wished."

Accordingly, I have provided a wife for my reader. She is not regularly handsome ; but she has one of those faces which are justly accounted more beautiful than beauty. A person who goes by says,

" What a lovely expression ! "   There is intelligence
in her eyes, and an infinite sweetness about her mouth.
Whenever she turns her face upon you in kindness,
she seems to thank and bless you, and wish you all
happy things.   Sorrow might cut her to pieces, ere
she would say a word to distress you : or if she did,
she would repent it forever.   But in joy, — I advise
you to bring a world of vivacity along with you,
for she will give as good as you bring.   She is fond
of books and music.   If you do not have some exquisite casts and engravings to adorn your parlor
with, you will not do her justice.   When females of
her own rank come to see her, they long to play
the rustic as she does.   When the peasant girls bring
her provision, they desire more than ever to be ladies.   She meets them half way, and will pin their
handkerchiefs for them, if got loose.   Between ourselves (for it must not be mentioned to everybody),
she can make an excellent pudding.   It was a whim
of her grandmother to teach her; and she insists
that her children will be the better for it, and not
at the mercy of a cook; for I must own, that although not yet married, she has the face to speak
of the family she may have some day; and has even
been heard to say, that she should not like to make a
very poor match, because she hopes to have leisure
enough to be her husband's companion; which, added she, is after all the first business of a wife : though
she blushed when she said it.   Her vivacity and address serve to extricate her gentleness out of its difficulties.   Her brother, who is a collegian, and loves
somewhat maliciously to call her " a 'Blue," caught

her one day, to his great triumph, in the act of
loitering over a dumpling she was making, and read·
ing a book. She was forced to blow open the
leaves, her fingers being all over flour. In vain she
protested that it was an offence extraordinary, and
that the pudding should not be the worse for it.
He takes an unfair advantage, and brings her out to
us in the garden, holding her by the helpless arms,
upon which, what does my lady, but suddenly slip
aside, smear his ears all over with the flour, and
scamper away! But I shall never make an end if I
say more.

Now, what does any bachelor say to such a cottage
with such a mistress? Is it not a pretty mixture of
the polite and the rustic? I once heard a nobleman
observe, that it was natural to men of rank to like
peasant girls, and for plebeians to like ladies. I am
not of his opinion. I think that whenever men prefer
women of an inferior station — (unless they do it for
the sake of a libertine variety, or because they have
undergone some particular disgust) — it is owing to
want of address. The peasant renders them bolder.
Their superior station enables them to substitute airs
of condescension and familiarity, for approaches which
they know not how to manage. But nothing is so delightful in a woman, as a mixture of habitual gentility
with the simple and healthy tastes which might adorn
the heroines of a genuine pastoral. The Peggy of
Allan Ramsay is a promising specimen. If I had
married out of the Lizard family in the Guardian —
(which, by the way, is the sort of family I spoke of in
my last) — I should have wished Miss Cornelia to

have more of " the Sparkler " in her composition, or
the Sparkler more of Cornelia. Since I saw them
last, they both want mending a little. I used to prefer
the Sparkler, till she made that unsparkling observation in No. 31 ; which, however, I trust the self-love
of the old gentleman induced him to misrepresent.
But Mrs. Cornelia's romance, in the same number,
would have been more to my taste, had she acknowledged at once, that she intended to make somebody
happy, instead of beating about the bush in that
manner.*

---

* The old gentleman referred to above is Nestor Ironside, the imaginary
writer of the Guardian. The account of the Lizard family is by Steele. This is
his character of the Sparkler : "Mrs. Mary, the youngest daughter, whom
they rally and call Mrs. Ironside, because I have named her the Sparkler, is the
very quintessence of good nature and generosity , she is the perfect picture of her
grandfather ; and if one can imagine all good qualities which adorn human life
become feminine. the seeds, nay, the blossom of them, are apparent in Mrs.
Mary." Here is what he says of Mrs., or, as we should call her, Miss Cornelia :
"Mrs. Cornelia passes away her time very much in reading, and that with so great
an attention that it gives her the air of a student, and has an i l effect upon her,
as she is a fine young woman ; the giddy part of the sex will have it she is in love ;
none will allow that she affects so much being alone, but for want of particular company. I have railed at romances before her, for fear of her falling into those deep
studies : she has fallen in with my humor that way for the time, but I know not
how. my prohibition has, it seems, only excited her curiosity ; and I am afraid she
is better read than I know of, for she said of a glass of water in which she was going
to wash her hands after dinner, dipping her fingers with a pretty lovely air, ' It is
crystalline.' I shall examine farther, and wait for clearer proofs." Here is
also the Sparkler's "unsparkling observation," made in the course of some
profitable conversation upon happiness: "My favorite, the Sparkler, with an
air of innocence and modesty, which is peculiar to her, said that she never expected such a thing as happiness, and that she thought the most any one could
do was to keep themselves from being uneasy ; for, as Mr. Ironside has often
told us, says she, we should endeavor to be easy here, and happy hereafter. '
The romantic Cornelia "was for living in a wood among choirs of birds, with
zephyrs, echoes, and rivulets to make up the concert. She would not seem to
include a husband in her scheme, but at the same time talked of cooing turtles,
mossy banks, and beds of violets, that one might easily perceive she was not
without thoughts of a companion in her solitudes." — ED.

I will conclude this paper with two old French songs, which are much to the purpose. The first of them is by Maynard, an author of a caustic turn, who agrees with the nobleman above mentioned in preferring peasants to ladies. The other is from the good-natured pen of Froissart, the old chronicler, and makes the lady partake of the peasant. If Froissart wrote many such songs, his poems deserve to be reprinted as well as his Chronicles.

ADIEU TO LADIES,

Hélène, Oriane, Angelique,
    Je ne suis plus de vos amans ;
Loin de moi l'éclat magnifique
    De noms puisès dans les romans.

Ma passion, quoiqu'Amour fasse,
    Ne fera plus son paradis
Des beautés qui tirent leur race
    De la chronique d'Amadis.

Vive Barbe, Alix, et Nicole,
    Dont les simples naïvetés
Ne furent jamais à l'ecole
    Des ruses et des vanités.

Une sauté fraiche et robuste
    Fait que toujours leur teint est net ;
Et lorsque leur beauté s'ajuste,
    La campagne est leur cabinette.

Leur âme n'est pas inhumaine
    Pour tirer mes vœux en longueur ;
Jamais je n'ai perdu l'haleine
    En courant apres leur rigueur.

Adieu, dames, dont l'habit riche
    Sous un lux vain et trompeur
N'est autre chose que la niche
    D'une carcasse à faire peur.

J'en veux aux femmes de village,
    Je n'aime plus en autre part ;
La nature en leur beaux visages
    Fait la figue aux secrets de l'art.

TRANSLATION.

Helens, Clelias, Orianas,
    I am no longer of your train ;
Far from me be your sultanas,
    With their splendor, proud and vain.

I can love, and feel a passion ;
    But no more I place my bliss
Upon dames of lofty stations,
    Who descend from Amadis.

Long live Alice, Barbara, Molly !
    Girls whose little simple hearts
Never went to school with folly
    To pick up your airs and arts.

Strong and fresh with healthy duties,
    Theirs the tint is, theirs the bloom ;
When the rouges adjust their beauties,
    Fields are all their dressing-room.

They, good creatures, keep no man in
    Vile suspense, to show their power ;
None need lose their breath with running
    After them, from hour to hour.

Farewell, ladies, patch'd and painted,
    Who beneath your stately clothes
Hide but limbs with luxury tainted,
    Bodies fit to scare the crows.

Morning eyes and milkmaid faces
    Henceforth rule an honest heart :
Nature, in their rustic graces,
    Snaps her fingers at your art.

THE BEAUTY WHO WAS TOLD TO BE PROUD.

Jeune Beauté doit, dit-on,
Etre orgueilleusette;
On reconnait à ce ton
Noble pucellette.

Hier au hasard me levai
Dès la matiné;
Au jardin me promenai
Dessous la feuillé.

Déjà me couchais parmi
La naissante herbette,
Quand je vis mon doux ami
Cueillant la fleurette.

Comment gronder un amant
De sa diligence?
J'écoutais son compliment
Avec complaisance.

D'un bouquet il me fit don,
Simplette, doucette;
J'oubliai cette leçon,
Que l'on m'avait faite.

Jeune Beauté doit, dit-on,
Etre orgueilleusette;
On reconnait à ce ton
Noble pucellette.

TRANSLATION.

A beauty ought, they say,
To be a little proud;
It is the only way
To know her from the crowd.

I rose at early morning,
Upon this truth intent,
And down the garden turning,
Beneath the trees I went.

I laid me in the bloom,
Among the grassy bowers,
And saw my lover come,
A-gathering of flowers.

8

How could a lady look
  On such a work askance?
His compliments I took,
  I own, with complaisance.

A bunch of flowers he gave me
  From his own coat-button,
And, as I hope to save me,
  My lesson was forgotten.

Good Lord! and yet they say
  A beauty should be proud;
It is the only way
  To know her from the crowd.

MISCELLANEOUS

ESSAYS AND SKETCHES.

Peace be with the soul of that charitable and courteous author who introduced the ingenious way of miscellaneous writing. — SHAFTESBURY.

ESSAYS AND SKETCHES.

PERSONAL REMINISCENCES OF LORDS.

THE first time we saw any Lords, we were too young to receive such impressions of them as should remain in after life. The earliest man of any note we remember, was an American projector, who had a talent for ship-building. We were told of the extraordinary things he could do to make ships sail fast and well; and him we have never forgotten. We have his face this minute before us.

The next time we were blessed with the sight of Right Honorable and Most Noble faces, was in the House of Lords itself. We had just been shown the House of Commons, where the nonchalant appearance of a few members, with their hats on, lounging upon the benches, struck us as no very dignified sight, though we thought them sharp looking men and mightily unaffected. From there we were taken to see the Lords; and we state, with perfect candor, the impression they made on us, when we say that they looked like a parcel of linen-drapers. If the Commons were free and easy, we expected to find the Noble Lords noble and lordly; we thought we should

see the dignity which we missed among the others.
Not an atom of it. Both houses, it is true, were very
thinly attended, and the most dignified members of
both may have been absent; but we found that a
number of lords might be collected and not look a
bit superior to any other collection of decent men.
We had absolutely seen our chamberlain of London
a few days before, who surpassed every man of them
in dignity of appearance. Nor had we any prejudice
against lords. On the contrary, our prejudice was
in their favor, and we were greatly disappointed.
"What!" said we to ourselves, "are *these* lords?
Why, they look like men just come from behind
counters, and those of the least manly description."
It was the fashion at that time to wear light-colored
small clothes and white stockings, and this custom
added to the effeminacy of their appearance. But
their faces! What poor-looking expression was
there! What weakness! What a negation of all
purpose and energy! We came away, quite mortified for our chivalrous notion of the peerage, — of
the relations of the Bolingbrokes and Peterboroughs,
and never heartily recovered the impression afterwards.

From time to time we were shown a lord in a
stage-box or on horseback. They were nothing
different from other men, except that we fancied
a look of higher self-possession, — perhaps because
they were lords. Doubtless there was often a conscious look which the spectator might take for self-
possession, or assumption, or pride, or dignity,
according to his preconceived notions. Pope talked

of the " nobleman look," but said that Wycherley had
it as well as Bolingbroke, which shows that it had
nothing to do with rank.* He meant the look of
self-possession, in its most graceful aspect. The person the most answering to the received idea of a
nobleman, whom we ever saw, was the late Duke of
Grafton. We remember him coming out of the Unitarian chapel in Essex Street, with his staid gloved
hands, tall person, hook nose, and cocked hat sur-
mounting all, like the father of a generation of Sir
Charles Grandisons. Junius would have given a different account of his inner nobility. It was conscientious in him, however, to go to the Essex Street
Chapel, and he was a very respectable-looking man,
— *not* in the gig-keeping sense.

Lord Castlereagh, the only time we saw him, —
which was many years before his death, — struck us
as being something of a dandy. He was in nankeen
pantaloons and a green coat; but he had as fine a
face as man could well have, with little intellect in it.
If nobility could have a patent face, — a countenance
appropriated to rank, apart from the look of wit and
talent, — it would look like him. But then he had
been occupied in important work. No lord looks
good for anything who is a mere lord, and by far the
greatest number we have seen were of this class.
Lord Eldon, who is a judge, and of plebeian origin,
casts as fine an eye upon you in passing along the
streets some years ago, as could be looked for in a
" learned gentleman ; " and yet law has made it come

---

* Hazlitt writes admirably on this subject in the paper On the Look of a
Gentleman, in The Plain Speaker. — ED.

to nothing. Lord Ellenborough had the glance of a
clever man, but his face was clouded with a look of
burly stubbornness. The face of the nobleman we
have always looked at with the greatest interest is
Lord Holland's. We felt thankful for his elegant
literature, his advocacy of liberal opinions, and above
all, his never-failing protests in the House of Lords
when an ignorant or ungenerous measure was carried. But we have seen him only at a distance. Let
his black eyes and his shrewd looks, however, say
what they may, they say nothing in behalf of his
rank : for he is a wit, and could do without it.

We were once going down Bedford Row, when we
saw a little mean-looking man ascend the steps of a
house, give a good knock, and ask the footman a
question. The footman answered with a face, the
expression of which amounted to contempt. It was
as much to say, " What does such a shabby-looking
fellow as you want with my master, and why do you
take upon yourself to give such a knock?" The little
man, turning to go away, took out a card, and gave it
the footman. The reader should have seen the fellow's manner at sight of this card ! He saw " Lord "
upon it; and his face, shoulders, arms, legs, and soul
fell instantly into a profound respect and humiliated
repentance. We omit this lord's name, but nobody,
most assuredly, would have taken him for a nobleman, — unless, indeed, a footman might have done
so ; for footmen, being conversant with lords, ought
to know of what aspects they are capable.

Not long after this we happened to sit next a lord
in a box, who swore much at a *debutante* in a com-

edy, and said she was the " d—dest impudent little
devil he ever saw in his life." At the same time he
clapped a speech of hers with as much energy as his
hands could bring together, for he too was a fragile
little fellow. We begged to know the reason of this
apparent contradiction ; and he said, " O, I like her
impudence of all things ; it's devilish amusing."
This was candid, and we had nothing to object. It
was also professional, — of the "order," — for it up-
held claims without merit, and stood by a sort of
" privilege of peerage," — the right that impudence
has to be on a par with impudence.

The next lord we remember seeing, whose patent
was put to the test, was the colonel of a body of vol-
unteers, who were assembled in the courtyard of a
great house in Piccadilly, in expectation of seeing
him for the first time. Suddenly it was announced
that he was coming. The great gates were thrown
open, the band struck up, the regiment presented
arms : enter my lord on a white charger, and, by way
of introduction to his men, is pitched right over the
horse's head. Thus (as the moral of a fable would
say) the being a lord does not render a man a good
horseman any more than it renders him modest, or
wise, or handsome, or strong, or genteel, or even
such a man as can be safe in the experience of a
footman.

We were standing once at a book sale behind two
gentlemen, one of whom, by his voice, we recognized to be the late John Kemble. The other was of
the same stature as the actor, not so gentlemanly
in appearance, and had his hat set knowingly on the

top of his head. Mr. Kemble, addressing him as
"My Lord," made us curious to see his face. The
actor's face we saw very well. It was turned side-
wise towards the great unknown, exhibiting all the
dignity of its Roman profile; and the tone, high in
dignity as in sound, in which the actor spoke, interested us extremely, considering the rank of the person
he was conversing with. On a sudden this person
turned rapidly towards his acquaintance, exhibiting
his profile in turn, and letting us into the secret of
his voice. The effect was ludicrous. The nobleman's person had given us a manly idea of him
enough, though there was a dandyism in his bearing
not of the genteelest kind; but his face! and his
voice! The first was like a premature old woman's,
the second worthy of it, — at once high, mumbling,
and gabbling. A little staring eye surmounted this
odd imbecility. He rapidly uttered a few shuffling
sentences, forming a most singular contrast with the
lofty and measured tones of the actor; and we thought
how much better the latter would have acted the
nobleman off the stage than the former upon it. How
ludicrous, indeed, the noble lord would have appeared
in any serious character, on or off!

The next time we fell in company with a lord, he
was talking on the subject of art, which he did very
badly. We did not know who he was, nor was
he acquainted with all the persons present. Somebody made a remark in dissent; we expressed (in all
civility) our agreement with it. The stranger, who
had a very insipid countenance, said nothing, but contrived to throw into his face an air of nonchalant

assumption, which appeared very odd. The secret was explained when we learnt who he was. But are these, we thought, the manners of high life? Are such the people that think to dispense with objection, and are these the faces their absurdity begets them? Who would have known this lord from an arrogant, mean citizen? His appearance is not a jot better.

Does the reader remember a little, withered old man, who used to emerge on fine days into his balcony in Piccadilly, take a chair there,

"And sun himself in Huncamunca's eyes"?

His business, it was said, was to watch the ankles of the ladies and the conscious giggle of the serving-maids. But he mixed it with wiser matter. He was taking a "reverend care of his health." Stories of milk baths were told by the smiling passengers, of the doctor ever in attendance, and of the good done to old gentlemen by the company of pleasing faces and milk-maid breaths, without of necessity involving anything erroneous. This old lord (the Duke of Queensbury) had been a great turf-man in his youth ; we know not what he was famous for in more advanced life. In old age he was eminent for sitting in a balcony and looking stupid. He was immensely rich. He probably could have had eighty thousand beefsteaks for his dinner every day. The money for these he left at his banker's, while he dabbled with a little spoon-meat, and his neighbors toiled all day to get a steak for their wives and children.

We leave this point to the reader's reflection. — 1830.

A LETTER

On, to, and By the Book-Personage known by the Name of "The Reader."

DEAR Sir, or very dear Madam: Among the various phenomena of the literary world (to begin in proper book style), you have heard, doubtless, of editors who write letters to themselves, and are very much their humble servants, "Quidnunc," and "Philalethes." In other times the highest and the lowest periodical writers were equally given to this species of correspondence; the former in the excess of their wit, the latter because they get nobody but themselves to be their Constant Readers.* Of late years, such is the exuberance of literature, in Mr. Jerdan's, as well as the grammatical sense of the word, that we believe the custom survives with none but the very newest and worst setters-up of a publication. These gentlemen, here and there, are still auto-epistolary. One of them is his own "Impartial Observer," and differs with himself, "though with

---

* Mr. Spectator gleefully confesses that he is guilty of writing letters to himself. "I often choose," he says, "this way of casting my thoughts into a letter, for the following reasons. First, out of the policy of those who try their jest upon another before they own it themselves. Secondly, because I would extort a little praise from such who will never applaud anything whose author is known and certain. Thirdly, because it gave me an opportunity of introducing a great variety of characters into my works, which could not have been done had I always written in the person of the Spectator. Fourthly, because the dignity spectatorial would have suffered had I published as from myself those severe ludicrous compositions which I have ascribed to fictitious names and characters.' Spectator, No. 542. — Ed.

deference to his superior judgment." Another is
happy to subscribe to his own opinion, being, at the
same time, a subscriber to his "interesting miscel-
lany;" and a third, sitting in his editor's room, and
despairing of success with his "widely-circulated
journal," is his "sincere well-wisher and admirer,
Thomas Jones, Appleby." A certain description of
gentlemen "about town" are said to have made great
use of this epistolary talent, and been half the women of their acquaintance; and a tribe of doctors,
resembling them, have been enabled to bear such
grateful testimony to their own merits as to acquire
an extensive correspondence of the ordinary kind, and
write themselves into an equipage and a mansion.

But you have yet to learn that a man may write a
letter to himself and not be aware of it; nay, that all
his readers but one may join him in the correspondence, and all be in the same predicament. You are
now this minute doing it, so are they; and, what is
more, myself, who am the sole exception, are you
and they too. I am the editor and all his readers. I
am a lady of quality and a blacksmith; I am a soldier, and at the same time a clergyman; a dandy and
a quaker; an old lady and a young one; a man of
yesterday, and yet Martial addressed epigrams to me;
an intimate friend of Sophocles, and yet Sir Walter
is continually bespeaking my good opinion. In short,
I am the little, big, slender, robust, young, old, rich,
plain, poor, handsome, male, female, and neuter personage, known by the name of "The Reader." I
am *you*, Reader, whatever you may think of it, and
you are all of us. You address your prefaces to me,

and have others addressed, for the same reason, to yourself. I am the Benevolent Reader of the old books; also the Courteous, the Indulgent, and the Impartial, but, above all, the Discerning. The affectation of independence in modern writers has induced them to leave off addressing me by some of these epithets, yet my good word is still bespoken as the Indulgent and the Candid; and if I am not always styled the Discerning, it is not the less given me to understand that I am so. I should like to see the author that ventured to treat me otherwise. It is true, a hint is now and then ventured about "commonplace readers," and "readers of the ordinary description:" but these are mere words. I will venture to affirm, that if *the* Reader ever chose to inquire whether it was *he* that was intended by those petulant appellations, the writer would infallibly say no. *The* Reader is always treated with respect. The least thing said to him, is, that he is "requested:" — the Reader is requested to do so and so; to "observe," or to "bear in mind." It is also asked whether he will be "kind enough" or "good enough" to do this and that. Furthermore, being a man, he is of necessity a gentleman, as surely as the cobbler before the hustings; and inasmuch as he is of the female sex, he is fair; — the fair Reader; — "our fair Readers will do us the honor to observe," &c.

It is in this corporate character that I now address you. Being *The Reader*, I am everybody who reads, and therefore may safely speak in the first person; for nobody quarrels with himself in the person of another, however willing he may be to contemplate **his** merits in him; at least, it requires a rare stretch of philosophy to do so, and the modesty is sure to be accompanied by something that consoles it.

As a reader of a ripe age, who was deep in the gilt nursery books of the last century, it may be allowed me to regret the cessation of those quaint old dreams of wood-cuts, now confined to ballads on the walls, or only reprinted for the benefit of the curious. I acknowledge the superiority of the present engravings, and allow our new infant self, if he has any taste for the fine arts (which is not always the case), to " quiz " the stuck-up attitudes, blotted eyes, and impossible legs and arms of our old King Pepins and worthy London apprentices. But there was something remote and ideal in those very deficiencies in the likeness to things known. *Such* a London apprentice as that *might*, for aught you know, thrust his arms down the throat of two lions, conveniently gaping on each side of him, and pluck out their hearts. *Such* a little boy as King Pepin, all eye and flapped waistcoat, *might* come to be a man wonderful, and ride in his coach. We do not defend the rewards generally promised in the infant literature of that period, such as coaches and great puddings, though the private taste seems to lie a good deal that way still. Neither will we stand by the morality of Master Jemmy the bad boy, and Master Jacky the good one, the former of whom is bound to be eaten by lions, while the latter becomes Lord Mayor; for it is now doubted by philosophers in the city, whether every Lord Mayor was a good little boy; and also, whether every naughty boy goes to Africa or comes to the poorhouse. Such determinations of events will not be allowed in this refining age, philosophers themselves being sometimes poor, and rich men not always having been good. We are aware that the great eye of this generation looks rather to the general good than the particular example of success, and inculcates a handsome prudence, which, allowing folly its excesses, saves it from bad blood, and encourages it to grow wiser. We have nothing to say against that; but still we may be allowed to admire the picture-cuts of Master Jemmy and Master Jacky, now so happy at home, playing their battledoor and shuttlecock, and then both, methinks, so unhappy afterwards, — the one devoured by roaring lions, and the other stuck up in his fine coach without his brother. To the impressive dead bodies of " Smith, Jones, and Robinson," in Mr. Dilworth's Spelling-Book (was it not?), who would swim in the water when they were told to remain on dry land, and to the awful admonitory figure of the schoolmaster in his cocked hat, with one finger up, we cannot refuse our respect. It is somewhat begged of us, we grant, by early habit, and by the sight of those stark-naked, pale pieces of stiffness on the ground ; to say nothing of the warm and well-clothed teacher. " The great teacher, Death," and the hardly inferior solemnity of the teacher academical, divide the awfulness between them. Otherwise we could have wished that Death and a little daring had not been brought so peremptorily together. But things may have been good at a former period which are not desirable at present.

As " the reader" of the present times, nothing

comes amiss to us. We find all ages and conditions agreeably lumped up together in the food provided for them. The little children's books are fit for grown people to read; and the grown people are obliged to be universal in their knowledge, for fear of not having answers to give to the little children. Pictures also, the realization of the dreams of books, abound more than ever.

Even our amiable old friend, the Elements of Morality, rich with its " fifty copper plates," is nothing to the " one hundred and fifty " in a modern volume of Arabian Nights; and then for cheapness, we have the same delicious work for five and sixpence; all Shakespeare for ten shillings, and loads of acted plays and farces at threepence the set, like gingerbread. As to songs, we get them at a penny the hundred. I'd be a Butterfly is about the value of a wafer and a half, and so is that public piece of privacy, O, no, we never mention Her, which piece of reserve, when it first came out, we heard two fellows whispering in the ear of the town along Regent Street, with all the delicacy of a couple of gongs.

We are afraid there may appear some confusion in this letter between the reference to our general character as " The Reader" and our own particular book inclinations. But something of this must be pardoned, if it be not of too exclusive a description. *The Reader*, after all, is a human being, and must sometimes be content to represent particular bodies of men rather than the whole fortuitous world of perusers. Above all, it is to be presumed that he is a genuine Reader; — that is to say, really fond of books; and as such,

9

there are many feelings which he will have in common with the whole genus of bookworms.   There is
sometimes a false *The Reader*, — that is to say, one
who is appealed to by authors whom nobody reads,
or who is a mere chance taker-up of a book, in which
he has no more right to recognize himself under that
title than a fly who should walk over it.   Mr. Jacob,
an unheard-of name in our times, was a reader of this
sort a hundred years ago ; and our friend Mr. Jerdan
is one at present.   I shall, therefore, proceed to consider myself in one light as the Reader appealed to by
authors ; in another, as the Reader fond of reading
them.

And here, my dear friends, I cannot but lament the
cessation of those pleasing epithets of Benevolent
and Candid, which I have before mentioned, and
which tended to keep up the good qualities they
spoke of.   It was easy to see whether the author was
trying to cajole us, or only paying the proper compliment to our virtue.   If he was a good fellow, it was
all as it should be ; if otherwise, he was only in the
right with regard to *ourselves; we*, the Reader, were
still candid, and benevolent, and intelligent, but we
smiled at his endeavors to deceive us, and called to
mind what the philosopher says about hypocrisy, —
" the homage which vice pays to virtue."   It is true,
we dismissed the man a little more charitably than
might have been the case had he been less civil ; but
charity is desirable towards everybody.*

---

* " Why is it that we hear no more of Gentle Readers ? " asks Southey, in The
Doctor.   " Is it that, having become critical in this age of magazines and reviews, they have ceased to be gentle ? But all are not critical." With what

Lector benevole had a pretty sound in Latin; so had *candide* and *amice*. "To the Reader" is not so well; it is too unceremonious, or, at least, unsocial. There is neither respect nor cordiality in it; and, somehow, to an Englishman, the Italian *a chi legge* sounds worse. Neither is "Advertisement" altogether to be approved; — "Advertisement to the Reader;" it is too dry and official. In French it looks hardly decent — *Avis au lecteur*. I am aware that the same words in different languages have different shades of meaning, but the root is the same. "Advice to the Reader" is to be found in old English books. The French phrase has even passed into a proverb. It means putting a man on his guard. This, to be sure, is a useful proceeding with some books, and would be more so if other people, instead of the author, had the writing of the advice. How pleasant it would be to be able to preface one's enemy's book with such a warning: to forestall a criticism, or give a notice "*Sur la vie et les ouvrages.*" *Every man his own other man's preface* would be handsome dealing.

---

sweet reverence and loving humor Hawthorne, in the preface to The Marble Faun, writes of that "friend of friends, that brother of the soul," the Gentle Reader. 'The antique fashion of prefaces recognized this genial personage," he says, "as 'the Kind Reader,' the 'Gentle Reader,' the 'Beloved,' the 'Indulgent,' or, at coldest, the 'Honored Reader,' to whom the prim old author was wont to make his preliminary explanations and apologies, with the certainty that they would be favorably received. I never personally encountered, nor corresponded through the post with this representative essence of all delightful and desirable qualities which a reader can possess. But, fortunately for myself, I never, therefore, concluded him to be merely a mythic character. I had always a sturdy faith in his actual existence, and wrote for him year after year, during which the great eye of the Public (as well it might) almost utterly overlooked my small productions." — ED.

During the period when Latin was the common tongue of literature, and it required scholarship to read as well as write a book, it is agreeable to see the importance which the Reader bore in the mind of everybody connected with the work, — author, printer, and publisher. The book was, perhaps, dedicated to some lord or great man, some *Illustrissimo*, whose light has long since disappeared; or some *Vir Amplissimus* of a Dutchman. He was the ostensible patron. The titles were set forth in a grotesque of Dutch and Latin, rich as the efflorescence of his coat of arms; and perhaps his arms themselves were added, thirsty with leopard's faces, and threatening with daggers. But *he* was not " The Reader." Not he. Perhaps he could not read the work. Lords in those times were not the wits and geniuses they are now. Some little preface by itself was pretty sure to be added *lectori benevolo*, bespeaking his good opinion with a *tibi commendo*, and reminding him of it with a *vale!* We, " The Reader," now almost swallowed up in that more formidable noun of multitude, the Reading Public, were then one of a select portion of society, like the doctors of a university; and though we acknowledge ourselves reasonably lost among the many, and, indeed, assisted in bringing about the great light that has put out our college lamps, we cannot but take a pleasure in turning over those evidences of our old importance, and fancying ourselves bowing like a polite judge on the bench to the appeals of our learned brothers the Elzevirs and the Giunti. This is one of the secrets of the link between the Bibliomaniacs and saner readers. Any

ɔook was worth something in those times; and, by
the courtesy of scholastic habits, it remains so still.
But rarity made it a great deal more so, and therefore
nothing is so precious to the Bibliomaniac as the possession of a rare copy. It diminishes the advantages
of the rest of the world; — gives him a value in his
own eyes which he could not otherwise possess. We
do not say this invidiously. Partaking to a certain
degree of the Bibliomaniac ourselves, and at the same
time being liberal-minded towards all the world in
our capacity of *the Reader* universal, we live, either
to vindicate our dusty superiority, or allow our absorption in the common wit, just as the whim is upon
us; and as so many books are venerable in our eyes,
every book, in some measure, becomes so by reason
of its book-nature. *Bibliophilus sum; nihil biblici
a me alienum puto.* Only let a writer address us
handsomely, and it is hard if we do not find something to commend in his work, even should it be only
in the address. We confess that we love to respond
to those deferential appeals made to our wisdom and
good qualities. Nothing can be said out loud between
author and reader; but the sympathy is not the less
understood. " The Reader," says the author, "will
have the goodness,"— we *have* the goodness. " The
Reader will undoubtedly perceive," — undoubtedly
we *do* perceive. " We need not inform the intelligent Reader," — you certainly need not; but let us
have it.

Good-natured Ovid is the earliest writer we can
call to mind, who established a direct intercourse between the Reader and himself. We feel all the differ-

ence he describes between our comfortable situation
at home, and his cold and solitary exile; and doubly
sympathize with the man, from the compliment paid
us by so famous a poet. It is the only instance of
the kind we recollect, in which Rome cuts a domestic figure in one's imagination, instead of being the
great domineering city, paraded by consuls, and
looking warlike or Ciceronian. For Pliny, somehow,
does not make us enter cordially into his fine houses.
We, the Reader, were then a wit and fine gentleman
about town, under the eye of Augustus; hatless, and
gowned; and, as Arbuthnot says of that prince, without glass to one's windows or a shirt to one's back.
The Reader, to wit, ourself, need not be informed,
that ancient reading, being in manuscript, was much
more confined than it is at present. In Greece we
were a philosopher, an historian, a poet; latterly a
grammarian, a collector of epigrams, or a mystic.
What are ordinary readers now were then listeners
to the poet's lyrics, or audiences at an Olympic game
or a theatre. And it was the same in the age of chiv-
alry. Hence the addresses of the poets to their
harps and audiences. Milton covenanted with us
(" the Knowing Reader ") for the performance in due
time of an epic poem; but when he had gloriously redeemed his promise, he spoke of us as an auditor; —
" Fit *audience* find though few." For a long time
we were either a professed minstrel, or else a clerk or
ecclesiastically learned person, as distinguished from
the laity. Chaucer and others helped to extend our
jurisdiction. Our friend Caxton, in the reign of Edward the Fourth, addressed his History of Prince

Arthur to us, under the title of " the Christian Reader." By this time we had included the people of
quality, both male and female, to whom he accordingly proceeds to address himself. These gave rise
to the term " Gentle Readers," our gentleness at that
time consisting, not in its modern effeminate qualities,
but in having high blood in us, and being qualified
to knock people on the head. Caxton, however,
judiciously distinguishes between such as " desire
to read " and such as " desire to hear read." By a
subsequent edition of this work, it may be seen how
we had increased our body corporate among the plebeians; for the editor takes upon himself to be in-
solent. " Thus," says he, " reader, I leave thee at
thy pleasure to read, but not to judge, except thou
judge with understanding. The ass " (think of that
said nowadays to " the reading public ! ") " is no
competent judge between the owl and the nightingale, for the sweetness of their voices ; cloth of arras
or hangings of tapestry are not fit to adorn a kitch-
en ; no more are kettles, pots, and spits to hang in a
lady's bed-chamber ; neither is it becoming for a man
to censure that which his ignorance cannot perceive,
or his pride and malice prejudicate or cavil at." — This
fellow must have been a knight, at least.

An author who is uneasy with his readers has generally good reason to be so. We like him in proportion as he is the reverse ; that is to say, provided he is
worthy of our company ; and more especially, if as in
Ovid's case, he does it honor. With what reverence
do we not receive those personal communications
vouchsafed us by such writers as Milton, and imper-

tinently called impertinences by the critics! How
we love them in writers of a tenderer cast, and enjoy their gayety in the more lively! Scaliger, speaking of the delightful egotism of Montaigne (would
that all good authors were as modest as he, and not
afraid of committing their dignity!), asks " what the
devil it signifies whether he liked this wine or that?"
It signifies that he understood the social part of us,
and that he was not an arrogant critic, who thought
himself too good for his readers. When Fielding
arrests the progress of one of his narratives to tell us
of the little parlor in which he was writing with his
children about him, how thankful do we not feel for
his good-natured humanity in thus letting us into his
domestic difficulties, — in giving the picture at once
the zest of a pain and the cordiality of a pleasure!
How does it not make us wish, that all men, not ill-
inclined, could know and understand one another;
could see how much pain they can endure, and how
much pleasure bestow!

" The Reader's" loss of consequence nowadays,
as we have before observed, is his gain ; that is to say,
" The Reader" is going out, because all are readers.
The newspapers and magazines speak of us as "our
readers." We are sometimes directly called " the public," and scavengers and beadles address us, with talents
that used to be confined to the clergy. Still there is
" The Reader" properly so called, that is to say, the
Reader genuine and fond of reading ; and as such we
have still our tastes and our distinctions. We often
read at breakfast and tea ; are sometimes observed
reading even in the streets, — not out of ostentation,

but because we cannot leave our friend at home: nay, if dining alone, we like to have the book open beside us, or will stick it up against the loaf, and devour salad and Sir Walter at the same time.

We find no obstacles in the streets. We thread the multitude as easily as a fish does the sea among his fellows, or a blind bat avoids chairs and tables in a room. We keep a sort of eye, without seeing it, to the gutter; and have the path down a hill before us, without trying to keep it.* We prefer, however, green lanes, or a lane with bookstalls, stopping occasionally to compare notes with the blackbirds, and always stopping to look at the books. In the latter case, we make a display of the volume in our hand, lest the stall-man should confound it with one of his own. If we put it in our pocket, we fancy he will see it sticking out as we move off, and make hasty search before we get out of sight. We fancy he will think it a Waller, " price 9d.," or a description of the German Spa, or Marcus Antoninus's Meditations, or some modern writer (perhaps ourself!), " same as sells at five shillings ! "

A lounge in summer against a bank or the new-mown hay, has been too often described to be dwelt' on. In doors, if the season be fine and warm, a sofa

---

* Herein differing from book-loving Charles Lamb, who, in his Detached Thoughts on Books and Reading, says, " I am not much a friend to out-of-doors reading. I cannot settle my spirits to it. I knew a Unitarian minister, who was generally to be seen upon Snow Hill (as yet Skinner's Street was not), between the hours of ten and eleven in the morning, studying a volume of Lardner. I own this to have been a strain of abstraction beyond my reach. I used to admire how he sidled along, keeping clear of secular contacts. An illiterate encounter with a porter's knot, or a bread-basket, would have quickly put to flight all the theology I am master of, and have left me worse than indifferent to the five points." — ED

is the thing, after a walk, with the balmy substitution of slippers for boots, and a new work to begin ; or, say, the fifth chapter of a new novel, where you turned down a leaf, and were at a most interesting passage. The ivory knife to cut open the leaves with, is also pleasing. We cannot but think there is a kind of sensual pleasure in it. We must not dwell upon the pleasure of reading in bed, turning first one elbow and then the other, and finally lying upon one's back, wondering we did not choose that happy posture at once. The custom is dangerous, and conscientious readers leave it off, if they are not sure the candle will be put out. A book behind the pillow for morning, is another thing ; or even for the chance of reading, if you wish it, though you never do. But we shall be reverting to particular tastes. As to winter time, we believe it will be allowed by all catholic perusers, that an elbow-chair, and a foot on each hob, is the most luxurious enormity.

1830. "THE READER."

DR. DODDRIDGE AND THE LADIES.

THIS is another volume of the work * which excited so much attention and amusement, as disclosing the livelier part of Dr. Doddridge's character, and his fondness for the ladies. We mean to say nothing against the doctor's reputation. His fondness was kept within legal bounds, and only

* The Correspondence and Diary of Philip Doddridge, D. D., &c. Edited from the original MSS. by his Great-grandson, John Doddridge Humphreys, Esq. Vol. IV. London, 1830.

overflowed in a double stream of benevolence towards
the fair sex, — in a pleasing mixture of piety and
gayety, — a double wish to please and to be pleased.
But the public were amused to see a name, which
had hitherto partaken, however mildly, of the common gloom in which Dissenters stand with the world,
suddenly invested with a radiance of gallantry and
hilarity, as if Venus had taken an arch pleasure in
throwing a light upon him from the clouds, and showing that doctors are men.

It is a pity to think that there are persons who find
fault with this new light, and think it unbecoming
the seriousness of a dissenting minister's reputation.
It is lamentable to see how hard men can struggle to
keep up painful pretensions and false notions of piety,
— what ingenious steps they take to have as little
comfort and to maintain as great a portion of vice as
possible, in order to indulge upon the one the spleen
which the other occasions. A great scandal was
lately excited among the ascetics of the Catholic
church (luckily a very small body now) by the discovery that the celebrated Bossuet, the proud cham-
pion of the Roman faith, the St. Paul of the French
court, was in love, and wrote billets-doux. They
might well dislike it, for there was reason to believe that the poor bishop, on the strength of the aus-
terities exacted of him, had an actual mistress, and
so was made a hypocrite. If Doddridge had been
one of his clergy, he would very likely have been
a hypocrite too, though of a more charitable order.
The Catholic church, in this matter, is filled by its
tenets with lies and contradictions; the worst and the

best men are alike induced to sin, the former because
they are gross and double-dealing, the latter because
they have the strongest sympathies; and thus all come
to practise hypocrisy in common, and real vices are
propagated by false virtues. However, these absurdities are diminishing every day.

Dr. Doddridge was an amiable man, of a sprightly
blood, and of a hectic temperament, which ultimately
threw him into a consumption. His views were too
cheerful for his doctrines, which he was accused of
accommodating to different companies; that is to say,
his charity predominated, and he found out, in his various texts, something to enliven everybody he came
nigh. Men of other complexions, who were uneasy
with themselves, preached from uneasy texts: he took
up the cheerful ones, and made everybody grateful
wherever he went, talking to the old of Methusalem,
and comparing the ladies to Eve in Paradise. Accordingly he was adored by all classes and ages. Doors
flew open to receive him; men pressed his hands; old
ladies fell in love with him, and young ladies, who
were not allowed to fall in love, beatified his wife,
and wrought ornaments for her person. The first
characteristic thing we meet with in the volume before us is a " splendid apron " which " dear Miss
Scott" wrought on purpose for Mrs. Doddridge, and
with which the doctor felt himself "quite over-
whelmed." The editor speaking of it as now existing, says it is " one of the most costly and beautiful
that can be imagined. Groups of ranunculuses and
other flowers are represented by colored silks, relieved with gold; and a butterfly is introduced with so

much skill, that it may almost deceive the eye." The
doctor, who was an elegant poet, addressed her the
following seraphical lines upon it : —

TO MISS SCOTT,

ON HER PRESENTING MRS. DODDRIDGE WITH AN EMBROIDERED APRON.

> Too *lovely* maid, possess'd of every art
> To charm the fancy and command the heart,
> The bloom of Paradise thy needle paints,
> Thy song's the echoes of celestial saints ;
> And the blest youth, to whom thy love is given,
> *Will pass through Eden, on his way to Heaven.*

Alas ! no blest youth (more shame for him) took a
road so delightful. Miss Scott, whom her father
called a " Protestant Nun," from her devotion to works
of charity, and who was a poetess as well as a pain-
tress, died a maid. There were not enough Dr. Dod-
dridges to appreciate her. It is astonishing how many
people one longs to have married in old times, purely
to rescue one's sex from the disgrace of unfeelingness.

This poor girl subsequently fell into a state of religious gloom (owing to those infernal doctrines of
Calvinism, which the doctor's happier condition enabled him to throw off) ; but it does not appear to
have succeeded in overwhelming her. Her health
was bad, and she mistook the gloomy impressions
resulting from it for an irreligious state of mind. In
the present volume are some affecting letters which
passed between her and the doctor ; and pretty strong
instances of the light in which she regarded him.
We fear he ought to have turned Mussulman, or not
written verses.

The doctor was too ready an admirer of all charming women not to have the good wishes of any one

of them. Mrs. Doddridge should have secreted his·
letters from her fair friends. At page 91, he writes
thus to her: "On Tuesday I dined with Mr. Fawcett's mistress: a sweet girl truly (he had said in a
previous letter, that her temper was like his wife's),
fair as alabaster, with black eyes and hair, a pretty
little mouth, and wanting only a little more color in
her cheeks, *which now and then I gave her.* These
sons of Levi (Mr. Fawcett was a minister) take for
their wives the best of the flock, and *it is but fit they
should.*"

Mrs. Doddridge is somewhat startled at the " pretty·
little mouth," and musters up some correspondents in
his absence ; and a colonel, to give him a counter hint
with ; but all in great pleasantness and good humor.

" I heartily rejoice," she says, " in the prosperity
of all my friends; but permit me to tell you, my
dear sir, that I am a little in pain for your constancy, and think I have some reason, when you seem so
transported with those genteel young ladies, with
their black eyes and alabaster complexions! with
pretty little mouths too : indeed, I think I have much
more to apprehend from them than from the good
old lady of eighty-one you told me of some time
ago ; however, I will endeavor to comfort myself,
that notwithstanding all these powerful temptations,
your constancy will be as inviolably secure as my
own, and more I cannot wish it to be, though perhaps should I tell you this is the third letter I have
written by this post! so extraordinary a circumstance might give you a suspicion that I am carrying on some intrigue in your absence ; but I need

do no more to remove it than to tell you the names
of my correspondents."
The colonel was the famous Colonel Gardiner,
who from a man of pleasure became hypochondriacal, and saw a ghost.*

---

* This is the story, as related by Dr. Doddridge in his biography of Colonel
Gardiner: "The major had spent the evening (and, if I mistake not, it was
the Sabbath) in some gay company, and had an unhappy assignation with a
married woman, whom he was to attend exactly at twelve. The company broke
up about eleven; and not judging it convenient to anticipate the time appointed,
he went into his chamber to kill the tedious hour, perhaps with some amusing
book, or some other way. But it very accidentally happened, that he took up a
religious book, which his good mother or aunt had, without his knowledge,
slipped into his portmanteau. It was called, if I remember the title exactly,
The Christian Soldier, or Heaven taken by Storm, and it was written by Mr.
Thomas Watson. Guessing by the title of it that he would find some phrases of
his own profession spiritualized in a manner which he thought might afford him
some diversion, he resolved to dip into it ; but he took no serious notice of anything, and yet, while this book was in his hand, an impression was made upon
his mind (perhaps God only knows how) which drew after it a train of the most
important and happy consequences. He thought he saw an unusual blaze of
light fall on the book while he was reading, which he at first imagined might happen by some accident in the candle. But lifting up his eyes, he apprehended,
to his extreme amazement, that there was before him, as it were suspended in the
air, a visible representation of the Lord Jesus Christ upon the cross, surrounded
on all sides with a glory; and was impressed as if a voice, or something equivalent
to a voice, had come to him, to this effect (for he was not confident as to the very
words), 'O sinner! did I suffer this for thee, and are these the returns?' But
whether this was an audible voice, or only a strong impression on his mind
equally striking, he did not seem very confident; though, to the best of my
remembrance, he rather judged it to be the former." But, according to that
"shrewd, clever old carle," Rev. Dr. Carlyle of Inveresk, who knew Gardiner
well, Dr. Doddridge has marred this story, "either through mistake or through
a desire to make Gardiner's conversion more supernatural, for he says that his
appointment was at midnight, and introduces some sort of meteor or blaze of light
that alarmed the new convert." But this was not the case, adds Carlyle; "for
I have heard Gardiner tell the story at least three or four times, to different sets
of people, — for he was not shy or backward to speak on the subject, as many
would have been. But it was midday, for the appointment was at one o'clock ;
and he told us the reason of it, which was, that the surgeon or apothecary had
shown some symptoms of jealousy, and they chose a time of day when he was
necessarily employed abroad in his business."
Carlyle also maintains that as Gardiner told the story there was nothing super-

At page 102 is a letter to Mrs. Doddridge in the Somersetshire dialect, which shows the vivacity of the doctor's spirits. Certainly he was the gayest Calvinist on record. At page 44 we find him catching maids at sea. " If you consult the map (he observes), you will see, by comparing the date of my last, that, like the sun, which is still in the tropic of Cancer, or like the crabs which I yesterday caught, I am now in a kind of retrograde motion; or at least go sideways. I could not refuse the importunity of my friends here (happy for me that I was not a woman) ; but came back in a chaise which they sent for me on Sunday night, and preached (wicked worm that I was) an evening lecture after my other work ; but this being a singular instance, you will, I hope, excuse it, especially as I was well enough to rise at five yesterday morning, and to make a voyage down the river, which is ten miles to the sea : when I had the pleasure of meeting thirty-five sail of ships, and of catching a great number of soles, plaice, flounders, and crabs, with two lobsters, and a *fair* Maid ! who immediately threw herself into a very natural attitude, and frisked about with a strange kind of motion ; and as far as I could judge by the strong action of the muscles of her face, and especially of her mouth, made a very pathetic motion in a language I did not understand. The name, however, she had the honor to bear, and her *resemblance* to your very agreeable

natural in it. It was the book, and not a supernatural appearance that converted Gardiner. " He was so much taken with this book that he allowed his hour of appointment to pass, never saw his mistress more, and from that day left off all his rakish habits, . . . and the contempt of sacred things, and became a serious good Christian ever after." — ED.

sex, impressed me so far that had not my companions been less compassionate than myself, I believe she had still been sporting with the river nymphs, and perhaps celebrating the courtesy of that gallant knight to whom she became a captive. But I must assure you, my dear, that though she was detained in the vessel, nothing passed between us that could give you any reasonable umbrage; and, fair as she was, these lips have not yet touched her! nay, so insensible is my heart to the charms of her whole species, that I give it you under my hand that I had rather have a single shrimp, than as many of these fair creatures as would stock a Turkish seraglio."

Our gallant doctor is always paying compliments to his wife, who appears to have deserved them. His accounts of the compliments he receives from other ladies, and the charming reception he is always meeting with from the most amiable families, must have put her faith in him to some test. He does not spare it a handsome trial; and yet he contrives to make the trial a ground of homage. His kindness seems to have been on a par with his vanity; and that is saying much for a flattered man. He says at the close of the above letter about maids, — " But to be serious, it was a very pleasant day, and I concluded it in the company of one of the finest women I ever beheld, who, though she has seven children grown up to marriageable years, or very near it, is herself still almost a beauty, and a person of sense, good-breeding, and piety, which might astonish one who had not the happiness of being intimately acquainted with you.

10

" I am just returning in the vehicle in which I came from Ipswich; Providence has there also strangely cast my lot in one of the most friendly and agreeable families I have met with; and absolutely, as I am informed, the best in the whole town, though not that which I intended to have visited. Mr. Wood is extremely obliging. Everything is done that can be to make me, if possible, forget you! and yet every circumstance serves a contrary purpose. The more agreeable the persons I see about me, the more am I reminded of her who is most agreeable; and the more pleasurable the scenes I pass through, the more do I wish to share them with you, and by sharing to double them.

" But I forget that a young lady has done me the honor to invite me to breakfast with her; and pardon my vanity, when I tell you it is one who was pleased to say that she would have gone a thousand miles for such an interview with me as she enjoyed last week. She is, I perceive, mistress of a handsome house and independent fortune ; but believe me, that should such things as these happen to me every day, I should still rejoice that I am,

" My dearest Love,
" Securely and entirely yours,
"P. DODDRIDGE."

At page 50, he says, —
" I have been partaking of a most elegant supper; but I solemnly declare, that a crust of brown bread and a draught of water with you had been a feast far exceeding it. A thousand things which once

seemed romantic, grow plain sober sense when referred to you. But I can add no more. My dearest,
farewell. These tedious days of absence will come
to a conclusion, and I shall, for a while at least,
lose all my cares, were they a thousand times greater, in your delightful society."

The following passage, from one of the doctor's
scientific friends, reminds us of Buffon's theory of the
earth, which he thought was struck by a comet from
the sun.

" I do not know what use is usually assigned to
the sun's motion; but we know that motion is essen-
tial to all terrestrial fire; and why may it not be so
to the solar fire likewise? Motion produces fire, and
keeps it burning. And, by the way (since you are
upon experiments), let me hint to you a pretty micro-
scopical one, if you have it not already. Strike fire
with a flint and steel on a sheet of paper; gather
up the dust and put it into your microscope, and
you will see round iron balls; which shows that the
motion of striking heats the steel even to fusion, so
that every spark is a drop of melted steel, which
forms itself into a sphere, for the same reason that
the drops of rain are globular. Many of these liquid
spheres will be broken and thrown into irregular
shapes by their falling on the paper before they
are sufficiently cooled; but you will see many perfect spheres. My third magnifier shows them as big
as peas."

Behold (as the French say) a letter from Mrs.
Doddridge, which shows that she is resolved not to
be surpassed by the doctor in loving, however she
yields to him in other sciences.

" DEAREST AND BEST OF MEN : Did I know tenderer
epithets, I should certainly use them ; but even Mrs.
Evans herself cannot help me to one ; for though she
says you are an angel, even that does not suit me
so well whilst I myself am quite a mortal.

" She has formed a very dangerous conspiracy
against me upon your return ; fatal indeed to my repose, should it succeed ; but I make myself perfectly easy about it, and believe, how great soever
your friendship for Mr. Evans may be, you would not
choose to change wives with him, at least not at present.   But, indeed, my dearest, your three last delightful letters have made me a bankrupt in everything
but love ; that, however, is a stock on which you
may largely and freely draw ; and give me leave to
tell you, dear sir, you shall not, nor cannot, exhaust
it ; for, though I most readily yield you the superiority in everything else, here I must and will contend with you, at least for an equality, and could
you see my heart, you would there behold it written
in characters which neither time nor age can erase.
But, alas ! so great at present is our unhappy distance,
that, as Mr. Pope observes upon a like occasion, were
even the scheme of having a crystal placed in the
breast to take place, it could be of no service to us ;
and therefore we must, in this instance, as well as in
many others, content ourselves with believing what
we cannot perceive."

Hallo !   At page 182 we find Dr. Doddridge, the
grave divine, the Family Expositor, reading the
Wife of Bath's Prologue " to Nancy, this afternoon,"
and taking his share " in the laugh it raised."

"I slept last night as comfortable as I ever did in my life, and my cold is so well to-day, that, whereas I could scarcely speak five words together eight-and-forty hours ago, I have been able, without any difficulty, to read the Wife of Bath's Tale (Prologue, he means) to Nancy this afternoon, and to take my share in the laugh it raised. My fair auditor was particularly edified with those lines: —

> ' There swims no goose so gray, but soon or late
> She finds some honest gander for her mate.'

But of that by the way." * Nancy (a Miss Ann Moore) good-humoredly disdains the application of this couplet in a postscript. We hope she was the lady who boxed his ears at page 253. The doctor was certainly very provoking sometimes, betwixt the severity of his doctrines and the gayety of his conversation. He was bound, we think, either to have preached other doctrines, or not have been so lively. The above anecdote is a curious instance of the freedom of our pious ancestors, with regard to the books they would read in company. Do we think their descendants more virtuous in not reading them? Not a jot. We think them apparently more consistent with their doctrine, but more hypocritical in practice; though we see a preferment in the preceding, which it certainly does not look for. The truth is, their doctrines are not so fixed as they used to be;

---

* It was Pope's version of the Wife of Bath's Prologue that the doctor read to Miss Nancy. Here is the original of the lines quoted above: —

> "Ne non so grey goos goth ther in the lake,
> (As sayst thou) that wol ben withoute a make." — ED.

and they do not know whither such freedom might lead those, who are as little certain as they are.

In a letter from Warburton to Doddridge, we have the opinion of that celebrated robustious divine on the amount of happiness in human life. It is expressed with his usual force. " Though I be extremely cautious," he says, " what sect I follow in religion, yet any in philosophy will serve my turn, and honest Sancho Panza's as well as any ; who, on his return from an important commission, when asked by his master whether they should mark the day with a *black* or a *white* stone, replied, ' Faith, sir, if you will be ruled by me — with neither, but with good *brown ochre.*' What this philosopher thought of his commission, I think of human life in general: *good brown ochre* is the complexion of it."

Warburton had been living at his friend Allen's, and living too well. His blood was getting too buttery and episcopal. We recollect mentioning to the late Mr. Hazlitt, that a celebrated living writer had declared his belief in the predominance of evil in the world, calling it "an awful fact." — " He had just lost his money," said that shrewd observer. The French have a phrase of seeing things " in rosecolor." We have no such phrases in this country : we eat and drink too much, and get too much money, and think that evil predominates. There is enough evil, surely, to mend, particularly in our system ; but, for our part (and we have had care enough too), we no more believe that evil predominates, compared with good, than we believe the sensations of ordinary health to be disagreeable instead of pleasant. Man-

kind, generally speaking, enjoy a great deal of good,
and all their best impulses press them forward to the
attainment of more and better. The cheerful French
have found out these secrets, and we cannot do better
than follow them in promoting the discovery. Hear,
as one step towards it, Warburton's opinion of
Young's Night Thoughts. The book, to be sure, curi-
ously enough, is not so popular with us as in France ;
but the French can afford to like melancholy books.,
A luxurious contrast is furnished to their vivacity.
In England, a melancholy thought gets hold of us,
and worries us like a dog hanging at a bull's nose.
" I hope," says Warburton, " the MS. poem you
mentioned in your last, will be more in the Christian spirit than Dr. Young's ' Night Complaint,' — a
dismal rhapsody, and the more dismal for being full
of poetical images, all frightful, without design or
method ; so that I have thought, as Mr. Pope's motto
to his Essay on Man was, — *Know yourself:* so the
motto to this should be, — *Go hang yourself;* for
what has any man to do else under that perturbation
of mind the author seems to be in? Yet one does
not know what to think of him. He appears rather
to be under a poetical than a religious dilemma, by
the straining and heaving of his thoughts." The
secret was, that Young was a parasite and a preferment-hunter, who failed in his views, and only had
too much ! He was melancholy for want of a mitre.

We now come to the story of the Box on the Ear.
" While the doctor," says his editor, " was ever ready
to yield the chastening charms of female society their
proper influence, he was far from abrogating the just

prerogative of masculine sway — an amusing instance of which occurred in a mixed company, when the superior authority of the ' lords of the creation' was duly vindicated, as the following anecdote will avouch.

" Dr. Doddridge and a lady of his acquaintance were once disputing before a large company concerning the authority of the husband over his wife, when the doctor overcame in the argument; and the lady, unable to restrain herself on being vanquished in so tender a point, arose from her chair, and going up to the doctor, half in jest, half in earnest, gave him a stroke with her fan. The doctor, on receiving this rough treatment, looked a little grave, and after a silence of a few minutes, spoke the following lines, to the visible confusion of his blushing antagonist : —

' Fidelio once most unhappily said,
However, such nonsense came into his head,
That the Sex he had loved and studied so long
Had their fancies and passions a little too strong.
Sabrina grew warm at a charge so unjust ;
To plead for the Fair she was ever the first ;
And their wisdom at once in her anger appears,
When to answer his Reasons she boxes his ears.' "

We have said the doctor was a provoking man ! There was more in his provocations than appears on the face of them, and the present case was probably no exception. It is necessary to know who the lady was, before we can pronounce her conduct so unfeminine as it appears to have been. Was she married or unmarried? Was she rich or poor, healthy or sick, happy or unhappy? Considerations connected with any of these circumstances might have mingled with the argument, and warmed her blushes with

more glows than one. We will not condemn her till
we know, even though the flap of her fan was something equivocal; nor can we allow the justice of the
doctor's triumph, till we see what right he had to be
so very argumentative and superior. It was too bad,
in a man so amiable and so well off, to have the best
of an argument, as well as a charming wife, and heaps
of admiring friends, fair and brown. He should not
have overthrown the ladies in a dispute, and set himself to making verses, while they were getting up.

The heretical doubt respecting the lady of sixty, in
the following letter, would have perplexed poor Miss
Scott. " I had on Saturday," the doctor writes to his
wife, " the pleasure of seeing Shakespeare's tomb and
epitaph, as also the monument of a celebrated person
who died at sixty, and a maid, if her *tombstone fibs
not*. She came from *Nonsuch* (the Italics of this
word are the doctor's own), in Surrey, and is buried
at the feet of the Lady Carew, whose waiting-woman
she was, and who, that she (Lady C.) might continue
a maid no longer, is said to have jumped out of a
window three stories high." In the chancel of Strat-
ford church the doctor meets with " a charming lady,"
with whom he " would have been glad of further conversation," and who was " indeed a woman of surprising sense," though not equal to Mrs. Doddridge.
He is always meeting with ladies so charming, and
welcomes so delicious, and lives in such a world of
love, festivity, religion, and locomotion, that he reminds us of the famous John Buncle. We should
have thought John's character drawn from him, if he
had married five wives, and been a Unitarian. 1830.

CONFECTIONERY.

ONE cannot open this book * without fancying that one scents all the good things that we see mentioned in it, — the cakes, candies, creams, ices, preserved fruit, — the raspberry tarts, and the sirups of violet. Mr. Gunter, whom " the gods have made poetical," and who quotes Greek, Latin, and Italian for his purpose, justly claims for his art something of a superior elegance to that of all others connected with the table. We except the Fruiterer; but his is not more of an in-door than an out-of-door art. The Fruiterer belongs to all times of the day, and all places except the high street; whereas pastry and confectionery must be eaten housed. There is a sort of sophistication connected with them which does not do for pure nature. The little boy is the only person that can eat his bunn in the face of heaven and not be ashamed. And we suspect, that with all the helps of Mr. Gunter, no masticator of jelly cakes, or meringues, eats his felicity with half the satisfaction that he did his bunn when he was a little boy.

The superiority of confectionery and pastry over other cookery consists in its association with fruits and grain. A cookery-book reminds one of the

---

* The Confectioner's Oracle, containing Receipts for Desserts, &c., with others for Pastry-Cooks, and an Elucidation of the Principles of Good Cheer. Being a Companion to Dr. Kitchener's Cook's Oracle. By W. Gunter.

shambles. The Confectioner talks to us of sugars, and oranges, and violets. He lives in quite another world. He is of the garden and the dairy. Eve, who " tempered dulcet creams," was the mother of his pretty girls in the pastry shops. Cookery did not begin till after the fall. We confess, if our bad habits would let us, we would never eat joint more, but stick to this paradisiacal eating, and have blood made up of raspberries and the rose. It is not moral weakness that prompts us to the wish, any more than bodily weakness would follow it. To get out of the necessity of beef eating, would be to get out of the necessity of excitement and clouded energy. The weakest stomachs are those which assimilate best with flesh already made. To take to a sudden course of living upon fruits and farina might endanger it; but he that had never lived on anything else would probably beat us all. The late General Elliott, whose picture, by Sir Joshua, may be seen in Pall Mall, stout, military, with a nose as energetic as his cocked hat, lived entirely on fruit and vegetables.

But to our author. Mr. Gunter seems to be two, if not " three gentlemen at once," in his book. There is, first, the gay, bantering, scholarly Gunter, superior to his trade, and tossing his quotations about him, from the Greek and Latin; there is the professional Gunter, important in his undertaking, and piquing himself on the patronage of his lords and ladies; and, finally, there is the Gunter of the frontispiece, sitting beside a table with a fowl on it, and looking as melancholy as the first is gay. He seems to have

no appetite to his dish, but rather to be deploring the
bad digestion of some previous one, one of his hands
being in his waistcoat, and his face looking incredulous of the pleasures of this world.   This Gunter
may be the second, but he ought not to have been so
candid in his lemon peel.   Great men cannot always
afford to be seen in their simplicity.   He should
have given us a head of himself in its smartest condition, like Mr. Ude or Mr. Farley, and not have led
the reader to suppose that a Confectioner can look
mortal.

To the Gunter in his professional state we have
nothing to object.   We take it for granted that his
cakes and jellies are made after the most exquisite
fashion, otherwise the facetious Gunter could not
have introduced " Earl Powis " making a speech in
his favor.   In the Advice to Confectioners, we have
a sketch of the history of the science, more smart
than satisfactory ; and in the appendix we are presented, in a most unexpected and disinterested manner, with remarks on digestion, and earnest advice to
take care of one's health, by air, temperance, and
exercise.   Such is the march of intellect, like those
of the white ants, over one's very table, and so
thoughtful does an eater of pastry become in spite
of the vivacity of his set-to.   This reminds us that
Mr. Gunter may say what he pleases against cooks,
as distinguished from pastry-cooks, but of all the
substances taken into the daring stomachs of men,
the physicians tell us (and we believe them) that
there is none so difficult to conquer, and so provocative of horror in the struggle, as the compound of

flour and fried butter, known to the unsuspecting under the innocent name of pie-crust. The boy goes on bearing it for a long time, but, as he grows older, " shades of the prison house" begin to close in upon him, as Mr. Wordsworth says, — that is to say, of pie-crust; for it is clear, by the speculative melancholy of that poet, that he has been a large eater of it in his time. "The child," he says, "is father to the man," — that is, begets all the habits of the grown person ; and pie-crust, he may depend upon it, is the origin of much melancholy blank verse and theological dilemma.* We except this from the innocencies of our pastry, unless our readers are fox-hunters, or run about as they did in the days when pie was bliss. In that case they may eat anything.

But we have another objection to make to the elegant Gunter, which is, that in endeavoring to exalt his art into new regions of the sweet, he becomes profane, and talks of love and the ladies ! Now, we must never have two such things as love and the love of eating brought together. If eating, in its most innocent shape (as no doubt may be the case), is found in connection with love, care must be taken to distinguish one love from the other, and not confound their metaphors and their sympathies. Here is Dr.

---

* Holmes's Autocrat, you may remember, once took more of his landlady's pie than was good for him, and had an indigestion in consequence. "While I was suffering from it," he says, "I wrote some sadly desponding poems and a theological essay, which took a very melancholy view of creation. When I got better, I labelled them all ' Pie-Crust,' and laid them by as scarecrows and solemn warnings. I have a number of books on my shelves that I should like to label with some such title ; but as they have great names on their title-pages, —Doctors of Divinity some of them, — it wou.dn't do." — ED.

Kitchener, in the introduction, represented as talking of the "epicurism of the sex," and recommending Mr. Gunter to give " a sort of electrical and thrilling impulsion " to all the ladies ! We hope they will be on their guard the next time they see him. He is an accomplished but dangerous man. In the same place we are told that the eating of a delicate confection, compared with that of a ragout, is like the finer feeling of a "second love" compared with "the undistinguishing ardor of a first attachment ;" and in the appendix, an appetite, which requires exciting, is likened to " the lukewarm heart of a husband" made warmer by the "caresses of his wife." We beg the lady patronesses of Mr. Gunter to put a stop to these profane images. There is an elegance in the pleasures of confectionery, which does not extend to every sort of eating ; but the grosser part of both sexes have already a notion that eating and loving are entertainments of the same family ; and if those who understand the matter do not interfere, we shall have horrid women — or, rather, no women — laying down the laws of beef and affection over the dinner table, and making out that people have no mind to anything but body. Miserable creatures ! Nobody can have a mind to theirs. They never bring together the two ideas of love and woman. They are women and lobster sauce, and fit only to be loved by cannibals. They are "*fond*" of fish ! An ogre would be "fond" of them.

Ladies and sweetmeats may undoubtedly be brought together, and there are occasions when love and sweetmeats may be so. There is a pretty instance of it in a scene in La Fontaine's love-making novel, called the Family of Halden. Mr. Gunter tells us, that " English Meringues " are an especial favorite with the Marchioness of C——; in whose praises, and those of her lovely daughter, he could " almost " write a poem out of gratitude; that Lady De R—— was the first who introduced into high life the artificial jelly candy, which " melts in the mouth, leaving a charming titillation on the tongue;" and that jelly cakes owe their celebrity to Lady Julia H——d, of whom it is said that " the change of her maiden name of C. arose from the very elegant manner in which a plate of them was pointed out to her by her present lord, and the few words of his musical voice which accompanied the *politesse* of the moment.

" What great events from, &c., &c."

and then our author signs his initials to the note that conveys this interesting information, — " W. G." — This is innocent, but we should protest against hearing of the jelly cakes afterwards, and finding them turned into images of bliss.

1830.

A TREATISE ON DEVILS.*

IT is much easier to conceive a good spirit than a
bad one, not only because the latter is useless
and his sufferings absurd (nature refusing to allow of
suffering beyond a certain pitch, and no infliction of
ill warranting or making reasonable a further and
worse infliction, except for the good of all parties),
but because malignity, which is a devil's characteristic, and which is understood to mean the love of
injuring another for the injury's sake, is found, upon
a due knowledge of evil and its causes, to be a thing
altogether fictitious and impossible. The worst of
men does not injure another because, abstractedly, he
would do him a mischief, but in order to get rid of
some pressure of evil upon himself. Take the envi-
ous man, the revengeful, the murderer for the sake of
gain, — or what seems worst of all, the murderer for
the sake of murder, — and, tracing the causes of his
offence with a humane and a thoughtful eye, we shall
find that it is out of some imaginary disadvantage,
some sense of infelicity or inequality, or some morbid
want of excitement, frightening the poor inconsider-
ate wretch himself even more than he frightens others,

---

* This treatise was published soon after the appearance of Sir Walter Scott's
Letters on Demonology and Witchcraft, with the following preface or introduction : " Humbly submitted to those who require something more on the subject
than is to be found in the late work upon Demonology, and particularly to such
of them as are zealous for the extirpation of unworthy notions of God and
man." — ED.

that induces him, under the notion or the impulse of procuring relief to his own desires, to thrust his evil upon the head of another. And the worse and more wicked we could suppose a creature to be, the more (not to speak it profanely) woulu be his excuse; because the more dreadful would be the disadvantage under which he lay, the more tormenting his infelicity, and the more grievous (if it could never be made smooth for him) his wrong. Pain, like a heap of brambles, shows us our departure from a right path; and melancholy it seems that pain should be necessary, even supposing it to exist only in the younger period or first renewals of a world, after some catastrophe interrupting its bliss, and before the new wilderness can be cleared; but as all evils are not so evil as we suppose them, so we know from all that we *can* know (and nothing gives us a right to pronounce further, especially in contumely of what is good) that the worst evils are fugitive, and the greatest crimes are mistakes. For all these reasons (the world feeling them more and more as it grows enlightened), there comes up by degrees a suspicion that it is better to say as little as possible, in a serious way, of such anomalies as devils: — in a little while people are allowed to doubt them, then to laugh at them, and finally, except among the grossly ignorant or superstitious, devils remain fit subjects for nothing but jests, and caricature, and the voluntary gravity of the black-lettered.

As to those writers and others, who continue to preach a doctrine which they despise, out of a notion that the delusion is necessary to mankind, — that men

are so wicked as to require terrors to keep them in
awe, — and other half reasonings of that sort, it is a
great presumption in them, in the first place, to assume a privilege of exemption from those duties of
veracity to which they would fain tie the rest of the
world; and, secondly, they harm their own natures
by it, and maintain themselves in an ill opinion of
the world in which they take themselves to be the
wisest persons. They rule it (as they think) by falsehood, and yet are weak enough to lament that it is as
bad and false as it is, and a " vale of tears." Now, the
world is neither so bad nor so unhappy as many suppose it, though, assuredly, there is sorrow enough in
it to make us anxious to wipe the tears out of its
eyes; but this is not to be done by the use of the
very falsehood we lament, by adding to what is already evil in the world, — melancholy and perplex-
ing ideas of things beyond it, and all this at a time
when, the delusion being discovered, the signal is
given for its destruction. As men, let us think none
of us exempt from the virtues and sincerity of men;
nor, by taking ourselves for the gods of the foolish,
imagine we must have devils to keep the peace for
us. Truth will do very well without them, if we
suffer it to take its course. Are we to suppose ourselves better and wiser than all which it may find
out for us? Who has given us the clew to discover
that?

With regard to the existence of one supreme devil,
or conscious and wilful Principle of Evil (which has
been doubted by the most orthodox, upon a due con-

sideration of texts-and Scripture),* it is not only con-
tradictory to the received opinions respecting the
omnipotence and beneficence of the Deity, but is a
superfluity in common reasoning ; for as it is a maxim
in logic, that when anything can be accounted for on
one principle, it need not have recourse to another,
and as it ought equally to be a maxim in common
sense to choose the more agreeable principle of the
two, it is much better to refer the origin of evil to
that inert and insensible part of matter of which Plato
speaks, and the hardness of which causes a difficulty
in the working it, than to set up, for the amusement
of sluggish imaginations, the terrors of feeble ones,
and the poor views of the worldly, a gratuitous malignant spirit, equally absurd whether we consider
the attributes of God or the necessities of common
reason. And herein the celebrated living writer, who
is as delightful in fiction as he appears shallow in philosophy, and who has addressed a book to a little
child in which he condescends to preach the horrible
doctrine of hell torments, ought, we think, to have a

---

* As in the very word *devil*, which is a translation of the Testament, is
assumed to be the meaning of the Greek word *diabolos*, though the letters signify
an *accuser*, and admirably fit the passage in that sense. For instance, — "Be
sober, be vigilant," says the Apostle, "for your adversary the *accuser* walks
about, seeking whom he may devour." What can be better than this construc-
tion, or more natural in addressing a letter to an infant community, bound to be
on their good behavior ? and why should the word be translated *devil* ? So in
the famous passage in Isaiah, where the King of Babylon is so nobly apostro-
phized under the title of Lucifer, or the light-bringer, son of the morning. Why
should this be tortured into a prophecy of the devil, and the morning star be
made synonymous with an imaginary infernal being ? It appears to us that a
book written expressly on the subject, with the proper requisites of learning and
philosophy, might now settle the pretensions of this infernal personage forever.
We should envy the composer of such a work, and would do our utmost to
second his benefaction to mankind

deep sense of his shame and humiliation : for it is either a great weakness in him or a great insincerity. He says, in the preface to one of his novels, with an escape of cunning, brought upon him by the mortified vanity of a failure, that he will never go counter to public opinion; or, to use his own words, will never " sail against the stream." *   We need not say whether it is becoming in a man of genius to talk in this manner, for whatever reason ; but it is one thing not to sail against the stream, and another to go down with it in the company of the small craft of ignorance and hypocrisy. Imagination, however, carries a blessing with it in its own despite ; and the magic vessel, in this instance, while the captain is thinking of nothing but the flag he has hoisted in favor of old prejudices, has a stock of humanities on board that shall still benefit the world.

It hardly need be observed, at this time of day, that Milton's devil is no real devil, any more than his divinity is really divine. The divine things in Paradise Lost are the poetry and the humanity. As far as his devil partakes of these, the devil himself becomes divine ; and as far as his Deity wants them, we feel that nothing can be flatter or more ungodly. Milton laughed at the vulgar idea of the devil, and disdained to degrade his fallen Archangel into horns

---

* In Captain Clutterbuck's Introductory Epistle to the Rev. Dr. Dryasdust, prefixed to the Fortunes of Nigel, the author of Waverley is made to say, in speaking of the failure of the White Lady in The Monastery, that no one shall find him "rowing against the stream." " I care not," he adds, " who knows it,— I write for general amusement : and though I never will aim at popularity by what I think unworthy means, I will not, on the other hand, be pertinacious in the defence of my own errors against the voice of the public." — ED.

and a tail. Had he delayed writing his poem some years longer, there is reason to believe that he would have disdained to degrade his Deity into a " school divine" and a sorry tyrant,* or to think that spirits in a state of perfect bliss and virtue could fall.† Such a god is not the natural God of a great poet; and from some remarkable evidences, not only in his later works, but that transpired on proving of his will, it appears certain that he retired more and more from the vulgarities that had been palmed upon his infancy into the sacred recesses of his own thought, and found there no longer an unworthy deity. He had "edified" a chapel to himself;‡ and the music of his own organ now ascended into a nobler sky, giving to his sightless eyeballs a right to look tranquil.

No; the only genuine devil now extant is the proper old woman's devil, with horns and a tail, and he begins exceedingly

"To pale his ineffectual fire."

* " And God the Father turns a school-divine." — POPE.

† " What to me is more wonderful," says the author of Robinson Crusoe, "and which, I think, will be very ill accounted for, is : — How came seeds of crime to rise in the angelic nature, created in a state of perfect, unspotted holiness ? How was it first found in a place where no unclean thing can enter? How came ambition, pride, or envy to generate there? Could there be offence where there was no crime? Could untainted purity breed corruption? Could that nature contaminate and infect which was always drinking in principles of perfection?

" Happy it is to me that writing the history, not solving the difficulties of Satan's affairs, is my province in this work: that I am to relate fact, not give reasons for it or assign causes: if it was otherwise, I should break off at this difficulty, for I acknowledge I do not see through it : neither do I think that the great Milton, after all his fine images and lofty excursions upon the subject, has left it one jot clearer than he found it." — *History of the Devil*, p. 41. edit. 1777.

‡ " A littel wyde
There was an holy chappel edifyde." — SPENSER.

The old women themselves desert him. He loses his believers by wholesale; is a very sorry and poor devil, and people quote Burns, and wish him out of his durance. Formerly he was identified with emperors and archangels; he was called the Prince of the Air; he had all the spirits of the terrestrial world given him for subjects; the whole Pagan mythology was turned over to him, and when gods were forgotten, devils were made out of the fairies. He is now "himself alone," deprived of his property, like Job, and sits amidst the ashes of his ruin in shabby misery. He has lost even his power to joke, which was one of the ghastliest things about him. He no longer laughs, and says, *Ho! Ho!* like another Henry the Eighth. He has nothing to say it for. If he is still black as a coal, with talons and saucer eyes, he is also lean as a rake; no longer fat, as when he used to have those delicious dinners with the old wives, like a favored Methodist parson. His talons are of no use to him but to serve him like Job's; and his saucer eyes now, indeed, for the first time,

"Witness huge affliction and dismay,"

rolling about like a starved owl's in a trap, who has been caught there at noonday.

Formerly he and his ministers were everywhere round about us, tempting us to ill, doing us all sorts of mischief, and laughing at it, and now and then raising storms of wind and rain, and thunder and lightning (which, not having been to school, they did not know were good things for us). The powers granted him were no less prodigious than odd. If you wished anything at the devil, he took it. He disputed possession of you with your good angel; and a silly old woman, in whom indigestion confounded dreaming with waking, and who went flying on the wings of her head vapors, had the power of making him a present of an immortal soul. What is more extraordinary, and shows us the danger of giving an inch of ground to assumptions and things unproved, is, that old women, both male and female, having much to do with education, they habituated some of the most exalted understandings to believe in these rascalities of superstition, and we should infallibly have all believed in them to this day had not the excess of the demand upon their credulity in some other matters roused men of spirit and genius to vindicate the invaluable right of doubting and inquiring, some of them (Luther for one) being all the while fastened with the grossest chains of superstition by the one hand, while they wrote against them triumphantly with the other. Let us be modest when we think of these things, but do not let us prove our modesty by adhering to errors upon which we have been enlightened. Let us reflect, rather, upon how many points we may still be mistaken, and resolve to carry on the good work of improvement in which those illustrious men set us so noble an example.

We lay before our readers some amusing extracts from an old writer, both serious and comic, which will show them what was thought of devils by the contemporaries of Shakespeare. Not that *he* believed in any such nonsense, though he knew how to turn the poetical parts of it to account; and in matters of speculation, as well as practice, was doubtless the most undogmatical of men. He and the other great poets of that time were accused of being exceedingly sceptical, and there is evidence in them to show that, in a proper sense of the word, the opinion was true. We do not make an exception of old Heywood, who was author of some beautiful simple dramas, and from whom the chief number of extracts are taken : for though a touching writer, he was little of a poet. He had great feeling, but no imagination ; and it is not paradoxical to affirm, that if he had finer eyes for fiction, he would have seen farther into truth.* And so it is, *vice versa*, of the mechanical philosophers. But to the passages in question. The first is very ghastly, on account of the quiet familiarity of shape in which the alleged devil makes her *entrée*. This is a great secret in horrid stories.

"In the easterne part of Russia," saith Heywood, "about harvest time, a spirit was seen to walk at midday, like a sad, mourning widow; and whoso-ever she met, if they did not instantly fall on their knees to adore her, they could not part with her without a leg or an arm broken, or some other as great mischiefe." — *Hierarchie of Angels.*

The chief of these noon-devils, according to the Rabbis, is a very singular personage. He has a head like that of a calf, with a horn shooting out of his

---

* Thomas Heywood, who, says Charles Lamb, in his Specimens of English Dramatic Poets, "is a sort of *prose* Shakespeare. His scenes are to the full as natural and affecting. But we miss *the poet*, that which in Shakespeare always appears out and above the surface of *the nature*." — ED.

fcrehead ; is all over ox's hair, full of eyes, and *rolls along like a tub.** We shall take this opportunity of observing that, according to the Jews, all male devils have plenty of hair on their heads, while, on the contrary, female devils are bald. This is the reason, they say, why Boaz laid his hand on the head of Ruth. It was in order to assure himself that he had not a female devil in his chamber.† With us the shock would be great, but we should certainly acquit the lady of enchantment. No Christian would say, " Eh, you little devil !" to a girl with a bald head.

A STORY OUT OF NIDERIUS.

" Niderius telleth this story: In the borders of the kingdom of Bohemia lieth a valley, in which divers nights together was heard clattering of armour and clamours of men, as two armies had met together in picht battel. Two knights that inhabited near unto this prodigious place agreed to arm themselves and discover the secrets of this invisible army. The night was appointed, and, accommodated at all assayes, they rode to the place, where they might descry two battels ready ordered for present skirmish ; they could easily distinguish the colours and prevant liveries of every company ; but drawing neere, the one (whose courage began to relent) told the other that he had seene sufficient for his part, and thought it good not to dally with such prodigies ; wherefore, further than he was, he would not go. The other called him coward, and

---

* Rabbinical Literature., Vol. II., p. 118.   † Id., p. 104.

prickt on towards the armies, from one of which a horseman came forth, fought with him, and cut off his head. At which sight the other fled, and told the sight the next morning. A great confluence of people, searching for the body, found it in one place, and the head in another; but neither could discern the footing of horse or man, only the print of birds' feet, and those in miry places." — *Hierarchie of Angels.*

This reminds us of the Tempter's Feast, in Milton, which vanishes,

"With sound of harpies' wings and talons heard." *

Birds' and goats' feet were thought to be unalterable accompaniments of devils, and rendered the boldest of them coy in their extremities.

The following illustration, out of Heywood, of the promptitude of devils to avail themselves of any expression in their favor is one of the best stories about them we ever read. The reason is, that it is domestic, and touches upon the affections. The peril of the innocent and unconscious child in the hands of the swarthy visitors, furnishes a striking picture of contrast.

THE BLACK DINNER.

" In Silesia, a nobleman having invited many guests to dinner, and prepared a liberal and costly feast for their entertainment, when all things were in great

---

* Paradise Regained, Book II., v. 403. Warton observes upon this passage, "that the sound of the wings and talons is much finer than if the harpies had been seen, because the imagination is left at work, and the surprise is greater than if they had been mentioned before."

forwardness, instead of his friends whom he expected, he only received excuses from them that they could not keep his appointment. Whereat the inviter, being horribly vexed, broke out into these words, saying, ' Since all these men have thus failed me, I wish that so many devils of hell would feast with me to-day, and eat up the victuals provided for them ;' and so in a great rage left the house, and went to church, where was that day a sermon ; his attention to which having tooke away the greatest part of his choler, in the interim there arrived at his house a great troupe of horsemen, very blacke, and of extraordinary aspect and stature : who, alighting in the court, called to a groome to take their horses, and bade another servant run presently to his master and tell him his guests were come. The servant, amazed, runneth to church, and with that short breath and little sense he had left, delivers to his master what had happened. The lord calls to the preacher, and desiring him for that time to break off his sermon, and advise him by his ghostly counsel what was best to doe in so strict an exigent, hee persuades him, that all his servants should with what speed they can depart the house. In the mean time, they, with the whole congregation, come within view of the mansion : of which all his servants, as well men as maids, had with great affright delivered themselves, and for haste forgotten and left behind a young child, the nobleman's sonne, sleeping in his cradle. By this the devils were revelling in the dining-chamber, making a great noise, as if they had saluted and welcomed one another : and looked through the case-

ments, one with the head of a beare, another a
wolfe, a third a cat, a fourth a tygre, &c., filling
bowls and quaffing as if they had drunke to the
master of the house. By this time the nobleman,
seeing all his servants safe, began to remember his
sonne, and asked them ' what had become of the
child'? These words were scarce spoke, when one
of the devils had him in his arms, and shewed him
out of the window. The good man of the house
at this sight being almost without life, spying an old
faithful servant of his, fetched a deep sighe, and
said, ' O me, what shall become of the infant!' The
servant, seeing his master in that sad extasie, replied,
' Sir, by God's help I will enter the house, and fetch
the childe out of the power of yon devils, or perish
with him.' To whom the master said, ' God prosper
thy attempt, and strengthen thee in thy purpose.'
Whereon, having taken a blessing from the priest, he
enters the house, and coming into the next room
where the devils were then rioting, he fell upon his
knees, and commended himself to the protection of
heaven. Then pressing in amongst them, he beheld
them in their horrible shapes, some sitting, some
walking, some standing. Then they all came about
him at once, and asked him what business he had
there. He, in a great sweat and agonie (yet resolved in his purpose), came to that spirit which
held the infant, and said, ' In the name of God, de-
liver this child to mee.' Who answered, ' No, but
let thy master come and fetch him, who hath most
interest in him.' The servant replied, ' I am come
to do that office and service which God hath called

me, by virtue of which, and by his power, loe, I seize upon the innocent: and snatching him from the divell, took him in his arms and carried him out of the roome. At which they clamoured and called after, 'Ho, thou knave, ho, thou knave, leave the childe to us, or we will teare thee in pieces.' But he, unterrified with their diabolical menaces, brought away the infant, and delivered it safe to the father. After some few daies the spirits left the house, and the lord re-entered into his antient possession. In this discourse is to be observed, with what familiaritie these Familiar Spirits are ready to come, being invited."— *Hierarchie of Angels.*

Chaucer has a pleasant story to similar purpose, which is too long to repeat: but we cannot resist giving an abstract. A summoner (a bailiff of the ecclesiastical court) riding out on his vacation, overtakes a yeoman under the trees, in a green cloak, also on horseback. He bids him good-morrow, and the yeoman asks him whether he means to go far that day.

> "This sompnour him answered, and said, 'Nay ι —
> Here, fast by,' quoth he, 'is mine intent
> To riden, for to raisen up a rent,
> That longeth to my lord his duety.'
> 'Ah! art thou then a bailiff?' quoth he
> (He durst not, for very filth and shame,
> Say that he was a sompnour for the name),
> '*De par Dieux !*' quoth this yeoman, 'leve brother,
> Thou art a bailiff, and I'm another.' "

The two horsemen get social, and the summoner asks the yeoman where he lives, in order that he may know how to find him. The yeoman, " in soft speech," tells him that he lives " far in the North

Countree " (the supposed quarter of the devils) : and adds, that he hopes to see him there shortly, and will give him such directions as he cannot possibly miss.

After comparing notes, and agreeing that it is idle to have a conscience, the sompnour, who is very curious, requests to know his fellow's name.

> **ə**   " This yeoman gan a little for to smile ;
> 'Brother,' quoth he, 'wilt thou that I thee tell?
> *I am a fiend; my dwelling is in hell:*
> And here ride I about my purchasing,
> To wot whether men *will give me anything.*' "

" Benedicite ! " cries the sompnour ; " what say ye ? " — The frightened church officer recovers himself, and after some conversation, they agree to stand by one another in their callings. The yeoman is to take whatever people give to him ; the summoner what he can get ; and if there is an overplus on either side, they are to share it.

. They come into a town, where a carman is swearing at his horses for not getting on with a load of hay :

> " Heit, Scot ! heit, Brock ! what, spare ye for the stones !
> The fiend (quoth he) you fetch, body and bones :
> The dev'l have all, both horse, and cart, and hay."

The summoner wonders that his friend does not take the man at his word, and seize on the team ; but the devil tells him that he does not mean what he says, as he will see presently.

> " This carter thwacketh his horse, upon the croup,
> And they began to drawer and to stoop,
> Heit, now ! (quoth he) there — Jesus Christ you bless,
> And all his handy work, both more and less !

That was well twitch'd, mine own liard [*] boy:
I pray God save thy body, and Saint Eloy."

" There," said the devil, " you see ! " — The companions quit the town, and arrive at the hut of a poor widow, against whom the summoner has a warrant. He agrees to compound the matter, if she will give him twelve pence (a good sum in those days) : the poor woman protests that she could not raise such a sum in the whole world : the summoner gets enraged, says he will take away her " new pan," and calls her names : upon which the woman gets angry in turn, and wishes him at the devil.

"Unto the devil, rough and black of hue,
Give I thy body, and my pan also.
And when the devil heard her cursen so
Upon her knees, he said in this mannère :
'Now, Mabily, mine own mother dear ;
Is this your will in earnest that ye say ?'
'The devil,' quoth she, 'so fetch him ere the day,
And pan and all, but he will him repent.'
' Nay, old stot, that is not mine intent,'
Quoth this sompnour, 'for to repenten me
For anything that I have had of thee :
I would I had thy smock and every cloth.'
' Now, brother,' quoth the devil, 'be not wroth :
Thy body and this pan be mine by right,
Thou shalt with me to hellè yet to-night,
Where thou shall knowen of our privity
More than a master of divinity.'
And with that would the foule fiend him hent :
Body and soul he with the devil went."

The devils formerly in request may be divided into ten classes: First, the old Oracular Devil, or Devil Pagan, who took upon himself to be Apollo or Jupi-

---

[*] Liard, a name for a gray horse.

ter, and is said to have occupied the shrines of those deities; an opinion which good old Plutarch (who was, in fact, the Reverend Mr. Plutarch, clergyman at Delphos) would have thought a blasphemy too horrible to be endured.

Second, the Devil Vagabond, just mentioned, who went about seeking what he might devour, from a summoner down to a sauce-pan. He has since turned out to be a common shoplifter or thief; that is, when he takes a sauce-pan; when he takes a summoner, he is an apoplexy.

Third, the Possessing Devil, or Devil of the Exorcist, who was fond of inhabiting people's bodies, and made himself famous among the nuns. This turned out to be the chaplain.

Fourth, the Amatory Devil, or Incubus, who partook of the nature of the second, and who, according to Chaucer, had disappeared in his time, being displaced by the Friar; at which period perhaps the word Incubus was first rendered Incumbent. He is still clerical sometimes, but oftener a layman; and may be seen haunting milliners' apprentices down Regent Street, in the likeness of a foolish youth; or standing at a tavern door, sly and stupid, eying the women's ankles as they pass. He is also the Nightmare.

Fifth, the Devil Grim, or General Devil, who appeared in a proper diabolical shape, or was at least black and swarthy, and often went in a company, as may be seen in the story of the Black Dinner. He has totally disappeared.

Sixth, the House Devil, or Devil Pranksome, with whom the Fairies were confounded. He was a minor kind of class the second, and contented himself with knocking and making a noise, displacing furniture, and making the good people " knowe not what to think." He has been discovered to be a maid-servant.

Seventh, the Wayside, or Out-of-Door Devil, also confounded with Fairies. He was a kind of Satyr. — " They sit," quoth Burton, " by the highway side, to give men falls, and make their horses stumble and start as they ride (if you will believe the relation of that holy man Ketellus, in Nubrigensis, that had an especial grace to see devils). . . . . If a man curse or spur his horse for stumbling, they do heartily rejoice at it; with many such pretty feats." *

Eighth, the Necromancer's or Astrologer's Devil, who came up when he was called by art; explained the mysteries of the universe ; was a great statesman ; and promised riches and power. Some of his tribe (to use the libellous language of those days) were " mighty Dukes" and " Princes," having brute heads, and riding on horseback.†

Ninth, the Attendant Devil, or Familiar, who was of various degrees of rank, from the accomplished imps that waited on Faustus and Agrippa, down to the cat of the old crone. See Goethe's and Marlowe's tragedies, and The Witch of Middleton.

---

* Anatomy of Melancholy, Part I., Section 2.
† See Reginald Scot's Discovery of Witchcraft, p. 229.
" Their first and principal king (which is of the power of the East) is called *Baell* ; who, when he is conjured up, appeareth with three heads : the fi st like a toad, the second like a man, the third like a cat ; he speaketh with a hoarse voice. He maketh a man to go invisible : he hath under his obedience and rule sixty and six legions of devils.
" The first duke under the power of the East is named *Agares*. He cometh

12

Tenth and last, the Devil Proper, or devil himself, the Apollyon of John Bunyan. He was " the black man " of the nursery and the coal-hole ; and used to be called upon to take away children or swallow them up.* To his friends the witches, he used to appear either as a satyr or sort of clergyman, in black clothes, very reverend, dressed at it were for the evening. But his proper establishment consisted of a tail with a sting to it, " horns on his head, fire in his mouth, eyes like a bason, fangs like a dog, claws like a bear, a skin like a *nigger*, and a voice roaring like a lion ; whereby (quoth Reginald Scot), we start and are afraid when we hear one cry *Bough.*" † A facetious churchman, being asked why the devil took such

---

up mildly in the likeness of a fair old man " (there is something striking in this) "riding upon a crocodile, and carrying a hawk on his fist. He has under him thirty-one legions.

" *Valefer, alias* Malephar, is a strong duke, cometh forth in the shape of a lion and *the head of a thief.* He is very familiar with them to whom he maketh himself acquainted, till he hath brought them to the gallows ; he ruleth ten legions.

" *Furfur* is a great earl, appearing as an Hart with a fiery tail. He lieth in everything.

" *Furcas* is a knight, and cometh forth in the similitude of a cruel man, with a long beard and hoary head. He sitteth on a pale horse.

" *Gamigin* is a great marquess, and is seen in the form of a little horse.

" Another marquess is a liar and horse-stealer. ' *Zepar*, a great duke,' makes women incontinent and barren. *Berith* is a 'great and a terrible duke,' and 'also a liar.' "

* According to the author of *Malleus Maleficarum*, and " the residue of that crew," says Scot, in speaking of the etymology of the word devil, " *Dia* is *Duo* and *Bolus* is *Morcellus ;* whereby they gather, that the devil eateth up a man, body and soul, at two morsels." — *A Discourse concerning Devils and Spirits,* Book I., Chapter 32.

† Discovery of Witchcraft, page 85. ["From him who had not lost all his original brightness, to this dirty fellow who leaves a stench, sometimes of brimstone, behind him, the descent is a long one," says Lowell, in the learned paper on Witchcraft, in Among My Books. — ED.]

a strange liking to old women, quoted a passage, in which it had been said of him, that he " loved to walk in dry places." * Another wag, undertaking to show the people the devil himself, " to the satisfaction," as Swift terms it, " of the beholders," held out to them an *empty purse!* A solider account of him has never been given. An Italian poet makes mention of a devil who dwelt in the smoke of roast meat. †

---

* "That the prince of the powers of darkness, passing by the flower and pomp of the earth, should lay preposterous siege to the weak fantasy of indigent eld — has neither likelihood nor unlikelihood, *à priori* to us, who have no measure to guess at his policy, or standard to estimate what rate those anile souls may fetch in the devil's market." — *Charles Lamb.* — ED.

† Berni, Orlando Innamorato, Canto 51, st. 42. For a thorough knowledge of devils and all that has been said of them, the curious reader may consult Glanville on Witches, Wierus, *De Præstigiis Dæmonum*, Stehelin's Rabbinical Literature, the Lives of the Saints, and above all, Reginald Scot's Discovery of Witchcraft, the title of which ought to be given at large to do honor to the writer who could produce such a work at a period so early: for it was printed in 1584. But the sapient Scotch monarch had not then come to England to encourage people to be as sottish and half-witted as himself. Scot's book is entitled "The Discovery of Witchcraft, — proving that the compacts and contracts of witches with devils and all infernal spirits or familiars are but erroneous novelties and imaginary conceptions, &c. Wherein likewise the unchristian practices and inhumane dealings of searchers and witch-tryers, upon aged, melancholy, and superstitious people, in extorting confessions by terrors and tortures, and in devising false marks and symptoms, are notably detected : and the knavery of jugglers, conjurers, charmers, soothsayers, figure-casters, &c., fully opened and decyphered : all which are very necessary to be known for the undeceiving of judges, justices, and jurors, before they pass sentence upon poor miserable and ignorant people : who are frequently consigned, condemned, and executed for witches and wizards." It was avowedly to confute these "damnable opinions," as he calls them, that King James wrote his *Demonologie.* Reginald Scot was a learned and spirited English gentleman, one of the most worthy of that title that ever existed, and ought to be held in eternal honor by those who feel interested in the cause of humanity. Think of a king putting forth the strength of his authority amidst bowing courtiers and churchmen, in order to retain a superstition by which it has been calculated that *twenty thousand people were burnt in the course of one hundred and fifty years ;* and then figure to yourself this gallant English gentleman (whose book it is said was burnt by the hangman) disdaining in secret these attempts of

Before the devil's existence was denied, people began to perceive that considerable doubts might be
entertained as to the extent of his operations, and
how far King James and others had a right to palm
upon him the offences of their "corrupted flesh." *
We speak in courts of law of criminals being " moved
and instigated by the devil ; " but nobody but a Methodist doubts nowadays that the real instigators are
folly and bad education, or poverty, or disease.   The
sight of injustice is also a great instigation.   Whit-
field, in his Life, attributes his aberrations from virtue
to the devil ; who watched for him, he said, and " took
his usual advantage : " — upon which Bishop Laving-
ton observes, that the man was only excusing himself
at the devil's expense, and that Satan had reason to
complain, and to look upon himself as an ill used
gentleman.   To be serious ; — why should we set up

---

the royal driveller, and looking forward to a time when his book would be quoted
in favor of common sense and feeling, and with the gratitude of posterity. We
should take care to bear the names of such men in golden preservation ; for it is
sometimes the lot of the most precious labors to become obsolete and unremem-
bered by reason of the very good they have done us. We are too apt to fancy, that
what is a commonplace to us, was the same to our benefactors.

* *Demonologie*, Book III., Chapter 2. The King says, that those who deny the
power of a devil, would likewise deny the power of God, if they could for shame ;
that is to say, those who deny the existence of the worst contradiction to good,
must deny the power of the good itself ; for such is really his argument. "Since
a divel," he says, "is the very contrarie opposite to God, there can be no better
way to know God, than by the contrarie, as by the one's power (though a creature)
to admire the power of the great Creator, by the falsehood of the one to consider
the truth of the other ; by the injustice of one to consider the justice of the other :
and by the cruelty of the one, to consider the mercifulness of the other : and so
forth in all the rest of the essence of God, and qualities of the Divell." — *Id.*,
Book II., Chapter 7. What a contempt must Scot have felt for such logic as
this ! There is one point founded upon it that might have been granted to the
king ; viz., that by reading his book you may know by contraries what a book
ought to be.

an imaginary malignant being to warn our mistakes and our anger with ;' to learn how to hate and persecute in behalf of the very doctrines that protest against hatred and persecution ; and to endanger a confusion in all our notions of justice, benevolence, and common sense? Sterne, in his Tristram Shandy, has copied a form of excommunication once in use against thieves and malefactors, and by which their eyes, limbs, and every particle of them, body and soul, were damned forever and ever in the name of all that was held sacred and good.* Dr. Slop was employed to read it out loud ; Uncle Toby whistled lillibullero all the while in ecstasy of astonishment ; observing at one

---

* A translation is to be found in Scot, who proceeds to make the following remark: "This terrible curse with Bell, Book, and Candle, added thereunto, must need work wonders: howbeit, among thieves it is not much weighed, among wise and true men it is not well liked, to them that are robbed it bringeth small relief: the priest's stomach may well be eased, but the goods stolen will never the sooner be restored. Hereby is bewrayed both the malice and folly of Popish Doctrine, whose uncharitable impiety is so impudently published, and in such order uttered, as every sentence (if opportunity served) might be proved both heretical and diabolical. But I will answer this cruel answer with another cure far more mild and civil, performed by as honest a man as he that made the other, whereof mention was lately made.

"So it was that a certain Sir John, with some of his company, once went abroad a jetting, and in a moonlight evening robbed a miller's weir, and stole all his eels. The poor miller made his moan to Sir John himself, who willed him to be quiet : for he would so curse the thief and all his confederates, with Bell, Book, and Candle, that they should have small joy of their fish. And therefore the next Sunday Sir John got him into the pulpit, with surplice on his back and his stole about his neck, and pronounced these following in the audience of the people : —

> "All you that stole the miller's Eeles,
> *Laudate Dominum* de Cœlis ;
> And all they that consented thereto,
> Benedicamus Domino.

"Lo, (saith he) there is sauce for your eeles, my master."

passage, " our armies swore terribly in Flanders, but nothing to this : — for my own part I could not bear to treat and curse my dogs so ! " Dr. Slop continues : " May St. John the Precursor, and St. John the Baptist, and St. Peter, and St. Paul, and St. Andrew. and all other Christ's Apostles, curse him. May the holy and worshipful company of martyrs and confessors, who by their holy works are found pleasing to God Almighty, curse him. May the holy choir of the Holy Virgin damn him. May all the saints who from the beginning of the world and everlasting ages are found to be beloved of God, damn him. May he be damned wherever he be, whether in the house or stables, the garden or the field, or the highway, or in the path, or in the wood, or in the water, or in the church. May he be cursed in living, in dying. May he be cursed in all the faculties of his body. May he be cursed inwardly and outwardly. May he be cursed in the hair of his head. May he be cursed in his brains, and in his vertex." (That is a sad curse, quoth my father.) " In his temples and in his forehead, — in his ears, in his eyebrows, in his eyes, in his cheeks, in his jaw-bones, in his nostrils, in his arms, in his hands, in his fingers.

" May he be damned in his mouth, in his breast, in his heart and purtenance ! down to the very stomach.

" May he be cursed in all the joints and articulations of his members, from the top of his head to the sole of his foot. May there be no soundness in him.

" May the Son of the living God, with all the glory of his majesty " — (here my Uncle Toby, throwing back his head, gave a monstrous long, loud *whew —*

w — w, something betwixt the interjectional whistle of hey-day! and the word itself) — "curse him," continued Dr. Slop, "and may Heaven, with all the powers which move therein, rise up against him, curse and damn him, unless he repent, and make satisfaction. Amen. So be it, — so be it. Amen."

"I declare," quoth my Uncle Toby, "my heart would not let me curse the devil himself with so much bitterness." "He is the father of curses," replied Dr. Slop. "So am not I," replied my uncle. "But he is cursed, and damned already, to all eternity," replied Dr. Slop.

"I am SORRY FOR IT," quoth my Uncle Toby.

"Dr. Slop drew up his mouth, and was just beginning to return my Uncle Toby the compliment of his *whu — w — w*, or interjectional whistle, when the door hastily opening in the next chapter but one — put an end to the affair." — Tristram Shandy, Book III., Chap. xi.

But the affair was not put an end to. It has flourished, and brought forth good fruit. When people were led to consider that Jews had organs and dimensions like themselves, they first began not to loathe them, then they pitied them, and at last they did them justice. A similar process of reflection took place in behalf of birds and beasts : it was discovered that horses and dogs had limbs to be hurt, as well as ourselves; and it is now doubted by some whether we ought to shut in a cage a winged animal, whose region is the air. (By and by we shall begin to have commiseration for fish, and anglers will cease to think themselves the humanest of men.) At length the

devil himself was done justice to ; and noble-hearted
Burns finally wished him out of his coal-hole.   So

> " Fare you well, auld Nickie-ben !
> O wad ye tak a thought and men' !
> Ye aiblins might — I dinna ken —
> Still hae a stake —
> I'm wae to think upo' yon den,
> Even for your sake ! "

1830.

A FEW WORDS ON ANGELS.

AS we have said so much about Devils, we
thought we could not complete these supernatural discussions better, nor leave off with a pleasanter " taste in the mouth," than by adding what we
know of Angels.   We hope it will prove like a
dessert after the " hot dishes."

Angel comes from the Greek word Aggelos (pronounced Angelos), and signifies a messenger.   Mer-
cury in Hesiod is called the Angel of Jupiter.   Any
messenger, literally speaking, is an angel.   A ticket-
porter might write on his card, " Thomas Jones,
Angel."   A beautiful woman, coming to us with
an errand of peace or joy, is literally, as well as
metaphorically, an angel.   But in modern language
(and herein we desire to speak with a seriousness becoming the idea of " the sweet and loving angels,"
as Luther calls them *) the word signifies one of the
multitudes of those winged spirits, who, according
to the Jews and Christians, enjoy the beatitude of the

---

* Table-Talk.

divine presence, are eternally glorifying it with hymns and harpings, and are occasionally despatched to us on messages or with aid. Luther is of opinion, that while occupied in heaven, they are, nevertheless, fighting for us on earth ; " for," says he, in his home-ly way, and with that vein of familiarity in his re-spect, which does not diminish the real reverence of enthusiasm, " the angels have long arms." * But it has been the general opinion of the churches, that every man has a guardian angel assigned him, who helps him in his ways, encourages his virtues, and supplies proper trouble on occasion to turn him from his vice. This is the Good Demon of the Platonists ; nor is it possible to make inquiry into the nature of the one spirit without hearing of the other. . Nothing is here meant to be insinuated against the existence of myriads of heavenly creatures. We have

---

* " And is there care in heaven ? And is there love
   In heavenly spirits to these creatures base,
   That may compassion of their evils move ?
   There is : — else much more wretched were the cace
   Of men then beasts : But O l th' exceeding grace
   Of Highest God that loves his creatures so,
   And all his workes with mercy doth embrace,
   That blessed Angels he sends to and fro,
   To serve to wicked man, to serve his wicked foe l

 " How oft do they their silver bowers leave
    To come to succour us that succour want l
    How oft do they with golden pineons cleave
    The flitting skyes, like flying pursuivant,
    Against fowle feendes to ayd us militant :
    They for us fight, they watch and dewly ward,
    And their bright squadrons round about us plant t
    And all for love and nothing for reward : .
    O, why should Heavenly God to men have such regard ? "

So Spenser beautifully sings in The Faerie Queene, Book II., Canto viii. —. En.

the same hope of their existence as we have of thousands of other things, good and lovely, and the same tendency to disbelieve in their useless opponents. But the most orthodox believers may, according to the divines, be too anxious and too peremptory on these points; and therefore we shall not follow them in their flights with St. Dionysius, who pretended to draw up a peerage of the angelic noblesse. We shall not venture to say with the great poet (who, after all, made a bad business of it), —

"Into the heaven of heaven I have presumed
An earthly guest ; "

neither shall we discuss with the churchmen whether angels have or have not bodies; whether they are always exercising their understandings ; how long it would take them to come down from the eighth heaven, reckoning at the rate of a thousand miles an hour ; or how many of them could dance on the point of a needle without jostling. A Jesuit, of the name of La Cerda, informs us that a single angel whirls the heavens, and all the orbs about with it, at the rate of 26,000 German miles an hour.* We cannot take his word for it ; and, indeed, the greater and more angelical the hopes of mankind become, the less will they take people's words for anything, a dogma by its essence containing the principles of falsehood, which is the reason why so many fine ones come to nothing, and endanger the virtues they pretend to support.†

* *De Excellentia Spirituum Cœlestium*, Cap. 2.
† The learned reader need not be informed that the word *angel*, like a great many other words in Scripture, is capable of having other interpretations put upon it than that of a winged messenger from above. See a work entitled the Oriental Missionary.

Yet, on reflection, we give a list of the alleged hierarchy of angels, and of some of their names. The poets, having made use of them, have rendered them a warrantable part of fiction; and there is a music in the sound. Milton, in the addresses of Satan, does not observe the due order of the hierarchy, which stands as follows : —

The SERAPHIM . . . who excel in love.
CHERUBIM . . . . knowledge.
THRONES . . . . superiority to sin, and in influence upon those below them.

DOMINATIONS . . . . freedom of service and the regulation of the divine glory.
VIRTUES . . . . execution of the divine will.
POWERS . . . . subjection of evil spirits.

PRINCIPALITIES are the . . . chief governors of the divine messengers.
ARCHANGELS . . . . chief messengers.
ANGELS . . . . messengers.

These are the " trinal triplicities" of which Spenser talks; the whole hierarchy consisting of three classes, and every class of three sections. Upon the subject of their employment round the " throne" of the divine being, we would rather not dwell; our respect for the mystery of the Deity being too great, and not choosing to degrade it even to the heights of poetry. We may remark, however, that the placing Seraphim before Cherubim, — or love before knowledge, — can hardly be thought unworthy of anything divine, and is a fine moral. The distinction of offices and faculties in these lists of angels is, it must be confessed, not always very distinct. It is not so in the one before us ; and they differ in various authors.* Of the names of angels, the following comprise the most received and the most musical. There are four celebrated archangels : —

MICHAEL, who is said to preside over the East Wind, and the Nations in that quarter.

RAPHAEL . . . . the West.
GABRIEL . . . . the North.
URIEL . . . . the South.

Whether by accident or system, this assignment of quarters is very suitable to the characters given to the respective archangels, Michael being the fierce and more dictatorial virtue, Raphael " the affable archangel," and Uriel the angel of the sun. It has been observed, on a similar ground, that the names of the two princes of painting, Raphael and Michael Angelo (the most visible angels ever possessed by the Romish Church, and very lucky ones for her) were singularly expressive of their different qualities, as well as of the rank they held in their paradise. Corelli's name of Arcangelo was a like felicity ; no

---

* See Heywood's Hierarchie of Angels ; a Treatise of Angels, by John Salkeld, London, 1613 ; a Theological Discourse of Angels and their Ministries, by Benjamin Camfield, &c. ; and for matters relative to angels in general, consult also La Cerda, before mentioned, and a work entitled Rabbinical Literature, by the Rev. J. P. Stehelin, in two vols., 8vo., 1748. La Cerda contains a number of celestial anecdotes ; and Mr. Stehelin's work is a curious compilation of things fantastic, but, upon the whole, showing a kindliness of imagination which Christians would hardly expect from Jews, and which they would be more Christian in some points if they would imitate. The Jews, for instance, like our sect of Universalists, believe that the devils themselves may be saved. There is one very grand notion in this book. The Jews believe that there are three voices constantly going through the world, unheard of mortal ears : the *Voice of the globe of the sun*, the *Voice of the soul departing from the body*, and the *Voice of the murmuring of Rome*. This is the most magnificent idea of the Roman capital ever conceived.

musician, except Handel, touching forth a more angelical note than he did, with his air-drawn bow.
Handel, in addition to this, fairly sets the angels floating, with his wafting symphonies ; and, when he con-
cludes, you lose their feet in heaven.   Let the reader
allow me to mention in this place, as no unsuitable
one, the divine air of " Waft her, angels," and the
still diviner one, " There were shepherds abiding
in the fields," with its Raphaelesque recitative.
Nothing can be simpler, more touching, more sincere.   You are conscious of the innocent shepherds
keeping their flocks in the cool night.   Their very
looks are painted in the artless notes, and the angels
speak to them in a few others, equally simple and
beautiful.

Other names of angels : —

Hamabiel.	Maion.	Ophaniel.
Ambriel.	Malthidiel.	Arean.
Zamiel.	Jeremiel.	Zuriel, and
Varchiel.	Ariel.	Muriel.
Jurabatres.		

" El " is a termination, denoting God.   Thus, Uriel
signifies the Light of God ; Raphael, the Medicine of
God, — the Celestial Healer.   These and other angels
were supposed to preside over the zodiac, the planets,
the elements, &c., and indeed over everything that
could be presided over, down to a weed in the grass.
The Rabbis were of opinion that they made themselves bodies to appear in, out of the snow under the
Throne of Glory ; and that if they were absent from
heaven seven days in succession they were unable to
return.

It is not our intention to speak of the Fallen Angels or of their " Loves." It is much easier to conceive a loving than a fallen angel ; but our present object is to describe the happy winged spirit, as he appears to the eye of innocence and imagination. Infants, when they smile without an apparent cause, are supposed to see angels.* It is these whose faces we would behold.

Our guesses as to the nature of any being may be unlimited ; but we can paint images of him only from what we know, and hence we draw happy spirits in the happiest human shape.

> "To whom the angel with a smile that glowed
> Celestial rosy red, love's proper hue." — MILTON.

> " Her angel face
> As the great eye of heaven shined bright,
> And made a sunshine in the shady place." — SPENSER.

> "Occhi avea neri, e chioma crespa d'oro,
> Angel parea di quei del sommo coro." — ARIOSTO.

> " Black eyes he had, and sunny curls of hair ;
> He seem'd an angel, newly from the air."

Ariosto's heroine, who is a personification of Beauty, is named Angelica. So we call a beautiful boy a cherub ; and though sophisticate ladies may find fault with being called angels, and not think it very sincere, it is still one of the best and most natural appellations which the rapture of love can bestow on beauty and goodness.

---

* "Some," says delightful old Thomas Fuller, "admiring what motives to mirth infants meet with in their silent and solitary smiles, have resolved (how truly I know not) that then they converse with angels, as indeed such cannot amongst mortals find any fitter companions." — *Epistle Dedicatory to A Pisgah-Sight of Palestine.* — ED.

Our friend the Jesuit, above quoted, makes mention indeed of old angels. He describes one, who appeared to the mother of St. Eucherius, and who told her that she was about to be brought to bed of an archbishop.* This venerable anticipation looks as much like an old angel as anything well can ; but still we cannot fancy an elderly seraph, or a cherub of two-and-sixty. Jesuits are famous for having odd notions of things divine. They are celebrated in particular for not understanding the exact limits of what may be feigned and what not: and accordingly, in our friend's book we have a story of an angel, who imposed himself upon a farmer for one of his ploughmen, in order that the latter might cultivate his love of the truth at chapel.† Yet in the same book we have an account of another pious person, who, being extremely addicted to angels ("*addictissimus angelis*"), would never tell a lie, not even to save his life ; that is to say, would not do what the angels would. The best story in La Cerda is one which Massinger made the ground of his Virgin Martyr. An extract or two from the tragedy we keep for the conclusion of this article, as the best part of it, and as boys keep the sunny side of their apple for the last relish. The angel proper, as the heralds would call him, is neither old nor false, but young, beautiful, ingenuous, rosy bright, with wings, and a white vest. La Cerda gives us to understand (and here he is innocent enough) that he is " sometimes clothed in blue, rarely in purple." Some of the poets have made

---

* La Cerda, Cap. 43.   † La Cerda, Cap. 2.

his wings to be put on and off at pleasure, and many
have painted them as of gorgeous color.

> "Of silver wings he *took* a shining pair,
> Fringed with gold, unwearied, nimble, swift." — FAIRFAX'S *Tasso.*

Cowley, in the Davideis, is still more particular to
this point, but the passage is in his worst style, and
therefore must not be quoted. It is doubtful whether
the word *wore* in the following passage of Milton
does not imply the same thing. Speaking of Raphael, when he came down on his message to Adam,
he says, —

> "Six wings he *wore*, to shade
> His lineaments divine: the pair that clad
> Each shoulder broad, came mantling o'er his breast
> With regal ornament; the middle pair
> Girt, like a starry zone, his waist; and round,
> Skirted his loins and thighs with downy gold,
> And colours dipt in heaven: the third his feet
> Shadowed from either heel with feather'd mail,
> Sky-tinctur'd grain. Like Maia's son he stood,
> And shook his plumes, that heavenly fragrance filled
> The circuit wide." — *Par. Lost*, Book V.

Which last image is taken from a beautiful couplet of
Fairfax, never to be too often repeated: —

> "On Lebanon at first his foot he set,
> And shook his wings with rosy may-dews wet."

Again, in the passage where Milton describes Satan
in the likeness of a cherub: —

> "And now a stripling cherub he appears
> Not of the prime, yet such as in his face
> Youth smiled celestial, and to every limb
> Suitable grace diffused, so well he feigned.
> Under a coronet, his flowing hair
> In curls on either cheek play'd; wings he *wore*
> Of many a coloured plume, sprinkled with gold;
> His habit fit for speed succinct, and held
> Before his decent steps a silver wand."

This description has been much admired ; and indeed
Milton cannot dilate into any description in which
something admirable is not to be found. In gorgeousness of color his angels are not to be surpassed ;
yet we cannot help thinking that there is something
too princely, and conscious, and full-dressed : not
native enough to the sweetness and simplicity of
heaven. They do not announce themselves so much
by the delightfulness of their presence as the dazzling
of it, which is surely the inferior thing. It ·is doubtful whether Raphael has not too much *bird-coating;*
and there is something in the " silver wand " which
the youthful Cherub bears before him, which, to our
minds, is positively poor and in the way. Milton·
seems to have had a regard for a stick. He has given
one to Satan to support his uneasy steps over the,
burning soil of Hell ; and here he gives him another
in heaven to look becoming with. Princes in those
times walked with a stick, — perhaps the poet himself did ; and he has, unquestionably shown more
regard for the kingly character in heaven than he did
on earth. His angelic notions are full of " regal
ornament," of " coronets," and kingly state.

> " He, *kingly,* from his state
> Inclined not " ——

says he, speaking of Michael. But they have worse
moral failures than these. To say nothing of the
contradictions into which his story compelled him ;
and to sum up in one specimen all the faults to which
polemics had rendered his divinity liable, what are
we to think of his making his angels guilty of positive, gratuitous malignity? Satan, travelling towards

13

earth, comes to a sea of jasper, on which is a staircase which descended from heaven.

> " The stairs were then let down, whether to dare
> The fiend by easy ascent, or *aggravate*
> *His sad exclusion from the doors of bliss.*"
>
> Book III., v. 553.

This is a piece of malignity more worthy of hell than
heaven; if, indeed, hell could be imagined capable
of at once being in a state of bliss and desirous of
giving sorrow.   In fact, this is the most infernal passage in Paradise Lost.   Luckily, it is mere talking:
no being could be guilty of a mockery so inhuman; for
there is, in reality, no such thing as malignity for its
own sake.   The most wilful inflictors of suffering are
themselves in a state of suffering, which they think to
alleviate by thrusting a part of it on others; and angels, having no suffering at all, would be the only
true devils, if they would act as the poet's slip of the
pen has here made them.

There is a pretty passage of an angel in Spenser;
and there the heavenly creature is at his proper work:
he is doing good.   The poet has given him pied
wings like a' jay, which is perhaps not so well.   They
would better have suited a Cupid.   But the picture
is in his happiest manner.   It is attended with those
circumstances of verisimilitude which make the most
supernatural things appear natural.   On turning to
the passage, I find that Spenser has compared his
angel to Cupid, and this too in a stanza which is the
more displaced by reason of the very perfection of its
paganism.   It is as if Poussin had lumped together
a Scripture piece and a Bacchanal.   A pilgrim finds

Guyon sleeping in "a shady delve," and somebody sitting by him.

> "Beside his head there satt a faire young man,
> Of wondrous beauty and of freshest yeares,
> Whose tender bud to blossome new began,
> And flourish faire, above his equall peares :
> His snowy front, curled with golden heares.
> Like Phœbus' face adorned with sunny rayes,
> Divinely shone ; and two sharpe winged sheares,
> Decked with divers plumes like painted jayes,
> Were fixed at his back, to cut his ayery wayes."
>
> *Faerie Queen*, Book II., Canto 8.

There are the wings of Titian's Cupid, in the picture where his mother is blinding him. Perhaps it was a consciousness to that effect which led the poet into his comparison. We omit the latter as unsuitable; but we must not omit what follows. The stranger delivers up his charge to the pilgrim ; and then, says the poet, —

> " Eftsoones he gan display
> His painted nimble wings, and vanisht quite away.
> The palmer seeing his left empty place,
> And his slow eies beguiled of their sight,
> Waxe sore affraid, and standing still a space
> Gaz'd after him, as fowle escapt by flight."

Where the " blessed bird" goes to (as Dante calls him), we do not presume to say ; nor what he does when he has ended his journey:

> " What know we of the blest above
> But that they sing, and that they love?"

says Waller. To say we know it, is to say a little too much ; but to imagine it is reasonable enough, considering that singing and loving (provided they be genuine of their sort) are two of the highest pleasures on earth, and may be fancied to touch upon heaven. Milton has said some fine things about the loves of angels, to which we content ourselves with referring the reader. Taken out of their context, and of that " celestial colloquy sublime," we might do them an injustice. The angel, in this article of ours, may be said to become our property, as soon as we can descry him with earthly eyes, and no sooner ; or we may fancy we hear before we see him.

> " And now 'tis like all instruments,
> Now like a lonely flute ;
> And now it is angel's song, .
> That bids the heavens be mute."
> COLERIDGE'S *Ancient Mariner.*

We must humanize everything before we can love it. To fancy an angel rising in the east like a star, is making him too potent and gigantic. He must come near to us, and in our own shape ; must be guarding innocence or consoling adversity, or suggesting wisdom and sweeter thoughts to those who fancy themselves wicked, or conversing with the glad eyes and inarticulate raptures of infancy ; for infants, when smiling and babbling to themselves, are supposed to be talking with angels. Even those beautiful gorgeous wings, in which he is invested by the poets, hardly seem to be an apparel in which he is to *stay* with us. They are for a sudden vision, a *stoop* out of the lustre of heaven. It is remarkable that the painters have never given colored wings to their angels. The temptation would seem to be great, — the palette looks like a wing ready made, — and yet they have not given way to it. No : *the* angel is the angel of one's infancy, the blooming white-vested boy with the spot-

less wings ; and thus is he painted by the Guidos and
Correggios.

We think we see him now, looking out of one of
their divine pictures, young, blooming, innocent, natural as unconscious perfection, beautiful as truth. He
is a boy on a noble scale, but still human ; and his
large curls are tawny with the noons of Paradise.

An angel is the chorister of heaven, the page of
martyrdom, the messenger from the home of mothers. He comes to the tears of the patient, and is in
the blush of a noble anger. He kisses the hand that
gives an alms. He talks to parents of their departed
children, and smooths the pillow of sickness, and
supports the cheek of the prisoner against the wall,
and is the knowledge and comfort which a heart has
of itself when nobody else knows it, and is the play-
fellow of hope, and the lark of aspiration, and the
lily in the dusk of adversity. All this we believe
him, even should we hold his appearance to be a
fable, and though we deny the letter of a thousand
things out of which we would extricate the spirit ;
for wherever there is goodness and imagination, there
of necessity are thoughts angelical, winged indestruc-
tible hopes. The dryest line of the geometer, if he
knew all, were a wand of as much wonder as Prospero's ; or if it were not so, Prospero's itself were
none, and our most exalted aspirations would still be
as warrantable as the earth we touch. If anything
unwise could be unpardonable, the only fault not to
be forgiven were dogmatism ; and yet where could
an angelical thought exist, and forgiveness not be
discovered?

We conclude with the lovely scene out of Massinger. Drayton gives us to understand that angels
converse in poetry. We know not how that may be ;
but if ever a blooming, angelical boy was visible in a
book, and talked on paper, it is here.

ANGELO, an Angel, attends DOROTHEA as a Page.   ANGELO, DOROTHEA.
The time midnight.

Dor. My book and taper.

Ang. Here, most holy mistress.

Dor. Thy voice sends forth such music, that I never
Was ravish'd with a more celestial sound.
Were every servaut in the world like thee,
So full of goodness, angels would come down
To dwell with us : thy name is *Angelo*,
And like that name thou art. Get thee to rest :
Thy youth with too much watching is opprest.

Ang. No, my dear lady. I could weary stars,
And force the wakeful moon to loose her eyes,
By my late watching but to wait on you.
When at your pray'rs you kneel before the altar,
Methinks I'm singing with some quire in heaven,
So blest I hold me in your company.
Therefore, my most loved mistress, do not bid
Your boy, so serviceable, to get hence :
For then you break his heart.

Dor. Be nigh me still, then.
In golden letters down I'll set that day,
Which gave thee to me. Little did I hope
To meet such worlds of comfort in thyself,
This little, pretty body, when I, coming
Forth of the Temple, heard my beggar-boy,
My sweet-fac'd godly beggar-boy, crave an alms,
Which with glad hand I gave, with lucky hand ;
And when I took thee home, my most chaste bosom
Methought was filled with no hot wanton fire,
But with a holy flame, mounting since higher,
On wings of cherubims, than it did before.

Ang. Proud am I that my lady's modest eye
So likes so poor a servant.

Dor. I have offer'd
Handfuls of gold but to behold thy parents.
I would leave kingdoms, were I queen of some,
To dwell with thy good father ; for the sou

Bewitching me so deeply with his presence,
He that begot him must do't ten times more.
I pray thee, my sweet boy, show me thy parents ;
Be not ashamed.

Ang. I am not : I did never
Know who my mother was ; but by yon palace,
Filled with bright heav'nly courtiers, I dare assure you,
And pawn these eyes upon it, and this hand,
My father is in heav'n ; and, pretty mistress,
If your illustrious hour-glass spend his sand
No worse than yet it doth, upon my life,
You and I both shall meet my father there,
And he shall bid you welcome.

Dor. A bless'd day ! *

We had a great mind to conclude with this scene,
but there is another in the same play which presents
us with so beautiful a picture of the angel, — somewhat between the gorgeousness of the poets in general and the simplicity of the painters, — that we
cannot resist copying it. Theophilus, the persecutor,
who has been the cause of the martyrdom of Dorothea, and who is converted and becomes a martyr
himself, is soliloquizing upon the torture he will wreak
upon those who differ with him, when Angelo comes
in with a basket of fruit and flowers. The Roman
does not see him at first, and so continues talking.

---

* "This scene," says an excellent critic, "has beauties of so high an order,
that with all my respect for Massinger, I did not think he had poetical enthusiasm
capable of furnishing them. His associate, Decker, who wrote Old Fortunatus,
had poetry enough for anything. The very impurities which obtrude themselves
among the sweet pieties of this play (like Satan among the sons of heaven), and
which the brief scope of my plan fortunately enables me to leave out, have a
strength of contrast, a raciness and a glow in them, which are above Massinger.
They set off the religion of the rest, somehow, as Caliban serves to show Mi-
randa." — *Specimens of English Dramatic Poets*, by Charles Lamb.

Thus it is that fine natures know how to turn fugitive or imaginary evil to
account, instead of thinking themselves called upon to show that they cannot
think too much evil about it ; as some critics have done, whom it were a poor
thing to name in so sweet a place.

Theoph.   This Christian slut was well,
A pretty one : but let such horror follow
The next I feed with torments, that when Rome
Shall hear it, her foundation at the sound
May feel an earthquake. How now !   [*Music.*
Ang. Are you amazed, sir ?
So great a Roman spirit, and doth it tremble ?
Theoph. How cam'st thou in ? To whom
Thy business ?
Ang. To you :
I had a mistress, late sent hence by you
Upon a bloody errand ; you entreated,
That when she came in to that blessed garden
Whither she knew she went, and where now happy,
She feeds upon all joy, she would send to you
Some of that garden fruit, and flowers ; which here,
To have her promise saved, are brought by me.
Theoph. Cannot I see this garden ?
Ang. Yes, if the master
Will give you entrance.   [*He vanisheth.*
Theoph. 'Tis a tempting fruit —
And the most bright-cheeked child I ever viewed, —
Sweet smelling, goodly fruit. What flowers are these ?
In Dioclésian's gardens the most beauteous,
Compared with these, are weeds : is it not February,
The second day she died ? frost, ice, and snow,
Hang on the beard of winter : where's the sun
That gilds the summer ? Pretty, sweet boy, say,
In what country shall a man find this garden ?
My delicate boy, — gone ! vanished ! Within there,
Julianus ! Geta !

Enter JULIANUS and GETA.

Both. My lord.
Theoph. Are my gates shut ?
Geta. And guarded.
Theoph. Saw you not a boy ?
Jul. Where ?
Theoph. Here he entered ; a young lad ;
A thousand blessings danced upon his eyes,
A smooth-faced, glorious thing, that brought this basket.
Geta. No, sir ?
Theoph. Away — but be in reach, if my voice calls you.
                                        [*Exeunt.*

We need not point out to our readers the "bright-cheeked child," the "smooth-faced glorious thing," that brings a basket, — a thousand blessings dancing upon his eyes; — but we notice the words that we may enjoy them in their company. — And so with this perfect taste of the angel and his Eden fruit, we conclude. 1830.

CHILD-BED.

A PROSE POEM.

AND is child-bed among the graces, with its close room, and its unwilling or idle visitors, and its jesting nurse (the old and indecent stranger), and its unmotherly, and unwifely, and unlovely lamentations? Is pain so unpleasant that love cannot reconcile it; and can pleasures be repeated without shame, which are regretted with hostile cries and resentment!

No. But child-bed is among the graces, with the handsome quiet of its preparation, and the smooth pillow sustaining emotion, and the soft steps of love and respect, and the room in which the breath of the universe is gratefully permitted to enter, and mild and venerable aid, and the physician (the urbane security), and the living treasure containing treasure about to live, who looks in the eyes of him that caused it and seeks energy in the grappling of his hand, and hides her face in the pillow that she may save him a

pain by stifling a greater. There is a tear for what
may have been done wrong, ever ; and for what may
never be to be mutually pardoned again ; but it is
gone, for what needs it? Angelical are their whis-
pers apart; and Pleasure meets Pain the seraph, and
knows itself to be noble in the smiling testimony of
his severity.

It was on a May evening, in a cottage flowering
with the green-gage, in the time of hyacinths and
new hopes, when the hand that wrote this, took the
hand that had nine times lain thin and delicate on
the bed of a mother's endurance ; and he kissed it,
like a bride's.   1827–1837.

ROUSSEAU'S PYGMALION.

W E are not aware that this piece of Rousseau's
has hitherto appeared in English. It is a
favorite in France, and very naturally so, on all accounts. To our countrymen there will perhaps appear to be something, in parts of it, too declamatory
and full of ejaculation ; and it must be. confessed,
that if the story alone is to be considered, the illustrious author has committed one great fault, which
was hardly to be expected of him ; and that is, that
he has not made the sentiment sufficiently prominent. The original story, though spoiled by the rake
Ovid, informs us, that Pygmalion, with all his warmth
towards the sex, was so disgusted at the manners of
his countrywomen, that instead of going any longer

into their society, he preferred making images, in
his own mind, and with his chisel, of what a woman ought to be; informing her looks, of course,
with sentiment and kindness, as well as with the
more ordinary attractions. It appears to us, therefore, that instead of making him fall in love, almost
out of vanity, as Rousseau has done, it might have
been better, in the abstract point of view above mentioned, to represent him fashioning the likeness of
a creature after his own heart, lying and looking at
it with a yearning wish that he could have met with
such a living being, and at last, while indulging his
imagination with talking to her, making him lay his
hand upon hers, and finding it warm. The rest is,
in every respect, exquisitely managed by Rousseau.
But now we must observe, that while the charge of
a certain prevailing air of insincerity over the French
style in these matters appears just in most instances,
a greater confidence is to be put in the enthusiasm
of the Genevese; for he was a kind of Pygmalion
himself, disgusted with the world, and perpetually,
yet hopelessly, endeavoring to realize the dreams of
his imagination. This, after all, is perhaps the most
touching thing in his performance. Pygmalion's self
predominates over the idea of his mistress, because
the author's self pressed upon him while he wrote.
The only actual difference between the fabulous solitary and the real one was, unfortunately, that Pygmalion seems to have been willing enough to be
contented, had he found a mistress that deserved
him; whereas Rousseau, when he was really beloved,
and even thought himself so, was sure to be made

the ruin of his own comfort; partly by a distrustful. morbidity of temperament, and partly, perhaps, by a fastidious metaphysical subtilty, which turned his eye with a painful sharpness upon the defects instead of humanities of his fellow-creatures, and made the individual answer for the whole mass.

THE SCENE represents a sculptor's work-shop, in which are several blocks of marble, sculptured groups, and sketches of statues. In the midst of these is another statue, concealed under a drapery of a light and shining stuff, ornamented with fringes and garlands.

Pygmalion is sitting, supporting his head with his hand, in the attitude of a man who is uneasy and melancholy. On a sudden he rises; and taking one of his tools from a table, gives some strokes of the chisel to several of the sketches; then turns from them, and looks about him with an air of discontent.

Pygmalion. There is neither life nor soul in it; it is but a mere stone. I shall never do anything with all this.

O, my genius, where art thou? What has become of thee? All my fire is extinguished, my imagination is frozen; the marble comes cold from my hands.

Make no more gods, Pygmalion; you are but a common artist—ye vile instruments, no longer instruments of my glory, ye shall dishonor my hands no more.

(He throws away his tools with disdain, and walks about with his arms crossed, as in meditation.)

What am I become? What strange revolution has taken place in me?—Tyre, proud and opulent city, your illustrious monuments of art no longer attract me.

I have lost my taste for them. All intercourse with artists and philosophers has become insipid to me: the society of painters and poets has no attraction for me; praise and renown have ceased to elevate me; the approbation of posterity has no interest for me; even friendship has to me lost all her charms.

And you, young masterpieces of nature, whom my art has presumed to imitate, you, in whose train the pleasures ever led me, you, my charming models, who consumed me at once with the flame of love and genius, — since I have surpassed you, you are all become indifferent to me.

(He seats himself, and contemplates the figures around him.)

Detained in this room by an inconceivable charm, I know not what to do here, and yet I cannot leave it. I wander from group to group, from figure to figure, my weak and uncertain chisel no longer acknowledging its master. These rude sketches are left untouched by the hand which should have given them life and beauty —

(He rises impetuously.)

It is over, it is over: I have lost my genius! So young — and yet I have survived it!

And what, then, is this internal ardor which consumes me? What is this fire which devours me? Why, in the languor of extinguished genius, should I feel these emotions, these bursts of impetuous passion, this insurmountable restlessness, this secret agitation which torments me? I know not; I fear the admiration of my own work has been the cause of this distraction: I have concealed it under this veil —

my profane hands have ventured to cover this monument of their glory.   Since I have ceased to behold
it, I have become more melancholy and absent. How
dear, how precious, this immortal work will be to
me !   If my exhausted mind shall never more produce anything grand, beautiful, worthy of me, I will
point to my Galatea, and say, " There is my work.".
O my Galatea ! when I shall have lost all else, do
thou alone remain to me, and I shall be consoled.

(He approaches the veiled statue; draws back;
goes, comes; stops sometimes to look at it, and
sighs.)

But why conceal it?   What do I gain by that?
Reduced to idleness, why refuse myself the pleasure
of contemplating the finest of my works?   Perhaps
there may yet be some defect which I have not perceived; perhaps I might yet add some ornament to
the drapery: no imaginable grace should be wanting to so charming an object.   Perhaps the contemplation of this figure may re-animate my languish-
ing imagination.   I must see her again; I must examine my work.   What do I say?   Yes; I have
never yet examined it; hitherto I have only admired
her.

(He goes to raise the veil, and lets it fall, as if
alarmed.)

I know not what emotion seizes me when I touch
this veil.

I feel a tremor, as though I were touching the
sanctuary of some divinity. — Pygmalion, it is but a
stone ; it is thine own work — what can it mean?
In our temples, they serve gods made of the same
material, and formed by the same hand as this.

(He raises the veil trembling, and prostrates him-, self before the statue of Galatea, which is seen placed on a pedestal, raised by semicircular steps of marble.)

O Galatea! receive my homage. I have deceived myself. I thought to make you a nymph, and I have made you a goddess. Even Venus herself is less beautiful.

O vanity, human weakness! I am never weary of admiring my own work; I am intoxicated with self-love; I adore myself in that which I have made. —No, never was there anything in nature so beautiful; I have surpassed the work of the Gods.— What! so many beauties formed by my hands; my hands then have touched them; my mouth has — I see a defect. This drapery too much conceals it. I must slope it away more; the charms which it shades should be more displayed.

(He takes his mallet and chisel, and advancing slowly, begins with much hesitation to ascend the steps towards the statue, which, it seems, he dares not touch. He raises the chisel, — he stops.)

What is this trouble — this trembling? I hold the chisel with a feeble hand — I cannot — I dare not — I shall spoil everything.

(He endeavors to conquer his trouble, and at last, raising the chisel again, makes one stroke, and lets it fall, with a loud cry.)

Gods! I feel the quivering flesh repel the chisel!

(He descends, trembling and confused.)

— Vain terror, blind folly ! — No — I will not touch her — the Gods affright me. Doubtless she is already deified.

(He contemplates her again.)

What would you change, Pygmalion? Look! what new charms can you give her? Alas! her only fault is her perfection. — Divine Galatea! less perfect, nothing would be wanting to thee.

(Tenderly.)

Yet a soul is wanting. That figure should not be without a soul.

(With still increasing tenderness.)

How fine should be the soul to animate that body!

(He stops a long time; then returns to his seat, and speaks with a slow and changed voice.)

What desires have I dared to form! What senseless wishes!

What is this I feel? — O Heaven! the illusion vanishes, and I dare not look into my heart. I should have too much to reproach myself with.

(He pauses a long time, in profound melancholy.)

This, then, is the noble passion which distracts me! It is on account of this inanimate figure that I dare not go out of this spot! — A figure of marble! — a stone! — A hard and unformed mass, until worked with this iron! — Madman, recover thyself, see thine error, groan for thy folly —   But no —

(Impetuously.)

No, I have not lost my reason; no, I am not wandering; I reproach myself with nothing. It is not of this marble that I am enamoured; it is of a living being whom it resembles; the figure which it presents to my eyes. Wherever this adorable form may be, whatever body may bear it, whatever hand may have made it, she will have all the vows of my heart. Yes, my only folly is in the power of discerning beauty; my only crime is being sensible to it. There is nothing in this I ought to blush for.

(Less lively, but always with passion.)

What arrows of fire seem to issue from this object to burn my senses, and to carry away my soul unto their source! Alas! she remains immovable and cold, while my heart, consumed by her charms, longs to quit my own body to give warmth to hers. I imagine in my delirium that I could spring from myself, that I could give to her my life, that I could animate her with my soul. Ah, let Pygmalion die, to live in Galatea ! — What do I say, O Heaven? If I were she, I should no longer see her; I should not be he that loves her ! — No, let my Galatea live; but let not me become Galatea. O! let me always be another, always wish her to be herself, to love her, to be beloved —

(Transported.)

Torments, vows, desires, impotent rage, terrible, fatal love — O! all hell is in my agitated heart — Powerful, beneficent Gods ! — Gods of the people, who know the passions of men, ah, how many miracles have you done for small causes ! Behold this object, look into my heart, be just, and deserve your altars !

(With a more pathetic enthusiasm.)

And thou, sublime essence, who, concealing thyself from the senses, art felt in the heart of men, soul of the universe, principle of all existence, thou who by love givest harmony to the elements, life to

14

matter, feeling to bodies, and form to all beings; sacred fire, celestial Venus, by whom everything is preserved, and unceasingly reproduced! Ah, where is thy equalizing justice? Where is thy expansive power? Where is the law of nature in the sentiment I experience? Where is thy vivifying warmth in the inanity of my vain desires? All thy flames are concentrated in my heart, and the coldness of death remains upon this marble; I perish by the excess of life which this figure wants. Alas! I expect no prodigy; already one exists, and ought to cease; order is disturbed, nature is outraged; restore to her laws their empire, re-establish her beneficent course, and equally shed thy divine influence. Yes, two beings are left out of the plenitude of things. Divide between them that devouring ardor which consumes the one without animating the other. It is thou who hast formed by my hand these charms, and these features, which want but life and feeling. Give to her the half of mine. Give all, if it be necessary. It shall suffice me to live in her. O thou! who deignest to smile upon the homage of mortals, this being who feels nothing, honors thee not. Extend thy glory with thy works. Goddess of beauty, spare this affront to nature, that a form so perfect should be an image of which there is no living model!

(He gradually re-approaches the statue with an air of confidence and joy.)

I resume my senses. What an unexpected calm! What unhoped courage re-animates me! A mortal fever burned my blood, a balm of confidence and

hope flows in my veins, and I feel a new life. Thus
the sense of our dependence sometimes becomes our
consolation. However unhappy mortals may be,
when they have invoked the Gods, they are more
tranquil. — And yet this unjust confidence deceives
those who form senseless wishes. — Alas! in the condition I am in, we call upon every one, and no one
hears us; the hope which deceives is more senseless
than the desire.

Ashamed of so many follies, I dare no more to contemplate the cause of them. When I wish to raise
my eyes towards this fatal object, I feel a new trouble,·
a sudden palpitation takes my breath, a secret tremor
stops me —

(With bitter irony.)

O, look, poor soul! summon courage enough to
dare behold a statue.

(He sees it become animated, and turns away with
alarm ; his heart oppressed with grief.)

What have I seen? Gods·! what have I imagined
that I saw? A color on the flesh, a fire in the eyes,
even movement. — It was not enough to hope for a
miracle ; to complete my misery, at last I have seen —

(With expressive melancholy.)

Unhappy creature, all is over with thee — thy delirium is at its height — thy reason as well as thy
genius abandons thee. Regret it not, Pygmalion, for
the loss will conceal thy shame.

(With indignation.)

The lover of a stone is too happy in becoming a
visionary.

(He turns again, and sees the statue move and de·

scend the steps in front of the pedestal.   He falls on
his knees, and raises his hands and eyes towards
heaven.)

Immortal Gods!   Venus, Galatea!   O, illusion
of a furious love !

(Galatea touches herself and says) Me !

(Pygmalion transported) — Me !

(Galatea touching herself again) — It is myself.

(Pygmalion) — Ravishing   illusion, which   even
reaches my ears !   O, never, never abandon me.

(Galatea moves towards another figure and touches
it) — Not myself.

(Pygmalion in an agitation, in transports which he
can with difficulty restrain, follows all her movements,
listens to her, observes her with a covetous attention,
which scarcely allows him to breathe.   Galatea advances and looks at him ; he rises hastily, extends his
arms, and looks at her with delight.   She lays her
hand on his arm ; he trembles, takes the hand, presses
it to his heart, and covers it with ardent kisses.)

(Galatea, with a sigh) — Ah ! it is I again.

(Pygmalion) — Yes, dear and charming object —
thou worthy masterpiece of my hands, of my heart,
and of the Gods!   It is thou, it is thou alone — I
have given thee all my being — henceforth I will live
but for thee.   1820.

ON THE SUBURBS OF GENOA AND THE COUNTRY ABOUT LONDON.*

D EAR N.: I could bear my large study † no
longer; so I have mounted into my third
story, and intrenched myself, as usual, in a little
corner room. It is about the size of the study in
————, where we all adjourned on the morning of
Twelfth Night, to take breakfast. Do you remember
that night? how we sung " To ladies' eyes a round,
boys;" and how the eyes were as sparkling and triumphant at six o'clock in the morning, as they were
at six in the evening? " *Can* I forget it?" say you:
" Can anybody forget it?" I think not. The very
walls must remember it. A living poet, whom we
were near killing with laughter at two in the morning, has doubtless written his best things upon eyes
since the appearance of that ocular constellation. I
am sure a living novelist would have made his heroines equal to the rest of his characters, and done
himself a world of good into the bargain, had he not

---

* This essay was carefully corrected for republication by the author, who
ruthlessly drew his pen through many of its graceful sentences. Though we
gladly avail ourselves of most of his verbal emendations, we have not the heart to
omit the pleasant passages which he marked for suppression, and therefore re-
print the article in its entirety, without the loss of a paragraph. We do not
think the reader will blame us for retaining the anecdote of Shelley, and the
description of the suburbs of Genoa. — ED.
† There is a description of this study in the chapter on My Books, in the Indicator. The "dear N." to whom this article is addressed is Vincent Novello,
" my good Catholic friend Nov.," of Elia's Chapter On Ears. — ED.

had that extra-judicious hackney coach call for him at one. Be assured, that pleasant spirits have haunted that house ever since. I know (without the maid servants informing me) that a noise of crystal ringings and sweet voices is heard every Twelfth Night through the rooms; and that the gallant occupier and his wife cannot sleep for the life of them, for exquisite imaginations.

But you must know I have another reason for mounting into this nest of mine, in addition to those I have given to B. It lifts me above a sense of the lanes and stone walls of this suburb of Genoa. Albaro is a pretty name, and a very pretty looking hill at a distance. It has also some fine retreats and gardens, for those who can afford them. But for a place to walk about in, and enjoy one's neighbor's goods (to which you know I have a propensity), it only shows me how very pretty some hills as well as women can look at a distance, and what stony-hearted creatures they turn out upon inspection. When you behold Albaro from the sea, you cry out, "What a delicious place to live in!" Imagine a gentle green hill, full of olive trees, vineyards, and country seats, beheld from a blue sea, glittering under a blue sky, and with the Apennines at the back of it. Enter it, and the charm is dissolved. Eternal lanes, with eternal stone walls, intersect it in all directions. The best are paved like the carriage part of the London streets, with a stripe of smoother walk in the middle, made of tiles laid edgewise. The worst are compounded of bits of broken walls, stones, and occasional pushings forth of the native rock. Some are merely the beds of torrents : but all are lanes, lanes, lanes, — all stone, brick, and mortar, with seldom even a hole to look through. Your only resource, as in the worst passages of human life, is to imagine what may be on the other side ; but then the tantalization is in proportion. In the summer, the vines look over the walls, here and there, and afford a relief; but the lanes, for the most part, are then hot and close, and in those that lead down to the sea the footing is still a nuisance. Furthermore, the sea has no beach. In winter (which is quite severe enough in this quarter of Italy to make you feel it) the promenade is intolerable. Sometimes a wind comes down from the snowy mountains, sharp set as a wolf, and more searching than any east wind with us. Besides, Genoa being situate between the sea and the mountains, is famous for wind ; and Albaro, I suppose, is the most famous place for wind about Genoa. Last winter one would have thought the whole army of tempests had come by sea to pass over the mountains, and go and trample down some incorrigible tyranny. The whole cavalcade seemed to sweep over us with their " sightless horses," their whistling hair, and mad outcries.

It is little better, for the most part, in the rest of the suburbs ; in some of them, not so good. There is one good road, which circles the hill ; and on the other side of Genoa, there is a wider piece of plain to get footing upon. But, generally speaking, your path lies up and down hill, through the stoniest of all stony alleys. Even the road which I speak of, round Albaro, and which would make a beautiful figure in a picture, presenting depths of olive grounds below, and the sea in the distance, tantalizes you with the sight of pleasant places in which it is impossible to enter, and which, if you did enter, it would be impossible to walk in. The olive grounds are all walled in, as usual, and all raised upon terraces of artificial earth, lest the torrents should wash them away. But what care the Genoese? Nature, with them, is but a slave in the hands of the slave merchant. All her beauties consist in what they will fetch. Their olive trees produce nothing but quattrini and minestra; their bunches of grapes are but so many purses of soldi. They care for nothing but care itself, and a good oleaginous dinner to make it worse.

Now, tell it not in Scotland, lest the cocknies of the Canongate rejoice; but give me, dear N., before all the barren suburbs in the world (bits of mountain included) the green pastures and gentle eminences round about glorious London. *There* we have fields : — there one can walk on real positive turf; there one can get trees that are of no use, and get under trees, and get among trees; and have hedges, stiles, field-paths, sheep and oxen, and other pastoral amenities : —

> "Sometimes walking, not unseen,
> By the hedge-row elms on hillocks green ;
> While the ploughman, near at hand,
> Whistles o'er the furrowed land,
> And the milkmaid singeth blithe,
> And the mower whets his scythe,
> And every shepherd tells his tale
> Under the hawthorn in the dale."

How pleasant it is to read one of our poets in a foreign country! I pass from page to page, as I used from meadow to meadow, not omitting to enjoy the *style* by the way.

> "Straight mine eye hath caught new pleasures,
> While the landscape round it measures;
> Russet lawns and fallows gray,"

Observe the coloring!

> " Where the nibbling flocks do stray ? "

Mark the nicety!

> "Mountains — "

Mountains! what does he mean by that?

> " Mountains on whose barren breast
> The laboring clouds do often rest."

Genoa pitched in the vale of Thames! He must have seen Genoa by a sort of unnatural second sight. I beg you to look upon this as an impertinent vision, foreign to the subject, or only brought in to show the beauty of the rest by the force of contrast.

> " Meadows trim, with daisies pied,"

There he comes home again.

> "Shallow brooks and rivers wide ?
> Towers and battlements it sees,
> Bosomed high in tufted trees,
> Where perhaps some beauty lies,
> The Cynosure of neighboring eyes ?
> Hard by a cottage chimney smokes
> From betwixt two aged oaks."

Complete justice is never done to a fine passage in a poet, if you do not know the one that preceded it : just as a new key in a musician demands a comparison with that of the previous air. How admirably contrasted, and yet with the properest and mellowest gradation, is the richness and elevation of this passage about the tufted trees and the high-born beauty in their turrets, with the " two aged oaks," and the peasant's habitation that smokes between them ! — Alas, there are no such oaks here, and no such tufted trees ! — Do you remember our picnics on the grass in the Hampstead Fields? Do you remember our books, our lounges, our trios, our crowns of field flowers for heads " not our own "? Do you recollect that strange Centaur of a squire, who came riding in his meadows with a monster of a footman behind him, and could not help being delighted at seeing our dinner trespassing on his premises?

I fancy you discern to what all this leads, — the sketch that I promised you a long while back, of pleasant memories connected with the country about London ; similar to those which I have touched upon in a former Indicator, connected with the inside of it. You are right. I could not delay it longer, if I would.

> " Ah, happy hills ! ah, pleasing shade !
>   Ah, fields beloved in vain !
> Where once my careless childhood strayed,
>   A stranger yet to pain !
> I feel the gales that from ye blow
> A momentary bliss bestow,
>   As waving fresh their gladsome wing,
> My weary soul they seem to soothe,
> And redolent of joy and youth,
>   To breathe a second spring."

And yet the fields are not " beloved in vain ; " neither was my childhood a stranger to suffering. My life has had strong lights and shades upon it from its commencement; but, upon the whole, I am grateful ; and the pleasures I have enjoyed make me love even the memory of some of the pains.

"A dram of sweet is worth a pound of sour."

How could Gray say that his fields were " beloved in vain," when the sight of them, in pain and melancholy, could still please him in this manner ; and when he cultivated flowers in his college window to the last? Nature is never beloved in vain. Shakespeare, after running the whole round of humanity, went to live and to die among his native fields. Rousseau's botany never forsook him. The oaks are firm friends ; and we can love the most blooming of roses in our old age.

In taking my circuit round London, I will begin with the east, in order that I may end with the north. It is the least pleasant side, yet two out of our four greatest names in poetry are connected with it, — Spenser and Milton. I have already noticed that Spenser was born in East Smithfield. Bunhill Fields has the most unromantic of sounds, and yet there Milton not only lived, but seems to have delighted to live. It is probably the " noble suburban spot," of which he speaks in his Latin poems, and contained the elm trees of which he was so fond. I do not remember whether I have mentioned before, that Steele amused himself with a laboratory at Poplar, which is still extant. You may gather from some of the works of De Foe, who was a hosier in Cornhill, that he was a great walker about the neighborhood of the river. An unaccustomed eye, suddenly emerging from the narrow streets upon Tower Hill, is met by a crowd of grand and tragical recollections, — by murdered patriots and heroes, infants, lovers, and kings. There breathed out the souls of the Raleighs and Sydneys. There Hutchinson prepared himself to die in patient endurance; and Guilford Dudley and Jane Grey went one after the other to the scaffold, instead of the retirement that suited their innocence. The death of another Jane is said to have given its name to Shoreditch. This was Jane Shore, the life of the voluptuous retirements of Edward the Fourth, who was seen there in her old age, wrinkled, and gathering watercresses. What a difference from the picture of her, in which she is described as having risen " out of her bed in the morning, having nothing on but a rich mantle cast under one arm over her shoulder, and sitting in a chair, on which her naked arm did lie ! " This portrait, by the way, argues a taste, and an eye for coloring, which one should hardly have looked for in the paintings of those times. It was, perhaps, the work of an Italian. But I shall never get out of town. Of Hackney, and all that region, famous for giving a name to Hackney coaches, I know nothing more illustrious than what is said of it in some quaint periodical work ; — namely, that

"Homerton and Clapton do declare,
The many country seats that there are there."

They tell me, however (is this true?), that I am to like a place a little more to the north, the name of which I shall not allow myself to be sure of till I hear further advices. Let it be as good a name as you

can, for I shall "like it most horribly." I remember
now that I used to go that way to bathe. Besides,
you have C. L. The great men of the court of Elizabeth must have resided much about the neighborhood
of Stoke Newington and Highbury, for every old
mansion thereabout is dignified with the title of one
of her palaces. A house is still shown at Islington,
for Raleigh's. At Stoke Newington lived the late
Dr. Aikin, who was a clever man and did good;
though he should not have said, that Spenser's Epi-
thalamium "wants only judicious curtailment to
make it a very pleasing piece." I would as lief have
had the bride curtailed, had I been the hero of it. Dr.
Aikin's sister, Mrs. Barbauld, still renders the place
interesting by her residence. Here lived Dr. Watts,
whose logical head did not hinder his little frail person from being hypochondriacal, and whose hypo-
chondria, unfortunately, drove him into Calvinism
instead of the Bowling-green. But I believe he extri-
cated himself at last. There wants a good account
of the last years of men who get rid of their super-
stitions, as well as of those who are said to have been
overcome by them.

To return to the river's side, and cross the water.
At Greenwich, famous for its green woods and white
sails, — for its old weather-beaten pensioners, who sit
eying the placid stream, — and for lasses who kiss
their mother earth all the way down hill in fair time,
and their cousin John at the bottom of it, — Queen
Elizabeth held her court; such a court, as princes
and courtiers can seldom contrive to muster up. Flattery there had a sort of right; and, accordingly, the

old Queen was a "nymph" to the last, scorching up the Hattons and Raleighs with the retrospective beauties of seventy. Furthermore, she walked abroad among them with a wrinkled face, black teeth, little sparkling gray eyes, a hand and arm so white that it transported even Dutchmen, and a new gown for every day in the year. How she contrived to maintain her charms, while dancing and playing on the lute, in order to convince a Scotch ambassador of her juvenility, who was to look through a crevice, none but a Scotchman can say; and, accordingly, I leave it to Sir Walter. If he discovers something to venerate in the fumbling of King James, he will surely not be at a loss in the tumbling of old Elizabeth. At Redriff (vainly spelt Rotherhithe) some story-book hero cuts a figure; but I cannot remember his name. Down the Kent Road, Chaucer's pilgrims took their way to Canterbury, telling stories that have outlasted St. Thomas's shrine, and will outlast a thousand others. I think I see him now, looking downwards; the Wife of Bath grinning; the Friars and Summoners in all their varieties of hypocrisy and impudence; the Squire dancing on his horse, conscious of the Prioress; the experienced Knight, his father; the busy Sergeant at Law, who seemed still "busier than he was;" the reckless Sailor; the unhealthy Cook; the lean meek Scholar, upon his lean horse; the lean choleric Steward, upon his plump one; the bull of a Miller, &c., &c., and Harry Baillie, the host, venting his admiration of a pathetic story in a volley of oaths. Kent Street derives a minor lustre from Goldsmith's Madame Blaze. Newington Butts, as its name de notes, was famous for archery. With the suburb fields, that now contain prisons and bedlams, the great poets and wits of Shakespeare's time must have been conversant, owing to the neighborhood of the theatre in the Borough. Their club, at the Mermaid in Cornhill, was as convenient a spot as they could well choose, between the theatre on one hand, and the court and country seats of Elizabeth on the two sides of the water on the other. Camberwell was lately remarkable for the proud villa of a Quaker physician. Clapham looks unnatural, with its bankers' houses on a bit of wild common. Armstrong, in his poem upon preserving health, recommends Dulwich as " yet unspoiled by art." I believe it still retains its character, though more houses have come, and the gypsies gone away. It touches upon Norwood. Here is Dulwich College, founded by one of Shakespeare's fellow-players, Allen, — a name which seems to belong to people of worth. I know one myself. The original of Fielding's Allworthy was another: and the first countenance I remember at school was an Allen's, — so good and handsome that an old stall-woman, against whom he happened to run in the street, and to turn round upon in the course of her abuse, exclaimed, " Confound your great, ugly, driving — — sweet face, God bless it!" Poor Allen! he died aboard ship, a surgeon, vainly forewarned by Roderick Random. What had his blushing maiden face to do in a gangway? And yet what would the hard places of the world become, if such faces never shone on them! — To Dulwich College. Sir Francis Bourgeois bequeathed his collection of pictures, which it is a holi-

day to go and see. Between Dulwich and Beckenham is a pretty, rustic, out-of-the-way spot, called
Penge, which an acquaintance of yours thinks the
charmingest place in the world. Her first child was
born at Beckenham. The white spire of Beckenham
church, issuing out of the trees, is a truly English and
sylvan spectacle. I think Johnson was in the habit
of visiting somebody at Beckenham. In the church
is Gray's epitaph on Mrs. Clarke, " Lo ! where the
silent marble weeps." Sydenham, another pretty village with a green, has long been the residence of Mr.
Campbell. Lewisham was immortalized by Queen
Elizabeth in a strain of alliterative abuse, which, not
being a queen, I have not the face to repeat. Returning
westward, we come to Thrale and Johnson at Streat-
ham. There Mrs. Thrale encouraged his bile with
good dinners, and soothed it with gay curtains; and
there, it seems, he had a desk on each side a window, upon which he used to write his Lives of the
Poets, — a " mechanical operation of the spirit"
somewhat too prophetic of the point of criticism at
which he would stop short. But admiration ever be
paid to the hero of Boswell, and reverence to the
good Samaritan who took up the female in the street,
and put her to bed while other people were chatter-
ing ! At Merton, a pretty place with a pretty appellation (so at least it seemed to me, when I spent my
holidays there) lived the illustrious little withered
lion, Nelson. But it once contained a personage much
more interesting in my eyes ; to wit, an aunt of mine ;
a true West Indian of the best sort, somewhat wilful,
very idle and generous, and a lady to the heart of

her. If the mention of these two personages together looks like an anticlimax, take the following out of a master of the "bon goût," which I think beats it hollow. It is Chaulieu addressing the Countess of Stafford : —

> " Vous n'aurez jamais besoin
> De Muse qui vous anime,
> Ni qu' Apollon prenne soin
> De vous montrer le sublime ;
> Car vous trouverez chez vous
> *Dans un Oncle fort aimable,*
> Un maître plus que capable
> De vous former au bon goût."

But what has this impertinent Frenchman to do with one's young days and one's natural affections? Talking of Queen Elizabeth and her Nymphals, I remember writing an elegy on the death of this kins-woman, in which I called her a " nymph " also, though she was between fifty and sixty. Why did she not live to be called a damsel? There was such an elegance about her in my eye that I never thought her wrinkled face old. And where are you, dear cousin F., that in the pride of your tuckers and dressed locks you are not still calling me "*petit garçon,*" and throwing down peaches from the trees to my adoring eyes? What had trouble to do with your warm strip of West Indianism, that it did not dance and flutter all its life in perpetual youth? She had the cruelty to give me a little crystal heart, as if it signified noth-ing to the "*petit garçon ;*" and I wore it next my own at school, with an infinite mixture of pride and pensiveness. Few things are better than these fan-cies, or even the recollections of them ; and those that are, partake of the same character. Let me try

15

as I may, I feel I have nothing greater, much less
happier in me, than I had when a boy; nor can I do
anything better than draw out, as it were, what was
in me then. Business has only made me uneasy to
others, and remorseful to myself. My tasks take
another direction. I am formed by nature to suffer
and imagine alone, or in company with some friend;
and in public to do nothing but impart a sense of the
joys which love and patience reward me with.

But what have the peach trees done with me, that
I stand here in a dream, when I have to make half
the circuit of London? Yet I must not forget the little
River Wandle, which runs by Merton, and in which I
once saw a vision bright and ideal as any in a picture.
It was nothing, too, but a girl with long flaxen hair
and blue eyes, washing some linen with naked feet
among the pebbles. Her hair was flaxenest of the
flaxen; her eyes blue as sapphire; — it was August;
and the

> " Cærule stream, rambling in pebble-stone,
> Crept under moss as green as any gourd."

What she must have thought of me in my school
petticoats I know not; but her surprise had the advantage of fixing her in a beautiful posture, and
making her open all her blue eyes. I wish Mr.
Wordsworth had flourished then, and set " us youth "
upon attempting to write naturally. I made " a copy
of verses " afterwards upon the Wandle, which might
have been a little better for it. When I met with the
lines upon it in Drayton's Polyolbion, the vision came
upon me again in all its beauty, only not quite so
" plump."

"Then Wandal cometh in, the Mole's beloved mate,
So amiable, so fair, so pure, so delicate,
So plump, so full, so fresh, her eyes so wondrous clear ;
And first unto her lord at Wandsworth doth appear,
That in the goodly court of their great sovereign Thames,
There might no other speech be had amongst the streams
But only of this nymph, sweet Wandal, what she wore,
Of her complexion, grace, and how herself she bore."

Polyolb., Song 17.

At Wimbledon, when a child, I was taken to see
Horne Tooke, who patted me on the head, and gave
me a very different benediction from the bishop. In
a wood near the same place I saw, many years afterwards, one of the most successful of ministers, who
seemed one of the most miserable of men. I have
pitied him ever since.

At Putney Gibbon was born, and at Battersea lived
Bolingbroke. A pretty infidel neighborhood! I
think I see Bolingbroke and Swift sitting at the open
window over the Thames, waiting for Arbuthnot and
Gay to come from London, and Pope from Twickenham. Bolingbroke is lounging, with an end of his
peruke over his shoulder. Swift is fidgeting with
the girdle of his cassock, or cutting his nails to the
quick with a penknife. All the banks of the Thames
upwards are classic ground. At Richmond, in that
lazy undress of a fat body, called Thomson, lived one
of the freest, most cordial, and most unexclusive of
poetical spirits, the most *un-Scotch* of Scotchmen.
He was seen eating peaches off a tree with his hands
in his waistcoat pockets; which is what he ought to
have done. Out of his enjoyments have come ours.
Garrick must not be passed by at Hampton, nor old
Jacob Tonson at Barn Elms, since Congreve and

Vanbrugh used to dine with him; * nor Horace
Walpole, with his toy-shop and his two-penny notions, at Strawberry Hill. He would have been a
man, if he had not been a lord. But Twickenham
and Pope! What a burst of beauty and wit is there!

> "What lady's that, to whom he gently bends?
>   Who knows not her? Ah, those are Wortley's eyes,
> The sweet-tongued Murray near her side attends;
> · Now to my heart the glance of Howard flies;
> Now Harvey, fair of face, I mark full well,
> With thee, youth's youngest daughter, sweet Lepell.
>
> " I see two lovely sisters hand in hand,
>   The fair-haired Martha, and Teresa brown;
> Madge Bellenden, the tallest of the land,
>   And smiling Mary, fair and soft as down.
> Yonder I see the cheerful duchess stand
>   For friendship, zeal, and blithesome humors known:
> Whence that loud shout in such a hearty strain?
> Why, all the Hamiltons are in her train." — GAY.

We fancy Pope always reading or writing; at intervals entertaining Bolingbroke, Swift, or Arbuthnot,
or all three; or undergoing his pleasing provocations
betwixt the humors of

> " The fair-haired Martha, and Teresa brown."

---

* See a pleasant parody by Rowe, on the Dialogue between Horace and
Lydia. The speakers are Tonson and Congreve. Tonson says, —

> " I'm in with Captain Vanbrugh at the present,
>   A most sweet-natured gentleman, and pleasant;
>   He writes your comedies, draws schemes and models,
>   And builds duke's houses upon very odd hills."

Yet he ends with saying, that he would give up even Vanbrugh to be reconciled
with Congreve, and would set up a bed for him in his dining-room at Bow Street
if he would come and see him. Jacob cuts a better figure here than when he inserted bad money among his payments to poor Dryden for his Virgil. — See the
letters at the end of Walter Scott's edition of Dryden.

Further up, at Chertsey, died good-hearted and fine-headed Cowley, — Pope says, of a fever, which he caught in consequence of having been drinking too freely, and lying out all night in the fields, with Dean Sprat. The story is in Spence's Anecdotes, but was omitted by Johnson, less out of tenderness, I dare say, to the Tory poet, than to the Tory bishop, whom he was anxious to exalt. Pope added, that " the parish still talked of *the drunken Dean.*"

Brentford, as Sir Hugh Evans would have said, " hath strange reputations." It was celebrated in the wars of the King and Parliament. The " two kings" of it are renowned in the Rehearsal. A poet, who lived at Richmond, records it as " a town of mud ;" * and a king, who lived at Kew, chose it for his prospect from the other side of the river. At Hammersmith Richardson had a country box. He used to bring unexpected nosegays from his garden there to his printing office in the city, in order to tempt his compositors to be early at their work.

Kensington is eminent for the heaviest part of the gossipping history of courts ; but there are one or two literary anecdotes connected with it, which I cannot refer to for want of books. There is a poem on the Gardens by Tickell. I believe Kent first displayed his genius in improving them. There was once some

---

* Castle of Indolence, the last stanza.

"Ev'n so, through Brentford's town, a town of mud,
An herd of bristly swine is prick'd along," &c.

Gay records, —
" Brentford's tedious town,
For dirty streets and white-legged chickens known."

inconvenience, perhaps, in walking in them at late hours; but all the rest of the time it was as it should be. Now, for "satyrs and sylvan boys," they have beadles, who take care that you cultivate nature with propriety, and remind you at every turn of the Board of Green Cloth. Who can dine on the grass with beadles looking at them? Eating their veal pie under favor, and merry by authority?

At Holland House, still in becoming hands, lived, loved, and died Addison; none of them very happily, though much is said about the death. I do not use the word "happy" in a physical sense, but as a question of good taste. Christians can die well undoubtedly: so can good people of all religions; especially if their blood is in a state for reasonable circulation, and they are not haunted with fears for others. I do not know how Steele died. Very pleasantly, I dare say, if he had his wits about him; for Young said, that "in his worst state of health, he seemed to desire nothing but to please and be pleased." But at all events, his last years are preferable to those of Addison, even though he had given up his property to his creditors and retired into Wales.. He used to amuse himself there with sitting out of doors in a chair, and giving prizes to be contended for by the village damsels. His more prudent friend, who put executions in his house to instruct him (which was about as good-natured, as Steele thought it, and about as wise as damming up a torrent for a fortnight), flourished and faded in his grand house under the contempt of his wedded countess, and resorted to consolations, which, in such a man, and such a man only, provoke

one to forget the charity which he lost sight of. It is
a tradition, I believe, in Holland House, that Addison
used sometimes to compose while pacing up and
down a long room that had a window at each end,
and in each window a bottle. What the bottle contained, more or less, stronger or weaker, is matter of
speculation. If he thought of poor Steele, I beg his
pardon ; but why did he not *say* something about it?
Addison's tavern habits were too much for Pope, who
was obliged to leave off sitting up with him. Dennis,
according to Spence's Anecdotes, said, that Dryden
" for the last ten years of his life was much acquainted
with Addison, and drank with him more than he ever
used to do ; probably so far as to hasten his end."
Addison was then a young man. This was beginning
betimes for the great moralist of the circles. When
the story of his death-bed is told, it should be added
(and doubtless would obtain equal admiration) that,
a fortnight before, he sent for Gay, and told him with
much penitence, that he had " injured him greatly,"
but would make it up to him, if he lived. What the
injury was, does not appear. " Better late than never ; " but did he husband this good thing all the while
he was writing the Spectator, and the charming Saturday articles? The lecture which he wrote to the lady
who made love to him, and which somehow or other
transpired, is of a piece with the rest. Little did
Calista know of *him*. Addison had wit at will, a
delightful style, little things of all sorts in profusion,
especially when he was in his cups : but he wanted
greatness of every kind. His virtue, even in its hum-
blest moment, was but a species of good breeding,

equally useful to him, he thought, in and out of the presence; a mixture of prudence, egotism, and sub-mission. He was perplexed neither by his sympa-thies nor his wisdom (at least he has not suffered any such misgivings in the long room to transpire); and he went to heaven, as he would have gone to court, dressed in his most becoming graces *à la mode*, and preparing himself for a good reception, if not by the consciousness of his rank, by the smiling zeal of his deference, and the politeness of his security.

In the burying-ground between Bayswater and Oxford Street lies " poor Yorick."

Paddington, " base, common, and popular" as it may now seem, is a very old village, that once had an abbey with a flourishing abbot, famous for his pomp and hospitality. One side of the road still belongs to the church. I have had many reasons for loving it, man and boy :— but here begins the ground of my affections, continuing through mead and green lane till it reaches beyond Hampstead. In the church-yard, by the green, with the fine trees on it, lie two of the most irritable spirits that ever disseminated lib-eral opinion, — Curran and Dr. Geddes. The tomb of Geddes has an epitaph upon it worth a Christian's going to see. In front of one of the houses between Paddington and Oxford Street, is an almond tree: not " on top of green Pelinis," but " all alone " never-theless, and in its due season

" With blossoms brave bedecked daintily."

Proprietor of that house and tree, and occupier of the house next door, was an old lady, whom I recol

lect, or think I recollect, in my childhood, as a sort
of perpetual thin-visaged old girl. In vain she walked
out with a lap-dog, a hood, and an umbrella that was
also a walking-stick. Her lap-dog, a jealous cur, was
the only unpleasant thing about her. Her merry
voice "piped as though it should never grow old."
And yet, whether I know her best from my own experience, or those of my brothers, I forget. At all
events, her image appears as vivid to me as if I saw it
carved at the top of her stick. She was the terror
and delight of all children ; alternately frightening
them to death with goblin tricks, and putting them in
Paradise with indescribable dumplings. What a difference between her and another old lady whom I
knew, who lived in a great house by Paddington
Church, and was herself frightened to death, and
worse, by Calvinism ! She was one of the kindest
women in the world ; but she " lived well," and did
not move about like the other, which would have
kept her blood from stagnating in that infernal lake.
I know not to which of the houses it was, but I think
to the smaller one that belonged those divine green
rails, which used to dance before me by anticipation
all the way from home, like a fairy prospect. There
are no such rails now, as the old gentleman in Gil
Blas said of the peaches. And yet I have a pleasure
in seeing *imitations* of them too, especially in a poor
suburb.

I know not which is the pleasanter way to Hampstead, the one up Kilburn Lane through West End, or
the one over the beautiful meadows that ascend to the
church. Upon the whole, however, I am for the

latter, and you generally go that way; so here is a *vade-mecum* to read *again*, as you take your journey; for that you *must* read it in the fields, and in those identical fields, is certain. If you are obliged to read it aloud, I shall not quarrel; nor even if you are all happy in hearing it; since I shall only gnash my teeth with impatience, when I receive the news, which is what I am inclined to do every week when I think of every friend I have; so it does not much signify. Out of forty thousand impatiences comes patience. I am " used to it," like the eels. B. shall write me an account of it, and put me at my worst; when I shall, of course, grow better.

Kilburn (the Kele or Cold Bourne) had its abbey, as well as Paddington. It is said to have stood on that pretty green slope on the right hand, as you enter the village from London. The Bourne runs at the foot of it, and forms afterwards the sheet of water facetiously called the Serpentine River. Out of the left side of Kilburn runs a lane to a little rustic hamlet called Wilsdon, one of the most secluded spots about London, and celebrated in the Literary Pocket Book with a due and united *gusto* of alehouse and pastoral. I dined there one time in company with an elegant living poet, whose fancy retreated from the " cakes and ale " into a contemplation of the white-curtained room up stairs, which he thought very amiable. White-curtained rooms are amiable. There are no such little draperied simplicities here, with woodbine and diamond windows; though there are heads of hair that would look well, looking out. Another time I had a delightful dinner

with W. C., in a room hung with Honbracken's engravings of the poets. There was a " niece" to wait
on us (may nobody make her look less happy and
pretty than she did then !), and a considerable appetite on both sides. C. acknowledged it was " the sort
of thing."

The lane leading on the right hand up to Hampstead winds pleasantly through thick hedges and fer-
tile fields, and opens at West End upon a beautiful
view of Hampstead and the Church. From the retirement of West End, fate once pitched me into a
very different sort of seclusion in *Horsemonger* Lane
(think of the name !), as if I had been no better than
a quoit. It was a quoit, however, that had shattered
some very hyacinthine locks.

We have now entered Hampstead, the region of
all suburban ruralities, of paths leading upward and
downward, of groves, of prospects, of meadows and
wood, of remote-looking lanes, of a remnant of wild
nature, of classical recollections. When I returned
from the very different lane just mentioned, I hastened
to re-occupy a bench that stood in a delightful slope,
and overlooked West End. I found it pushed away
by the fantastic house that now stands there, mystify-
ing the fields, and mocking antiquity. C. L. could not
have been more startled when he saw the chimney-
sweeper reclining in Richmond meadows. Had the
chimney-sweeper found the wonderful lamp he might
have raised just such a structure.

> " With twenty murders of good taste upon it,
> To push us from our stools."

Near this alarming fact (not the tenement next to it, but the first one on the right hand as you look up the lane) is a white house, in which Dr. Johnson took lodgings for his wife, crossing the fields to come to her of an evening. The road leads straight on from here to the heath. Let me leave the church on my right, with my usual reverence and silence. Every spot from this place is sacred to me for some recollection. Good God, how clearly I see everything! how vividly every corner turns upon me, with its trees, its gateways, or its mounds! On the right, in the first floor of a cottage, lived the last of the Mulsos, — at least, so I fancy her, for she was a maiden lady, and ought to have been the last, if she was not. (Not that I have any objection to the Mulsos, but Richardson and a continuation of the species somehow do not agree; though Pamela thought otherwise.) On the left I stood with dear S. and M. S., drawing ideal pictures of housekeeping. On the right again I kissed somebody that shall be nameless. Here I read; there I wrote something; there I used to turn down on horseback; and there I was thrown from my horse, to the great displeasure of a lady's maid, who, upon my assuring her I was not hurt, was angry that I had made her so nervous. Let me rest a while in the grove overlooking the heath, and fancy I am reading my Spenser. — I'll get up and cross to North End. At North End, across the heath, under the wing of his friend Dyson, lived Akenside. He calls the slope leading into the Hendon Road, Goulder's *Hill;* and altogether made as much of his suburb as the greatest cockney of us all. Milton could

not have said more for his "noble suburban spot," or
for the boarding-school girls whom he used to deify.
"Hampstead's airy summit" anybody may speak of,
but none but a lover could have talked of "climbing"
its "steep aerial way," especially on the north. He
was then, however, weak and sick, — sick, too, in the
lungs; though so fond was he of the place, that even
the north wind did not come amiss to him. See his
Odes; where, amidst a great deal of what is prosaical, and nothing that is lyrical, the real poet occasionally looks forth.

> "Thy verdant scenes, O Goulder's Hill,
> Once more I seek, a languid guest;
> With throbbing temples, and with burdened breast,
> Once more I climb thy steep aerial way.
> O faithful care of oft-returning ill!
> Now call thy sprightly breezes round,
> Disso've this rigid cough profound,
> And bid the springs of life with gentler movement play.
>
> "How gladly, 'mid the dews of dawn,
> My weary lungs thy healing gale,
> The balmy west, or the fresh north, inhale!
> How gladly, while my musing footsteps rove
> Round the cool orchard or the sunny lawn,
> Awaked I stop, and *look to find*
> *What shrub perfumes the pleasant wind*,
> Or what wild songster charms the Dryads of the grove."

All this reminds me, but too painfully, of another
and greater poet, a lover of Hampstead, of whom
more presently. North End, seen from the heath
above it on the south-east, presents one of the prettiest
village pictures I am acquainted with, — trees, gardens, and smoking cottages, with a mansion here
and there. The road that runs over the heath between this and the Vale of Health is a remnant of

the old Roman Road or Watling Street, and is praised by Camden for the beauty of its prospects. You can see from it to Windsor, and the borders of Buckinghamshire. The clumps of pines before the place where Lord Erskine lived, are of Italian origin, having been, in fact (as I understand), brought from Italy by the person who built the mansion that looks down them. Nearly opposite, on the other side of the road, are nine elms, under which it is recorded that Pope and Lord Mansfield used to sit. It must not be omitted, to the eternal honor of Mr. Coxe, poet and auctioneer, and also of Lord Mansfield's eminent successor, that the noble lord having an intention of cutting down these nine elms, Mr. Coxe made a becoming petition in the name of the Nine Muses, which it was impossible for an Erskine to resist. So the elms are where they used to be, with, I hope, a better seat under them. At Caen Wood, the fine seat of the Mansfields, there is a portrait of Betterton the player, which is said to be from the hand of Pope. On the right of the Highgate Road, pleasant meadows lead over to pleasant places, — Hendon and Finchley; on the left a lane turns off to Highgate and Kentish Town, justly christened Poet's Lane, both on account of its rural beauty and the walks here enjoyed by Mr. Coleridge, Mr. Keats, and others. There is a beautiful cottage and farm in it (only the cottage is too near the lodge) that belonged to Lord Southampton. The path over the fields to Highgate, or back again to the Vale of Health or the Heath, is quite lovely. Who knows it better than yourself? But you like me to repeat it. It was from a house on the eastern part of the heath that Keats took his departure to Italy. Melancholy as it was, and the more so from his attempt to render it calm and cheerful, it was not the most melancholy circumstance under which I saw him there. I could not hinder him one day from going to visit the house, in which, though he was himself ill and weak, he attended with such exemplary affection his younger brother that died. Dead almost himself by that time, the circumstance shook him beyond what he expected. The house was in Well Walk. You know the grove of elms there. It was in that grove, on the bench next the heath, that he suddenly turned upon me, his eyes swimming with tears, and told me he was " dying of a broken heart." He must have been wonderfully excited to make such a confession ; for his spirit was lofty to a degree of pride. Some private circumstances pressed on him at the time ; and to these he added the melancholy consciousness, that his feeble state of health made him sensible of some public annoyances, which no man would sooner otherwise have despised. His heart was afterwards soothed where he wished it to be ; and when he took his departure for Italy he had hope, or he would hardly have gone. Even I had hope. — My weaker eyes are obliged to break off. He lies under the walls of Rome, not far from the remains of one, who so soon and so abruptly joined him. Finer hearts, or more astonishing faculties, never were broken up than in those two. To praise any man's heart by the side of Shelley's, is alone an extraordinary panegyric.

You know what I must think of Hampstead, when

the memories of two such men come in aid of all that
endeared me to it before. Its beauty and its classical
associations are enough to render it interesting to
everybody; but love and friendship of all sorts have
also hallowed it to me. It pleases me to think, that
kindred hearts with these have delighted in the place
before. A little after you enter the town from London is a mansion which belonged to Sir Henry
Vane, — the most exalted and extraordinary intellect,
except Milton, of an age of great men; and one,
perhaps, who saw still farther than Milton into the
capabilities of society, in spite of the puritanical cloud
in which he wrapped up his Platonism. Here also
Day, the manly-spirited author of Sandford and Merton, brought his new-married wife, who talked and
walked with him to his heart's content; and in the
long room in Well Walk, now the chapel, but then
the pump-room for the mineral waters, used to be seen
one of the most amiable of men of wit, Arbuthnot,
who came there to get the health which he distributed
to thousands. I was going to say the most amiable
of physicians, but' I recollected Garth. Garth was
often at Hampstead, if he never lived there, for he
used to come to join the Kit-Kat Club at their summer dinners. He lies buried at Harrow, purely to
oblige one's prospect. The club met at the last
house on the hill, before you turn down into the
Vale of Health. It is now a private residence; —
a long low house, with trees before it. I write this
for your fellow-readers. There is a series of his-
tories belonging to this house. In the first place,
it was the scene of the summer meetings of the

Club aforesaid, consisting of Steele, Addison, Con-
gréve, Garth, Vanbrugh, and other wits and great
Whigs. When Steele was hiding from his duns in
a cottage on Haverstock Hill (which is still remaining), they used to call for him by the way.
After this, Richardson made it the scene of one
of Clarissa's flights: on which account a Frenchman is said to have made a pilgrimage on purpose to see it. It was hitherto an inn, known by
the name of the Upper Flask. Being afterwards
converted into a private dwelling-house, it became
the residence of George Steevens, the commentator
on Shakespeare, who used to walk to London every
morning at daybreak to correct the press. But
another anecdote remains, not the least in interest.
I will repeat it for the benefit of the readers above
mentioned. Some years ago, when the house was
occupied by a person whose name I forget (and I
should suppress it in common humanity if I did not),
I was returning home to my own, which was at no
great distance from it, after the opera. As I approached my door, I heard strange and alarming
shrieks mixed with the voice of a man. The next day
it was reported by the gossips that Mr. Shelley, no
Christian (for it was he who was there), had brought
some " very strange female " in the house, no better,
of course, than she ought to be, — the consequences
of which, of course, were no other than what *they*
ought to be, and what decent imaginations might
guess. Alas, their decent imaginations would never
have got at the truth, had they carved it and Chris-
tianed it till doomsday. The real Christian had

16

puzzled them.   Mr. Shelley, in coming to our house
that night, had found a woman lying near the top of
the hill in fits.   It was a fierce winter night, with
snow upon the ground ; and winter loses nothing of
its fierceness at Hampstead.   My friend, always the
promptest as well as the most pitying on these occasions, knocked at the first houses he could reach, in
order to have the woman taken in.   The invariable
answer was that they could not do it.   He asked for
an outhouse to put her in while he went for a doctor.
Impossible.   In vain he assured them she was no
impostor, — an assurance he was well able to give,
having studied something of medicine, and *even
walked the hospitals*, that he might be useful in this
way.   They would not dispute the point with him ;
but doors were closed, and windows were shut down.
Had he lit upon worthy Mr. Park, the philologist,
he would assuredly have come, in spite of his Calvinism.   But he lived too far off.   Had he lit upon you,
dear B—n, or your neighbor, D—e, you would,
either of you, have jumped up from amidst your books
or your bed-clothes, and have gone out with him.
But the paucity of Christians is astonishing, considering the number of them.   Time flies ; the poor
woman is in convulsions ; her son, a young man, la-
menting over her.   At last my friend sees a carriage
driving up to a house at a little distance.   The knock
is given ; the warm door opens ; servants and lights
pour forth.   Now, thought he, is the time.   He puts
on his best address, which anybody might recognize
for that of the highest gentleman as well as an interesting individual, and plants himself in the way of

an elderly person who is stepping out of the carriage with his family. He tells his story. They only press on the faster. " Will you go and see her?" " No sir, there is no necessity for that sort of thing, depend on it: — impostors swarm everywhere : — the thing cannot be done : — sir, your conduct is extraordinary." " Sir," cried Mr. Shelley at last, assuming a very different appearance, and forcing the flourishing householder to stop out of astonishment, " I am sorry to say that *your* conduct is *not* extraordinary : and if my own seems to amaze you, I will tell you something that may amaze you a little more, and I hope will frighten you. It is such men as you who madden the spirits and the patience of the poor and wretched ; and if ever a convulsion comes in this country (which is very probable) recollect what I tell you ; — you will have your house, which you refuse to put this miserable woman into, burnt over your head." " God bless me, sir ! Dear me, sir ! " exclaimed the frightened wretch, and fluttered into his mansion. The woman was then brought to our house, which was at some distance, and down a bleak path ; and Mr. S. and her son were obliged to hold her till the doctor could arrive. It appeared that she had been attending this son in London, on a criminal charge made against him, the agitation of which had thrown her into the fits on their return. The doctor said that she would inevitably have perished had she lain there only a short time longer. The next day my friend sent mother and son comfortably home to Hendon, where they were well known, and whence they returned him thanks full of gratitude. Now go, ye

Pharisees of all sorts, and try if ye can still open your hearts and your doors, like the good Samaritan. This man was himself, too, brought up in a splendid mansion, and might have revelled and rioted in all worldly goods. Yet this was one of the most ordinary of his actions.

Dear N., I know I cannot delight you more than by repeating the praises of another friend : — so richly in this respect has heaven compensated me, for a thousand evils, in things of which even death cannot deprive me.

P. S. — Among other suburban dwellers about London, I have omitted to mention in the course of this article, that Sir Thomas More lived at Chelsea ; that Thomas Moore hummed a short time at Hornsey ; and that Coleridge resides at Highgate, a " stroller with a book." 1823.

DR. JOHNSON, THE DEVIL, AND MR. COBBETT.

" THE office of the Register, and my shop, are now at No. 11 Bolt Court, Fleet Street. It is curious that I am now in the very house in which Old Dread-Devil, Dr. Johnson, lived and wrote so many years ! I have been a long while wanting to get it, on account of the cleanness, neatness, and stillness of the court, and the nearness of the house to the printing-office ; but until three days ago, I was not at all aware, that the melancholy moralist ever lived in it.

There is a neat coffee-house in the court, called ' *The Dr. Johnson* ; ' and though I cannot forgive the doctor for having given, in his own person, an example to illustrate the definition in his dictionary, where, against the word ' Pensioner,' he puts *a slave of state;* though I cannot forgive him for this, to see, as I do, from my window, *his name* put over a coffee-room, with a view to attract custom to it, is very pleasing : his name, thus used, is a mark of respect for his great mental endowments and vast literary labors, while his statue in St. Paul's is only a memorial of his having been *a slave of state.*" — *Cobbett's Register.*

We like these self-references of Mr. Cobbett, when his humanities are upon him, and he has a good word to say for another. A piece of sympathy, from him, is the more pleasant, inasmuch as he seems to think it to be his duty to be full of antipathies ("a good hater," as Johnson called it), and to push them to the utmost. We think he might relent a little during this fine, promising weather in the political world, and give us a few more of his "primroses" and pleasant anecdotes.

Dr. Johnson was one of the last of our great men, who had reason, throughout life, to curse the superstition inflicted upon him in childhood. His mother, poor woman, when he was just able to learn what she meant, was so eager to impress upon him the doctrine of eternal punishment, that she not only made him get out of his bed on purpose to infix it the more on his recollection, but called up the servants to aid the calamity. Mr. Cobbett, therefore, has too much reason to call him "Dread-Devil ; " but our politician, in proceeding to say something to his advantage, might have added another good word for the " melancholy moralist," since it was into his house, in this very Bolt Court, if we mistake not, that the doctor, who was a kind-hearted man, notwithstanding the asperities of his temperament, acted the very unusual Christian part, like a proper Samaritan, of bringing a poor girl on his shoulders, whom he found destitute in the streets, putting her into his own bed, making her well, and sending her home to her relations.

In Bolt Court, Johnson wrote the Lives of the Poets. He lived there from the year 1776 till he died. He had a garden to the house (Mr. Cobbett, who is horticultural, should revive it), with stone seats at the door. Boswell describes a conversation he had with him one day, when each took a seat in the open air, and the doctor was " in a placid frame of mind, and talked away easily."   1830.

COFFEE-HOUSES AND SMOKING.

SMOKING has had its vicissitudes, as well as other fashions. In Elizabeth's day, when it first came up, it was a high accomplishment: James (who liked it none the better for its being of Raleigh's invention) indignantly refused it the light of his countenance: in Charles's time it was dashed out by the cannon; lips had no leisure for it under Charles the

Second : the clubs and the Dutch brought it back again with King William : it prevailed more or less during the reign of the first two Georges; grew thin, and died away under George the Third ; and has lately reappeared, with a flourish of Turkish pipes, and through the milder medium of the cigar, under the auspices of his successor.

The last smoker I recollect among those of the old school, was a clergyman. He had seen the best society, and was a man of the most polished behavior. This did not hinder him from taking his pipe every evening before he went to bed. He sat in his arm-chair, his back gently bending, his knees a little apart, his eyes placidly inclined towards the fire : and delighted, in the intervals of puff, to recount anecdotes of the Marquis of Rockingham and "my Lord North." The end of his recreation was announced to those who had gone to bed, by the tapping of the bowl of his pipe upon the hob, for the purpose of emptying it of its ashes.* Ashes to ashes ; head to bed. It is a pity that the long day of life cannot always terminate as pleasantly. Bacon said that the art of making death-beds easy was among the *desiderata* of knowledge. Perhaps, for the most part, they are easier than the great chancellor imagined ; but,

---

* This lover of "the great plant" was Leigh Hunt's father, who, as a smoker, is thus described in The Autobiography of Leigh Hunt: "He was one of the gentry who retained the old fashion of smoking. He indu'ged in it every night before he went to bed, which he did at an early hour; and it was pleasant to see him sit, in his tranquil and gentlemanly manner, and relate anecdotes of 'my Lord North,' and the Rockingham administration, interspersed with those mild puffs and urbane resumptions of the pipe." — ED.

no doubt, the most conscientious ones might often be bettered. A virtuous man shall not always take his departure as comfortably as a sinner with a livelier state of diaphragm. Frenchmen have died, sitting in their chairs, full-dressed and powdered. I have a better taste in mortality than that; but I think I could drop off with a decent compromise between thought and forgetfulness, sitting with my pipe by a fireside, in an old elbow-chair.

I delight to think of the times when smoking was an ornament of literature, a refreshment and repose to the studious head; when Hobbes meditated, and Cowley built his castles in those warmer clouds, and Dr. Aldrich his quadrangles. In smoking, you may think or not think, as you please. If the mind is actively employed, the pipe keeps it in a state of satisfaction, supplies it with a side luxury, a soft ground to work upon. If you wish to be idle, the successive puffs take the place of thinking. There is a negative activity in it, that fills up the place of real. Intruding notions are met with a puff in their teeth, and puffed into nothing. Studious men are subject to a working and fermenting of thought, when their meditations would fain be over: they cannot always cease meditating. Bacon was accustomed to take a draught of March beer towards bedtime, to settle this æstuary of his mind. I wonder he did not take a pipe, as a gentler carrier off of that uneasiness. Being a link between thought and no thought, one would imagine it would have been a more advisable compromise with his state of excitement than the dashing of one stream upon another in that violent manner, and forcing his nerves to behave themselves. There are delicate heads, I am aware, that cannot bear even a cigar. Smoking, of any sort, makes too sudden an appeal to the connection between their sensitive nerves and the stomach ; produces what the doctor's call predigestion, and is rebuked with a punishment of the weaker part, to wit, the brain. Bacon's might have been such in his old age, after all the service it had seen ; but I wonder, on that account, that he resorted to the jolly and fox-hunting succedaneum of beer. A walk would have been better. " After study walk a mile." The object is to restore the blood gradually to motion, arrested as it has been with many thoughts, and confused when they let it go. Now a pipe is a more gradual restorative than a draught. As it is a shadowing off between thinking and no thinking, so it is a preparer for sleep, and a reconciler with want of company.

But the genius of smoking, being truly philosophical, has its love of society too : and then it resorts to a cup. Among Mr. Stothard's agreeable designs for the Spectator, there is one of the club over a table, with their pipes and their wine. Captain Sentry is going to light his pipe at the candle ; Sir Roger is sitting with his knees apart, like the old gentleman I have been describing, in the act of preparing his, — perhaps thinking what a pretty tobacco-stopper the widow's finger would have made. One longs to be among them. As I never pass Covent Garden (and I pass it very often) without thinking of all the old coffee-houses and the wits, so I can never reflect, without impatience, that there are no such meetings nowadays, and no coffee-room that looks as if it would suit them. People confine themselves too much to their pews and boxes. In former times there was a more humane openness of intercourse. Different parties had indeed their respective places of resort; a natural consequence of politics, perhaps of letters; but this prevented ungraceful quarrels. Hostility might get in, but was obliged to behave itself. Dryden, who was the object of attack to an increasing horde of scribblers, was never insulted in his coffee-house. Even the bravos of Lord Rochester, or whoever it was that had him waylaid in Rose Alley, did not venture to disturb the peace of his symposium. The room in which he sat is described as open to all comers, and he occupied a prominent part in it. In winter a place was sacred for him at the fireside.

I confess, if I were a wit, I would rather have a room to myself and friends. I should like to be public only in my books. But this is a taste originating in the times. Dryden was a modest man in his intercourse; and was never charged, I believe, among all the accusations of vanity brought against him, of being the vainer for frequenting a coffee-room. Being a lover of wits, I should like to see the times alter in this respect, and the great men of all parties become visible. But where could they be so? Where could the pleasant fellows among our existing Whigs and Tories take up one of their respective tabernacles, and make a religion of our going to hear them, and aspiring to a pinch out of their snuff-boxes? I was thinking of this, as I passed through Covent Garden the other evening.

Above all, said I, where could we have the whole
warmth of the intercourse revived, the Spectator's
tobacco-pipe and all, especially when it is no longer
the fashion to drink wine?   It would take a great
deal to fetch Englishmen again out of their boxes.
They do not allow smoking in the best coffee-houses;
and where they do, so many other things are allowed,
that no gentleman would remain.   Where shall I
place my imaginary coterie, and fancy myself listening to the Drydens and Addisons of the day?   It
is the fashion now for your wilder writers in magazines to patronize, or pretend to patronize, some
house of call, or vociferation, the mediocrity of which
shall give them an air of vigor and defiance in the
patronage, and prove them men of originality.   There
is something pleasant in this where it is not an affectation of superiority to prejudice, arising out of an
absolute sense to the contrary, and betraying itself
by a tone of bullying.   But real or not, and with
all my regard for those honest houses, where the
only sophisticate thing is the presence of some of
their panegyrists, they will not do for the purpose
before us.   Due is my consideration for the *Dog* and
the *Coal-hole:* pungent my sense of the *Cheshire
Cheese:* the *Hole in the Wall* has a snug appellation; and as for Dolly's *Beef-Steak House*, great
would be my ingratitude, did I forget its hot pewter-
plate, new bread, floury potatoes, foaming pot of
porter, and perfect beefsteak.   The man that cannot
enjoy a beefsteak there, can enjoy a stomach nowhere.   But it is not what I was seeking the other
night.   Neither is the Hummums, nor the Bedford,

nor the Piazza, nor the Southampton, nor the Salopian.*

During these meditations, I approach my friend Gliddon's snuff and tobacco-shop, in King Street. Ay, here, said I, is wherewithal to fill the boxes of the Steeles and Congreves, and the pipes of the Aldriches and Sir Roger de Coverleys. But where is the room in which we can fancy them? Where is the coffee-house to match? Where the union of a certain domestic comfort with publicity, — journals of literature as well as news, — a fire visible to all, — cups without inebriety, — smoking without vulgarity? On a sudden, I find carriages stopping at the door; I recognize an acquaintance of mine, a member of Parliament, who does not easily come out of his way to fill a snuff-box: I hear a gentleman inquiring about the coffee-room, and " whether Prince Esterhazy is to be turned away again by a stress of company." I enter, and ask my old acquaintance what miracle he has been about. He points to a board in his shop, and then takes me through a door in the wall into the very room that I was looking for. It was rather two rooms thrown into one, and with a fire in each; a divan of ample dimensions runs

---

* The Salopian House is immortalized in Elia's essay on The Praise of Chimney-Sweepers. It was at the Southampton tavern that Hazlitt's " Coffee-House Politicians " met to read the papers and discuss the news of the day. The Bedford Coffee-House was frequented by Colman and Thornton, the lively authors of the Connoisseur. "This coffee-house," says Mr. Town, in his survey of London, "is every night crowded with men of parts. Almost every one you meet is a polite scholar and a wit. Jokes and *bon mots* are echoed from box to box; every branch of literature is critically examined, and the merits of every production of the press, or performance at the theatre, weighed and determined." — Connoisseur, No. 1. — Ed.

round it; lamps of ground glass diffuse a soft, yet
sufficing light; the floor is carpeted; two cheerful
fires offer double facility of approach, a twofold
provocation to poke and be self-possessed; around
are small mahogany tables, with chairs, in addition
to the divan; and in the midst of all, stands a large
one, profusely covered with the periodical works of
the day, newspapers, magazines, and publications
that come out in numbers. I sit down, and am
initiated with the hospitality due to an old friend,
in all the amenities of the place. A cigar and an
excellent cup of coffee are served. "But will you
have as good coffee at the end of the year?" —
"Can you ask me that question, Mr. Honeycomb *
— you, who have known me long?" — " Well, if
anybody that ever kept a shop can do it, it is you:
and I tell you what; — if you do, depend upon it,
no success will be like yours. Good fortune produces
abuse of it; but the abuse is always as impolitic,
compared with a genuine policy, as cunning is inferior to wisdom. If there were any one shop in
London, in which the customer for a series of years
were sure to find one undeviating goodness of article, the phenomenon would attract and retain all
eyes. And these cigars: the boy tells me they are
excellent also. Is this true?" — "I can tell
you one thing they say of them, by which you may
judge for yourself; they say they are smuggled." —
" O, ho! "

"And snatch a grace beyond the reach of law."

---

* This paper was published under the signature of Harry Honeycomb, a pretended descendant of the famous Will Honeycomb of the Spectator. — ED.

You know how the law picked my pocket once.
Before that time, I was so tender of conscience,
that when I was at Hastings I would not purchase a toy or a pair of gloves that was contra-
band; whereas *now*—I will not ask you to make
me certain whether the articles are smuggled or not
— say no more — rest your insinuating fame on that.
But a prettier-tasted cigar — a leaf with a finer tip of
flavor in it, — pray, how many cigars might a man
smoke of an evening? I have a great mind to try.
But I must look at your publications. By the way,
you have no pipes, I see; and I observe no bottles.
Have you neither pipes nor wine?"—"No, we are
exclusively cigar; we have coffee, sherbet, lemonade,
all reasonable Oriental drinks to harmonize with our
divan, but nothing to disturb the peace of it. Thus
we secure a certain domestic elegance in-doors, and
can prevent drunkards from coming in to get drunker.
A gentleman may come from his dining or drawing-
room, and still find himself in a manner at home.
Besides, a cigar is the mildest as well as most fashionable form of tobacco-taking; and as it is no longer
the mode to drink wine, wine is not sought after." *

---

* In the article entitled Of the Sight of Shops, as published in the original
edition of the Indicator, there is a very graceful and handsome mention of Mr.
Honeycomb's friend Gliddon, of King Street, formerly of No. 31 Tavistock Street.

"We presume that snuff-takers delight to solace themselves with a pinch of
Thirty-seven; and we accordingly do so in imagination at our friend Gliddon's in
Tavistock Street, who is a higher kind of Lilly to the Indicator, — our papers lying
among the piquant snuffs, as those of our illustrious predecessor The Tatler did
among Mr. Lilly's perfumes at the corner of Beaufort Buildings. Since the
peace with France, the shops of our tobacconists have become as amusing as
print-shops; though not always, it must be confessed, in a style of delicacy becoming their enamoured boxes. At our friend's in Tavistock Street everything is

— " That is all very good for you ; but for me, who
have been casting a wistful eye, as I came along, at
the old haunts of Sir Roger and his friends, I confess
it is a drawback on a certain fancy I had, when I first
came in.   However, we must consider what Steele
and Addison would have liked had they lived now,
and witnessed the effect of the Spectators of other men.
It is they that have helped to ruin their own pipes and
wine, and given us a greater taste for literature and
domesticity ; and I comfort myself with concluding,
that they would have come here, at least *after* their
bottle, to take their coffee and look over your papers
and magazines.   There he sits, over the way, —
Steele, I mean, — the man with the short face ; for I
perceive there is wit at that table.   Opposite him is
Addison, in black, looking something like a master
in chancery.   The handsome man, always on the giggle, must be Rowe ; and the other one, an officer, is
Colonel Brett.   But who is this tall formal personage
coming up?   Look at him, — the very man, Ambrose
Phillips.   Who would think that his muse was a little dancer in octosyllables, — a dandler of young
ladies of quality?"

Mine host left me alone to complete my initiation.
Another cup of coffee was brought me, and five several publications ; to wit, a newspaper, a twopenny
sheet, a number to be continued, a magazine, and a
review ; for I am fond of having too many books at

managed in a way equally delicate and cordial ; and while the leisurely man of
taste buys his Paris or his Indicator, the busier one may learn how to set up his
gas-light in good classical style, and both see how completely even a woman of
true feelings, can retain the easiest and pleasantest good-breeding in the midst
of observant eyes and humble occupation." — ED.

once. I looked over these, and then, contented with
the power to read them further, continued giving
bland puffs to my cigar, and speculating around me.
The conversations were maintained in very quiet
and gentlemanly tones: now and then was heard
the sound of a leaf turning over; sometimes a hem
consequential or otherwise; my own puffs were always distinguishable to myself; and at intervals I
could discern those of others, and hear the social
crackling of the fire. No noisy altercation here; no
sanded floors or cold feet; no impatient waiting for the
newspaper; * while the person in possession keeps
it the longer because you wait: all is warm, easy,
quiet, abundant, satisfactory.

I conclude the principal visitors of the divan to be
theatre-goers, officers who have learnt to love a cigar
on service, men of letters, and men of fortune who
have a taste for letters, and can whirl themselves from
their own firesides to these. If you are in the city, on
business, go for a steak to Dolly's; if midway between
City and West End, go to the first clean-looking lar-
der you come to; if a man of fashion, and you must
dine in your altitudes, go to the Clarendon; but after
any of these, man of fashion or not, go if you can, and
get your cigar and your cup of coffee at Gliddon's.
It is finishing with a grace and a repose.

By the way, I spent a pretty afternoon the other
day. It was a complete thing, one thing excepted:
but — she's at Paris. I dined, I will not say how

---

* As at Nando's. " What an eternal time that gentleman in black, at Nan-
do's, keeps the paper! I am sick of hearing the waiters bawling out incessantly,
'The Chronicle is in hand, sir.'" — Elia's Detached Thoughts on Books and
Reading. — ED.

early; but took only a couple glasses of wine; which will retrieve my character on that point. I then made tour of the book-stalls, at Covent-Garden; bought some comedies and a Catullus; went to the theatre, and saw Der Freyschutz and Charles the Second; re-issued from among the perukes, with a gallant sense about my head and shoulders, as if I carried one my-self; went and settled my faculties over a cup of the New Monthly at Gliddon's; got home by eleven (for I would not go to a party where she was not); and fell to sleep at the words " Lulling hope," in a song I am writing.   1826.

WIT MADE EASY, OR A HINT TO WORD-CATCHERS.

A. HERE comes B., the liveliest yet most tiresome of word-catchers. I wonder whether he'll have wit enough to hear good news of his mistress. Well, B., my dear boy, I hope I see you well.

B. I hope you do, my dear A., otherwise you have lost your eyesight.

A. Good. Well, how do you do?

B. How? Why, as other people do. You would not have me eccentric, would you?

A. Nonsense. I mean how do you find yourself?

B. Find myself. Where's the necessity of finding myself? I have not been lost.

A. Incorrigible dog! Come now, to be serious.

17

(*B. comes closer to A. and looks very serious.*)

A. Well, what now?

B. I am come to be serious.

A. Come, now; nonsense, B.; leave off this. (*Laying his hand on his arm.*)

B (*looking down at his arm*). I can't leave off this. It would look very absurd to go without a sleeve.

A. Ah, ha! You make me laugh, in spite of myself. How's Jackson?

B. The deuce! How's Jackson! Well, I never should have thought that. How can Howe be Jackson? " Surname and arms," I suppose, of some rich uncle? I have not seen him gazetted?

A. Good by.

B. (*detaining him*). " Good by ! " What a sudden enthusiasm in favor of some virtuous man of the name of By! " Good by!" To think of Ashton standing at the corner of the street, doting aloud on the integrity of a Mr. By!

A. Ludicrous enough. I can't help laughing, I confess. But laughing does not always imply merriment. You do not delight us, Jack, with these sort of jokes, but tickle us; and tickling may give pain.

B. Don't accept it, then. You need not take everything that is given you.

A. You'll want a straight-forward answer some day, and then —

B. You'll describe a circle about me, before you give it. Well, that's your affair, not mine. You'll astonish the natives, that's all.

A. It's great nonsense, you must allow.

B. I can't see why it is greater nonsense than any other pronoun.

A. (*in despair*). Well, it's of no use, I see.

B. Excuse me: it is of the very greatest use. I don't know a part of speech more useful. It performs all the greatest offices of nature, and contains, in fact, the whole agency and mystery of the world. It rains. It is fine weather. It freezes. It thaws. It (which is very odd) is one o'clock. " It has been a very frequent observation." It goes. Here it goes. How goes it? — (which, by the way, is a translation from the Latin *Eo, is* it; *Eo,* I go; is thou goest; it, he or it goes." In short —

A. In short, if I wanted a dissertation on it, now's the time for it. But I don't; so good by. (*Going.*) — I saw Miss M—— last night.

B. The devil you did! Where was it?

A. (*to himself*). Now I have him, and will revenge myself. Where was it, eh? O, you must know a great deal more about it than I do!

B. Nay, my dear fellow, do tell me. I'm on thorns.

A. On thorns! very odd thorns. I never saw a thorn look so like a pavement.

B. Come, now, to be serious.

(*A. comes close to B., and looks tragic.*)

B. He, he! very fair, egad. But do tell me where was she. How did she look? Who was with her?

A. O, ho! Hoo was with her, was he? Well, I wanted to know his name. I could not tell who the devil it was. But I say, Jack, who's Hoo?

B. Good. He, he! Devilish fair! But now,

my dear Will, for God's sake, you know how interested I am.

A. The deuce you are! I always took you for a
disinterested fellow. I always said of Jack B., Jack's
apt to overdo his credit for wit; but a more honest,
disinterested fellow I never met with.

B. Well, then, as you think so, be merciful. Where
is Miss M——?

A. This is more astonishing news than any. *Ware*
is Miss M——. I know her passion for music; but
this is wonderful. Good heavens! To think of a
delicate young lady dressing herself in man's clothes,
and going about as a musician under the name of
Ware.

' *B.* Now, my dear Will, consider. I acknowledge
I have been tiresome; I confess it is a bad habit, this
word-catching; but consider my love.

(*A. falls into an attitude of musing.*)

B. Well.

A. Don't interrupt me. I am considering your
love.

B. I repent; I am truly. sorry. What shall I
do? (*Laying his hand on his heart.*) I'll give up
this cursed habit.

A. You will? Upon honor?

B. Upon my honor.

A. On the spot?

B. Now, this instant. Now and forever!

A. Strip away, then.

B. Strip! For what?

A. You said you'd give up that cursed habit.

B. Now, my dear A., for the love of everything that is sacred, for the love of your *own* love.

A. Well, you promise me sincerely?

B. Heart and soul!

A. Step over the way, then, into the coffee-house, and I'll tell you.

Street Sweeper. Please, your honor, pray remember the poor swape.

B. My friend, I'll never forget you, if that will be of any service. I'll think of you next year.

A. What, again?

B. The last time, as I hope to be saved. Here, my friend, there's a shilling for you. Charity covers a multitude of bad jokes.

Street Sweeper. God send your honor thousands of them.

B. The jokes or the shillings, you rascal?

Street Sweeper. Och, the shillings. Divil a bit the bad jokes. I can make them myself, and a shilling's no joke, anyhow.

A. What? really silent? and in spite of the dog's equivocal Irish face? Come, B., I now see you can give up a jest, and art really in love; and your mistress, I will undertake to say, will not be sorry to be convinced of both. Women like to begin with merriment well enough; but they think ill of a man who cannot come to a grave conclusion.

1825.

THE FENCING-MASTER'S CHOICE.

A S we have a great aversion to the repetition
of old jokes, and in our ignorance of what
is going forward in the festive parts of the town,
can never be certain that any story we take for a
new one is not well known, we always feel inclined
to preface a relation of this kind with something
that should serve for an apology in case of necessity, or give it a new grace in default of newness of
a better sort. And this reflection always reminds
us of that pleasant Milanese, whom nature made a
wag and a jolly fellow, and Francis the First made
a bishop; to wit, Master Matthew Bandello, the
best Italian novelist, after Boccaccio, and one who
could tell a grave story as well as a merry one.
Monsignore Matteo, before he proceeds to relate
how "*a jealous* enamoured himself" of a young
widow, or how a pleasant "*beff*" was put upon a
priest who became "furious of it," and "remained
stordited," makes a point of informing the reader
where he first heard the story, who told it, and in
whose company, and how much better it was told
than he, with his Lombardisms, can have any pre-
tence to repeat it; on all which accounts he wishes
to God, that people could have heard it fresh from
the lips of that very amiable and magnificent Signor, the before-mentioned Signor Antonio, whom he
recollects as if it was but yesterday, because he was

standing at the time with a right joyous and genteel company by the balustrade of the gardens of
the very illustrious and most adorned Signor, his
singularly noble friend the Signor Gherardesco dei
Gherardi, Conte di Cuviano, where there happened
to be present the ladies equally eminent for their
high birth and most excellent endowments, to wit,
the right courteous, virtuous, and most beautiful ladies the Lady Vittoria, Princess of Colombano, and
the Lady Hippolita d'Este, widow of the most valor-
ous and magnificent Signor, the ever-memorable Al-
fonso, Prince of Ferrara ; which ladies, being very
affectionate towards all argute sayings and witty deeds,
did nigh burst themselves for laughter, in the which
the very illustrious Signor Gherardesco aforesaid did
heartily join, to the great contentment of that princely
company, and all who overheard those urbane con-
ceits and most graceful phrases, which he (the bishop)
utterly despairs of rendering anything the like to the
reader. But he will do his best ; and as the story is
exceedingly curious (to wit, a little free), he had addressed it to the right virtuous and most adorned with
all feminine dowries, the Lady Lucretia di San Don-
nato, in return for one of a like nature which she was
graciously pleased to relate to him one day ; to wit, on
the eve of the day of Corpus Domini, sitting in the
windows of the Palazzo Rospoli, at that time inhabited by the very magnificent, most adorned, and most
worthily given Signor, the Signor Prince Cesare Otto-
boni, nephew of the most Holy Father.

By this process, the reader feels bound to like the
story, if only out of a proper sense of the company he

is in, and the respect that is due to all those fair and magnificent names; and then follows the *novella*, or new tale, perhaps not at all new, and no longer than the one we are about to relate.

We should like to call to ourselves an aid of this sort, and be able at the head of every one of our stories to state how it was told us by this person or that; how that, sitting one day in the gardens of Kensington, at a time when the dust of the streets rendered an escape into those green and quiet places agreeable, we had the pleasure of hearing it from the lips of that very adorned and witty Mister, the Reverend Mister Samuel Smith, or the extremely magnificent and choice in his neckcloths, the admired Mr. Tomlinson; or how, dining with the very magnificent and grave Esquire, the Squire Jinks, of Jinks Hall, it was related to us by the facetious and extremely skilled in languages, the bachelor of arts, the hopeful Dick Watts, cousin of the high born and most beautiful lady, the Lady Barbara Jinks, consort of the said esquire, who, being at that moment in the act of swallowing a cherry, was nigh to have thrown all the lovers of wit and elegance in those parts into mourning, in consequence of the extreme difficulty she found in swallowing the fruit and the facetiosity at once.

The story is this: that in the year of our Lord one thousand seven hundred and ninety-nine, the celebrated fencing-master, Monsieur de la Rue, being at that time fencing-master to the gentlemen of the University of Cambridge, and grievously tormented in his vocation by the said gentlemen, who made no end of mimicking his grimaces, groaning out of measure at his

thrusts, not repenting at his remonstrances, and showing themselves otherwise insensible of the dignity and
painstaking of his profession, did one day, towards
the end of the month of June, the weather being hot,
the said Monsieur de la Rue in his jacket and nightcap, and divers of the said gentlemen standing idly
about, laughing and making a vain sport, instead of
pinking him, as they ought to have done, — he, the
said Monsieur de la Rue, did, I say, then and there sit
down on the floor in the room in which he was fencing, and placing, one on each side of him, the two foils
which he then happened to be holding in his hands,
and being provoked out of the ordinary measure of
his patience by the eternal gibes and ungrateful levities of those his tormentors, the said gentlemen, was
moved to utter the following speech, or representation expostulatory ; which he did with great passion
and vehemence, his eyes wide open, his hands and
face trembling, and emphasis rising at every sentence : —

"Jentlemens, —
" If *Got Almaighty* — vere to come *down* from *hev-
ven*, — and vere to say to me, ' *Monsieur de la Rue*,
—vill you be fencing-master at Osford or Cambreege,
— or vill you be ETAIRNALLY dam?' —
"I should answer and say, —
"' SARE, — if it is *all* the same to you, —I vill be
ETAIRNALLY dam.'"
1828.

TWILIGHT ACCUSED AND DEFENDED.

A MONSTROUS thing has happened.   Here is
a correspondent of ours, and a pleasant one too,
and witty withal, aiming a blow at our gentle friend,
Twilight!   What possible mood could he have been
in?   Did he expect a friend who had disappointed
him? or a new book? or a letter?   Was his last bottle of wine out?   Or did he want his tea?   Or was
he reading and could not go on, the servant not being
in the way to bring candles?   Or was the evening
rainy?   Or had he said anything wrong to any one
else, and so was out of temper?   Or had he been
reading something about twilight, badly written, a
" twaddle," and so was disposed to go to an extreme
the other way, and be perverse in his wit?   His first
verse looks like it.   Or had he a toothache? or a
headache? or nothing to do?   Or had his fire gone
out?

We should almost as soon have expected a blow
from him at gentleness itself, as at our gentle dusk
friend, the mildest and most unpresuming of the
Hours, meek, yet genial withal, like some loving *Mes-
tiza*, or Quadroon, something between fair and dark,
or dusk and dusker, who, by her sweet middle tone
between merit and the want of pretension, and by
having nothing to arrogate, and much to be prized,
charms the amorous heart of some contemplative
West Indian, who is tired out between the flare of

his whiter favorites, and the undiscerning presumption of his black. Certain it is, that, vehemently
howsoever he speaketh, we hold him not to be in
earnest (the less so by reason of that enormity) ;
but, in order to prevent the peril of any false conclusions, in minds accustomed not to such facetious
perversity, and still more to take the opportunity of
vindicating the character of our gentle friend, and
make our correspondent remorseful the next time
he sees her (for having even appeared to treat her
ill), we have thought it incumbent upon us to follow up his hard words with others more fitly soft
and overwhelmingly balmy. O, there is nothing like
defending a good easy cause, and a tender-hearted
client! It makes one, somehow, so sure of triumph,
so able to trample on one's enemy with the softest
foot and the most generous reputation — so gifted
(dare we say it?) with the pleasure of malignity by
the very exercise of benevolence. Mark you, dear
reader, with what a tender savageness we will set
him down. Yet he rails in good set terms. There
is no denying that. Far be it from us to deny it,
who shall only gain the greater praise from our ref-
utation. Hear him how he sets out with the ingenious impudence of his pun and his alliteration : —

A TRIMMING FOR TWILIGHT.

How I despise the twaddle about twilight,
That most unserviceable sort of sky-light ;
Weak, wavering gleam, that, wending on its way
Towards the night, still lingers with the day.

Twilight's a half-and-half affair, that would
With all its heart be moonlight if it could;
Dim, but not dark; you pause at the bell handles ;
'Tis scarce worth while to conquer it with candles.

Twilight is eve grown gray before its time,
Mystified mummer, aping the sublime
Day with its eye half closed, and half a-peep ;
The afternoon, making believe to sleep.

'Tis like that forming frown yet undefined
That yon half-smiling female face has got,
As though it hadn't quite made up its mind
Whether it should look angrily or not.

Twilight's an interloper in the sky ;
The face of nature painted with one eye :
Something between blank darkness and broad light,
Like dotard day coquetting with young night.

A dame *passé*, who, growing old and wan,
Affects to veil the charms she feels are gone ;
Knowing her day is o'er, the wily jade
Inwraps the ruin where the sunshine play'd.

Lovers love twilight, but I'm not a lover ;
And why *they* love it I could ne'er discover :
For light is passion's parent : do ye deem
Beauty no debtor to the radiant beam
That lamps its loveliness ; say, can we know
That beauty lives, and one bright glance forego ?
Or, is't a fancy of love's selfish art,
To close the eyes, and see but with the heart ?

Haply 'tis so ; in love's delirious trance,
The raptured soul, grown jealous of the glance
That has a joy beyond it, dims the light
To lend to young imagination sight.

Fancy, that peoples darkness with bright rays,
And makes a darkness that it thus may gaze :
How is't that *every* feeling, fond, intense,
Tempts us to lose a while our visual sense?

Is it superfluous? We drink love through it :
'Tis then in us; we can no longer view it
By gazing outwards ; now, a glance to win,
Our eyelids close, and turn their sense within.

This is digressive, but enough for me;
Lovers, in fact, are no authority;
So, as I said at first, old twaddling twilight,
Be still the lover's gleam, you shan't be *my* light.

Thou'rt day declared a bankrupt, offering round
A dividend of ten-pence in the pound:
Plague take such compositions; I'll for one
Have twenty shillings' worth of light or none.

Not daybreak, but day *broken;* light fades fast;
Do as thou wilt, thou'rt sure to *fail* at last.
"Come, sealing night," before thee twilight flies;
Put out the mocker with your starry eyes.
Dusky-hued coward! hast begun the race,
Dar'st thou not look Dame Dian in the face?

Now flickering fainter, now more darkly dull,
" I, that am cruel, am yet merciful:
I would not have thee linger in thy pain:"
Come, light the candles; struggle not, — 'tis vain.

Is that thy shadow, lingering on the moor?
No matter; you shall never come in-door.
The stars come out at thee, pale day-diminisher;
Now the moon gleams at full, — ay, that's a finisher.

Beneath the hillock's shadow, cloaked in gray,
Cautiously creep before the light away;
But when the morning moon grows sick and pale,
Then, stealthy stepper, come across the vale.

Child of the mist, isthmus 'twixt light and shade !
Shadow of Chaos, from which earth was made !
Day dying of decline ! doubt-dreaming ray !
Thy presence saddens me — away — away !

W. I. R.

" Away — away ! " Our correspondent must have
been in a great hurry, to speak thus to the poor gentle
twilight, which has not a word to say for itself, unless
it be the muffin-bell, the next thing in humbleness of
sound to the sheep-bell. We take him to be a prodi-
giously active and eager spirit, with an ultra flow of
health and life, and never easy but when occupied,

perhaps not then, unless the occupation perfectly suits him. But he has a soul withal; you may know it even by what is implied in his style of abuse; and therefore it is not the twilight he hates, but the absence of something which he wanted instead of it. Yes; assuredly he has been "snubbing" the poor Quadroon, like some lordly planter, because somebody else has not brought him his sangaree.

He lets — we cannot say the "cat out of the bag" — but the dove out of the cage — in what he says about lovers. He tells us he is "no lover," merely in order to avoid what he knows to be conclusive against him; and, in fact, he runs into a digression about love, on purpose to disprove his own argument. Besides, if he happens to be so limited or so unlucky in his circle of acquaintances as to be in love with nobody, he must love all sorts of lovable things, otherwise how could he write so well about loving? and if a man loves anything at all, he must needs love so mild and loving a thing as the twilight. (Here are a great many repetitions of the word "love;" but it is a pleasant note, and will bear reiteration like the nightingale's.)

Furthermore, in this passage of our correspondent's about love, compared with certain letters which he has written to us privately, urging us to give an article on Coleridge, we have detected him in the fact of his disingenuousness; for this very passage has manifestly been suggested by some stanzas of that favorite of his, in the poem entitled the Day-Dream. It is a lover's picture of twilight in a room, and is so beautiful and true, that it might serve alone, as an answer to all the stanzas of this pretending rogue : —

" My eyes make pictures, when they are shut : —
  I see a fountain, large and fair,
  A willow and a ruined hut,
  And thee, and me, and Mary there.
O Mary! make thy gentle lap our pillow!
Bend o'er us, like a bower, my beautiful green willow!

  *   *   *   *   *   *   *

  The shadows dance upon the wall,
    By the still dancing fire-flames made ;
  And now they slumber, moveless all!
    And now they melt to one deep shade !
  But not from me shall this mild darkness steal thee ;
  I dream thee with mine eyes, and at my heart I feel thee! "

Very beautiful and spiritual, and truly loving. But
lovers, the most honorable and delicate, have a trick
of taking other advantages of the good-natured twilight ; and the poet goes on to let us know as much : —

    "Thine eyelash on my cheek doth play."

Far be it from us to deny the merits of light and seeing. Beauty was surely meant to be seen as well as
loved, or why is it so beautiful? But it is a maxim
with us never to deny the merits of one good thing
because there is another ; and twilight, where love is,
has its loveliness also, as well as lamp and daylight.
One of the greatest tests of true love is the sense of
joy imparted by the mere presence of the beloved
object, apart from light, speech, or anything else ; and
twilight, somehow, rewards us for the sincerity and
generosity of this feeling, by bringing us nearer to the
object of our affection, in its abolition of intermediate objects, and a general sense of its mild embrace-
ment.

  Come — let us consider what our correspondent
would say further in behalf of the twilight, if he

were in the humor for it. We wish we had time to
say it in verse; but here we heave a great sigh (one
of the sighs of our life); and as we always feel
ashamed of sighing in the midst of this beautiful
creation (of which to be able to discern a millionth
part of the beauties, is to waken up as many con-
solatory angels, who lie in wait to become visible to
loving eyes), we shall proceed to express ourselves
in our accustomed prose, from which, at all events,
the love of what is poetical cannot be excluded.

Twilight is the time between light and darkness,
when the facility afforded for action by the daylight
is over, and the aid of candle-light, for the renewal
of action, awaits our pleasure to renew it or not.
It is therefore the precise time, of all others, which
seems designed by nature for meditation. We say,
by nature; for though we hold it to be man's nature
to be artificial as well as natural, yet it is natural
for him, being a thinking being, to "take pause;"
and nature, in this gentlest and most intermediate
hour, seems to offer it him. The greatest part of
his duty is over (we hold, that in a more civilized
state of society it will *all* be over, except for purposes of entertainment); he cannot see to work; he
cannot see to travel very actively; his very book begins to fail him, unless he has determined to keep up
the train of his reading, and goes nearer and nearer
to the window, and at last he must give it up. He
is therefore thrown upon his meditations.

Now " *think* a little."

Not of your cares, dear reader, if you can help it; not
of your work; not of other people's faults; not of your

own. There is time enough to attend to those, when
we have more light — unless, indeed, you do it in great
charity, first towards the faults of others, and then
towards yourself (having earned the right), and always provided you end, as indeed you must, if true
charity meditates with you, in resolutions befitting
the mildness and considerateness of the hour. We
would not even have you think of the sufferings of
others, provided you think of them at any other
time, and do what you can to help them. Twilight is a placid hour, and you must entertain it
with placidity or not at all. You must have so
acted, or so wished to act, at other times, as to be
able to give gentle welcome to gentle guest. You
must be *worthy* of the twilight.

(Here our correspondent gives a great wince ; and
begins to inquire of his conscience, whether he has
ever cracked any one's skull, or written any impiety except the above.)

Now let us think of all mild and loving things —
of our childhood, of the fields, of our best friends,
of twilight itself and its shadows, of the quiet of
our fireside, and the fanciful things we see in the
glowing coals, of the poets who have spoken of
evening, of the beauty of stillness, of scenes of rural
comfort, of the travels of the winds and clouds, of
stories of good angels, nay, of dear friends whom
we have lost, provided we have lost them long
enough or loved them well enough to consider them
with reference to the beauty of their own spirit
rather than to their absence from ourselves. Perhaps they are commissioned to be good angels over

18

us : — perhaps they are now this minute in the room,
smiling in the certainty of their own lovingness, and
the knowledge of our future good; ay, and (as far as
their sympathy with our present struggles will permit) smiling to think even how startled we should be
to see them, if it were within Heaven's knowledge of
what is best for us that we should do so.   For God is
the author of mirth as well as seriousness, and considering what security of belief in good there must be in
celestial natures, we may conceive some little stoop-
ing to it even in the happiness of heavenly cheeks.

"Let us think" of that, and of all other possibilities
beyond the regions of mere earthly utility, not excepting it nevertheless.   It is the privilege of the imaginative, that they include everything which is good, besides
seeing a germ of it at the core of the thorniest evil.

We put these words, " let us think," within marks
of quotation, for a reason very proper to mention in
this place ; for we scarcely ever begin meditating at
twilight without calling them to mind as uttered to
us by the beloved parent to whom we are indebted for
most of our aspirations after anything useful or beautiful.   She would say to us sometimes at this hour,
when our spirits appeared to her to be a little too in-
cessant, " Come — let us *think* a little."   And then
we used to sit down on a stool at her side, and look
at the fire, and be led into a sedate mood by some
story she would tell us of her own mother, or of the
sea, or of some great and good people of old.

So now this is good hushing time, is it not, reader?
and fit for keeping a little from the candles ; and not
what our ultra lively friend (now growing remorseful)

would make of it. You and we are sitting on each side of the fireplace, one of us with a knee between his hands, the other with a child between his knees, and there is a fair friend with us, and we are all as quiet as mice, our faces lit up by the fire, and our shadows shifting on the wall. When we speak, it is in a low voice; for twilight has this also in common with the sweetest of its friends : —

> "Its voice is ever soft, gentle and low —
> An excellent thing in Twilight."

W. L. R. shall come in among us, if he is " very good."

W. L. R. You see before you, sir, a penitent.

Writer. I see before me a suspicious quoter of impudent plays.

W. L. R. I appeal to the lady's face, sir.

Writer. O, you're a very cunning appellant, sir, and the lady's face will get you a pardon for anything. — There — don't tumble over the little boy. But with what face you can come in, after saying you are " no lover " —

W. L. R. Excuse me. Whatever I might have said before, real or pretended, and whatever new presumption I may be guilty of now, nobody can look on this lady's face without —

Writer. Hush, hush ; not so very loud and enthusiastic. (*All laugh.*) You see how little he was in earnest. The moment he hears of a comfortable party and a charming woman, he is for being in the midst of it, twilight and all. — Come, as we are Christian people, we will give him, by way of penance, what shall be no penance at all. He shall recite to us Coleridge's poem, entitled Frost at Midnight. There is mention in it of a fireside and of the little fluttering film on the bars before us ; and the spirit of the whole piece is suited to the occasion, quiet, reflective, and universal. The last line is the perfection of ideal sympathy.

W. L. R. (Suppressing the vehemence of his enthusiasm, in order to recite with a gentleness fitted to the lines, and gradually growing softer and more seasonable, till nothing can be better given.)

FROST AT MIDNIGHT.

The frost performs its secret ministry,
Unhelped by any wind. The owlet's cry
Came loud—and hark, again ! loud as before.
The inmates of my cottage, all at rest,
Have left me to that solitude, which suits
Abstruser musings : save that at my side
My cradled infant slumbers peacefully.
'Tis calm indeed ! so calm, that it disturbs
And vexes meditation with its strange
And extreme silentness. Sea, hill, and wood,
This populous village ! Sea, and hill, and wood,
With all the numberless goings on of life,
Inaudible as dreams ! the thin blue flame
Lies on my low-burnt fire, and quivers not ;
Only that film, which fluttered on the grate,
Still flutters there, the sole unquiet thing.
Methinks, its motion in this hush of nature
Gives it dim sympathies with me who live,
Making it a companionable form,
Whose puny flaps and freaks the idling spirit
By its own moods interprets, everywhere
Echo or mirror seeking of itself,
And makes a toy of thought.

But O ! how oft,
How oft, at school, with most believing mind,
Presageful, have I gazed upon the bars,
To watch that fluttering stranger ! and as oft
With unclosed lids, already had I dreamt
Of my sweet birth-place, and the old church-tower,

Whose bells, the poor man's only music, rang
From morn to evening, all the hot Fair-day,
So sweetly, that they stirred and haunted me
With a wild pleasure, falling on mine ear
Most like articulate sounds of things to come!
So gazed I, till the soothing things I dreamt
Lulled me to sleep, and sleep prolonged my dreams!
And so I brooded all the following morn,
Awed by the stern preceptor's face, mine eye
Fixed with mock study on my swimming book:
Save if the door half opened, and I snatched
A hasty glance, and still my heart leaped up,
For still I hoped to see the *stranger's* face,
Townsman, or aunt, or sister more beloved,
My playmate when we both were clothed alike!
Dear babe, that sleepest cradled by my side,
Whose gentle breathings, heard in this deep calm,
Fill up the interspersed vacancies
And momentary pauses of the thought:
My babe so beautiful! it thrills my heart
With tender gladness, thus to look at thee,
And think that thou shalt learn far other lore
And in far other scenes! For I was reared
In the great city, pent 'mid cloisters dim,
And saw nought lovely but the sky and stars.
But thou, my babe! shalt wander like a breeze
By lakes and sandy shores, beneath the crags
Of ancient mountain, and beneath the clouds,
Which image in their bulk both lakes and shores
And mountain crags: so shalt thou see and hear
The lovely shapes and sounds intelligible
Of that eternal language, which thy God
Utters, who from eternity doth teach
Himself in all, and all things in himself.
Great universal Teacher! he shall mould
Thy spirit, and by giving make it ask.

Therefore all seasons shall be sweet to thee,
Whether the summer clothe the general earth
With greenness, or the redbreast sit and sing
Betwixt the tufts of snow on the bare branch
Of mossy apple-tree, while the nigh thatch
Smokes in the sun-thaw: whether the eavedrops fall,
Heard only in the trances of the blast,
Or if the secret ministry of frost
  Shall hang them up in silent icicles,
  Quietly shining to the quiet moon.

1834.

TABLE WITS.—A BREAKFAST.

IT is expected, we understand, that we shall begin our second volume * with something very piquant. This is an awful announcement. To be called upon for a bon-mot is embarrassing. To be expected to be amusing for eight good octavo pages, is at least equal to calling upon a man for half an hour's much interesting chat, all on his own side. Then there is the sensation which singers have, when they are told that the company are " all attention."

Some persons, when they expect you to be witty, do not even reconcile the announcement by an implied compliment. They look upon it as all in the way of business. As a baker has his hot rolls by eight o'clock, so an author, they think, is to have his essays. Twopenny loaves are the trade of one; twopenny Indicators of the other. The same expense of the faculties is supposed to go to the making of either. The printer composes for his bread; so does the author. The cook melts down another animal's brains with great equanimity; the author, of course, likewise.

As we are to be full of good things in our present number, we take a refuge very common to those who have no better, and invite the reader to discuss (a word, by the by, of much injured metaphorical commonplace, which we hereby restore to its ingenuity) †

---

* Of that pleasant little periodical, The Indicator. — ED.

† "Table and conversation interchange their metaphors," says Hunt, in his Table-Talk. "We *devour* wit and argument, and *discuss* a turkey and chine." — ED.

some rolls and ham with us. It is astonishing what good company a gentleman can make himself by means of this kind. A breakfast may be eloquent; a dinner is sure to be so. The very decanting of his wine shall " discourse excellent music " for him. His good things are all of the best, substantial, and intelligible. He is solid over his beef. His *jeu d'esprit* is a bottle of soda. " A leetle more of the sounds? " — " a leetle stewed lobster? " — " a leetle more lemon to the currie? " — " some stuffing? " — " more grouse? " " let me recommend this blanc-mange — this cream pancake — this custard with your tart — these brandy apricots — these olives — a devil — hah ! (smacking his lips) this is the old wine I told you of, sure enough : " — phrases of this kind, judiciously administered, shall outrival twice as many bon-mots. They shall produce a profound sensation, — an absolute severity of satisfaction. We have known a gentleman, remarkable for a certain festive taciturnity, sit at the head of his table ; and, by dint of these commendatory syllables, united to the reputation of knowing more than he said, make a wit feel doubtful of the merit of being facetious, and fearful how he interrupted so intense a conviviality.

And here (before the rolls come up) we may notice a compromising kind of it, which would see fair play between ideas and no ideas, and might be imitated to advantage by those who would willingly say something and yet nothing. Polite conversation, as detailed by Swift, has had its day ; so that if the genteel have no new novel or scandal to discourse of, they will rather say nothing than not appear knowing or literary. The jokes about " my Lord Mayor's fool," and " none the better for seeing you," and " Tom, how is it you can't see the wood for trees," have been superseded by the periodical publications. Now the wittock we speak of (to use a Scotch diminutive) is akin to punning, inasmuch as it plays upon words; so that at any rate, some verbal knowledge is requisite for those who handle it; and herein the advantage proposed to the dining circles is evident. It is practised with great applause by a friend of ours, and may be called the Art of Translating a Language into itself. Thus, to break, signifying also to fracture, and fast, being, in one sense, the same as rapid, the wag in question calls breakfasting, Fracturing one's Rapid. Cold mutton he translates into Frigid Sheep. Foreign pickle is Peregrine Pickle. Some bacon is a Piece of the Viscount St. Albans; — or in removing bacon for some other dish, he recommends you to put it

"Nigh where the goodly Verulam stood of yore."

Greens are Verdants, and as verd means green, and green means inexperienced, and ants has a sound like aunts, he calls them, by a diffuser version, Inexperienced Sisters of one's Father. Pulling the bell, is Romping with the Beauty; and bringing up the urn, Educating the Sarcophagus. There is eminent authority for this kind of translation into other languages, — as the Latin conversion, attributed to Dr. Johnson, of a tea chest into the second person singular of the verb doceo, to teach; and Hogarth's epistolary drawing, inviting a friend, in three Greek letters, to Eta Beta Pi. But our friend contrives to be learned, while adhering to his own language, and pours forth a profusion of synonymous trifling, which we, of all persons, shall certainly not quarrel with, seeing that he does it out of the delight of escaping from his studies, and feeling his kindred or his friends about him. We were much pleased the other day, for his sake, in hearing of an eminent living philosopher of our acquaintance who, in the midst of his white locks, still retains his love of verbal joking, and delights to help his young companions to a jest as well as some soup. He lets, in particular, his political spleen take breath by it. One dish, which he is fondest of cutting up, he calls after such and such a statesman. He shakes his head at another, and says there is too much High Church in it. To your veal he recommends a squeeze of the judge.

· An old schoolfellow of ours, with whom we used to breakfast, in high glee, in a study four feet square, possesses, almost beyond any man we ever met with, this talent of converting one idea into another, and being equally merry in his mirth and his gravity. We remember the irresistible effect which his reception of a beating from the master used to have upon us all. His gesticulations of agony were so abrupt, varied, and extravagant, that the master and the boys used to be equally perplexed, — the latter how to keep themselves from laughing out loud, and the former whether to take it as something extremely wretched or contemptuous. Either expression was equally unusual in a school so well attempered as ours. He was found out at last, and compelled to take care of his jokes. His gravity, however, was under

suspicion to the last. When the master was about
to retire from his office, he received, for an exercise,
a set of Latin verses from him, in which there was a
pathetic adieu, apostrophizing him under the title of
" Reverende Magister." The old gentleman, not
much accustomed to the melting mood at any time, or
to the dry one often, turned round to him with a face
of ludicrous gratitude, and said, " Thank ye, P." He
used to perplex him also, as well as us all, by taking
advantage of a permission we had of being facetious
in verse-making, and giving up the most extravagant
versions of English nursery songs, such as Jack and
Gill, and When I was a Bachelor. Like all young
wits who are scholars, he liked to give ludicrous dignity to commonplaces by the gravity of a learned
language. He kept his tea and sugar memorandums
in Latin; used to call out for the boy who kept a
door, under the title of Janitor Aulæ; and gave us a
little pocket edition of Buchanan, which we have now
by us, as a pledge and MONUMENT of his friendship, — " Pignus et monumentum." He said of a
fellow-wag, who was accustomed to exaggerate,
" When so and so relates a story, you must multiply
by hundreds, divide by thousands, and make allowance in the quotient for Oriental grandeur." The
same spirit accompanied him to college, where, it is
understood, he might have got what classical honors
he pleased, had not the gravity of his answers at exam-
ination been questionable. He then went into orders,
and became remarkable for the dignity of his voice and
manner in the pulpit, while he retained all the jocose
part of his character among his friends. " What words"

(literally) " have we not heard at the Mermaid? " —
No man ever got up a little festive meeting with a more
orthodox grace.   If port was not liked by any one, he
found a bottle of claret by his plate ; and we shall
always retain a grateful recollection of his olives.   It
is a fault sometimes found with wits, and justly, that
their animal spirits carry them away from a proper
attentiveness to others.   This never was his case.   He
had a handsome faculty, not only of being pleasant
himself, but of extracting all that could be got out of
others.   To strangers he would sometimes be more dis-
concerting, like Swift ; to whom, by the way, he bore
some resemblance, if the Dean's picture in Sharpe's
edition of the Spectator is a good likeness.   He turned
round once upon a man in Holborn, and asked him,
with an air of zealous appeal, whether he had ever
injured his wife and family ; upon which the astonished passenger declaring he had not, " Then, sir,"
said he, " I will thank you, another time, not to tread
my shoe down at heel."   There was a huge fellow
one evening making a great noise in a coffee-house,
about a prize ox he had seen.   " I have heard of the
carcass," says P.   " The carcass ! " cries the other, with
a sort of triumph of knowledge : — " it's alive, sir ;
it's alive ; and live bodies are not called carcasses."
" Good," says the other, looking at him, " but I presume
they may deserve the name."   He said this with so indifferent and yet so particular an air, that neither the man
could be offended nor the company refrain from laughing.   At another time, being in the cider cellar in
Maiden Lane, and one of our party having said something in Latin, without the least intention of being

overheard, a military gentleman, somewhat irritable with having more wine than wit, said out loud, that he did not conceive a public room a fit place to talk Latin in. We forget what our schoolfellow said to this: but in consequence of his enlisting the company on our side with his jokes, the captain proposed to give him his address. " Sir," says P., with great gravity, " you need not trouble yourself with a specimen: I never had any doubt of your being a man of address." " Sir," returned the captain more vehemently, his voice a little titubating with wine — " You will not — then — take my address?" " O, excuse me, sir," replied the other, " I do take it infinitely; and all the rest of us take it." By this time the amusement of the audience had much increased. " Sir!" repeated the officer, half rising from his seat, and tumbling a little towards him, with pipe in hand, and angry wonder in his eye, — " I say, sir, — do you mean to say, sir, — you know what I mean — I mean to say, sir, I'll give you my address; that's what I mean." " But, sir," retorted our inflexible companion, " you must allow me to say that your liberality is really superfluous; since, to confess the truth, I really don't at all approve of your address." At this the tottering man (who, you might see by his face was good-humored enough, and worth being parried in this way by a gentleman) staggered up to his antagonist, and held out his hand to him, declaring he was one of the pleasantest fellows he ever met with in the whole course of his life, and nothing should induce him to quarrel with him.

We do not profess any practical science in meals.

Those who do will despise us at once, when they hear that we prefer breakfast and tea to dinner, and that by breakfast, we mean a very common one." * But we know what belongs to a meal. There was a lay-schoolfellow of ours, who was always proposing to treat some of us at a tavern; though he never did. He contented himself with casting up what he called "the damages." He used to cry out on a sudden, "It doesn't signify talking, but we will have that dinner I spoke of this afternoon. Come, now; I'm serious. Let us see what will be the damages?" He would then take pen, ink, and paper, and fall to making out a grave list of fish, flesh, and tart; till the exceeding wish to realize it, almost made dupes of our cloistered imaginations for the seventh time. The worst of it was, that he himself used to go home and feast on what he had been speaking of; while we were rung up in the hall, and dined like the monks of La Trappe. We shall reverse the spirit of this vagary. Our breakfast will be upon paper, but our readers shall have more than we are in the habit of seeing on our table. Students are at once tempted to exceed, and obliged to be temperate. The exhaustion of their faculties excites them to indulge a morbid appetite; while the delicacy of stomach produced by that exhaustion, makes them cautious how they render it greater next time.

What shall we say then? For " it does not signify

* "It seems," says Fuller, in speaking of the ravens that brought Elijah bread and flesh in the morning and evening, "it seems dinners are but innovations, whilst breakfasts and suppers are men's most ancient and natural meals." — *A Pisgah Sight of Palestine*, chapter 3, paragraph 17. — ED.

talking." We will have the breakfast he spoke of.
And here it is, ready laid. Imprimis, tea and coffee,;
secondly, dry toast; thirdly, butter; fourthly, eggs;
fifthly, ham; sixthly, something potted; seventhly,
bread, salt, mustard, knives and forks, &c. One of the
first things that belong to a breakfast is a good fire.
There is a delightful mixture of the lively and the
snug in coming down into one's breakfast-room of a
cold morning, and seeing everything prepared for us;
a blazing grate, a clean table-cloth and tea things, the
newly-washed faces and combed heads of a set of
good-humored urchins, and the sole empty chair at
its accustomed corner, ready for occupation. When
we lived alone, we could not help reading at meals:
and it is certainly a delicious thing to resume an entertaining book at a particularly interesting passage,
with a hot cup of tea at one's elbow, and a piece of
buttered toast in one's hand. The first look at the
page, accompanied by a coexistent bite of the toast,
comes under the head of intensities. But when in
company, unless it is of a very private and pardoning
description, it is, of course, not to be done, unless all
read; and a general reading in company is a sort of
understood talking. The most allowable perusal is
that of a newspaper. It involves a common interest,
and is in itself a very sufficing and matutine thing. But
we have enlarged on the pleasure of a breakfast paper elsewhere, in an article entitled A Day by the
Fire; which, by the way, will prevent us from indulging ourselves in other particulars appertaining to
the present subject. We have it not by us, nor are
we aware that we have before mentioned what we are

going to notice : but we wish to observe, that ladies, always delightful, and not the least so in their undress, are apt to deprive themselves of some of their best morning beams by appearing with their hair in papers. We give notice that essayists, and of course all people of taste, prefer a cap, if there must be anything : but hair, a million times over. To see grapes in paper bags is bad enough, but the rich locks of a lady in papers, the roots of the hair twisted up like a drummer's, and the forehead staring bald instead of being gracefully tendrilled and shadowed! — it is a capital offence, — a defiance to the love and admiration of the other sex, — a provocative to a paper war : and we here accordingly declare the said war on paper, not having any ladies at hand to carry it at once into their headquarters. We must allow, at the same time, that they are very shy of being seen in this condition, knowing well enough how much of their strength, like Samson's, lies in that gifted ornament. We have known a whole parlor of them flutter off, like a dovecot, at the sight of a friend coming up the garden.

But to return to our table. Ham is a good thing, but it is apt to fever our sedentary notions. We prefer cracking the round end of an egg with the back of a silver spoon, — not a horn spoon, which is flimsy and inefficient. A judicious jerk of the former upon a good, fair, dome-like shell issuing out of the egg cup, maketh a pretty result to the sensations. We cannot, in conscience, recommend hot buttered toast ; but it is a pleasing guilt. The best adventure to which it can give rise, is when you have modestly taken one of the outside pieces, and find your gentility rewarded by carrying off the whole of the crumb part of the inner one, the crust of which has been detached. Chocolate has a nutty taste, but is heavy. Coffee is heating, but has a fine, serious flavor in it, if well done. You seem to taste the color of it. We used to prefer it at all times, but tea has become preferable to the meditative state of our digestion. How the Chinese came to invent it, as Sancho would say, we do not know: but it is the most ingenious, humane, and poetical of their discoveries. It is their epic poem   1820.

GOING TO THE PLAY AGAIN.

WITH the exception of Oberon, we have not witnessed a theatrical performance till the other night for these six or seven years. Fortune took us another way; and when we had the opportunity we did not dare to begin again, lest our old friends should beguile us. We mention the circumstance, partly to account for the notice we shall take of many things which appear to have gone by; and partly out of a communicativeness of temper, suitable to a Companion. For the reader must never lose sight of our claims to that title. On ordinary occasions, he must remember that we are discussing morals or mince-pie with him; on political ones, reading the newspaper with him; and in the present instance, we are sitting together in the pit (the ancient seat of

criticism), seeing *who* is *who* in the play-bill, and
hearing the delicious discord of the tuning of instruments, — the precursor of harmony. If our companion is an old gentleman, we take a pinch of his snuff,
and lament the loss of Bannister and Mrs. Jordan.
Toothache and his nephew occupy also a portion of
our remark ; and we cough with an air of authority.
If he is a young gentleman, we speak of Vestris and
Miss Foote ; wonder whether little Goward will show
herself improving to-night ; denounce the absurdity
of somebody's boots, or his bad taste in beauty ; and
are loud in deprecating the fellows who talk loudly
behind us. Finally, if a lady, we bend with delight
to hear the remarks she is making, " far above " criticism ; and to see the finer ones in her eyes. We
criticise the ladies in the boxes ; and the more she
admires them, the more we find herself the lovelier.
May we add, that ladies in the pit, this cold weather,
have still more attractions than usual ; and that it is
cruel to find ourselves sitting, as we did the other
night, behind two of them, when we ought to have
been in the middle, partaking of the genial influence
of their cloaks, their comfortable sides, and their conversation? We were going to say, that we hope this
is not too daring a remark for a Companion : — but
far be it from us to apologize for anything so proper.
Don't we all go to the theatre to keep up our love of
nature and sociality?

It was delightful to see " the house " again, and
to feel ourselves recommencing our old task. How
pleasant looked the ceiling, the boxes, the pit, everything ! Our friends in the gallery were hardly noisy

19

enough for a beginning; nor, on the other hand, could
we find it in our hearts to be angry with two companions behind us, who were a little noisier than they
ought to have been, and who entertained one another
with alternate observations on the beauty of the songs
and the loss of a pair of gloves. All is pleasant in
these recommencements of a former part of one's life;
this new morning, as it were, re-begun with the lustre
of chandeliers and a thousand youthful remembran-
ces. Anon the curtain rises, and we are presented
with a view of the lighthouse of Genoa, equally delicious and unlike, — some gunboats returning from
slavery, salute us with meek puffs of gunpowder,
about as audible as pats on the cheek, — the most con-
siderate cannon we ever met with: — then follow a
crowd and a chorus, with embraces of redeemed captives, meeting their wives and children, at which we
are new and uncritical enough to feel the tears come
into our eyes; and, finally, in comes Mr. "Atkins,"
with a thousand memories on his head, — husband
that was of a pretty little singer some twenty years
back, now gone, Heaven knows where, like a black-
-bird. It seemed wrong in Atkins to be there, and
his wife not with him. Yet we were glad to see him
notwithstanding. We knew him the instant we heard
him speak.

Native Land (a title, by the by, which looks like
one of the captives, with an arm off) is worth going
to see, for those who care little about plot or dialogue,
provided there be good music. Part of the music is
by Mr. Bishop, the rest from Rossini. It is seldom
that any of Mr. Bishop's music is not worth hearing,

and one or two of the airs are among Rossini's finest.
There is *Di piacer*, for instance ; and we believe another, which we did not stay to hear. We fear it is a
little out of the scientific pale to think Rossini a man of
genius ; but we confess, with all our preference for such
writers as Mozart, with whom, indeed, he is not to be
compared, we do hold that opinion of the lively Italian. There is genius of many kinds, and of kinds
very remote from one another, even in rank. The
greatest genius is so great a thing that another may
be infinitely less, and yet of the stock. Now Rossini,
in music, is the genius of sheer animal spirits. It is
a species as inferior to that of Mozart, as the clever-
ness of a smart boy is to that of a man of sentiment ;
but it is genius nevertheless. It is rare, effective, and
a part of the possessor's character : — we mean, that
like all persons who really affect anything beyond the
common, it belongs and is peculiar to him, like the
invisible genius that was supposed of old to wait
upon individuals. This is what genius means ; and
Rossini undoubtedly has one. " He hath a devil,"
as Cowley's friend used to cry out when he read Virgil ; and a merry devil it is, and graceful withal. It
is a pity he has written so many commonplaces, so
many bars full of mere chatter, and overtures so full
of cant and puffing. But this exuberance appears to
be a constituent part of him. It is the hey-day in his
blood ; and perhaps we could no more have the good
things without it than some men of wit can talk well
without a bottle of wine and in the midst of a great
deal of nonsense. Now and then he gives us something worthy of the most popular names of his coun-

try, as in the instance above mentioned. *Di piacer*
is full of smiling delight and anticipation, as the words
imply. Sometimes he is not deficient even in tenderness, as in one or two airs in his Othello; but it is
his liveliest operas, such as the *Barbiere di Séviglia*
and the *Italiana in Algieri* that he shines. His
mobs make some of the pleasantest riots conceivable;
his more gentlemanly proceedings, his bows and compliments, are full of address and even elegance, and
he is a prodigious hand at a piece of pretension or
foppery. Not to see into his merit in these cases, surely implies only, that there is a want of animal spirits
on the part of the observer.

As we are not so fond of sharp criticism, as when
we were young and knew not what it was to feel it,
we shall say nothing of one or two of the fair singers
on this occasion, except that they did not appear to
have a sufficient stock of the spirits we have been
speaking of. To animal spirits, animal spirits alone
can do justice. A burst of joy will be ill represented
by the sweetest singing in the world that is not joyous, and that does not burst forth like a shower of
blossoms. Of Miss Goward's singing we can yet
form no judgment, as she had a very bad cold; but
she did her best with it, and did not apologize, which
gave us a favorable opinion of her; and her acting
increased it. If she does not turn out to be a very
judicious person, with a good deal of humor, she will
disappoint us. Madame Vestris, though she does not
insinuate a sufficient stock of sentiment through her
gayeties to complete the proper idea of a charmer to
our taste, is always charming after her fashion; but

from what we recollect of her, we doubt whether her performance in this piece is one of her favorite ones. The song of Is't art, I pray, or Nature? she gave with too little vivacity; and her part in the *bolero* she seemed to go through more as a duty than a pleasure — which is anything but *boleresque*. Mr. Wood has great sweetness of voice, with taste and sensibility; and the sweetness is manly. He was encored in the " romance " — Deep in a Dungeon ; but we preferred him in his first pleasing air, Farewell, thou Coast of Glory. We shall be glad to see him again, and to say more of him. We suspect he has more power than he yet puts forth.

There is no necessity to criticise the dialogue. The author himself probably regards it as being nothing more than one of our old unpretending acquaintances, yclept " vehicles for music ; " carriers of song, as Messrs. Clementi's are of piano-fortes. There is one scene, however, upon which we shall say a word. It is that in which a maimed husband comes back from the wars, and is received by his wife with aversion and ridicule. It is true the caricature is evident ; it is the only way in which such feelings can be made ludicrous; but there is something in it from which the heart revolts. It is a dangerous point to divert ridicule from its proper objects, and give degrading representations of humanity. There is something, too, on these especial occasions, when the joke is carried far (as is the case in violent double meanings in company), by which privacy itself is turned into publicity, and we become painfully conscious of the presence of those, with whom we could best interchange the most pleasurable ideas. We profess to be anything but prudes; we have no objection, for instance, to Zanina's being reconciled to " little fellows," whose ways are delightful; — but because we are not prudish, we become the more jealous in behalf of what may be called the humanities of license.

We must own we could not help laughing at some passages of Miss Goward's acting in this scene; and perhaps we scan the matter somewhat too nicely. Those who laughed most would probably have been among the first to hug the remnant of their maimed friends to their heart. But the experiment is dangerous. There is not too much sentiment in society after all; and it is better not to risk what there is. With what relief did we not call to mind, in our graver moments, the sight we had once, in those boxes, on the left hand, of a charming woman sitting next her gallant husband, Colonel C., who had returned from the wars with the frightful loss of his lower jaw. His wife married him after his return; and this, we were told, was she. He had his mouth and chin muffled up. But how did he not seem more than repaid in her sweet and loving presence, which we fancied that she pressed still closer to him than was visible in that of any other woman seated by her husband's side. When she looked in his face, we felt as if we could almost have been content to have lost the power of kissing with lips, that we might have received in all its beauty that kiss of the soul.

1828.

LADIES' BONNETS IN THE THEATRE.

IN default of having anything better to write about in our present number, we beg leave to remonstrate with certain bonnets, and other enormities, with which the ladies put out our eyesight in the theatres. The bonnet is the worst. If you sit right behind it, it shall swallow up the whole scene. It makes nothing of a regiment of soldiers, or a mountain, or a forest, or a rising sun ; much less of a hero, or so insignificant a thing as a cottage and a peasant's family. You may sit at the theatre a whole evening and not see the leading performer. Liston's face is a glory obscured. The persons in your neighborhood, provided they have no bonneted ladies before them, shall revel in the jocose looks of Farren or Dowton, and provokingly reflect the merriment in their own countenances, while you sit and rage in the shade. If you endeavor to strain a point, and peep by the side of it, ten to one (since Fate notoriously interferes in little things, and delights in being " contrary," as the young ladies say) — ten to one but the bonnet seizes that very opportunity of jerking sideways, and cutting off your resources. We have seen an enthusiastic playgoer settle himself in his seat, and evidently congratulate himself at the evening he was about to enjoy, when a party of ladies, swimming into the seats before him, have been the ruin of all his prospects. Even a head-dress, without the bonnet,

shall force you to play at bo-peep with the stage half
the evening; now extinguishing the face of some favorite actress, and now abolishing a general or a
murder. The other night, at the Queen's Theatre,
we sometimes found ourselves obliged to peep at the
Freemasons in a very symbolical manner through the
loops of a lady's bows. But the bonnet is the enor-'
mity. And we are sorry to say that the fair occu-
pants who sit inside them, like the lady in the lobster,
too often show a want of gallantry in refusing to take
them off; for, as we have said more than once, we
hold gallantry, like all the other virtues, to be a thing
mutual, and of both sexes; and that a lady shows as
much want of gallantry in taking advantage of the
delicacies observed towards her by the gentlemen, as
a man does who presumes upon the gentleness of a
lady. We felt, the other night, all the reforming
spirit of our illustrious predecessors of the Tatler and
Spectator roused within us, and in the same exact
proportion to our regard for the sex upon witnessing
the following prodigious fact: A lady, who came
with a party into one of the boxes at Covent Garden,
joined very heartily in expressing her disapprobation
of some person in a seat below her, who was dilatory
in taking off his hat. It chanced that this lady got
into the very seat that he had occupied, and her bonnet turning out to be a much greater blind than the
hat, what was the astonishment and the merriment of
the complainants, upon finding that she was still less
accommodating than the gentleman? Nothing could
induce her to perform the very same piece of justice
which she had joined in demanding from the other.

We are aware that in modern, as in ancient theatres, ladies come to be seen as well as to see.

" Spectatum veniunt, veniunt spectentur ut ipsæ."

But we are desirous that they should not pay themselves so ill a compliment as to confound their dresses
with themselves; it is the bonnets that are seen, in
these cases, and not the ladies. When seen themselves, they make a part of the spectacle, but who
cares to look upon these great lumps of gauze and
silk? Something is to be allowed to fashion, but the
wearers might be content with showing that their
heads could be as absurd as other people's, and then
lay aside the absurdity, and show that they understood the better part of being reasonable. They urge,
when requested to take their bonnets off, that they
" cannot" do it; meaning, we suppose, besides the
" will not," which " cannot" so often signifies, that
their heads are not prepared to be seen — that their
hair is not dressed in the proper manner; but it would
be easy to come with it so dressed; the bonnet is *not*
the only head-dress in fashion; and, above all, it
would be a graceful and a sensible thing to remember,
that in coming to a place where the object is to enjoy
pleasure, their own capability of pleasure is interested
in considering that of others. We never feel angry
with a woman except when she persists in doing
something to diminish the delight we take in complimenting the sex.

1831.

MOLIÈRE'S TARTUFFE.

THERE is something very delightful in the friend-
liness of intercourse that has sprung up between
France and England since the late troubles. Cabi-
nets may quarrel again, and wars be renewed; but
the more intimacy there is in the mean time between
the two nations, the less they will be disposed to be
gulled into those royal amusements. Formerly this
kind of intercourse was confined to kings and courtiers; and whenever these gentlemen were disposed to
pick a quarrel with one another, the people were sent
on to fight, like retainers to a couple of great houses;
their employers all the while making no more of the
business than if they were playing a game of chess.
Nations are growing wiser on this head; and nothing
will serve better to secure their wisdom than an interchange of their socialities and an acquaintance with
the great writers that have made them what they are.

It was with singular pleasure, therefore, that we
found ourselves, the other night, sitting at a French
play in the British metropolis, and that play Molière's.
There, on the stage, was Molière, as it were himself;
there spoke his very words, warm as when he first
uttered them; there he triumphed over hypocrisy,
and was wise and entertaining and immortal. But
what, in the mean time, had become of Louis the
Fourteenth and his splendor? What of all those lords
and courtiers, who used to make a brilliant assemblage

around him (we could not help fancying them in this
very pit), and praising or withholding their praise of
the immortal man, as the king spoke or held his
tongue? Gone is all that once filled that splendid
" parterre," like the flowers of any other garden :
gone all their plumes, and ribbons, and pulvilio, and
their bowing gallantries, and the very love that here
and there lurked among them, like a violet among
the tulips : but there stood the spirit of Molière, as
fresh as ever, and casting on their memory (when
you thought of it) its only genuine lustre.

It is curious to think how this great writer had to
win his way into toleration through the prejudices
attached to a stage life ; and how he depended upon
men who were comparatively nothing for an intima-
tion to the rest of the world, that a great and original genius was really worth something. It is to the
credit of Louis, that he managed his kingship in this
matter in good taste, and allowed the genius of Molière to be pitted against the marquises and grimaciers
of his court. If he had not stood by him, those butterflies the *petits-maîtres*, and those blackbeetles the
priests, had fairly stifled him. It was lucky that he
wrote when the king was no older, and before he had
become superstitious. It gives one a prodigious idea
of the assumption of those times, and the low pitch at
which an actor could be rated in spite of his being a
great genius, that a shallow man of quality having
found something ridiculous in Molière's mention of
a " cream tart " in one of his comedies, and not liking
the raillery with which the author treated his criticism, contrived to lay hold of his head one day as the

actor made him a bow, and crying out, " *Tarte à la crême, Molière! Tarte à la crême!*" rubbed his face against his cut-steel buttons, till it was covered with blood. For this brutality it never entered any one's head that an actor could have a remedy except in complaining to the king; which the poet did, and the peer was disgraced. Another anecdote, to the same purport, is more agreeably relieved. Molière, by way of being honored, and set on a level with gentlemen, had been made one of his Majesty's valets-de-chambre. Presenting himself one day to make the royal bed, his helper abruptly retired, saying that he should not make it " with an actor." Bellocq, another valet-de-chambre, a man of a good deal of wit, and a maker of pretty verses, happening to come in at this juncture, said, " Perhaps M. de Molière will do me the honor of allowing *me* to make the king's bed with him." Molière was a man of great heart, very generous, but sensitive also, and subject, in the midst of his pleasantries, to that melancholy which is so often found in the company of wit. Any delicacy towards him must, therefore, have been extremely felt, though on the subject of scorn and arrogance he, doubtless, had no proportionate soreness at heart. His wisdom and genuine superiority must have saved him from that. It was on the side of his sympathies, and not his antipathies, that Molière was weak. He troubled himself with a wife too young for him : and after having ridiculed jealousy in his comedies, was fain to acknowledge that he felt it in all its bitterness himself. Candor takes away the degrading part of these mortifications, but the sting is there, nevertheless.

What endears us the more to his sincerity, and to the
habitual kindness of his heart, is his saying to his
friend Chappelle, whom he made his father confessor
on this occasion, that " finding how impossible it was
to conquer his jealousy, he began to think that it
might be equally impossible in the object of his affections to get rid of her coquetry." The worst of
it was, that their ages were unequal. His young wife
(the daughter of an actress in his *corps dramatique*,
which gave rise to a scandal refuted by the date of
their connection) was herself an actress, beautiful,
and surrounded with admirers. She probably loved
the poet as well as she could, but found that she loved
people of her own age better; while he, taking his
undying admiration of beauty for a right to possess it,
forgot, till too late, that poets' hearts remain young
much longer than their persons. The consequence
was, that two people, both of them, perhaps, very
worthy, became a grief and torment to one another,
merely because incompatible marriages are permitted ;
for Molière had been a great ridiculer of marriage,
and there, no doubt, lay a good part of the sting. He
should have gone abroad more out of the society of
his *corps dramatique*, and found some charmer to
love less unsuitable to his time of life. There are
born poetesses, in their way, among the women, whom
temperance and the graces help to keep young even
in person, and often in a more touching manner than
the young and thoughtless. Molière should have laid
his laurelled head in the lap of one of these. She
might have repaid his candor and tenderness with a
like generosity.

But we are forgetting the play. — The house (the Lyceum) opened for these performances last Wednesday. It has been newly fitted up for the purpose, with fresh mouldings or compartments round the boxes (we forget exactly what), and a drapery of scarlet and white, very handsome. The prices, to nearly the whole of the pit, remain the same as before, three and sixpence ; but six shillings are paid for seats on a bench or two, and seven for those in a part of the orchestra. Some boxes may be taken by the evening at two, three, and four guineas, according to the number of persons and the situation of the box. The rest are let for the season at prices which look enormous ; being eighty, one hundred and twenty, or one hundred and sixty guineas for forty nights. The performances will be three times a week, Monday, Wednesday, and Friday, till Lent. Money is not taken at the door. There is a list of the places where you can get tickets, at the bottom of the play-bill, such as the booksellers, in Bond Street ; Marsh's, in Oxford Street ; Wilson's, at the Royal Exchange, &c. We bought ours at Mr. Neele's, a door or two on the left of the main entrance to the theatre out of the Strand ; which we mention in order to show that people may go as usual, with no more trouble than if they paid at the door.

The performances of the evening were Tartuffe, followed by a coronation of the bust of Molière ; *La Fille mal gardée*, a vaudeville in one act, and *L'Ambassadeur*, another, in which Perlet, who acted Tartuffe, and who is the principal performer of the company, reappeared in the chief character. We shall confine ourselves to the first piece, which, in-

decd, is the only one we saw, and which is quite
sufficient to see and to think about for one time. Our .
observations upon it will not be directed to scholars
only, and readers of French; but, agreeably to the
plan pursued by us in a former publication, we shall
endeavor to give all such readers as have a relish for
what is good, a taste of it somehow or other, let them
have missed scholarship, great or small, as they may.
French is a very common acquirement; yet there are
numbers unable to read even French, who very much
deserve to do so, and who have a genuine perception
of a good thing when it comes before them.

Few readers need be informed, but all will be glad
to know, that the comedy of Tartuffe (from which our
popular play of the Hypocrite is taken, which made
the selection of it on this occasion every way judicious) may be ranked among the *avant couriers* of
the knowledge and liberality of these times. It is a
masterly satire upon religious hypocrisy; and on its
first appearance at Paris, in an age full of well-fed devo-
tees and gallant confessors, was received accordingly.
The first three acts were brought out originally before
the court at Versailles, in the year 1664; but what
may be called the first public representation of the
entire piece did not take place till 1667, when it was
performed at Paris, and prohibited next day by an
order from the First President of Parliament. Molière himself had to announce the prohibition, which
he did in the following manner: " Gentlemen, we
reckoned this evening upon having the honor of presenting you with the Hypocrite; but Monsieur the
First President does not wish us to play him." Our

author must have reckoned very confidently on the
- king's protection to be able to joke in this manner.*
The time, indeed, was lucky for him so far. Louis
was then young and gay, and equally victorious in war
and gallantry. He had a minister the avowed patron
of men of letters (Colbert), and a general who loved
humor and original genius (Turenne).† He did not
think fit to let the piece re-appear for a year or two ;
but Molière remained on the best terms with him ;
and, in 1669, Tartuffe rose again in spite of its enemies, and has remained ever since a stock acting
piece, — the glory of the French stage and the hatred
of bigots and impostors. Perhaps they are more bitter against it in their hearts this very moment than
they have been for these hundred years ; the Jesuits
having trimmed their dark lanterns once more, and
pieces of this kind offering the most insurmountable
barriers against the reaction of priestcraft.‡

It has been thought curious by some, that in the

---

* Another turn was given to this bon-mot in one of the provinces. The bishop, in a place where they were going to perform the comedy, had lately died.
His successor was not equally disposed in favor of theatrical representations ; and
orders were given to the actors that they should quit the town before he made his
appearance, which he was to do the next day. Accordingly, when the time was
come for giving out the performances of the next evening, the announcer, affecting not to know that his lordship was to arrive so soon, said, " The Hypocrite,
gentlemen, to-morrow."

† See in the works of La Fontaine a pleasant account of a chat that took place
on the road between Turenne and that poet, when the former was on his way to
one of his campaigns.

‡ The speech of Father Nitard to the Duke of Lerma may be taken as a specimen of the pitch of insolence, worthy of Tartuffe, to which priests could be transported in those days. He was a Jesuit, and *confessor* to Louis's mother-in-law,
the Queen of Spain. He told the duke one day, "that he ought to treat him
with more respect, as he had every day his God in his hands (the Eucharist) and
his Queen at his feet."

English Hypocrite the ridicule should be confined to
sectarians, while in the original it attacks hypocrites
of the establishment. This is to be accounted for on
a variety of grounds. In the first place, the Catholic
establishment, especially as it existed in France at
that time, did not make such an exclusive matter of
difference of opinion as the hierarchy in England;
while, on the other hand, certain disputes in it were
so fierce, and yet all parties pretended pretty nearly
to such an equal measure of piety, that to make a
heterodox person of the Tartuffe would have been
absolutely to neutralize the satire on hypocrisy. It
would have been a mere party libel. An English
Methodist pretends to peculiar sanctity; but formal-
ists of a similar description in France were hardly
known till a later period. Again, a Catholic establishment is of a much more miscellaneous nature
than a Protestant; admits a host of lay members, and
otherwise affords pretences for quacks and hypocrites
of all sorts. It is a much larger world, in which vice
may be found in the particular, with less offence to
the main body. Then, again, there is confession, and
the admission of interferers and regulators into the
tenderest privacies of life. These people were very
often at variance with the rest of the families whose
heads they lorded it over (as Molière has taken care
to show); they were sometimes very officious in state
matters and at court, where, indeed, the clerical power
claimed a kind of sovereignty of its own, independent
of that of the civil and executive (a pretension against
which our anti-popery men are still warning us);
and, above all, at the time when Molière wrote, the

20

king was not only young and gay, and inclined to
" cut " his religious mortifiers, but the Great Condé,
then in favor, was a sworn enemy of bigots ; the Pope
had not long since been bearded by the French au-
thorities in Rome ; cardinals and bishops were, for
the most part, laymen at heart, and mixed not only
with politics but with the pleasures of life ; in short, the
" cloth," as a matter of any solemnity, was at a disadvantage ; and to pretend to an unusual measure of
sanctity was, in some sort, to offend priests as well as
laymen. Molière himself tells us that he had the
approbation of the Legate ; and that the greater part
of the bishops, to whom he had taken care to read
his work, were " of the same way of thinking as his
Majesty." * Nevertheless, a tremendous cry was
raised against it, even before it appeared. The author
was called, he tells us, a libertine, a blasphemer, a
devil incarnate ; and no sooner was it brought out,
than very worthy people, acted upon by the cries of
bigotry, joined in the wish to have it suppressed. The
President of Parliament, who agreed to become the
instrument of the suppression, was the celebrated
Lamoignon, the friend of Boileau, and reckoned one
of the best men in the world. Boileau helped him,
perhaps, afterwards to a better judgment. Ménage
tells us expressly, that he himself spoke to the President about it, and told him that the moral of the
play was excellent, and calculated to be of public
service.†

Ménage, in the same passage of his book, ventures

---

* "Premier Placet, présenté au Roi, sur la comedie du Tartuffe."
† Menagiana, p. 43. Edit. 1694.

to prefer Molière's prose to his verses. That learned wit had no very great taste in verses at any time, and had been accustomed to a very bad taste in particular, which Molière rooted out. The classical scholar was judicious and generous enough at the time to acknowledge the reformation ; but, perhaps, he never heartily forgot his old propensities. Perhaps, also, he grudged Molière that extraordinary facility in versifying, which Boileau has recorded with astonishment.*

The happy power for which Boileau here praises his friend, is one of the most remarkable things in the Tartuffe. Those who know the Hypocrite of the English stage, know the other in a certain way ; and know it well. But there is no comparison in the two styles ; every word telling with double force in the Frenchman's mouth, and uniting with the familiarity of prose the terseness of wit in rhyme. Let the reader imagine the best colloquial verses of Dryden or Pope, full of wit and humor, uttering the finest knowledge of life, comprising a plot no less interesting than simple, agitating the feelings deeply before they have done, and dismissing the audience in the most generous disposition for truth ; and they have a picture of this great and perfect comedy. An English audience, in their own language, could not relish a comedy in rhyme so well as the French can. Their manners are less conscious and mixed up. They could not so easily take an artificial grace for a natural one. But heard through the dimness of a language not habitual

---

* Ménage tells us, that when he himself sat down to write verses, he first 'got together " his "rhymes ; " and that his rhymes sometimes took him three or four months to "fill up " ! — Id. p. 261.

to us, we become just enough sensible of the grace and power of the versification to admire the comedy the more, without being the less sensible of its truth and nature.

In venturing to lay a scene of it before the reader, we have, therefore, not ventured to do it in rhyme. It is, indeed, an injustice to the author, in one sense, not to do so (supposing we were able to do it) ; but it would be hurting the effect of his truth and humor, which are the greater matters. We have selected the scene more particularly, because it exhibits what we conceive to be the greatest and most original trait in the author's genius; to wit, his delight in putting a good, broad, sustained, and even farcial-looking joke, knowing it to be founded in exquisite truth, and re-solving to relish it with us, unalloyed, for that reason. It is the spirit and *gusto* of the truth, taking place of the formal image ; and only making us hail and in-corporate with it the more. The scene is between Orgon, the credulous master of the house, who makes an idol of Tartuffe, and Dorina, the servant, a great enemy of the impostor, and burning to see him de-tected. Tartuffe has not yet made his appearance, and this is the first time Orgon has made his. Let the reader admire the singular skill with which, in the midst of this " joke run down," the audience are let into the interior of the host's credulity, and of Tartuffe's power and worldliness. Orgon says but two things alternately throughout ; and the performer must be imagined at once giving us a sense of this monotony of ideas, and varying the expression of them for the true comic effect. A little pause must be fancied occasionally, and a face full of meaning. The author of the Hypocrite has not ventured upon it; — but imagine it in the hands of Munden! To complete the scene, Orgon's brother-in-law, another enemy of Tartuffe's, is present, wondering all the while at his infatuation. Orgon has just come from the country, and after interchanging civilities with his brother, begs him to excuse him a little while he talks with the servant, and asks after the welfare of his house. He addresses her accordingly : —

"Well, Dorina, has everything been going on as it should do these two days ? How do they all do? And what have they been about?

Dor. My mistress was ill the day before yesterday with a fever. She had a headache quite dreadful to think of.

Org. And Tartuffe !

Dor. Tartuffe ! O, he is wonderfully well ; fat and hearty, a fresh complexion, and a mouth as red as a rose.

Org. (turning about with an air of fondness). *Poor soul !*

Dor. In the evening my mistress was taken with a sickness, and could not touch a bit of supper, her head was so bad.

Org. And Tartuffe !

Dor. O, seeing she could not eat, he eat by himself; and very devoutly swallowed two partridges, with a good half of a hashed leg of mutton.

Org. Poor soul !

Dor. My mistress did not shut her eyes all night. The fever hindered her from getting a wink of sleep, and we were obliged to watch by her till morning.

Org. And Tartuffe !

Dor. Tartuffe, happy gentleman, with a comfortable yawn, goes right from table to bed, where he plunges into his warm nest, and sleeps soundly till morning.

Org. Poor soul !

Dor. At last we prevailed upon Madame to be bled, which gave her great relief.

Org. And Tartuffe !

Dor. Monsieur Tartuffe was very much relieved also. He found himself charming, and to repair the loss of the blood which Madame had sustained, took four draughts of wine with his breakfast.

Org. Poor soul !

Dor. In short, both are very well now ; so I'll go and tell my mistress you are coming, and how happy you are to hear she is recovered.'"

We have left ourselves very little room to speak of
the actors. In fact, we must see them again before
we can venture to speak much; and then we shall
feel diffident, except in speaking of what all the world
may judge of. French nature is, in some respects, so
different from ours, — we mean that the same nature,
where great passions are not concerned, exhibits
itself in such various ways through the medium of
national manners, — that all critics ought to be cautious how they pronounce upon it, especially those
who know more of the language in books than as it
is spoken; which we confess to be our case. We
shall therefore wait, and judge cautiously. Mean-
time, we cannot help saying, that M. Perlet appears
to us a performer of the very first merit, full, both of
sensibility and judgment, relishing, self-possessed,
various, — " up," as the phrase is, to every situation,
and every part of it; and with an equal perception
of the gravest as well as the lightest things he has to
say. There was an air of singular depth and intention throughout his performance; and when he turned
with that preternatural insolence of heart, after his
detection, and pausing before he spoke, with his arm
up, and an air of frightful preparation, told the master
of the house " to go out of the house himself, for it
was his," — there was something ghastly and awful
in it. The house was so still we felt as if we could
almost have heard the rain out of doors. Yet the
same man, we are told, is wonderful in clowns and
idiots, and is but a young actor. We must not forget
Madame Daudel, a sort of younger Mrs. Davison;
very pleasant. She acted Dorina. 1828.

HEREDITARY HOUSE OF PLAYERS.

THE other day we heard of an indiscreet young Lord; who took it in his head to perform on a private stage, and performed very badly. This is the consequence of people going out of their spheres: an eccentricity, which the wisest cannot be guilty of with impunity. Had this tyro of quality, by the decease of the Peer, his brother, found himself in his right element, that is to say, in the House of Lords, he would, of course, have displayed a talent for legislation, because he inherits it. He may appear, for the present, to be nothing but a dandy and a foolish fellow, but the moment he got there, we should have his first wise speech; and all the speeches that followed would be equally wise. To hear him talk just now, not being a Peer, we allow might lead people to suppose that he could do nothing but swear, and say " By G—d," and gamble, and babble of wine and women; but only let the Peer, his brother, make room for him, only let him seat himself on the magic bench and wisdom shall flow from his lips; no question, however knotty, shall come amiss to him : points, which the House of Commons could not decide, shall come before him to be settled, and he shall settle them well : the whole country shall be satisfied : his tenants shall rejoice, especially if he has given them reasons why three parts of them are to be ejected from their houses; he shall disburse, till one in the morning, jurisprudence, eloquence, wisdom, and taxation, all by virtue of the noble cock-fighter his ancestor, whom Charles the Second gifted with those accomplishments by patent, and then roll-to the gaming-house in his carriage to swear, and say "By G—d," and gamble, and babble of wine and women, out of pure refreshment after the fatigues of sapience.

Now only fancy an actor attempting to legislate by virtue of *his* ancestors. It is clear the man would be preposterous. Had the late Mr. Kemble stood up in the House of Lords, and after his best consideration of the matter in hand, attempted to make a speech, who supposes that he could have at all equalled my Lord Grey? Who fancies that Garrick could have risen there, and shewn any wit, however sharp and epigrammatic he may have been in the green-room? Who thinks that Mr. Kean could even have looked clever; that Mr. Charles Kemble, not having a Lord to his father, could have had the least aspect of nobility; or that Mr. Dowton or Mr. Farren could have been as facetious as the Duke of Newcastle?

On the other hand, if we could but discover the descendants of Garrick and the other actors of past times, great or small, what a House might we not have of hereditary performers! *That* polity would be quite feasible, and it is astonishing that no aristocrat of histrionic propensities ever thought of it. When Charles the Second had his Richmonds, Grafton, St. Albans, and other little dukes, he doubted whether some of them ought to have been dukes, seeing that their mothers were actresses. What a pity the idea did not come into his head of giving a new

kind of patent to Drury Lane, and making them and
their descendants actors forever! What a pity that,
while he was ennobling the children of the Cleve-
lands, Querouailles, and other illustrious ladies, and
rearing up legislators out of their lightness, he did not
en-histrionize the sons of the Nell Gwynnes, Bet-
tertons, Lacys, and others, whose hereditary powers
of performing *Hamlet* and *Macbeth* might have
charmed us to the end of time! That this might
have been done, whatever Jacobin critics pretend, is
proved by the existence of our hereditary lawgivers.
To give law is no easy task. Our peers are jealous in
vindicating its dignity, and in protesting that the vulgar are unfit for it. To be sure there is the House of
Commons, who are legislators and not hereditary;
but they would make sad work of it without the
peers. In fact, they do but represent the peers, just
as a lower house of players might perform under
the auspices of an upper, and say nothing but what
the great lords and box-mongers of Drury and Covent Garden allowed them. There is no talent
among them; no fit legislation. How can there be,
if legislability can be conferred by ancestry, and is
thus a thing *sui generis?* For either a talent for law-
making is hereditary, or it is not. If it is not, then
we could have no house full of hereditary wisdom,
whereas, it is manifest we have. If it is hereditary,
as we have seen it is, then it must depend upon being
inherited, or it would be a pure figment, and no great-
grandson would be capable of solving knotty points
because his progenitor was a Marquis; which would
be a very ludicrous conclusion, and *flat treason*
against the state,

The feasibility of an Hereditary House of Performers (*peer-formers* rather), being thus established,
the next thing is earnestly to recommend its adoption,
and the next to enjoy the imagination of it. We
fancy ourselves going to the Hereditary Play-house,
not, as now, doubting of the success of this and that
player, and vexed at the truth that is in us, because
we may have to record his failures, — but sure of fine
actors and actresses in all the parts, delighting in the
report we shall have to make of them, and wondering how that Jacobin fellow that criticises them in the
Tri-color, can dare to contradict the whole feeling
and intelligence of the community, which is a rapture of hereditary delight. For always let us bear in
mind, that if some tens among us inherit the power to
legislate, and may be made to inherit the power to
act plays, all the rest of the world inherit a natural
respect for them, and would be as much charmed to
pay money at the pit door to see the Right Theatrical
the actor of *Macbeth*, as they are to give up their
pound notes, daughters, and tenements to the Most
Noble the Ejector and Legislator.

The following may be taken as a specimen of the
criticism in which it would be the " pride and pleasure " of all the loyal critics to indulge : —

Last night the tragedy of *Othello* was performed
at the Hereditary House of Players. The part of
Othello by the Right Theatrical Joseph Garrick ;
Desdemona, by the Right Fascinating Mrs. Betterton ;
Emilia, by the Most Forcible Mrs. Pritchard ; Cassio,
by the Right Clever Mr. Williams ; Iago, by the
Most Acute and Insinuating Mr. Ebenezer Cooke ;

and the Duke of Venice, by his truly noble Representative Mr. Algernon Booth. We have only to
name these illustrious *peer-formers*, to show how
well they must have sustained their characters. The
speech of the great Joseph Garrick — *Had it pleased
heav'n*, &c., was all that could be expected from the
known pathos of the performer's house; it would be
needless to dwell on the hereditary tones of Mrs.
Betterton; the title of Most Forcible shows what a
hand and arm Mrs. Pritchard must derive from her
ancestors; Mr. Williams in Cassio, had all the drunk-
ness and incapability of speech for which his progenitor was conspicuous; and the Duke was most
ducal. It is well known to the critical reader, that no
part in the list of hereditary characters is better sustained than that of Duke: it has the singular good
fortune of being at once the most easy and most
noble of them all; and the Duke before us could not
have performed his part better if he had been the
founder of his title. The unhandsome critic who
writes in the *Tri-color*, and who is the antagonist of
everything established and all moral orders to the
private boxes, would in vain dispute the talent and
utility of this noble house, and its power to represent
adequately its original worthies. In vain he says
that the Right Theatrical Mr. Joseph Garrick is
laughable instead of pathetic; that the present Mrs.
Betterton is the transmitter, not of her great-great-
grandmother's face, but of the several foolish ones
that have intervened; that the Most Forcible Mrs.
Pritchard is as weak a woman as ever got in a passion; and that Mr. Algernon Booth, though good

enough for a Duke, is fit for nothing else, and has not
an idea in his head. Such opinions as these can
only end in bringing everything great and established
into contempt, and rendering the poor dissatisfied
with the salaries paid to these delightful servants of
the public. His enmity is the more absurd, when we
come to consider that it does not signify, after all,
whether the worthy progenitors of this noble house
were, in a certain sense of the term, worthy or not,
since it is the king that makes noble actors; so that
if the whole race were to be destroyed, he could
make as many again to-morrow, and therefore secure the blessings of hereditary genius to our posterity. It is true shallow minds might argue against
the necessity of demanding any talents in the first
possessor of a theatrical title : but a mixture of these,
as great stage-men well know, makes the system
" work better: " and whether such were the case or
not, there is this final argument to put down all
sneerers and innovators forever; to wit, that without an Hereditary House of Performers, to stand
midway between the royal and plebeian ends of the
town, there would be no safety for East-end or West.
The city, for want of a tragedy to keep them in awe,
would immediately go in an uproar, and get up a
tragic comedy at St. James's, to the great danger of
his Majesty's person ; or the executive powers, for
the want of a tragedy to remind it of the right of the
subject, would march into the city, and help itself to
all those pockets of the middle orders, out of which
the Hereditary House is at present maintained for
keeping them inviolate.

All which, if it is not the case in other countries, and vile untheatrical republics, *ought to be;* and so the argument holds as good as if it were.
1830.

———•◦•———

MADAME PASTA.

I.

GOING to the King's Theatre again is a very different thing from renewing one's acquaintance with the other theatres. We confess, with all our love of Italian and of singing, we do not like it so well. The quiet seems pleasanter at first; treading upon matting is a sort of polite and gingerly thing; and it is interesting to look around for those beautiful faces belonging to Lady Charlottes and Carolines, dropping their lids down upon us as if they wore coronets, and not always the better for it. But the cue of polite life is to take indifference for self-possession; and you are not seated long before you begin to feel that there is an air of neutralization and falsehood around you. The quiet is a dread of committing themselves; — people come as much to be seen as to see; — the performers in the boxes prepare for disputing attention with those on the stage; — men lounge about the alleys, looking so very easy that they are evidently full of constraint; the looks of the women dispute one another's pretensions; — if you have been long away, you are not sure that something is not amiss in your appearance; that you are not

guilty of some overt act of a wrong cape, or absurd
reasonableness of neckcloth; in short, you feel that
the great majority of the persons around you have
come to the Opera because it *is* the Opera, and not
from any real love of music and the graces. The
only persons really interested, with the exception of
a few private lovers of music here and there, are the
young and inexperienced; musicians, who come to
criticise the music; and foreigners, whom it is pleasant to hear speaking their own language. After all,
these last are the only persons who seem at home.
The musicians are apt to be thinking too much of
their flats and sharps, and compasses of voice. The
young people, though they dare not own it to themselves, soon get heartily tired of everything but looking at the company; and the private lover of music
gets as tired with the glare and commonplace of nine
tenths of the performance.

Thanks and glory to Pasta, who relieved us from
all this spectacle of indifference and pretension the
moment we heard the soul in her voice, and beheld
the sincerity in her face. Pit and boxes were at once
forgotten, quality, affectation, criticism, everything
but delight and nature. Like a lark, she took us up
at once out of that " sullen earth," and made us feel
ourselves in a heaven of warmth and truth, and
thrilling sensibility. If these are thought enthusiastic
phrases, they are so. What others could we use to do
justice to the enthusiasm of genius, and to the delight
it produces in those golden showers out of its sky?

We saw Madame Pasta, for the first time, years
ago, in the character of the page in *Figaro*, and

afterwards in that of the female (we forget her name)
in the *Clemenza di Tito*, who sings with her lover
the beautiful duet, *Deh prendi un dolce amplesso*.
In the page, if we recollect, we thought her heavy
and ungain. In the other part, we remember that
Begrez, a singer not given to too much passion, stood
while he was singing the duet with her, holding her
hand, not indifferently as they generally do, but with
tenderness and affection, cherishing it against his
bosom ; a piece of nature which we have since attributed to her suggestion. If we are wrong, we beg
his pardon. At all events, it was creditable to him,
suggested or not.

Since we have seen Madame Pasta again, the heavy
kind of simplicity which we recollect in her Figaro
must either have been the consequence of her having
a greater tact for nature and truth, than she at that
time felt experience enough to put forth, or her performance of the part may have been better suited to
the character than we took it for. The page, in that
very breath-suspended and conscious piece, which is
always hovering on the borders of strange things, is
in reality in a very awkward position, and extremely
sensible of it ; and we are not sure, if we could have
seen Madame Pasta in it, with as much knowledge
of her then as we persuade ourselves we have now,
that we should not have found her the exact person
for the character, and presenting a portrait, full of
truth, in its very ungainness and want of teaching.

Truth is the great charm of this fine vocal actress.
She waits upon it, without claim or misgiving; and
like a noble mistress, truth in turn waits upon her,

and loves her like her child. We never saw anybody
before on the stage who impressed us with a sense of
this sort of moral charm in its perfection. Even Mrs.
Siddons had always a queen-like air·in her nature,
which seemed to be conscious of the homage paid it,
and to crown itself with its glory. Madame Pasta,
as the occasion demands, is tranquil, grave, smiling,
transported, angry, affectionate, voluptuous; intent
at one minute as a bust, radiant as a child with joy
at the next; intellectual as a Muse, full of wily and
sliding tones as a Venus; in short, the occasion itself,
and whatever it does with the human being. Imagine
a female brought up in solitude, with a natural sincerity that nothing has injured, walking quietly about
a beautiful spot, reading everything that comes in
her way, accomplished, at ease, getting even a little
too fat with the perfection of her comfort and her
ignorance of anything ungraceful; and imagine this
same female gifted with as much sensibility as truth,
and weeping, laughing, and undergoing every emotion that books can furnish her with, as she turns
over the leaves; and you have a picture of this noble
performer, and the extraordinary effect she produces
without anything like theatrical effort. Not that she
cannot indulge the critics now and then with the idea
of a stage actress, and set herself to make her *bravura*
effective; but truth is at the bottom even of that, and
she is sure to throw in some tone and sweet reference·
to nature; as much as to say to the lovers of it, " Do
not imagine I have forgotten you." She is like a
nature full of truth, brought out of solitude into the
world; — and too much habituated to sincerity, too

sweet in the use of it, and too conscious of the power it gives her, to forego so rare, so charming, and so triumphant a distinction.

We do not pretend to make any discovery in this matter. The accounts we heard of her in *Medea* showed us that the discovery had been made already; and it has been set forth by a critic, worthy of that name, in an article comparing this " perfection of natural acting " with that of the French. With a reference to this article, which is to be found in the Plain Speaker, Vol. II., and which we regret we have no room to quote, for nothing need be said of the opera itself, we must conclude. *Tancredi* is said to be one of the most popular of Rossini's operas, but is by no means one of his best; being crammed, in fact, as full of commonplaces and old threadbare recitative as nine tenths of it can hold. It is theatrical clothesman's music. But there is good in the remainder; and the fine air, *Di tanti palpiti*, is part of it. If any one thinks he has heard this air a hundred times, till he has got tired of it, let him never mind, but go and hear it from Madame Pasta; he will then find he has never heard it before. We have left ourselves as little room to speak of the other performers, some of them excellent in their way, especially Madame Cara-dori; but after our new, true, and most original acquaintance, even the best of conventional singers become comparatively uninteresting. Caradori is like a sweet and perfect musical instrument, by the side of her; not that she does not act too better than most singers; she even contrives, in her manners, to give us an amiable as well as clever idea of her;

but Pasta, coming upon all this, even in her most tranquil moments, seems like the very noontide of humanity risen upon a cold morning of it. There is more
effective grace in the least of her movements, though
she is too fat, and sometimes looks heavily so, than
in all the received elegancies of the stage ; — so beautiful as well as great is truth. By the way, we had
forgotten to say that her voice is not perfect. Who
asks whether any voice is so, when sensibility and
sincerity speak together, and the sound is hugged into
one's heart !

II.

We wish to add something to our last article respecting the truth and beauty of this singer's performance. It has been suggested to us, that Madame
Pasta is not so much absorbed as people may think
her in the business of the scene ; that she finds time,
like other singers at the opera, for those little inter-
changes of by-jokes and grown-children's play, by
which they occasionally refresh themselves from a
sense of their duties ; and that, in a concert-room or
an oratorio, where no illusion is going forward, we
should find more defects in her as a singer than we
are aware of. Finally, another friend tells us, that
we make a good deal of what we see ; and in our
gratitude for a favorite quality, find more of it to be
grateful for than exists anywhere but in our own
imaginations.

We doubt whether we are not committing the dignity of the critical character in thus admitting that

our opinion can be disputed privately. A corre-
spondeut is another matter. He approaches his critic
with a curtain between, and the latter retreats farther
into the mystery and multiplicity of his plural " we,"
leaving his questioner uncertain how many secrect
faculties and combined resources of experience he
may not have ventured to differ with. But to acknowledge that we are mortal and individual men,
" singular good " fellows, who can be disputed with
over one's wine and tea, face to face, and be forced to
say " I ; " and give a reason, with more privilege to be
wrong than any other man's reason ; all this would be
very frightful to us, if instead of being critics or judges,
sitting aloof above sympathy, and ·periwigged with
imposture, we did not profess to be what we really
are, nothing but Companions: men who get from
sympathy all they know, and do not care twopence
for anything but truth and good-fellowship.

We say, then, to these our objectors, public or
private (for after all there is no difference between
them, except as to the dry matter of fact ; we take a
real bottle with one, and an imaginary one with the
other) — we say, filling our glass, and looking them
in the face, with all that bland beatitude of certainty,
so convincing in any man, especially if he does not
proceed to argue the point (as we have an unfortunate propensity to do) — My dear So-and-so, you are
most horribly in the wrong. I wonder at a man of
your intelligence. You surprise me. Do you think
so, indeed? Well, you astonish me. I'm sure, if
you would but reflect a little. Well, I never. You
are the last man I should have thought capable

of using that argument. Nothing will ever persuade *me*, &c.

These answers ought to be convincing. But as some unreasonable persons may remain, who are not so easily convinced, and as we have a conscience that induces us not to leave them out, we shall proceed to observe, that all which is urged against us on the point in question may be very true, and Pasta yet remain just what we have described her. In the first place, it is not necessary to suppose her absorbed in the business of the scene in order to do it justice. It would be impossible she could do so, if she were. " If a man," said Johnson, " really thought himself Richard the Third, he would deserve to be hung." All we contend for is, that Madame Pasta has the power, to a surprising extent, of pitching herself into the character of the person she represents. The greater this power, the more suddenly she can exercise it. She touches the amulet of her imagination in an instant, and is the person she wishes to appear. It is a voluntary power of the extremest degree, in one sense : and yet, in another, it is the most involuntary ; that is to say, she can abstract herself at a moment's notice from circumstances not belonging to the scene, and yet in the next she is under the influence of the character imagined, as much as if she were a child. We will venture to illustrate this by a reference to authorship and to ourselves. We shall be talking, for instance, in the midst of half a dozen friends: they shall all be talking with us : and we shall be thinking no more of authorship than of the Emperor Nicholas. On a sudden it becomes necessary that we should

look at our paper, and give a turn to some story or
other piece of writing, serious or merry. In a moment we are as abstracted as if we were a hundred
miles off. We hear the conversation no more than
people hear the rumbling of the coaches when they
are not thinking about them; and, with the laugh
hardly off our lips, become as grave as the heroine of
our story; or, with the tears almost in our eyes, sit
down to give the finish to a joke, and tickle ourselves
into laughter with the point of it. Now why should
we not believe, that what we ourselves can do, others
cannot do twenty times as well?

That Madame Pasta should not feel everything just
as strongly as she imagines it, and that she should
give evidences to near observers that she can occasionally amuse herself, as other favorite performers
do, with certain quips and cranks among one another,
takes away nothing of the imaginative truth of what
she has to do, and only adds to the evidences of the
voluntary power. We certainly doubt whether she
could do this so well in some characters as in others.
We should guess that she was least able to do it
much, and most inclined to do it at all, when performing characters that tried her feelings the most
severely. There are stories of Garrick's turning round
with a comic grin in the thick of the distresses of
King Lear; and similar stories have been related of
Mr. Kean. Believe them if you will; but do not
believe that those great performers felt less the truth
of what they were about. Perhaps what they did was
necessary, as a relief to their feelings; just as sensitive
men will shock company sometimes by cracking jokes

upon some topic of distress. It is not because they do not feel it, but because they do, and because some variety of sensation is necessary to enable them to endure their feelings. If an actor were to feel, unmixed, all he seems to feel in such characters as Lear, he would go nigh to lose his senses in good earnest. Tragic actresses, the most eminent, have been known to faint and go into fits upon the performance of a trying character. Perhaps they would not have done so had their personal character contained variety and resource enough in it to call in the aid of this occasional volatility. Even Garrick is known to have looked prematurely old. Yet Garrick had everything to support him — fortune, prudence, and a good constitution. When we hear actors, equally great in their way, but less happy in bodily frame, rebuked severely for certain excesses alleged against them, we sometimes think it a pity that the rebukers do not know what it is to go through all that wear and tear of sensation, and to be at a loss how to keep up a proper level of excitement in their general feelings. We are not sure that Madame Pasta does not unconsciously let herself grow fatter than might be wished, out of an uneasy feeling of something to be supported and strengthened in this way; especially when it is considered that persons of her profession lead artificial lives, and cannot so well be kept healthy as others, by good hours and a life otherwise uninterfered with.

As to a concert-room or an oratorio, it is a dull business compared with singing amidst the feelings of a scene. Such places are fittest for instrumental performances, and for instrument-like singers. In the concert-room the audience expect little passion, and find it. They are themselves in a dull and formal state ; there is often a majority of musicians present, and a majority of musicians cannot be of the first order, nor do they desire anything of the first order in others. They wish the singers to act up simply to their own notions of excellence, which are but a reflection of themselves. All is quiet, mechanical, mediocre. Up gets a lady or gentleman, book in hand, and out of this is to disburse us the proper quantity of notes, checked by that emblem of reference to the dead letter. She does so; is duly delivered of a B, or a D, and everything is " as well as can be expected."

So in an oratorio. The audience are all assembled, as grave as need be ; the season, and the usual dull character of oratorios, helps to formalize them ; there is a good deal of mourning in the house, and sacred music is to be performed, mixed with a little illegal profane. That is to say, there is nothing real in the business, and nobody can be either properly merry or mournful. Which is just the case. In comes a gentleman, dressed in black, hitching his way along sideways, and leading a lady up the alley behind the orchestra ; another follows, and another, equally polite and preparatory : it is Madame So-and-so, in a hat and feathers ; it is Miss W. or Mrs. Z., all dressed like other gentlewomen, which is odd ; and like other gentlewomen they take their seats, and look as if they ought to drink tea. Music books make their appearance, as in the concert-room, and up rises the lady or

gentleman to sing in the same formal manner, and be
discreet in their flats. The sacred music drags, the
profane music hops, and the audience wish themselves in their beds.

Madame Pasta may probably not excel at such ex-
hibitions as these. We do not desire that she should.
It would not be easy to persuade us that, sing where
she may, her singing would not be better than the
most formal perfection; but the worst thing we can
say of an oratorio is, that not even she can take us
there. Put her on the stage, or in a company among
friends, let loose her feelings, and then we have the
soul of music; and this is the only real music in the
world.

That we make what we find on such occasions,
and listen with our imaginations upon us, is only
saying, in other words, that the occasion is fit to
excite the enthusiasm; otherwise how does it happen
that it is not equally excited on others? Doubtless
there must be enthusiasm and imagination to do fit
justice to the same qualities in the performer. Loveliness must have love. But how is it that love is
excited by some things and not by others? How is
it that multitudes are wound up to enthusiasm by one
orator and not by another, and that Madame Pasta
produces the same sensation from Naples to Berlin?
She is not an unknown singer, trumped up by a solitary enthusiast. Cities are her admirers; and she
would take hearts by storm everywhere, whether
critics explained or not by what magic she did it.

It is nevertheless very pleasant to us to know what
the magic is. We never feel the value of criticism,

except when it enables us to double our delight in this manner; for none can hold in greater contempt than we do the common cant of criticism, or less pride themselves in finding out those common defects to which critics in general have a natural attraction. It is truth that gives Madame Pasta her advantage; the same truth, yes, the very same spirit of sincerity and straightforwardness which is charming in conversation and in matters of confidence; which enables one face to look at another, unalloyed with a contradiction, and makes the heart sometimes gush inwardly with tenderness at the countenance that little suspects it. The reason is, that some of the most painful infirmities with which the state of society besets us are then taken away, and we not only think we have reason to be delighted, but are sure of it. For this we know no bounds to our gratitude; and it is just; for you could not more transport a man shaken all over with palsy by suddenly gifting him with firmness, than you do any human being, in the present state of things, by making him secure upon any one point which he ardently desires to believe in. There is, therefore, a moral charm, of the most liberal kind, in Madame Pasta's performances, which argues well for her personal character; and personal character, wish as we may, always mingles, more or less, with the impression created by others upon us. It is, indeed, a part of them, which helps to make them what they are, off a stage or on it, pretending or not pretending. It is true there is a difference between moral truth and imaginative; and it does not follow that, because Madame Pasta tells the truth in every-

thing she does on the stage, she should be an example
of the virtue elsewhere.   It is an argument, however,
that she would be so; just as the taste for an accomplishment implies that a person is more likely to
excel in it than if there were no such taste.   Madame
Pasta has to look sorrowful, and no sorrow can be
completer: — she has to look joyful, and her face is
all joy, — as true and total a beaming as that of a girl
without a spectator, who sees her lover hailing her
from a distance.   We have seen such looks, and they
have stood us instead ·of any other certainty.   Madame Pasta knows the truth well, and knows how to
honor it; and this is an evidence that the inclination
of her nature is true, whatever the world may have
done to spoil it.   We are aware, mind, of no such
spoliation.   Our impulse, if we knew this charming
performer (which is a pleasure incompatible with
the confounded critical office we have taken upon us),
would be to give as implicit belief to everything she
said off the stage as on it.   But we wish to guard
against a wrong argument, and to show the triumph
and the beautiful tendencies of truth, whether borne
out in all their quarters or not.

   1828.

OPERA OF THE WHITE AND RED ROSE.
— MADAME PASTA IN THE LOVER.

MAYER'S opera of the White and Red Rose (*La Rosa Bianca e la Rosa Rossa*) was brought out at the King's Theatre on Saturday evening, Madame Pasta being the hero of it. We remember noticing a playbill of this piece once at Genoa, and making up our minds not to go and see it, because it was historical. Song is for passion in its own shape, and not mixed up with the squabbles and pretences of history. Great writers, as a musical friend observed to us, have rarely laid their scenes in the midst of these impertinences, which augur ill for the composer. It is true, there is apt to be very little history after all in such pieces; but what there is does them injury. We do not want a singing Earl of Derby, singing foot-guards, and a warbling sheriff. These matters of the Court Calendar jar against one's enthusiasm, and the case is worse because it comes home to us in our own country. Fancy a love adventure mixed up two centuries hence with the differences between our Military Premier and Mr. Huskisson; the king going in and out, singing *Oh Dio;* Lord Goderich tender in a cavatina, the ladies all mystified, and a chorus of journalists at midnight (*Numi* and *lumi*) calling upon the powers above to throw a little light on the business.

Signor Huski.   Dice di si, come io, il
                 Vellingtonne.
(*Entra il Duca.*) Di si? Di no.
Coro di Giornalisti. Or cosa dice Huskisonne?

[*Mr. H.*   The Noble Duke says
            Yes; so all is done.
(*Enter Duke.*)   Says Yes? Says No.
Chorus of Journalists. Now what says Huskis-
                          son?]

READER. But, sir, this is a caricature.

CRITIC.   It is so, like the subject; but the spirit of
our objection is good, and opera goers feel it to
be so.

Signor Mayer's opera is not of the highest order,
nor is it by any means of the lowest. We do not
know whether this is the same composer who has
written several pleasing airs, — one of them with a
very striking and characteristic exordium; we mean
Chi dice mal d' amore. The emphatic drop on the
last syllable of the word *falsità* in that air, is a touch
of real genius. Madame Pasta would give it with a
corresponding beauty of gesture, impressing her firm
and indignant hand upon it with all the grace of a
noble scorn. There are two Mayers, we believe, both
writers of pleasing melodies; though, perhaps, we
are naming together two unequal men. One of them
is the author of a graceful ballad, beginning *Donne
l' amore escaltro poragletto.* At all events, the name
led us to expect more melody than we found in the
new opera; or, perhaps, we should say, more original airs: for there is a vein of rambling melody

throughout the piece, and, if not much invention, a great deal of taste and feeling. The music is so good that we expect it every minute to be better. There is now and then a very delicate commentary of accompaniment, throwing out little unexpected passages both learned and to the purpose. The best of the regular compositions are the duets. There are two between Madame Pasta and Curioni (*In tal momento* in the first act, and *E deserto il bosco* in the second) for which alone the opera is worth going to hear. Curioni, who has a manner of feebleness and indifference in general, seems inspired when he comes to sing with Pasta. Her part is one of the least effective ones she has had; but everything becomes elevated by that fine face of hers, and that voice breathing the soul of sincerity. The words *core* and *amore* are never commonplaces in her mouth. They resume all their faith and passion. They are no more like the same words in ordinary, than gallantry is like love, or than *scipio*, any walking-stick, was Scipio who supported his father. Pasta has a large heart in her bosom, or she could not have a voice so full of it. This it is that gives her the ascendency in the scene : that lifts her, " dolphin-like, above the element she lives in," and sports, and rules, and is a thing of life, in those deep waters of her song. Not that other singers have no hearts, and may not be excellent people, but that they have not the same faith in the very sounds and symbols of cordiality, and cannot be at a moment's notice in the world which they speak of. The common world hampers and pulls them back. It was well noticed by a lady in the pit, that she is

not hindered of her purpose by a break now and then
in her voice, the bubble of a note or so.   She slides
over it as if it were a molehill under her chariot
wheels, and abates nothing of her triumphant progress ; nay, adds a grace and a dignity on the strength
of it, as if it were a new proof how indifferent to the
spirit of the passage was the ground the most mate
rial to those who can look no higher.   Besides, there
is a suffering and permission in it that belongs em-
phatically to passion.   If it were for want of skill or
deliberation, it would be another thing.   But in the
rich haste of emotion, pearls are dropped as of no consequence.   The profusion of real wealth allows us to
notice them only as things that would make others
poor.

Being closer to Madame Pasta than usual this
night, we had a completer opportunity of noticing the
extraordinary grace of her movements.   She is never
at a loss, because she never thinks of being so.   She
leaves the whole matter to truth and nature, and these
settle it for her, as completely as they do for an infant.
You might make a picture from any one of her pos-
tures.   A favorite action of hers, and one extremely
touching, is, after venting a passion of more than usual
force, to put up her hands before her eyes, laying and
shutting up, as it were, her looks in them, as if to hide
from herself the sight of her own emotion.   When she
opens her arms in a transport of affection, leaning at
the same time a little back, and breathing and looking
as true as truth could wish, her heart seems to come
forward for one as real, and her arms to wait the
sanction of its acknowledgment.   For all arms, be it

observed, are not arms, whatever they pretend; any more than all that pretends to be love is love, or all eyes have an insight. Some arms are a sort of fore legs in air, merely to help people's walking. Others have machines at the end of them, to take up victuals and drink with, or occasionally to scratch out one's eyes. Others, more amiable, are to hang armlets and bracelets on, or to be admired for a skin or a shape; and then ladies put them in kid gloves, on purpose to take them off, and lift them indifferently to their cheek with rings on their fingers, and people say, What an arm Mrs. Timson has! But the real arms are to serve and love with, to clasp with; to be honest and true arms, content to be admired for their own sakes if the possessor be worthy, but happy to enable you to lose sight of them for the sake of the heart and the honest countenance. It is out of an instinct to this purpose (for the least of our gestures have their reason, if we did but scan it) that Madame Pasta throws back her arms, as if things only in waiting, and brings forward her heart, as if the approbation of that alone would sanction their use. It is for a similar reason, that we admire those women who can afford to make no display of the beauty of any particular limb, but reserve it for the objects of their love and respect to find out. It shows they are richer than in mere limbs. And, for the same reason, one hates all that French dancing, with fine showy limbs and senseless faces, which follows the musical performances at this house, and is just the antipodes of all that charms us in Pasta's singing. If her limbs were among the poorest in the world, they would become precious as warmth

and light, with that smile and those eyes; whereas,
if a French dancer could, by any possibility, have
limbs like a Venus, with a face no fitter to look at
for ten minutes, or for one, than nineteen out of
twenty of them possess, she might as well, to our
taste, be as wooden and pointed all over as a Dutch
doll; which, indeed, in her inanimate posture-mak-
ings and senseless right angles of toe, she very much
resembles. These people are made up out of the toy-
shop. They are dolls in their quieter moments, and
tee-totums in their livelier. A mathematician should
marry one of them for a pair of compasses.

We must not forget to mention that Madame Cara-
dori, whose illness had been previously stated to the
public, went through her part in the opera in spite of
it, though evidently in a state of suffering. She could,
of course, be expected to do little; but what she did
was good, and, at least, wanted nothing of its touch-
ingness. There is, at all times, something amiable in
the manner and appearance of this singer. Her more
than usual delicacy the other night, together with her
white dress, which had a long bodice with a cross
over it, and her hanging, uniform-looking sleeves,
gave her the appearance of a Madonna in one of
Raphael's pictures.

We must relate an anecdote of Madame Pasta,
highly corroborative of what has been said of her.
Some gentlemen, who knew her well, informed a
friend of ours when he was in Paris, that she would
come home from the opera, and sit in a passion of
tears at the recollection of what she had been acting.

They told him that nothing could be more unaffected, and that she would say she knew it to be idle, but that she "could not get the thing out of her head." This is just what imaginative people would expect her to say. She never pretended that she had taken herself for the character she represented, but she had sympathized with it so strongly that it became the next thing to reality; and if our hearts can be touched and our color changed by the mere perusal of a tragedy, how much more may not a woman's nature be moved that has been almost identified with the calamities in it; that, by force of imagination, has brought the soul of another to inhabit her own warm being; and has entertained it there as the very guest of humanity, giving it her own heart to agitate, and taking upon herself the burden of its infirmities!
1828.

----◦◦◦----

ON FRENCH OPERA DANCING.

DANCING is either the representation of love-making, or it is that of pure animal spirits, giving way to their propensity to motion. It is the latter, most probably, that strikes out the first idea of it, as an art; the former, that completes and gives it a sentiment. The rudest savages dance round a visitor. Politer ones treat him with a dance of the sexes.

But French opera dancing is neither the one nor the other. It pretends both, only to show how little it

has to do with either. There is love in the plot; there
is mirth in the stage directions: but you find it nowhere else. Think of a man making love, with no
love in his countenance! of a girl, as merry as a
grig, but destitute of the least expression of it, except
in her toe! A French ballet is like a rehearsal, with
the emotion left out. There is scenery; there are
dresses and decorations; some story is supposed to
be going on; but the actors are really apart from all
this; wrapped up in themselves, and anxious for
nothing but to astonish with their respective legs, and
fetch down applause from the galleries with a jump.

Enter, for instance, two lovers, with a multitude of
subordinate lovers to dance for them while they rest.
The scene is in Turkey, in Italy, in Cyprus; but it
might as well be in the dancing-master's school-room,
for anything it has to do with the performers. Forward comes the gentleman, walking very badly, like
all dancers by profession. He bridles, he balances
himself, he looks as wooden in the face as a barber's
block, he begins capering. That there is no meaning
in his capers but to astonish, is evident; for, in his
greatest efforts, he always pays the least attention to
his love. If it is love-making, it is the oddest in the
world, for the lady is forgotten, the gentleman capers
by himself, and he expresses his passion by seeing
how many jumps he can take, how often he can
quiver his feet before he comes down, how eminently
he can stand on one leg, and, finally, how long he
can spin round like a tee-totum, as if he had no brain
to be made giddy with. Suddenly he stops, like a
piece of lead; and having received his applause for

being a machine, stalks off as proud as a peacock, curving out his arms, holding his head up, and turning his toes east and west, as if it were a grace to be splay-footed. All this is certainly not " the poetry of motion."

It is now the lady's turn. She presents herself equally alone and enamoured; she looks grave and anxious, not at her lover, but the pit; no other emotion is in her face, but then her toes are very lively, and she begins by standing upon them. She seems to say, " You see what it is to love and be merry; it is to look like a school-girl before her master, and to have insteps as pliable as India-rubber." She then moves onward a little, and careers hither and thither, prettily enough as long as it resembles any real dancing; but this is not her ambition. On a sudden she stops like the gentleman, balances herself, tries her arms and legs, like a young crane learning to fly, then jumps up and down as high as she can, quivering her calves (those only seats of emotion), and finally gives a great spin round, as long as possible, looking like a bust and a pair of legs, with an inverted bowl for a petticoat. This she puts an end to by the usual leaden stop, as if rooted with fright; the tribute of applause is received with the due petrifaction of countenance, or a smile no less unmeaning; and off she walks like her inamorato, equally pompous and splay-footed, to stand cooling herself in the background, and to astonish the inexperienced with the shortness of her drapery and the corpulence of her legs.

Those legs are a sight, unquestionably. If any two balustrades of a bridge were wanting, here is the

remedy. There is a fair dancer now at the opera,
who, from a principle well known to the metaphysical, seems to be ostentatious of two phenomena of
this kind, in the exact proportion that she ought to
conceal them. She appears to consider them as prize
calves, and makes as great a show of her favorites as
an Essex grazier. The simile is not handsome, but
we forget the bearer is a woman when we look at
such legs. Not that very true women may not have
legs a little superfluous. Madame Pasta has them.
Mrs. Jordan's legs were handsome rather as a man's
than a woman's; and yet who ever doubted that she
was a very charming female? It is not the leg, but the
spirit with which it is worn; and, upon this principle, a woman with thick ankles may step about our
imaginations like a fairy, and another with thin ones
trample them as if they were lead. If a woman has
grace at her heart, her movements will be graceful and
her step soft, let her legs be what size they may. If
she has not, the downwardness of her spirit will put
a vulgar weight in her feet, let them be naturally as
light as a zephyr's. She shall shake the room as she
walks, like an ale-wife. But huge legs in a female
are not particularly valuable for their own sakes, as
our fair friend at the opera seems to think. Dancing
tends to make them so; but this is not what we go
to see dancing for. Here, however, lies the secret.
Body is everything in opera dancing, and mind nothing. To show a limb, they think, is — to show a
limb. So it is; *and nothing else.* But this is a
stretch of the intellectual to which they cannot arrive.
The audience instinctively know better; and though

they stay the afterpiece to admire more than they pretend, are at once amazed and disappointed; amazed
at the beauties lavished upon them, and disappointed
to find that the effect is not more beautiful. This is,
perhaps, as it should be, everything considered; but
then it is not dancing. There might be a great deal
less display, and a little more sense; and then people
might think of those they loved, and have their imaginations not unseasonably touched: for grace is the
link between body and soul; and a sprinkle of that
Attic salt on the public mind is not without its use.
At present, whatsoever their inclination to the contrary, the spectators, before the scene is half over, feel
only that there is a glare and an impertinence; that a
few half-naked-looking people are walking about, and
twirling, and looking stupid; and that if this is vo-
luptuousness, it is a very indifferent thing. The young
may be amused with the novelty, and the imaginative
may try hard to be kind to it, but if there are other
persons present, who have no greater ideas of what is
elegant and attractive, than the scenes they meet with
in French opera dancing, they are in as fair a way as
can be of being the commonest and weakest people
in the world, and realizing as little true pleasure as
the wooden faces they look at. Now and then there
is a single figure worth seeing; sometimes, though
rarely, a whole ballet. Des Hayes used to come
bounding on the stage like a deer. Angiolini was
interesting in Flora; and even Vestris (as long as
you did not see his face) had an effect beyond that of
his twirling, when he touched her round the waist as
Zephyr, and took her with him up in the air. But

there was poetry in the story. The air blew from the fields of Ovid and our childhood. The best opera dancer we ever saw was a female at Turin, of the name of De Martini. She united the activity of the French school with the grace and fervor of the Italian; and did not make her bounds and her twirlings for nothing. She would come, for instance, from the other end of the stage, in a series of giddy movements, and finish them with pitching herself into her lover's arms. Here was love and animal spirits too, each warranting and throwing a grace on the other. Surely a set of Italian or Spanish dancers would make a revolution in this matter, in the course of a season too, and put an end to a school which must be as little profitable in the comparison as it is unmeaning and delightless.

How different a French opera dance, and one of their dances on a green of a Sunday evening! We have had the pleasure of seeing the latter; and nothing could be merrier or to the purpose. But there is all the difference in the world between French nature and French art. The one is human nature—

"Dance, and Provençal song, and sun-burnt mirth;"

the other is Paris and affectation, the pedantry of pleasure. French opera dancing is like French painting,—a petrifaction of art, an attempt to set rules above the relish of the thing; and it ends in the same way, by being a kind of inanimate sculpture. Their dances on the green are as good as the dancing of birds. Spanish dancing is more passionate. We thought when we first saw a bolero we had never seen

dancing before. Those fervid alternations of court-
ship, and·that wild careering of one person round
the other, dancing in every limb, and seeming to
sweep the very ground as they went with the tips of
their fingers, the music fermenting all the while, and
the castanets cracking like joints, — it looked like a
couple of aboriginal beings newly made out of the
whole ardor of the south, and not knowing how to
vent the tormenting pleasure of their existence. De
Martini made us feel that all this might be controlled
into a sentiment; and Italian dancing, we should
guess, would be as fine, in its way, as Italian painting and music, if properly cultivated. The Germans
used to be violent dancers, as became their heavy-
laden tables. Of late years they have taken to the
most languid and voluptuous of all dances, as if they
had no alternative but to go to an extreme. We must
not omit to do justice to one French dance, the minuet, which is the perfection of artificial grace, the
dance of the courtier and fine lady, brimful of mutual
compliment, arising out of an infinite self-satisfaction.
A bow or courtesy is made, as if it were to nothing
under a prince or princess. A tip of the finger is
presented as if it were a jewel. How proud the
deference! How dignified the resumption! What
loftiness in the hat! What greater ascendency in
the very sink of the petticoat! What idolatry and
self-idolatry of approach! What intensity of separation, the parties retreating with high worship from one
another, as if to leave space enough for their triumph
to swell in! It seems as if none should dance a minuet after Louis the Fourteenth and his Montespans.

It is the excess of pretension, becoming something real on that account; and belongs to an age of false triumph and flattered assumptions. The *Minuet de la Cour* is the best minuet, and seems to have been inspired by its name. Mozart's minuet in Don Juan is beautiful and victorious; but it is not as pregnant with assumptions as the other, like a hooped petticoat; it does not rise and fall, and step about in the same style of quiet and undoubted perfection, like a Sir Charles Grandison or Lady Grave-airs: it is more natural and sincere, and might be danced anywhere by any two lovers, not the nicest in the world, proclaiming their triumph. We have seen Charles Vestris and somebody else, we forget whom, dance the *Minuet de la Cour*, but it was not the real thing. You missed the real pretenders, — the proper fine gentleman and lady. Mr. Kemble should have danced a minuet, if he could have danced at all; and Mrs. Oldfield risen in her " chintz and Brussels lace " to accompany him.

Let us not, however, be ungrateful to all stage-dancing in England. Three stage loves have we known in the days of our youth; as good love, and better, than is usually entertained towards persons one is not acquainted with; for it gave us an interest ever after in the fair inspirers: and two of these ladies were dancers. Our first passion of the kind was for the fine eyes and cordial voice of Miss Murray, afterwards Mrs. Henry Siddons; our second for the lady-like figure and sweet, serious countenance of Miss Searle, a dancer (since dead), who married the brother of Sir Gilbert Heathcote; and our third for the pretty *embonpoint* and ripe little black head of Miss

Lupino, since Mrs. Noble, whose clever self and husband may dancing preserve! We thought, when she married, she had made the fittest choice in the world. We hope these declarations, which are the first we ever made, are innocent; especially as we make them only to our Companion the reader. They are for nobody else to hear. We speak in a stage whisper. Our theatrical passion, at present, as he well knows, is for Madame Pasta; and we shall proceed, as we did in the other cases, to show our gratitude for the pleasure she gives us, by doing her all the good in our power, and not letting her know a word on the subject. If this is not a disinterested passion, we know not what is.

A word or two on our English manner of dancing in private: our quadrilles and country dances. A fair friend of ours, whenever she has an objection to make to the style of a person's behavior, says, " he requires a good shaking." This is what may be said of most of the performers in our ball-rooms, particularly the male. Our gentlemen dancers forget the part they assume on all other occasions, as encouragers and payers of compliment; and seem, as if in despair of equalling their fair friends, they had no object but to get through the dance undetected. The best thing they do for their partner is to hand her an ice or a lemonade; the very going for which appears to be as great a refreshment to them as the taking it is to the other. When the dance is resumed all their gravity returns. They look very cut and dry, and succinct; jog along with an air of indifference, and leave the vivacity of the young lady to shift for itself.

The most self-satisfied male dancer we ever saw, was
one who, being contented with his own legs, could
never take his eyes off them, but seemed eternally
congratulating them and himself that they were fit to
be seen. The next thing to this, is to be always
thinking of the figure; which, indeed, is the main
consideration both of gentlemen and ladies. Where
there is anything beyond, the ladies have it, out and
out. The best private dancer we know among the
male sex, is one who makes it his business to attend
to his partner; to set off with her as if she were a part
of his pleasure, and to move among the others as if
there were such things in the world as companionship, and a sense of it. And this he does with equal
spirit and modesty. Our readers may know of more
instances, and may help to furnish them; but the
reverse is assuredly the case in general. Perhaps it
was not so in the livelier times of our ancestors, when
taxation had not forced us to think so much of " number one;" and the general knowledge, that is preparing a still better era, had not unsettled the minds
of all classes of people as to their individual pretensions. Perhaps, also, dress makes a difference. Men
may have been more confident in cloaks and doublets than in the flaps and horse-collars of the present
day. To get up a dance on the sudden, nowadays,
on the green lawn, would look ridiculous on the men's
part. At least, they feel as if it would; and this
would help to make it so. On the other hand, a set
of gallant apprentices in their caps and doublets, or
of wits and cavaliers in their mantles and plumage,
had all the world before them, for action or for grace;

and a painter could put them on canvas with no detriment to the scenery. We are far from desiring to bring back those distinctions. It is very possible for an apprentice nowadays to know twice as much as a cavalier; and we would have no distinctions at all but between spirit and spirit. But a dress disadvantageous to everybody, is good for nothing but to increase other disadvantages. Above all, a little more spirit in our mode of dancing, and a little more of the dancing itself, without the formality of regular balls, would do us good, and give our energies a fillip on the side of cheerfulness. Families and intimate friends would find themselves benefited in health and spirits, perhaps to an extent of which they have no conception, by setting apart an evening or so in the week for a dance among themselves. If we have not much of " the poetry of motion " among us, we may have plenty of the motion itself, which is the healthy part of it; and the next best performer to such a one as we have described is he who gives himself up to the pleasure and sociality of the moment, whether a good dancer or not.

1828.

RECOLLECTIONS OF OLD ACTORS.

THE removal of our place of publication to Brydges Street has reminded us, that many years ago
we began writing theatricals at the house two doors
from us, where the paper (The News) is still published in which we made our *début*. May it live forever! We rejoice in its neighborhood, and hope it
is not sorry for ours. It must now be nearly thirty
years since we first wrote articles in the newspapers.
We were then in our boyhood, or rather lad-hood.
Not many years short of that period, we adventured
on the perilous task of criticism; and here we are
again, in the same street, almost on the same spot,
occupied with a new paper,* and pursuing the old

* The Tatler, a literary and theatrical paper, which Hunt edited from September 4, 1830, to February 14, 1832. "It was a very little work," he writes, in his
Autobiography, "consisting but of four folio pages; but it was a daily publication. I did it all myself, except when too ill; and illness seldom hindered me
either from supplying the review of a book, going every night to the play, or
writing the notice of the play the same night at the printing-office. The consequence was, that work, slight as it looked, nearly killed me; for it never pros-
pered beyond the coterie of play-going readers, to whom it was almost exclusively known; and I was sensible of becoming weaker and poorer every day.
When I came home at night, often at morning, I used to feel as if I could
hardly speak; and for a year and a half afterwards a certain grain of fatigue
seemed to pervade my limbs, which I thought would never go off. Such, nevertheless, is a habit of mind, if it be but cultivated, that my spirits never seemed
better, nor did I ever write theatricals so well, as in the pages of this most un-
remunerating speculation." According to Sir Thomas N. Talfourd, Leigh Hunt
gave theatrical criticism a place in modern literature. "In criticism, thus just
and picturesque," says Sir Thomas, "Mr. Hunt has never been approached;
and the wonder is, that instead of falling off with the art of acting, he even grew
richer; for the articles of the Tatler, equalling those of the Examiner in niceness
of discrimination, are superior to them in depth and coloring." — Talfourd's
Critical and Miscellaneous Writings, article On the Late William Hazlitt. — ED.

track. It makes us feel as if we were beginning life over again.

Drury Lane Theatre is not the same identical Drury Lane it was then. It is on the same spot, but its body has been altered. It is the old friend with a new face. Covent Garden has experienced the same rejuvenescence. Alas! why cannot actors and play-goers grow young again too! Why cannot they be old friends with new faces, — the interior spirit the same, but the body remoulded! How patiently one would stand to have the scaffold set up round about us, while the little genii (whoever they were that acted the part of bricklayers) should pursue their task of restoration, elevating one's front, extending the wings, and new glazing those dimmed windows, the eyes! Then to take down the scaffolding; and like the statue of Memnon, we would sing at the touch of morning.

It is a pity that some such thing cannot take place, for the sake of those that particularly desire it. Rabelais says that he was sure he must have been the son of a king, because nobody had more princely inclinations. We incline, in the same manner, to be so young in our feelings, and to desire such a good long life before us to do a world of things in, that it seems as if we had a right to it. Mortality is a good provision, considering that the world has not come to its state of enjoyment, and that people in general, by the time they are forty, hardly know what to do with their Sundays: but an exception might be made, we think, in favor of those who could occupy all their hours some way or other for a hundred years to come, and who have not yet got over their love even of gingerbread. It will take us at least twenty years longer before we arrive at an indifference to lemon-cake. A "book of pictures" we cannot conceive the possibility of not caring for; and as to the bright visions of nymphs, and goddesses, and Miss Smith, which filled our dreams, sleeping and waking, do we not take Madame Pasta for the very personification of truth? and did we not go seven times to see Miss Inverarity, because she has the very voice of cheerful girlhood, high and trusting, and we are sure, while we are hearing her, that there is one person among the audience of her own age? Did we, and do we not believe in the marvels of Cinderella, just as much as if we had come ten minutes ago, from reading the little gilt story-book on a school step? And did not the dance of the nymphs with torches appear to us as if a page out of Ovid had become true? Have we not, in short, faith infinite, hope,—we dare to add charity; yea, even more than we had at sophisticate seventeen, when people are for being something different from what they are? We beg leave to say, our age is *fifteen;* we have run the great circle, and come round to it: and we think it a little hard that we are forced to look so much older.

There is scarcely any one performer remaining at Drury Lane of all that we remember when we first began writing theatricals. We are not sure there is even one. Liston and Dowton came soon, but we recollect the *débuts* of both: — of the former certainly. Farren is quite a modern, and Harley.

Mrs. Orger made her appearance years afterwards, and we have none of the then old ladies, Mrs. Sparks, Mrs. Mattocks, Miss Pope. The reigning women then were, Miss Pope, with her precise bit of a voice, and genuine humor, — Mrs. Mattocks, who had a never-failing recipe of a sudden flash of laughter, starting out of an acrid face; — the beautiful and good-natured Mrs. Powell, with her honeyed tones (those who recollect them surely must do something for her in her old age); — Miss Murray (afterwards Mrs. Henry Siddons), with her sweet voice and eyes, the latter a little too rolling; — Mrs. Henry Johnstone, a slight, handsome creature, with a formidable power of looking vixenish; — Miss Duncan, now Mrs. Davison, long a most clever actress with a liberal style; Mrs. Jordan, delightful Mrs. Jordan, whose voice did away the cares of the whole house, before they saw her come in, and Mrs. Siddons, the mighty mother of the pall and sceptre. We always remember her as the mother, — as something elderly, and even gaunt. We suspect that, with all her talents, she was, by nature, something of a dowager, compared with such a queen as Pasta.

Mrs. Gibbs was flourishing at that time, but she was at the Haymarket, very good, and very pretty in chambermaids and black-mittened rustics.

There also was Mrs. Mills, a tight little actress, whose tightness led her to play drummers; and Madame Storace, loud, free, and clever, with a reedy voice; and Mrs. Crouch, once lovely, then going the way of all forsaken Princes' mistresses; and Mrs. Billington, the favorite great singer, looking like a

handsome apoplexy, and straining her throat till you
thought she would have one; and Mrs. Bland, the
favorite little singer, with a voice like her name,
and a short, thick person, and dark face to match,
which her sweet ballads made ever welcome. What
troubles did not all these people have! What pleasures too! And how much pleasure did they not
give!

With respect to the men, we begin to think that
Mathews was at Drury Lane in those days; but we
are not sure. We remember him at the Haymarket,
where Liston came out. Elliston was the great man
at Drury, and John Kemble at Covent Garden. We
used to be heretical enough to think the former the
greater natural genius of the two, though of a less
heroical turn for tragedy; and we think so still. As
a cordial and dashing comedian, in first-rate characters, we never saw him equalled. No gallant knew
how to make love as he did. He had a fervor and a
breath, as well as a cheerful eye and a most urgent
voice, that made his energy of some consequence.

Lewis surpassed him in airiness; but there was no
gentleman comedian who comprised so many qualities of his art as he did, or who could diverge so well
into those parts of tragedy, which find a connecting
link with the graver powers of the comedian in their
gracefulness and humanity. He was the best Wild-
air, the best Archer, the best Aranza; and carrying
the seriousness of Aranza a little further, or making
him a *tragic gentleman* instead of a comic, he became the best Mortimer, and even the best Macbeth,
of any performer who excelled in comedy. When

Charles Kemble acts comedy, he gives you the idea of an actor who has come out of the chivalrous part of tragedy. It is grace and show that are most natural to him, — the ideal of mediocrity. Elliston being naturally a comedian, and comedy of the highest class demanding a greater sympathy with actual flesh and blood, his tragedy, though less graceful than Charles Kemble's, was more natural and cordial. He suffered and was shaken more. The other, in his greatest grief, is but like the statue of some Apollo Belvedere vivified, frowning in beauty, and making a grace of his sorrow. The god remains impassive to ordinary suffering. Elliston's features were nothing nearly so handsome or so finely cut as the others; but they were more sensitive and intelligent. He had nothing of the poetry of tragedy; the other has the form of it; but Elliston, in Macbeth, could give you something of the weak, and sanguine, and misgiving usurper; and in Mortimer, in the Iron Chest, he has moved the audience to tears. It ought not to be forgotten, that he restored that character to the stage, when John Kemble had killed it with his frigidity.*

The tragedy of this accomplished actor was, however, only an elongation, or drawing out, of the graver and more sensitive part of his comedy. It was in comedy that he was the master. When Kean appeared and extinguished Kemble, Elliston seems prudently to have put out his tragic lamp. In comedy, after the death of Lewis, he remained without a rival.

---

* For a lively and caustic account of the manner in which Kemble performed the part of Sir Edward Mortimer, see Colman's preface to the first edition of The Iron Chest, reprinted in Hotten's edition of Broad Grins. — ED.

23

He had three distinguished excellences, — dry humor, gentlemanly mirth, and fervid gallantry. His features were a little too round, and his person latterly became a great deal too much so. But we speak of him in his best days. His face, in one respect, was of that rare order, which is peculiarly fitted for the expression of enjoyment : — it laughed with the eyes as well as mouth. His eyes, which were not large, grew smaller when he was merry, and twinkled with glee and archness; his smile was full of enjoyment; and yet the moment he shook his head with a satirical deprecation, or dropped the expression of his face into an innuendo, nothing could be dryer or more angular than his mouth. There was a generosity in his style, both in its greater and smaller points. He understood all the little pretended or avowed arts of a gentleman, when he was conversing or complimenting, or making love, everything which implied the necessity of attention to the other person, and a just, and as it were, mutual consciousness of the graces of life on his own. His manners had the true *minuet dance* spirit of gentility, — the knowledge how to give and take, with a certain recognition of the merits on either side, even in the midst of raillery. And then his voice was remarkable for its union of the manly with the melodious; and as a lover, nobody approached him. Certainly nobody approached a woman as he did. It was the reverse of that preposterous style of *touch and avoid*, — that embracing at arms' length, and hinting of a mutual touch on the shoulders, — by which the ladies and gentlemen of the stage think fit to distinguish themselves from the characters they perform, and even the Pollys and Macheaths propitiate our good opinion. Elliston made out that it was no shame to love a woman, and no shame in her to return his passion. He took her hand, he cherished it against his bosom, he watched the moving of her countenance, he made the space less and less between them, and as he at length burst out into some exclamation of " charming ! " or " lovely ! " his voice trembled, not with weakness, but with the strength and fervor of its emotion. All the love, on the stage, since this (with the exception of Macready's domestic tenderness), is not worth twopence, and fit only to beget waiters.

In calling to mind the pleasant hours that have been given us by the talents of Elliston, we must not forget to mention his defects. In tragedy, for want of a strong sympathy with the serious, he sometimes got into a commonplace turbulence, and at others put on an affected solemnity ; and he was in the habit of *hawing* between his words. The longer he was a manager, the worse this habit became. He was not naturally inclined to the authoritative ; but having once commenced it in order to give weight to his levity, he seems to have carried about the habit with him to maintain his importance. Unfortunately, he fancied that he was never more natural than on these occasions. He said once, at the table of a friend of ours, clapping himself on the knee, and breathing with his usual fervor, " Nature-*aw*, sir, is everything-*aw: I-aw* am always-*aw* natural-*aw*."

Theodore Hook had a ludicrous story of his calling upon Elliston at the Surrey Theatre, and having some conversation with him in the midst of his managerial occupations. In the course of their dialogue, Elliston would start in a grand manner from the subject, and give some direction to his underlings. He called for two of them successively in the following manner : —

Elliston — (turning suddenly to the right, and breathing with all his fervor). " Night watchman ! " — (Enter night watchman, and has a word or two spoken to him by the manager.)

Elliston — (scarcely having resumed the discourse, and turning suddenly as before). " Other night watchman ! " — (Enter other night watchman, and is spoken to in like manner. The histrionic sovereign then resumes his discourse with Mr. Hook, with tranquil dignity).

We had an hour's conversation with him once at Drury Lane ; during which, in answer to some observation we made respecting the quantity of business he had to get through, he told us, that he had formed himself " on the model of the Grand Pensionary De Witt." Coming with him out of the theatre, we noticed the present portico in Brydges Street, which had just been added to the front, and said that it seemed to have started up like magic. " Yes, sir," said he, " energy is the thing : — I no sooner said it, than it was done : — it was a *Bonaparte blow.*"

There was real energy in all this, and the right animal spirits, as well as an innocent pedantry : nor did it hinder him from being the delightful comedian we have described. He could not have been it, had he not been pleased with himself : and a little superfluous self-complacency off the stage was to be pardoned him. A successful actor would be a phenomenon of modesty if he were not one of the vainest of men. Nobody gets such applause as he does, and in such an intoxicating way, except a conqueror entering a city.

Then there was Bannister (now enjoying the *otium cum benignitate*), at the top of another line of comedy, not omitting homely domestic tragedy. His Walter, in the Children in the Wood, was as good, in its way, as Mrs. Siddons's Lady Macbeth; and his Job Thornberry, in John Bull, was as superior to Fawcett's, as a brazier is to his brass. Bannister was one of those actors who give you the idea of being genuine honest men, and make you happy. Fawcett was excellent also in his line, which was that of impudent servants and gambling pedagogues. No Pangloss and Caleb Quotem have ever been so good as his. The other men were John Kemble, the very statue of an old Roman set walking; Pope, who had a dashing tragic style, but was monotonous, and was always lifting up his arms, like St. Paul preaching at Athens; Raymond, a melodramatic sort of actor, more intelligent than any one of the present, though harsh; Henry Johnstone, another, of a more ideal cast, and more quietly effective, though his handsomeness made him somewhat foppish; Murray, the father of Miss Murray, a very sensible and pleasing actor in old gentlemen; Powell, the last of the declamatory, white-handkerchief mourners of an older school; Lewis, the essence of lightness, of whim, of the mercurial (we have often described

him : * he is not to be replaced) ; Munden, who made
every trifle of importance, and masticated his grins till
they were irresistible; Simons, the most filching of
filchers ; Emery, a perfect Yorkshireman, startling in
rustic tragedy; Wewitzer, the only Canton; Irish
Johnstone, of most lackadaisical potency, and a good
singer ; Blanchard, the best Marquis de Grand Cha
teau we have seen, a most petulant and palsied Signor,
— still extant, and much, in other things, as he was ;
and afterwards came Cooke, who took almost all the
ideal out of tragedy, but put some good stuff into
it, and was a painfully good Sir Pertinax ; then Master Betty, the plaything of declamation, whose clev-
erness deserved a better fate ; and after an interval,
with many others still flourishing, Kean, the finest
actor we ever beheld.

We ought to mention Robert Palmer, a dogged kind
of natural actor, especially in characters of sturdy im-

---

* Let the reader picture to himself a slight, youthful figure, of middle height,
with sprightly eyes half shut with laughing, a mouth that showed its teeth a little
when it smiled ; restless, and yet gentlemanly manners ; a pair of gloved hands
that went through all the varieties of illustration that hands can insinuate, and
thrust the point of a joke into your ribs with a finger, to the exclamation of "you
dog !"— light airy voice, harmonizing with the look of the face, often out of breath
with spirits, and reposing sometimes on long lower tones of ludicrous contrast : a
head full of nods, and becks, and flutterings ; and lastly, a habit of finishing his
sentences with indescribable exclamations of *hoo !* and *phoo !* and a look of pouting
astonishment, as if nothing remained on earth to wonder at but his triumphant
foppery, and he joined the astonishment in order to be in the fashion. We have
nothing like it nowadays : nothing so thin, so airy, so gentlemanly, so eternally
young : for Lewis was the very same to the last. His slenderness and his animal
spirits preserved his look of juvenility to the moment when he took leave of the
stage. It was in the *Copper Captain*, with his epaulets dancing on his shoulders.
He came forward at the end of the play to take leave, and for the first time in his
life, perhaps, when on the stage, the good-natured actor shed tears and caused
them. His gay voice failed him as he told the public that "for thirty years he
had not once incurred their displeasure;" and he was obliged to put up his
cocked hat before his face to hide his emotion.

pudence or sottishness; but we knew him only in his
decline. John Palmer was before our time. So was
Miss Farren: and Suett was before our critical days,
though we remember him well, with his quaint, thin
manner, and his little slippery laugh.

We heard an exquisite anecdote of Suett the
other day. It is not much to tell, but it is highly
characteristic. Suett, it must be observed, was both
one of the drollest and one of the simplest of mankind. His relish of a joke was infinite, but he gave
rise to many a one unconsciously; and hung upon the
world, in all things, betwixt a laugh and an astonishment. It was he that said when he was dying,
" O dear! O dear! Bobby going to die! Here's a
pretty job! Was there ever seen the like?"

Suett one day took it into his head, gravely,
to teach clergymen how to read the Lord's Prayer!
We forget the name of the public house from which
his card of announcement was addressed, but it ran
in some such manner as the following, and was in
perfect good faith: —

" *Clergymen taught to read the Lord's Prayer,*
By ROBERT SUETT, *Comedian.*
Address to the Cat and Feathers, No. 21 *Drury*
Lane."

1831.

CLARENDON'S HISTORY OF THE REBELLION.

HAVING been much interested by a re-perusal of Clarendon's History of the Rebellion, I sit down to look through it again with the reader. My object is not to write a criticism, still less to enter into a review of the period to which the book relates, but simply to point out and remark a little upon some of the most curious passages. Having felt a pleasure, I wish to impart it, and shall fancy myself in the reader's company as with a friend.

The edition I make use of is a foreign one, printed at Basil, which is not likely to be read in England: so that I can only refer to the number of the books without noticing the pages.

The work opens with an account of Prince Charles's romantic journey into Spain, and the way in which James the First was brought to consent to it. This has been copied by Hume; but though Hume relates the particulars more directly relating to the journey, such as the bullying conduct of Buckingham, and the ridiculous lamentations of the King, who threw himself on his bed, weeping and wailing, and exclaiming that he should lose "Baby Charles," he has omitted one or two passages highly characteristic of the courtiers of those times. I observe, by the way, that Hume represents Baby Charles (who was then a young man in the twenty-third year of his age) as having tears iu his eyes when his father wished him to give up the journey: but this is not mentioned by Clarendon. The appellation of Baby, and the wilful infirmities to which Royalty is subject, appear to have beguiled the historian of his usual precision.

Sir Francis Cottington, afterwards Lord Cottington, was a courtier of real courage for that period; yet, see how he behaves at an unexpected proposition: " Cottington," said James, " here is Baby Charles and Stenny "—(an appellation he always used of and towards the Duke) — " who have a great mind to go by post to Spain to fetch home the Infanta, and will have but two more in their company. What think you of the journey? " He (Cottington) often protested since, that when he heard the King, *he fell into such a trembling that he could hardly speak.* But when the King commanded him to answer him, what he thought of the journey, he replied, he could not think well of it, &c. — *Book I.*

This was the courage of a great courtier. Now see his delicacy. Cottington, to this offence against the Duke, subsequently added another; upon which Buckingham, after his usual open manner, vowed revenge on him. The courtier applied to him to know whether, by a proper obsequiousness, he could not be restored to his Grace's favor; and being answered in the negative, said, he at least hoped that his Grace would not condescend to gain by his loss; and so requested him to return a set of hangings he had presented to him " in hope of his future favor," and which cost him eight hundred pounds. The Duke answered " he was right ; " and the hangings were re-stored, or at least the amonnt of their value ; together with some sums of money, which Cottington had laid out, by his order, for jewels and pictures. — *Ibid.*

Cottington appears to have been bold enough with everybody except his first master ; but he knew his men, even when he was most daring. He most likely ventures to behave to Buckingham in this manner, out of a confidence that it was the safest thing he could do to a man of his temper, where his advances were not accepted. It was an avowal of meanness and inferiority, as well as a compliment to the other's spirit ; which tended to put him at a pardonable dis-tance from a lofty but not ungenerous temper. After the death of Buckingham, Cottington got into power. There were none of his old masters to overawe him. He felt secure of Charles and his weakness ; and having a turn for drollery as well as artifice, did not scruple to play a strange trick upon Laud, whom all the lay part of the government disliked. It was so contrived as at once to turn to their advantage, and disconcert the Archbishop with the King. The whole of the story is worth copying, inasmuch as it involves a Naboth-vineyard anecdote of Charles the First such as Hûme does not venture to repeat. "The King, who was excessively affected to hunting (says Clarendon) and the sports of the field, had a great desire to make a great park for red as well as fallow deer, between Richmond and Hampton Court, where he had large wastes of his own and great parcels of wood, which made it very fit for the use he designed it to ; but as some parishes had commons in those

wastes, so many gentlemen and farmers had good
houses and good farms intermingled with those
wastes, of their own inheritance, or for their lives or
years; and without taking of them into the park, it
would not be of the largeness, or for the use proposed.
His Majesty desired to purchase those lands, and was
very willing to buy them upon higher terms than the
people could sell them at to anybody else, if they had
occasion to part with them; and thought it no unreasonable thing, upon those terms, to expect this
from his subjects; and so he employed his own surveyor and others of his officers to treat with the owners, many whereof were his own tenants, whose
farms would at last expire.

"The major part of the people were in a short
time prevailed with, but many very obstinately refused; and a gentleman who had the best estate, with
a convenient house and gardens, would by no means
part with it; and the King being as earnest to compass it, it made a great noise, as if the King would
take away men's estates at his own pleasure." [As
if he would not! What else was it that he desired to
do?] "The Bishop of London, who was Treasurer, and the Lord Cottington, Chancellor of the Exchequer, were, from the first entering upon it, very
averse from the design; not only for the murmur of
the people, but because the purchase of the land, and
the making a brick wall about so large a parcel of
ground (for it is near ten miles about), would cost a
greater sum of money than they could easily provide,
or they thought ought to be sacrificed on such an occasion; and the Lord Cottington (who was more so-

licited by the country people, and heard most of their
murmurs) took the business most to heart, and endeavored by all the ways he could, and by frequent
importunities, to divert his Majesty from pursuing it,
and put all delays he well could do in the bargains
which were to be made, till the King grew very angry
with him, and told him he was resolved to go through
with it, and had already caused brick to be burned,
and much of the wall to be built on his own land.
Upon which Cottington thought fit to acquiesce.

"The building of the wall before the people con-
sented to part with their land, or their common,
looked to them as if by degrees they should be shut
out from both, and increased the murmur and noise
of the people who were not concerned, as well as of
them who were; and it was too near London not to
be the common discourse. The Archbishop (who
desired exceedingly that the King should be possessed
as much of the hearts of the people as was possible,
at least that they should have no just cause to complain), meeting with it, resolved to speak to the King
of it; which he did; and received such an answer
from him, that he thought his Majesty rather not informed enough of the inconveniences and mischiefs of
the thing, then positively resolved not to desist from
it. Whereupon, one day he took the Lord Cottington
aside (being informed that he disliked it), and, according to his natural custom, spoke with great
warmth against it, and told him, ' he should do very
well to give the King good counsel, and withdraw
him from a resolution in which his honor and justice were so much called in question.' Cottington

answered him very gravely, 'that the thing designed
was very lawful, and he thought the King resolved
very well, since the place lay so conveniently for his
winter exercise; and that he should·by it not be compelled to make so long journeys as he used to do in
that season of the year for his sport; and that nobody
ought to dissuade him from it.'

" The Archbishop, instead of finding a concurrence
from him, as he expected, seeing himself reproached
upon the matter for his opinion, grew into much passion, telling him, ' Such men as he would ruin the
King, and make him lose the affections of his subjects; that, for his own part, as he had begun, so he
would go on, to persuade the King from proceeding
in so ill a counsel; and that he hoped it would appear
who had been his counsellor.' Cottington, glad to
see him so soon hot, and resolved to inflame him
more, very calmly replied to him, ' that he thought
a man could not, with a good conscience, hinder the
King from pursuing his resolutions; and that it could
not but proceed from want of affection to his person;
and that he was not sure that it might not be high
treason.' The other, upon the wildness of his discourse, in great anger asked him, ' Why? from
whence had he received that doctrine?' He said,
with the same temper, ' They who did not wish the
King's health, could not love him; and they who
went about to hinder his taking recreation which
preserved his health, might be thought, for aught he
knew, guilty of the highest crimes.' Upon which
the Archbishop, in great rage and with many reproaches, left him; and either presently, or upon the

next opportunity, told the King, ' that he now knew who was his great counsellor for making the park ; and that he did not wonder that men durst not represent any arguments to the contrary, or let his Majesty know how much he suffered in it, when such principles in divinity and law were laid down to terrify them,' and so recounted the conference he had with the Lord Cottington, bitterly inveighing against him and his doctrines, mentioning him with all the sharp reproaches imaginable, and beseeching his Majesty ' that his counsel might not prevail with him ;' taking some pains to make his conclusions appear very false and ridiculous.

" The King said no more than but, ' My Lord, you are deceived : Cottington is too hard for you. Upon my word, he hath not only dissuaded me more, and given more reason against this business than all the men in England have done, but hath really obstructed the work, by not doing his duty as I commanded him, for which I have been very much displeased with him. You see how unjustly your passion hath transported you.' By which reprehension he found how much he had been abused, and resented it accordingly." — *Ibid.*

Hume ought not to have omitted this story. Everything connected with it deserves attention. In the first place, even Clarendon has thought proper to tell it, though he contrives to divide the interest as much as possible with Cottington's humor. This is a proof how much noise it must have made ; and how difficult the author found it, in that age, to leave it out of his history. The noise, indeed, is evident from every part of it; and what is remarkable, the courtiers agreed with the people. The design was not only unjust to others; it was inconvenient to themselves. The Chancellor of the Exchequer was puzzled for money for it. Laud, who had the direction of the King's conscience, and was already disliked by all classes for his arbitrary principles, was afraid he should be thought to encourage it. Something also is to be allowed him on the score of scandal to the Bible. Here was the scene of Naboth's vineyard reopened. The Archbishop finds himself in the situation of Nathan. Cottington hates him for his officiousness, perhaps envies him the chance of turning the King's intentions; and the King first leaves him to suppose that he had not made up his mind, and afterwards is not sorry to have an opportunity of rebuking him. His Majesty had been compelled, no doubt, to take to himself much of the reproach which the Prelate, in the course of his wrath, had vented against the supposed adviser. Finally, the project appears to have been obstinately gone through with, and there is no knowing how much of the subsequent bitterness between the King and his subjects, how much of the general indignation, or of the vindictiveness and apparent cruelty of individuals, may have been owing to this single circumstance.

Of this Lord Cottington, who was an amusing person, the reader shall have all that remains to be told. He followed the fortunes of Charles the Second during the civil wars; and in proportion as the Stuarts grew weak, appears to have become more impudent and entertaining. The King, in his exile, alarmed

his court by an intention to make Colonel Windham
Secretary of State; "an honest gentleman," says
Clarendon, "whose best pretension to the office was
that his wife had been his Majesty's nurse."—"One
day, the Lord Cottington, when the Chancellor (Clarendon himself) and some others were present, told
the King, very gravely (according to his custom,
who never smiled when he made others merry),
'that he had a humble suit to him on behalf of an old
servant of his father; and whom he assured him upon
his knowledge, his father loved as well as he did any
man of that condition; and that he had been many
years one of his falconers in England:' and there-
upon enlarged himself (as he could do very well, in
all the terms of that science), to show how very skilful he was in that art. The King asked him 'what
he would have done for him?' Cottington told him
'it was very true that his Majesty kept no falconers, and
the poor man was grown old, and could not ride as
he used to do; but that he was a very honest man,
and could read very well, and had as audible a voice
as any man need to have; and therefore besought his
Majesty, that he would make him his Chaplain;'
which, speaking with so composed a countenance,
and somewhat of earnestness, the King looked upon
him with a smile to know what he meant; when he,
with the same gravity, assured him the 'falconer
was in all respects as fit to be his Chaplain as Colonel Windham was to be Secretary of State;' which
so surprised the King, who had never spoken to him
of the matter, all that were present not being able to
abstain from laughing, that his Majesty was somewhat

out of countenance; and this being merrily told by some of the standers-by, it grew to be a story in all companies, and did readily divert the King from the purpose, and made the other so much ashamed of pretending to it, that there was no more discourse of it." — *Book XII.*

Cottington was of a Roman Catholic family. When he was in Spain on a former occasion, he was reconciled to the Church of Rome, and went regularly to mass; but on his return to England, he resumed his misconformity with the Protestants. It was convenient to his views of office. During the exile of Charles the Second he and Clarendon were sent by that prince in an embassy to the King of Spain, and Cottington, now aged and gouty, took the opportunity of "patching up his old body for heaven," and dying in the family faith.

He died not long after, at Valladolid, where he had taken up his abode for the remainder of his days. "He was *a very wise man*," says Clarendon, "by the great and long experience he had in business of all kinds, and by his natural temper, which was not liable to any transport of anger, or any other passion, but could bear contradiction, and even reproach, without being moved or put out of his way; for he was very steady in pursuing what he proposed to himself, and had courage not to be frightened with any opposition. It is true, he was illiterate as to the grammar of any language, or the principle of any science; but by his perfect understanding of the Spanish (which he spoke as a Spaniard), the French, and Italian languages, and having read very much of

24

them, he could not be said to be ignorant in any part
of learning, divinity only excepted. He had a fine
and extraordinary understanding in the nature of
beasts and birds, and above all in all kinds of planta-
tions, and arts of husbandry. He was born a gentleman
both by his father and mother, his father having a
pretty entire seat near Breton in Somersetshire, worth
above two hundred pounds a year, which had descended from father to son for many hundred years,
and is still in possession of his elder brother's children, the family having been always Roman Catholics. His mother was a Stafford, nearly allied to
Sir Edward Stafford, who was Vice-Chamberlain to
Queen Elizabeth, and had been Ambassador in
France; by whom this gentleman was brought up,
and was gentleman of his horse, and left one of his
executors of his will, and by him recommended to Sir
Robert Cecil, Secretary of State; who preferred him
to Sir Charles Cornwallis, when he went Ambassador
into Spain, in the beginning of the reign of King
James; where he remained for the space of eleven
or twelve years, in the condition of Secretary or
Agent, without ever returning into England in all
that time. He made by his own virtue and industry
a pretty fair estate, of which, though the revenue did
not exceed above four thousand pounds by the year,
yet he had four very good houses, and three parks,
the value of which was not reckoned into that com-
putation. He lived very nobly, well served and attended in his house; had a better stable for horses,
better provisions for sports (especially of hawks, in
which he took great delight), than most of his quality,

and lived always with great splendor; for though he loved money very well, *and did not warily enough consider the circumstances of getting it*, he spent it well all ways but in giving; which he did not affect. He was of an excellent humor, and very easy to live with; and under a grave countenance covered the most of mirth, and caused more than any man of the most pleasant disposition. He never used anybody ill; but used many very well for whom he had no regard. His greatest fault was, that he could dissemble and make men believe that he loved them very well, when he cared not for them. He had not very tender affections, nor bowels apt to yearn at all objects which deserved compassion. He was heartily tired of the world, and no man was more willing to die; which is an argument that he had peace of his conscience. He left behind him a greater esteem of his parts, than love to his person." — *Book XIII.*

This is a portrait of a clever, selfish, entertaining man of the world, whose success, after all, is a poor business. By his own knavery and folly to boot (for this "virtuous" money-getter, and "very wise man," was evidently not without both in their way), he gets rid of his good opinion of other men, and his real relish of life; eats and drinks himself into a good tormenting gout; and before he dies, is heartily weary of the world. His "peace of conscience" (which he had a perfect right to, considering the way he was brought up) means that he had little or no conscience of any sort; and what little he had, he satisfies, by reposing it "in the bosom of an infallible church," who, it must be confessed, owes her children a good deal of indulgence, in return for the pains she takes to spoil them.[*]

The wisdom and virtue of this courtier appear to have done little good to the character of his brother Ambassador.

Of the Earl of Arundel, who was sent by Charles against the Scots at the beginning of the troubles, Clarendon gives the following pithy character: "He did not love the Scots, he did not love the Puritans; which qualifications were much allayed by another negative; he did not much love anybody else." —*Book II.* Perhaps the author might have added something like what a friend of ours introduced at the end of a similar character drawn of a modern poet: —"He did not like *me.*" Arundel, though a court officer, was of a different way of thinking from Hyde on many points, and had probably crossed him with some of his stately manners. A good deal of personal pique is evident here and there in the writings of this statesman. Hume speaks ill of Arundel's talents. He seems to have been a selfish man,

---

* Here is Fuller's character of Cottington.

"Sir Francis Cottington, Knight, was born nigh Mere, in this county [Wiltshire], and bred, when a youth, under Sir —— Stafford. He lived so long in Spain, till he made the garb and gravity of that nation become his, and became him. He raised himself by his natural strength, without any artificial advantage: having his parts above his learning, his experience, and (some will say) his success above all: so that at the last he became Chancellor of the Exchequer, baron of Hanworth in Middlesex, and (upon the resignation of Doctor Juxon) Lord Treasurer of England, gaining also a very great estate. But what he got in a few years he lost in fewer days, since our civil wars, when the Parliament was pleased (for reasons only known to themselves) to make him one of the examples of their severity, excluding him pardon, but permitting his departure beyond the seas, where he died about the year 1650."—The Worthies of England, Nuttall's Ed., vol. 3, p. 329.— ED.

for he withdrew from the troubles, and lived and died in Italy. He was the possessor of the marbles known under his name.

The following anecdote of Windebank, Secretary of State, a favorer of the Papists, would have shone in Bandello: "I remember," says Clarendon, "one story brought into the house concerning him, that administered some mirth. A messenger (I think his name was Newton), who principally attended the service of apprehending priests, came one day to him in his garden, and told him that he had brought with him a priest, a stirring and active person, whom he had apprehended that morning; and desired to know to what prison he should carry him. The Secretary sharply asked him whether he would never give over this bloodthirsty humor? and in great anger calling him a knave, and taking the warrant from him by which he had apprehended him, departed without giving any other direction. The messenger, appalled, thought the priest was some person in favor, and therefore took no more care of him, but suffered him to depart. The priest, freed from this fright, went securely to his lodgings, and within two or three days was arrested for debt, and carried in execution to prison. Shortly after Secretary Windebank sent for the messenger, and asked him ' what was become of the priest he had at such a time brought before him?' He told him, ' that he conceived his Honor was offended with the apprehension of him, and therefore he had looked no farther after him.' The Secretary, in much passion, told him ' the discharging a priest was no light matter, and that if he speedily found him not, he should answer the default with his life; that the priest was a dangerous fellow, and must not escape in that fashion.' The messenger, besides his natural inclination to that exercise, terrified with these threats, left no means untried for the discovery, and at last heard where the man was in execution in prison; thither he went and demanded the priest (who was not there known to be such) as his prisoner formerly, and escaped from him; and by virtue of his first warrant took him again into custody, and immediately carried him to the Secretary; and within a few days after the priest was discharged, and at liberty. The jailer, in whose custody he had been put for debt, was arrested by the parties grieved, and he again sued the messenger, who appealed for justice to the House of Commons against the Secretary." — *Book III.*

From this and other charges, Windebank fled the kingdom. He was a creature of Laud's.

How TO BE PREVAILED UPON TO ERADICATE Bishops. — The House prepared a very short bill " for the utter eradication of Bishops, Deans, and Chapters; with all Chancellors, and officials, and all officers, and other persons belonging to either of them;" which they prevailed Sir Edward Deering, a man very opposite to all their designs (but a man of levity and vanity, easily flattered by being commended), to present into the House; which he did from the gallery, with the two verses in Ovid, the *application whereof was his greatest motive:*"—

" Cuncta prius tentanda; sed immedicabile vulnus
Ense recidendum est, ne pars sincera trahatur."

[I tried whatever in the godhead lay :
But gangrened members must be lopt away,
Before the nobler parts are tainted to decay.— DRYDEN.]

A good thing was said of this upon a bill by Lord
Falkland: "It was so late every day before the
House was resumed (the Speaker commonly leaving
the chair about nine of the clock, and never resuming
it till four in the afternoon), that it was very thin;
they only who prosecuted the bill with impatience
remaining in the House, and the others who abhorred
it, growing weary of so tiresome an attendance, left
the House at dinner-time, and afterwards followed
their pleasures: so that the Lord Falkland was wont
to say, ' that they who hated the Bishops, hated them
worse than the Devil ; and that they who loved them,
did not love them so well as their dinner.' "—*Ibid.*
This is true. But how should they? The dinner
was the more Episcopalian thing of the two.

MONTROSE. — Clarendon says, that when the King
arrived in Scotland, Montrose came privately to him,
and informed him, among other particulars, " that the
Marquis of Hamilton was no less faulty and false towards his Majesty than Argyle ; and offered to make
proof of all in the Parliament; but rather desired to
have them both made away;" which he frankly
offered to do ; but the King, abhorring that expedient,
though for his own security, advised " that the proofs
might be prepared for Parliament."—*Book IV.* The
following is a note of Hume's upon this passage, ap-
pended to the 58th chapter of his History: " It is
not improper to take notice of a mistake committed

by Clarendon, much to the disadvantage of this gallant
nobleman; that he offered the King, when his Majesty
was in Scotland, to assassinate Argyle. At the time
the King was in Scotland, Montrose was confined to
prison." He refers for his authority to Rushworth,
Vol. VI., p. 980. Montrose's imprisonment, however,
does not refute the charge of his having made the
offer. It only proves that he could not have made it
in person. Besides, Clarendon does not say that he
offered to assassinate Argyle, but to have him as-
sassinated. The additional words, " which he frankly offered to do," might indeed be construed otherwise; but not with probability, especially after so
direct a mention of the offer, enforced upon the reader by marks of quotation. It is observable that
Clarendon carefully makes use of these marks whenever he repeats the observations of another. Though
Montrose was imprisoned at that time, he was of an
active disposition, and might have conveyed the offer
by another person. Even if Clarendon represented
him as undertaking to be the assassin himself, the
time of his liberation might have been contemplated;
and the manners of those enraged and vindictive
times offer nothing very considerable against the likelihood of such a proposal; Clarendon, for one, clearly
believed in it, or he would hardly have mentioned the
proposal without expressing astonishment. At the
same time it should be mentioned, that Clarendon
was no friend to the Marquis's person, though he
joined in commending his exploits. He appears to
have been jealous of him; at least to have been mortified that Montrose did not pay more deference to his

opinion. See Book XII., where they have an interview near the Hague. The best argument in Montrose's favor might be drawn from his bravery, and
his open, defying nature; and yet very brave men in
those times could condescend to be assassins; and
Montrose, with all his gallantry, could play a tricking
and lying part. There were fanatics on all sides, and
of all descriptions; fanatics, too, in petty personal
feuds as well as in great party matters. Sir Walter
Scott has done his best to render Montrose a hero of
romance; and a very good one he is, as far as valor
and military conduct can make him; but he is much
fitter to be the hero of a modern Scotch ultra than
of an English gentleman at any time. Hume, himself a Scotchman and a Tory (though his philosophy
and cool temperament relieved him from many of
the absurdities connected with both of those watch-
words), was inclined enough to like Montrose and
his party, and yet hear how he begins his own account of the Marquis's history:—

" Before the commencement of these civil disorders,
the Earl of Montrose, a young nobleman of a distinguished family, returning from his travels, had been
introduced to the King, and had made an offer of his
services; but by the insinuations of the Marquis,
afterwards Duke of Hamilton, who possessed much
of Charles's confidence, he had not been received with
that distinction to which he thought himself justly
entitled. Disgusted with this treatment, he had for-
warded all the violence of the Covenanters; and agreeably to the natural ardor of his genius, he had employed himself, during the first Scottish insurrection,

with great zeal, as well as success, in levying and con-
ducting their armies. Being commissioned by the
Tables to wait upon the King, while the royal army
lay at Berwick, he was so gained by the civilities and
caresses of that monarch, that he thenceforth devoted
himself entirely, though secretly, to his service, and
entered into a close correspondence with him. In
the second insurrection, a grèat military command
was intrusted to him by the Covenanters; and he
was the first that passed the Tweed, at the head of
their troops, in the invasion of England. He found
means, however, soon after to convey a letter to the
King: and by the infidelity of some about that Prince
— Hamilton, as was suspected — a copy of this letter
was sent to Leven, the Scottish general. Being accused of treachery and a correspondence with the
enemy, Montrose openly avowed the letter, and asked
the generals, if they dared to call their sovereign an
enemy: and by this bold and magnanimous behavior, he escaped the danger of an immediate
prosecution. As he was now fully known to be of
the royal party, he no longer concealed his principles; and he endeavored to draw those who had
entertained like sentiments into a bond of association
for his master's service. Though thrown into prison
for this enterprise, and detained some time, he was
not discouraged; but still continued, by his countenance and protection, to infuse spirit into the dis-
tressed royalists."

Let justice be done to Montrose, and to everybody:
but that it may be done to everybody, let us take care
how we allow the most interested misrepresentations

of history to pass without notice, especially in these times. The servile have a sufficient re-action in their favor, from the events of the world, without being under the necessity of receiving further encouragement.

PARLIAMENT HOURS. — The old Parliament hours were from eight o'clock in the morning till twelve at noon. Afterwards, during the disputes of the House with Charles, Clarendon mentions a debate that lasted till after nine o'clock at night, which, he says, was the latest ever known, except that upon the Remonstrance. In his Life, an account is given of a bill, in which the Duke of Buckingham took so much interest, that, " contrary to his custom of coming into the House, indeed of not rising till eleven of the clock, and seldom staying above a quarter of an hour, except upon some affairs which he concerned himself in, he was now always present with the first in the morning, and staid till the last at night, for the debate often held from the morning till four o'clock in the afternoon, and sometimes till candles were brought in." It was thought late to meet at ten. " It is hard to tell," says Hume, in a note on the reign of Elizabeth, " why, all over the world, as the age becomes more luxurious, the hours become later. Is it the crowd of amusements that push on the hours gradually? or are the people of fashion better pleased with the secrecy and silence of nocturnal hours, when the industrious vulgar are all gone to rest? In rude ages, men have few amusements or occupations but what daylight affords them." These are undoubtedly among the causes; but the progress of commerce should be added. In proportion as traders and merchants become of importance, their hours must be considered; and they like to have as many of these as possible at a time. The rakes of Charles the Second's time, and the rich merchants of the ensuing reigns, became alike the encouragers of late hours; and fashion compelled what such opposite causes had begun. Parliaments now are in the habit of sitting up all night, and much worse they are for it. Their heads are muddled with wine; another line of separation is drawn between them and the people; and the spirit of dissipation, of fashion, and of money-getting, alike conspire to render them sorry guardians of public liberty. The true spirit of a House of Commons is now to be found in a few members inside, and those who canvass their actions out of doors. The great diffusion of knowledge and inquiry has rendered the represented superior to their representatives. Consider even the bodily vigor, the physical manliness of the old Parliament men who procured us our liberties, and then see what a poor set of shattered men of the world we have now for their successors, body as well as mind. And these two things are very apt to go together in men of public action, whether for good or evil. A solitary student who does his best, may have something to say in behalf of his infirmities; but how are a parcel of drinking, gambling, nervous, and gouty men to wage war with corruption at two o'clock in the morning.*

---

* Addison has an amusing little paper on late hours, in the Tatler. "It is very plain," he says, "that the night was much longer formerly in this island

NOTIONS OF REGAL PROPERTY. — The King asks (Book V.) " what title any subject of his kingdom had to his house and land, that he had not to his town of Hull." Compare this with the story of the house and grounds which he forced a man to part with, and then read the following passage from our author's own pen : —

" A man shall not unprofitably spend his contemplation, that, upon this occasion, considers the method of God's justice (a method terribly remarkable in many passages and upon many persons, which we shall be compelled to remember in this discourse), that the same principles, and the same application of those principles, should be used to wresting all sovereign power from the crown, which the crown had a little before made use of for extending its authority and power beyond its bounds, to the prejudice of the just rights of the subject. A supposed necessity was then thought ground enough to create a power, and a bare averment of that necessity, to beget a practice,

---

than it is at present. By the night, I mean that portion of time which nature has thrown into darkness, and which the wisdom of mankind had former'y dedicated to rest and silence. This used to begin at eight o'c'ock in the evening, and conclude at six in the morning. The curfew, or eight o'clock bell, was the signal throughout the nation for putting out their candles, and going to bed.

" Our grandmothers, though they were wont to sit up the last iu the family, were all of them fast asleep at the same hours that their daughters are new busy at crimp and basset. Modern statesmen are concerting schemes, and engaged in the depth of politics, at the time when their forefathers were laid down quietly to rest, and had nothing in their heads but dreams. As we have thus thrown business and pleasure into the hours of rest, and by that means made the natural night about half as long as it should be, we are forced to piece it out with a great part of the morning ; so that near two thirds of the nation lie fast asleep for several hours in broad daylight. This irregularity is grown so very fashionable at present, that there is scarce a lady of quality in Great Britain that ever saw the sun rise." — ED.

to impose what they thought convenient upon the
subject, by writs of ship-money never before known:
and a supposed necessity now, and a bare averment
of that necessity, is as confidently and more fatally
concluded a good ground to exclude the crown from
the use of any power, by an ordinance never before
heard of, and the same maxim of *salus populi su-
prema lex*, which had been used to the infringing the
liberty of the one, made use of for destroying the
rights of the other."

That it was ridiculous in one encroaching individual, or his court, to use the maxim of *salus populi*
for his own advantage, in contradistinction to theirs,
is evident; but it is not so evident that it was absurd
or vicious in the people themselves to use the same
maxim against the encroachments of the individual;
and by Clarendon's acknowledgment in many places,
however he may contradict it in others, the people at
large were really as much at issue with the King as
their representatives.   Clarendon, with all his superiority to the rest of the court, argues this question,
after all, like a lawyer.   The King is his client, the
people the defendants, and the most liberal concession
he makes is, that both have equal rights.   But by
his own account, the people were in the right in
this great quarrel.   Their representatives, no doubt,
sometimes committed great faults; and what was
worse, mean ones.   They had not escaped the con-
tagion of court example, and the cried-up craft of
King James.   But the great question had now come
up; of the many against the few.   It was the few
who began it; they would have trampled the many

into the dust forever; and the many had a right to bring them to their proper senses and situations. The King up to this period has always averred, and still avers, that he never intended to make war on the Parliament. He solemnly protested it. And yet Clarendon now says, as an excuse to those who reproached the King with not making war, that the fact was, he had no means of making it, not a barrel of powder, nor musket, nor money; but that he expected all these necessaries with impatience from the Queen. (See Book V., in various places towards the end.) The Parliament had notice of all these secret wishes and manœuvres: and yet both Clarendon and his master are constantly reproaching them for not putting faith in their practices!

GORING'S INFINITE HYPOCRISY, WHICH CLARENDON SEEMS TO ADMIRE. — "Colonel Goring came, upon the summons, with that undauntedness, that all clouds of distrust immediately vanished, insomuch as no man presumed to whisper the least jealousy of him; which he observing, came to the House of Commons, of which he was a member; and, having sat a day or two patiently, as if he expected some charge, in the end he stood up, with a countenance full of modesty, and yet not without a mixture of anger (as he could help himself with all insinuations of doubt, or fear, or shame, or simplicity in his face, that might gain belief, to a greater degree than I ever saw any man; and could seem the most confounded when he was best prepared, and the most out of countenance when he was best resolved, and to want words and the habit of speaking, when they flowed from no man with greater power), and told them, 'that he had been sent for by them, upon some information given against him, and that, though he believed the charge being so ridiculous, they might have received, by their own particular inquiry, satisfaction; yet the discourses that had been used, and his being sent for in that manner, had begot some prejudices to him in his reputation; which if he could not preserve, he should be less able to do them service; and therefore desired that he might have leave (though very unskilful, and unfit to speak in so wise and judicious assembly) to present to them the state and condition of that place under his command, and then he doubted not but to give them full satisfaction in those particulars, which possibly had made some impression on them to his disadvantage; that he was far from taking it ill from those who had given any information against him; for what he had done, and must do, might give some umbrage to well-affected persons, who knew not the grounds and reasons that induced him so to do; but that if any such persons would, at any time, resort to him, he would clearly inform them of whatever motives he had; and would be glad of their advice and assistance for the better doing thereof.' Then he took notice of every particular that had been publicly said against him, or privately whispered, and gave such plausible answers to the whole, intermingling sharp taunts and scorns to what had been said of him, with pretty application of himself and flattery to the men that spake it, concluding, 'that they well knew in what esteem he stood with others; so that if, by his ill carriage, he should forfeit the good opinion of that House, upon which he only depended, and to whose service he entirely devoted himself, he were madder than his friends took him to be, and must be as unpitied in any misery that could befall him, as his enemy would be glad to see.' With which, as innocently and unaffectedly uttered as can be imagined, he got so general an applause with the whole House, that not without some little apology for troubling him, they desired him again to repair to his government, and to finish those works which were necessary for the safety of the place; and gratified him with consenting to all the propositions he made in behalf of his garrison, and paid him a good sum of money for their arrears; with which, and being privately assured (which was indeed resolved on) that he should be Lieutenant General when it should be formed, he departed again to Portsmouth; in the mean time assuring his Majesty, by those who were trusted between them, ' that he would be speedily in a posture to make his declaration for his service, as he should be required;' which he was forced to do sooner than he was provided for, though not sooner than he had reason to expect." — *Book V.*

Goring afterwards surrendered Portsmouth back again to the Parliament, but was still trusted by anybody whom he chose to deceive, and went lying and cheating on all sides of him. It is impossible, in spite of one's indignation, not to admire the talents which he so perverted; but it is desirable in a writer who affects integrity like Clarendon, that the indig-

25

nation should be more prominent than he has chosen
to make it. Besides, a great deal of our admiration
of such men is diminished, if we reflect, that they
very likely succeeded in deceiving so many others,
not because they are more clever than many of them,
but because they possess one accomplishment the
less, — namely, a sense of moral beauty. I suspect
(which is extrely probable) that Goring very spe-
cially deceived Clarendon himself; who then became
willing to think as highly as possible of a man that
had overreached him; for it is difficult not to see
that his tendency, after all, is to value intellect and
political dexterity above every other consideration.
He confounded too often the instrument with its
work. In Book VIII. is a capital summary of the
character of Goring. Clarendon excels in portraits.
He has here painted two sovereign debauchees to the
life.

PORTRAITS OF TWO DEBAUCHEES — GORING AND
WILMOT. — " Goring, who was now General of the
Horse, was no more gracious to Prince Rupert than
Wilmot had been; had all the other's faults and
wanted his regularity, and preserving his respect with
the officers. Wilmot loved debauchery, but shut it
out from his business; never neglected that, and
rarely miscarried in it. Goring had a much better
understanding, and a sharper wit (except in the very
exercise of debauchery, and then the other was inspired), a much keener courage and presentness of
mind in danger. Wilmot discerned it farther off, and
because he could not behave himself so well in it,

commonly prevented, or warily declined it: and never drank when he was within distance of an enemy; Goring was not able to resist the temptation when he was in the middle of them, nor would decline it to obtain a victory: as in one of those fits, he had suffered the horse to escape out of Cornwall; and the most signal misfortunes in his life in war had their rise from that uncontrollable license. Neither of them valued their promises, professions, or friendships, according to any rules of honor or integrity; but Wilmot violated them the less willingly, and never but for some great benefit or convenience to himself; Goring without scruple, out of humor, or for wit's sake; and loved no man so well but that he would cozen him, and then expose him to public mirth for having been cozened; therefore he had always fewer friends than the other, but more company; for no man had wit that pleased the company better. The ambition of both was unlimited, and so equally incapable of being contented: and both unrestrained, by any respect to good nature or justice, from pursuing the satisfaction thereof: yet Wilmot had more scruples from religion to startle him, and would not have attained his end by any gross or foul act of wickedness. Goring could have passed through pleasantly, and would without hesitation have broken any trust, or done any act of treachery to have satisfied an ordinary passion or appetite; and, in truth, wanted nothing but industry (for he had wit, and courage, and understanding, and ambition, uncontrolled by any fear of God or man) to have been as eminent and successful in the highest attempts of

wickedness, as any man of the age he lived in or before. Of all his qualifications, dissimulation was his
masterpiece, in which he so much excelled, that men
were not ordinarily ashamed or out of countenance
with being deceived but twice by him."

There is a Bacchanalian " Health to Goring " in the
Poems of Robert Herrick. If any charitable person
wishes to find an excuse for Lord Rochester, let him
know, if he does not know it already, that. Wilmot
was his father.   1825.

---·◊·---

GEORGE SELWYN AND HIS CONTEMPO-
RARIES.*

T HERE is a charm in the bare title of this book.
It is an *open sesame* to a world of pleasant

---

* Edinburgh Review, 1844. — George Selwyn and his Contemporaries; with
Memoir and Notes. By John Heneage Jesse. 4 vols. 8 vo. London : 1843-4.
[The easy and idiomatic English of this paper, was not, it is to be feared, appreciated by Mr. Macvey Napier, Jeffrey's successor in the editorship of the
Edinburgh Review ; for upon Hunt proposing to send him a "chatty article,"
for the "buff and blue," he grew alarmed, and wrote the essayist a harsh letter on
dignity of style. The sensitive contributor was sorely wounded, and appealed to
Macaulay for counsel, who replied in a kind and cordial letter. See with what
tact Macaulay consoles the discomforted reviewer: " Napier would thoroughly
appreciate the merit of a writer like Bolingbroke or Robertson ; but would, I
think, be unpleasantly affected by the peculiarities of such a writer as Burton,
Sterne, or Charles Lamb. He thinks your style too colloquial ; and, no doubt, it
has a very colloquial character. I wish it to retain that character, which to me
is exceedingly pleasant. But I think that the danger against which you have to
guard is excess in that direction. Napier is the very man to be startled by the
smallest excess in that direction. Therefore I am not surprised that, when you
proposed to send him a *chatty* article, he took fright, and recommended dignity
and severity of style." — ED.]

things. As at the ringing of the manager's bell, the curtain rises, and discovers a brilliant *tableau* of wits, beauties, statesmen, and men of pleasure about town, attired in the quaint costume of our great-grandfathers and great-grandmothers; or, better still, we feel as if we had obtained the reverse of Bentham's wish — to live a part of his life at the end of the *next* hundred years — by being permitted to live a part of ours about the beginning of the *last*, with an advantage he never stipulated for, of spending it with the pleasantest people of the day.

Let us now suppose that only twenty-four hours were granted for us; how much might be done or seen within the time! We take the privilege of long intimacy to drop in upon Selwyn in Chesterfield Street, about half-past ten or eleven in the morning; we find him in his dressing-gown, playing with his dog Raton: at twelve we walk down arm-in-arm to White's, where Selwyn's arrival is hailed with a joyous laugh, and Topham Beauclerk hastens to initiate us into the newest bit of scandal. The day is warm, and a stroll to Betty's fruit-shop (St. James's Street) is proposed. Lord March is already there, settling his famous bet with young Mr. Pigot, that old Mr. Pigot would die before Sir William Codrington. Just as this grave affair is settled, a cry is raised of " the Gunnings are coming," and out we all tumble to gaze and criticise. At Brookes', our next house to call, Sir Charles Hanbury Williams is easily persuaded to entertain the party by reading his verses, not yet printed, on the marriage of Mr. Hussey (an Irish gentleman) with the Duch-

ess of Manchester (the best match in the kingdom),
and is made happy by our compliments; but looks
rather blank on Rigby's hinting that the author will
be obliged to fight half the Irishmen in town, which,
considering the turn of the verses, seemed probable
enough.   To change at once the subject and the
scene, we accompany him and Rigby to the House
of Commons, where we find the " great commoner "
making a furious attack on the Attorney-General
(Murray), who, as Walpole phrases it, suffered for
an hour.   After hearing an animated. reply from
Fox (the first Lord Holland), we rouse Selwyn,
who is dozing behind the treasury bench, and, wishing to look in upon the Lords, make him introduce
us.   We find Lord Chesterfield speaking, the Chancellor (Hardwicke) expected to speak next, the Duke
of Cumberland just come in, and the Duke of Newcastle shuffling about in a ludicrous state of perturbation, betokening a crisis; but Selwyn grows impatient, and we hurry off to Strawberry Hill, to join
the rest of the celebrated *partie quarrée*, or " out
of town " party who are long ago assembled.   The
petit souper appears on the instant, and as the champagne circulates, there circulates along with it a
refined, fastidious, fashionable, anecdotic, gossiping
kind of pleasantry, as exhilarating as its sparkle, and
as volatile as its froth.   We return too late to see
Garrick; but time enough for the house-warming fête
at Chesterfield House, where the Duke of Hamilton
loses a thousand pounds at faro, because he chooses
to ogle Elizabeth Gunning instead of attending to
his cards.

We shall, perhaps, be reminded that we have seen nothing of Fielding, Richardson, Smollett, Johnson, Collins, Akenside, Mason, or Gray; but our gay friends, alas! never once alluded to them, and for *us* to waste any part of so short a period in looking for men of letters, would be to act like the debtor in the Queen's Bench prison, who, when he got a day rule, invariably spent it in the Fleet.

According to Mr. Jesse, we owe this new glimpse into these times to a habit of Selwyn's, which it is difficult to reconcile with his general carelessness. " It seems to have been one of his peculiarities to preserve not only every letter addressed to him during the course of his long life, but also the most trifling notes and unimportant memoranda." Such was the practice of the most celebrated wit of the eighteenth century; the most celebrated wit of the nineteenth does precisely the reverse. " Upon principle," said the Rev. Sydney Smith, in answer to an application about letters from Sir John Mackintosh, " I keep no letters, except those on business. I have not a single letter from him, nor from any human being in my possession." * We should certainly prefer being our contemporary's correspondent; but we must confess that we are not sorry to come in for a share of the benefits accruing from Selwyn's savings to his posterity.

---

* Life of Mackintosh, by his Son, vol. ii., page 99. — "We talked of letter-writing. 'It is now,' said Johnson, 'become so much the fashion to publish letters, that, in order to avoid it, I put as little into mine as I can.' 'Do what you will, sir,' replied Boswell, 'you cannot avoid it.'" — Boswell's Life of Johnson, vol. vii, p. 80.

"To this peculiarity," continues Mr. Jesse, "the reader is indebted for whatever amusement he may derive from the perusal of these volumes. The greater portion of their contents consists of letters addressed to Selwyn by persons who, in their day, moved in the first ranks of wit, genius, and fashion. Independent of their general merit as epistolary compositions, the editor conceives that they will be found in a high degree valuable and entertaining, from the light which they throw on the manners and customs of society in the last age, from their presenting a faithful chronicle of the passing events of the day, and from the mass of amusing gossip and lively anecdote which they contain."

This is a rather injudicious paragraph. It excites expectations which are not fulfiled. There is very little anecdote — less altogether than will be found in any half dozen consecutive letters of Walpole; and two volumes would contain everything in the book calculated to throw the faintest light on manners. It is, indeed; precisely of that kind which Bacon says should be read by deputy, i. e., through the medium of a Review; for the real meaning of the aphorism — "Bad books make good reviews, as bad wine makes good vinegar" — is not, as the profane allege, because critics excel or exult in fault-finding, but because their chief utility consists in collecting scattered beauties, distilling essences, or separating the true metal from the dross. But it would be unjust to call this a bad book; it is certainly one which every possessor of a library should possess; yet it is one in which the quantity of print is out of all proportion to the useful or amusing matter; and the intelligent editor is evidently conscious of the fact; for, on what principle can his singularly liberal mode of annotation be defended, except as compensating for the poverty of the text? The legitimate use of editorial notes is

to clear up doubtful allusions, or supply knowledge
necessary to the understanding of the work. For example, it might be useful to tell us something about
Gilly Williams; but the youngest reader knows
enough of Garrick not to be puzzled by the incidental
occurrence of his name. Yet we are favored with a
biographical notice of the great actor, occupying ten
pages, *apropos* of this solitary line in one of Dr. Warner's letters — " The chapter of Garrick (his death)
is a very melancholy one for poor Harry Hoare and
me." This is book-making with a vengeance! At
the same time, this mode of proceeding has answered
the main purpose; it has made the book more reada-
ble, and may save the indolently curious much trouble, by placing all they can possibly wish to learn, or
refer to, within reach. Thus we find here a careful
compilation of most of the scattered notices regarding
Selwyn himself; and, with the help of the materials
thus collected, we will endeavor, before tapping (to
borrow Walpole's word) the chapter of his correspondence, to sketch an outline of his life.

George Augustus Selwyn entered the world with
every advantage of birth and connection; to which
that of fortune was added in good time. His father,
Colonel John Selwyn, of Matson, in Gloucestershire,
where the family ranked as one of the best in the
county, had been aide-de-camp to the Duke of Marlborough, commanded a regiment, sat many years in
Parliament, and filled various situations about the
court. His mother, a daughter of General Farring-
ton, was woman of the bedchamber to Queen Caroline,
and enjoyed a high reputation for social humor. As

his father was a plain, straightforward, commonplace
sort of man, it is fair to presume that he inherited his
peculiar talent from her; thus adding another to the
many instances of gifted men formed by mothers, or
endowed by them with the best and brightest of their
qualities. Schiller, Goethe, the Schlegels, Victor
Hugo, Canning, Lord Brougham, occur to us on the
instant; and Curran said, " The only inheritance I
could boast of from my poor father, was the very
scanty one of an unattractive face and person, like his
own; and if the world has ever attributed to me something more valuable than face or person, or than
earthly wealth, it was that another and a dearer parent gave her child a fortune from the treasure of her
mind."

Selwyn was born on the 11th August, 1719. He
was educated at Eton, and on leaving it entered at
Hertford College, Oxford. After a short stay at the
University, he started on the grand tour, and on his
return, though a second son, with an elder brother
living, made London and Paris his headquarters, became a member of the clubs, and associated with the
wits and men of fashion. Before he had completed
his twenty-first year, he was appointed clerk of the
irons and surveyor of the meltings at the mint: offices
usually performed by deputy. At all events, occasional attendance at the weekly dinner formerly provided for this department of the public service, was
the only duty they imposed on Selwyn; the very man
to act on Colonel Hanger's principle, who, when a
friend in power suggested that a particular office, not
being a sinecure, would hardly suit him, replied, " Get

me the place, and leave me alone for making it a
sinecure." The salary must have been small, for in a
letter from Paris (September, 1742), he says that his
entire income, including the allowance made him by
his father, was only two hundred and twenty pounds
a year; and he appears to have been constantly in
distress for money. In a letter to his former Eton
tutor, Mr. Vincent Mathias (Paris, November, 1742),
he entreats his advice as to the best mode of getting
the colonel to advance a small sum over and above
his yearly income; and gives a pitiable description of
circumstances, — "without clothes, linen, books, or
credit."

In 1744 Selwyn returned to Hertford College, and
resumed the life of a college student, — unaccountably
enough, for he was then a formed man of the world,
and twenty-five. Probably he had the thoughts of
pursuing a profession, or, to please his father, pretended that he had. His influential position in the
London world at this time, is shown by letters from
Rigby and Sir Charles Hanbury Williams.

" *The Right Hon. Richard Rigby to George Selwyn.*
" Tuesday, March 12 (1745), 7 o'clock.

" Dear George: I thank you for your letter, which I
have this moment received and read; and, that you may not
be surprised at my readiness in answering it, I will begin
with telling you the occasion of it. *I am just got home from
a cock-match*, where I have won forty pounds in ready money.
and, not having dined. am waiting till I hear the rattle of
the coaches from the House of Commons. in order to dine at
White's; and now I will begin my journal, for in that style
I believe my letters will be best received, considering our
situations.   .   .   .

" I saw Garrick act Othello that same night, in which I
think he was very unmeaningly dressed, and succeeded in

no degree of comparison with Quin, except in the scene where Iago gives him the first suspicion of Desdemona. He endeavored throughout to play and speak everything directly different from Quin, and failed, I think, in most of his alterations."

This was the occasion when Quin went to the pit to see his rival act. It was at a time when Hogarth's *Marriage à la Mode* was familiar to every one. One of the, prints of that series represents a negro boy bringing in the tea things. When Garrick, with his diminutive figure and blackened face, came forward as Othello, Quin exclaimed, "Here is Pompey, but where is the tray?" The effect was electrical, and Garrick never attempted Othello again. When Dr. Griffiths, many years afterwards, thoughtlessly inquired whether he had ever acted the part, "Sir," said he, evidently disconcerted, "I once acted it to my cost."

Sir Charles writes, —

"I hope you divert yourself well at the expense of the whole University, though the object is not worthy you. The dullest fellow in it has parts enough to ridicule it, and you have parts to fly at nobler game."

By disregarding this sensible hint Selwyn got into a scrape, which, had it happened in our time, would have fixed a lasting stigma on his character. In 1745 he so far forgot himself, in a drunken frolic, as to go through a profane mockery of a religious ceremony; and the circumstance having come to the knowledge of the heads of the University, he was expelled. Most of his gay friends looked on this affair in the same light as Sir William Maynard, who writes thus : —

"WALTHAMSTOW, July 3, 1745.

"DEAR·GEORGE : I have this moment received yours, and have only time to tell you the sooner you come here, the greater the obligation will be to me. *D—n the University! — I wish they were both on fire, and one could hear the proctors cry like roasted lobsters.* My compliments to Dr. Newton. Yours affectionately,

"W. M."

Indeed, the only palliation or apology, and that a poor one, that can be urged for Selwyn, is to be found in the bad taste and loose habits of his contemporaries. The famous Medenham Abbey club was founded soon afterwards. It consisted of twelve members, who met at Medenham Abbey, near Marlow, to indulge in ribaldry, profanity, and licentiousness. The motto (from Rabelais) over the grand entrance was, *Fay ce que voudrais.* Though the club became notorious, and their disgusting profanity was well known, it proved no bar either to the reception of the members in society, or to their advancement in the state. Sir Francis Dashwood, the founder, who officiated as high priest, became Chancellor of the Exchequer; Lord Sandwich, First Lord of the Admiralty; and Wilkes everything that the sober citizens of London could make him.

Selwyn's character at this time is given by one of the Oxford magnates: "The upper part of society here, with whom he often converses, have, and always have had, a very good opinion of him. He is certainly not intemperate nor dissolute, nor does he game that I know or have heard of. He has a good deal of vanity, and loves to be admired and caressed, and so suits himself with great ease to the gravest and the sprightliest."

Colonel and Mrs. Selwyn were, on this occasion, shocked and irritated in the highest degree; but the failing health of his elder brother John contributed to soften them, and procure him an extent of indulgence which would hardly have been granted, had it not become apparent that the family estate and honors must eventually devolve upon him. John Selwyn was the intimate friend of Marshal Conway, to whom, so early as 1740, Walpole writes, " I did not hurry myself to answer your last, but chose to write to poor Selwyn upon his illness. He deserves so much love from all that know him, and you owe him so much friendship, that I can scarce conceive a greater shock." He did not die till June, 1751, when George Selwyn was in his thirty-second year. By this event he became the heir, but the estate was unentailed, and his prospects were still dubious enough to excite the apprehensions of his friends. In November, 1751, Sir William Maynard writes, —

" The public papers informed me of your father's being dangerously ill, which was confirmed to me last post. As you have always convinced me of your love for your father (though I can't persuade the world you will be sorry for his death), I shall be glad to know, if you have one moment's leisure, how he does, as you are so nearly concerned in his doing well. I can't help thinking but it will be more for your interest that your father should recover, as I don't yet imagine you *quite* established in his good opinion, and as you have so powerful an enemy at home."

Who his powerful enemy at home was, does not appear. His mother is mentioned in a preceding letter as his advocate; yet one of Walpole's anecdotes implies that at one time he had forfeited the affection of both parents. The notorious Lady Townshend had taken an extraordinary fancy to the rebel, Lord Kilmarnock, whom she had never seen until the day of his trial. "George Selwyn dined with her, and not thinking her affliction so serious as she pretended, talked rather jokingly of the execution. She burst into a flood of tears and rage, *told him she now believed all his father and mother had said of him*, and, with a thousand other reproaches, flung up stairs. George coolly took Mrs. Dorcas, her woman, and made her sit down to finish the bottle. 'And pray, sir,' says Dorcas, 'do you think my lady will be prevailed upon to let me go and see the execution ? I have a friend that has promised to take care of me, and I can lie in the tower the night before.'"

His father died in 1751, without tying up the property, which brought with it the power of nominating two members for Ludgershall, and interest enough at Gloucester to insure his own return for that city. The change of circumstances made little change in his course of life. He had sat in Parliament for the family borough since 1747, when Gilly Williams writes, " I congratulate you on the near approach of Parliament, and figure you to myself before a glass at your rehearsals. I must intimate to you not to forget closing your periods with a significant stroke of the breast, and recommend Mr. Barry as a pattern, who I think pathetically excels in that beauty." Spranger Barry, the actor, is the intended model ; but Selwyn was not ambitious of senatorial honors, and when obliged to attend the House, and be in readiness for a division, he used either to withdraw to one of the committee-rooms for conversation, or to fall asleep. He gener-

ally sided with the court party, and was well rewarded for his constancy; being at the same time clerk of
the irons, and surveyor of the meltings at the mint,
registrar of the court of chancery in Barbadoes (where
he had an estate), and paymaster of the works — described as a very lucrative appointment. It was abolished in 1782 by Burke's economical reform bill; but
in the course of the next year he was made surveyor-
general of the works by Mr. Pitt.

In 1768 he was opposed at Gloucester by a timber-
merchant, and the manner in which his friends speak
of his opponent is characteristic of the times. Gilly
Williams calls him " a d—d carpenter;" and Lord
Carlisle asks, —

" Why did you not set his timber-yard afire? What can
a man mean who has not an idea separated from the foot
square of a Norway deal plank, by desiring to be in Parliament? Perhaps if you could have got anybody to have asked
him his reasons for such an unnatural attempt, the fact of
his being unable to answer what he had never thought about,
might have made him desist. But these beasts are mon-
strously obstinate, and about as wellbred as the great dogs
they keep in their yards."

It is currently related that Selwyn did his best to
keep Sheridan out of Brookes', and was only prevented from black-balling him for the third or fourth time
by a trick. According to one version, the Prince of
Wales kept Selwyn in conversation at the door till
the ballot was over. According to Wraxall's, he was
suddenly called away by a pretended message from
his adopted daughter. Some attribute his dislike to
aristocratic prejudice; others to party feeling; and
Mr. Jesse says it arose in a great degree from Sheri-

dan's " having been one of the party which had deprived Selwyn of a lucrative post " — that of Paymaster of the Works. Yet Mr. Jesse himself states that
the black-balling occurred in 1780, and that the place
was abolished in 1782. We are uncharitable enough
to think that an established wit would feel something
like an established beauty at the proposed introduction of a rival, and that a tinge of jealousy might have
been the foundation of the dislike.

Selwyn had taken to gaming before his father's
death — probably from his first introduction to the
clubs. In 1748, Gilly Williams asks, " What do
you intend? I think the almanac bids you take care
of colds, and abstain from physic ; I say, avoid the
knowing ones, and abstain from hazard." His stakes
were high, though not extravagantly so compared
with the sums hazarded by his contemporaries. In
1765 he lost a thousand pounds to Mr. Shafto, who
applies for it in language of an embarrassed trades-
man : —

"July 1, 1765.

" DEAR SIR : I have this moment received the favor of
your letter. I intended to have gone out of town on Thursday, but as you shall not receive your money before the end
of this week, I must postpone my journey till Sunday. A
month would have made no difference to me had I not had
others to pay before I leave town, and must pay ; therefore
must beg that you will leave the whole before the week is
out, at White's, as it is to be paid away to others to whom
I have lost, and do not choose to leave town till that is
done.

" Be sure you could not wish an indulgence I should not
be happy to grant, if in my power."

Mr. Jesse states, that latterly Selwyn entirely got the
better of his propensity to play ; observing, that it was

too great a consumer of four things — time, health, fortune, and thinking. But an extract from the late Mr. Wilberforce's Diary throws some doubt on the accuracy of this statement: "The first time I was at Brookes', scarcely knowing any one, I joined from mere shyness, at the faro-table, where George Selwyn kept bank. A friend who knew my inexperience, and regarded me as a victim decked out for sacrifice, called out to me, " What, Wilberforce! is that you?" Selwyn quite resented this interference, and turning to him said, in his most impressive tone, " O, sir! don't interrupt Mr. Wilberforce; he could not be better employed." This occurred in 1782, when Selwyn was sixty-three.

Previously we find him, in 1776, undergoing the process of dunning from Lord Derby; and in 1779, from Mr. Crawford, "Fish Crawford," as he was called, each of whom, like Mr. Shafto, "had a sum to make up."

Gaming was his only vice. He indulged moderately in the pleasures of the table. In 1765 Williams writes, " You may eat boiled chicken and kiss Raton (his dog) as well on this side the water." As regards gallantry, we have good authority for doubting whether he was quite so much an anchorite as was supposed; but his coldness was a constant subject of banter among his friends. Lord Holland says, " My Lady Mary goes (to a masquerade) dressed like Zara, and I wish you to attend her dressed like a black eunuch." Lord Carlisle — " In regard to her (a mysterious unknown), in every other light but as a friend, you shall see I shall be as cold as a stone, or as yourself."

Readers of the Rolliad may recall a broader joke; and Mr. Jesse has ventured to print one of Gilly Williams's levelled at Walpole as well as Selwyn, which we cannot venture to transcribe. As to his alleged intrigue with the Marchesa Fagniani, there is no better proof of it than his extreme fondness for her daughter (Maria, Dowager-Marchioness of Hertford), whom the gossips thence inferred to be his own. In contemporary opinion, Lord March shared the honors of paternity with Selwyn. He was equally intimate with her mother, and he left her an immense fortune at his death. Resemblance, too, must go for something; and Dr. Warner, after an interview with Lord March, says, " The more I contemplate his face, the more I am struck with a certain likeness to the lower part of it; his very chin and lips, and they are rather singular. But you will never be *d'accord* upon this interesting subject, as I am sorry to be too much convinced; but that you know better than I." In considering this question, it must not be forgotten that Selwyn's passion for children was one of the marked features of his character. Lord Carlisle's and Lord Coventry's, particularly Lady Anne Coventry (afterwards Lady Anne Foley), were among his especial favorites.

Selwyn paid frequent visits to Paris, and spoke French to perfection. " I shall let Lord Huntingdon know (says Lord March) that you are thought to have a better pronunciation than any one that ever came from this country." The queen of Louis the Fifteenth took pleasure in conversing with him. " I dined to-day (we are still quoting from Lord March) at what is called no dinner, at Madame de Coignie's. The Queen asked Madame de Mirepoix, ' Si elle n'avait pas beaucoup entendu médire de Monsieur Selwyn et elle?' Elle a répondu, ' Oui, beaucoup, Madame.' 'J'en suis bien-aise,' dit la Reine."

He was received on a perfect footing of equality, and, as it were, naturalized in that brilliant circle of which Madame du Deffand was the centre; and he often lingered longer in it than was agreeable to his English friends. "Lady Hertford (writes Lord March in 1766) made a thousand inquiries about you; asked how long you intended to stay, and hoped you would soon be tired of blind women, old presidents, and premiers," — alluding to Madame du Deffand, the president Hénault, and the Duc de Choiseul. Williams sarcastically inquires, "Cannot we get you an hospital in this island, where you can pass your evenings with some very sensible matrons? and, if they are not quite blind, they may have some natural infirmity equivalent to it."

Nothing proves Selwyn's real superiority more strongly than his reception in this brilliant coterie, and the enjoyment he found in it; for when he began making his periodical visits to Paris, national prejudice was at its height; — the French regarded the English as barbarians, and the English entertained a contemptuous aversion for the French. So late as 1769, Lord Carlisle thus amusingly alludes to the sentiments of the former: —

"I am very sorry to hear Mr. Wood's family were splashed by the sea. People who never travel know very little what dangers we run. I dare say most of your French acquaint-

ances here wonder you do not go to England *by land*. but
I believe they are very easy about us after we are gone.
They think we are very little altered since the landing of
Julius Cæsar; that we leave our clothes at Calais, having
no further occasion for them, and that every one of us
has a sun-flower cut out and painted upon his ——, like
the prints in Clarke's Cæsar. I do not think that all entertain this idea of us; I only mean the *sçavans;* those who
can read."

The French might be pardoned for supposing that
the English left their clothes at Calais, for the tailors
of Paris were then as much in requisition as the milliners; and Selwyn is invariably loaded with com-
missions for velvet coats, silk small-clothes, brocade
dressing-gowns, lace ruffles, and various other articles, by the gravest as well as the gayest of his
friends. As for the notion of reaching England *by
land*, geography and the use of the globes were rare
accomplishments in both countries. When Whiston
foretold the destruction of the world within three
years, the Duchess of Bolton avowed an intention
of escaping the common ruin by going to China.

Selwyn not only overcame the national prejudice
in his own individual instance, but paved the way
for the reception of his friends. It was he who
made Horace Walpole acquainted with Madame du
Deffand, and Gibbon with Madame de Geoffrin.

His habit of dozing in the House of Commons
has been already noticed. He occasionally dozed in
society. "We hear," says Williams, "of your falling asleep standing at the old President's (Hénault's), and knocking him and three more old women into the fire. Are these things true?" Walpole also hints at it. "When you have a quarter

of an hour, *awake* and to spare, I wish you would bestow it on me." He is by no means singular, as might be shown by many remarkable instances besides that of Lord North, who, according to Gibbon, " might well indulge a short slumber on the treasury bench, when supported by the majestic sense of Thurlow on the one side, and the skilful eloquence of Wedderburne on the other." Lord Byron, in one of his journals, records a dinner party of twelve, including Sheridan, Tierney, and Erskine, of whom five were fast asleep before the dessert was well upon the table. In another, he relates, " At the opposition meeting of the peers in 1812, at Lord Grenville's, where Lord Grey and he read to us the correspondence upon Moira's negotiation, I sat next to the present Duke of Grafton, and said, 'What is to be done next?' *Wake the Duke of Norfolk'* (who was snoring away near us), replied he; 'I don't think the negotiators have left anything else for us to do this turn.'" Considering the hours kept by modern wits and senators, they may be excused for dropping into a pleasing state of forgetfulness occasionally; but Selwyn had no such excuse. His mode of life is exhibited in a droll sketch, in a letter to himself, written by Lord Carlisle at Spa, in 1768. " I rise at six; am on horseback till breakfast; play at cricket till dinner; and dance in the evening till I can scarce crawl to bed at eleven. There is a life for you! You get up at nine; play with Raton till twelve in your night-gown; then creep down to White's to abuse Fanshawe; are five hours at table; sleep till you can escape your supper reckoning; then make two wretches carry you, with three pints of claret in you, three miles for a shilling."

Wits are seldom given to ruralities. Jekyll used to say that, if compelled to live in the country, he would have the road before his door paved like a street, and hire a hackney coach to drive up and down all day long. Selwyn partook largely of this feeling. The state of a gentleman's cellar was then, whatever it may be now, a fair indication of the use he made of his house, and Matson was very slenderly stocked. When Gilly Williams took up his quarters there in passing through Gloucester, he writes, "I asked Bell to dine here, but he is too weak to venture so far; so the Methodist and I will taste your new and old claret. I have been down in the cellar: there are about nine bottles of old, and five dozen of new." Yet Matson was a highly agreeable residence, charmingly situated, and rich in historical associations. Charles the Second and James the Second (both boys at the time) were quartered there during the siege of Gloucester by the Royalists in 1643; and they amused themselves by cutting out their names, with various irregular em-blazonments, on the window-shutters.

During one of his brief electioneering visits at Matson, Selwyn took it into his head to perform justiceship; for (as Fielding observes with reference to the similar attempt on the part of Squire Wes-tern), it was, indeed, a syllable more than justice. "What the devil," exclaims Gilly Williams, "could tempt you to act as justice of the peace? This is

Trapolin with a vengeance! What! evidence, party, and judge too! If you do not make it up with the man soon, some rogue of an attorney will plague your heart out in the King's Bench." His gardener had been guilty of some peculation, for which Selvyn, without ceremony, committed him.

A little over-eagerness might be excused, as one of his strongest peculiarities was a passion for the details of criminal justice, from the warrant to the rope. His friends made a point of gratifying it by sending the earliest intelligence of remarkable crimes, criminals, trials, and executions, as well as every anecdote they could collect concerning them. When Walpole's house in Arlington Street was broken open, his first care, after securing the robber, was to send for Selwyn. " I despatched a courier to White's for George, who, you know, loves nothing upon earth so well as a criminal, except the execution of him. It happened very luckily that the drawer who received my message has very lately been robbed himself, and had the wound fresh in his memory. He stalked up into the club-room, stopped short, and with a hollow, trembling voice said, ' Mr. Selwyn, Mr. Walpole's compliments, and he's got a housebreaker for you.'" Gilly Williams, having no housebreaker for him, sends him a story about one instead: "I will give you a Newgate anecdote, which I had from a gentleman who called on P. Lewis the night before the execution, and heard one runner call to another and order a chicken boiled for Rice's supper; ' but,' says he, ' you need not be curious about the sauce, for he is to be

hanged to-morrow.' 'That is true," says the other,
' but the ordinary sups with him, and you know he
is a devil of a fellow for butter.' If the continental
air has not altered you, this will please you ; at least
I have known the time when you have gone a good
way for such a morsel."

The best stories regarding his taste for executions
are related by Walpole, and well known. Innumer-
able are the jokes levelled at him for this peculiarity.
The best is the first Lord Holland's, who was dying.
" The next time Mr. Selwyn calls, show him up. If
I am alive, I shall be delighted to see him ; and if I
am dead, he will be glad to see me." Lord Holland was not the only statesman of the period who
could joke under such circumstances. Mr. Legge
(the story is Gilly Williams's) told a very fat fellow
who came to see him the day he died, " Sir, you are
a great weight ; but, let me tell you, you are in at the
death." Another of the same gentleman's stories is
probably meant as a warning — " I remember a man
seeing a military execution in Hyde Park, and when
it was over he turned about and said, ' By G—, I
thought there was more in it ! ' He shot himself the
next morning."

The writer of a letter in the Gentleman's Magazine, for April, 1791, supposed to be the Rev. Dr.
Warner, makes a gallant effort to rescue Selwyn's
memory from what he terms an unjust and injurious
imputation. After urging that nothing could be more
abhorrent from Selwyn's character, and that he had
the most tender and benevolent of hearts, he thus proceeds : " This idle but wide-spread idea of his be-

ing fond of executions (of which he never in his life attended but at one, and that rather accidentally from its lying in his way, than from design) arose from the pleasantries which it pleased Sir Charles Hanbury Williams, and the then Lord Chesterfield, to propagate from that one attendance, for the amusement of their common friends. Of the easiness with which such things sat upon him, you may judge from the following circumstance, which I have heard him more than once relate. Sir Charles was telling a large company a similar story to that of his attending upon executions, with many strokes of rich humor received with great glee, before his face, when a gentleman who sat next to the object of their mirth, said to him in a low voice, 'It is strange, George, so intimate as we are, that I should never have heard of this story before.' 'Not at all strange,' he replied in the same voice, ' for Sir Charles has just invented it, and knows that I will not, by contradiction, spoil the pleasure of the company he is so highly entertaining.' And such was his goodnature in everything." This may account for the pleasantries, but hardly for the facts stated by Walpole and others; or for such an epistle as the following: "I can with great pleasure inform you, my dear Selwyn, that the head is ordered to be delivered on the first application made on your part. The expense is a little more than a guinea; the person who calls should pay for it. Adieu, *mon cher mondain*. T. PHILLIPS."

As to tenderness and benevolence, there surely was no necessity for assuming that the taste in question was irreconcilable with such qualities. It was simply a craving for strong excitement; a modification of the feeling which still induces the Spanish women to attend bull-fights, and formerly lured the gentlest and noblest of the sex to tournaments. Moreover, people were by no means so refined or squeamish in Selwyn's time as now, when the spectacle of bloody heads over Temple Bar would not be tolerated for an hour. Crowds of all classes pressed round to gaze on those of the rebel lords in 1746; and telescopes were fixed for the use of the curious at a halfpenny a peep. " I remember " says Johnson, as reported by Boswell, " once being with Goldsmith in Westminster Abbey. While we surveyed the Poets' Corner, I said to him, —

> ' Forsitan et nomen nostrum miscebitur istis.'

When we got to Temple Bar, he stopped me, pointed to the heads upon it, and slyly whispered me, —

> ' Forsitan et nomen nostrum miscebitur *istis.*' "

Nay, not much more than twenty years ago, it was customary for the governor of Newgate to give a breakfast to thirteen or fourteen persons of distinction on the morning of an execution. The party attended the hanging, breakfasted, and then attended the cutting down, but few had any appetite for the second and third parts of the ceremonial. A very pretty girl (the governor's daughter, we believe), who spoke of the sufferers as " *our people*," distributed the tea and coffee. She assured us, in confidence, that the first call of the incipient amateur was invariably for brandy; and that the only guest who never failed to do justice to the broiled kidneys (for which she was famous) was the ordinary.

Storer (one of the Selwyn set) writes in 1774, "You will get by your edition of Madame de Sévigné's Letters enough to pay for as much *Vin de Grave* as ever she drank *en Bretagne*." Selwyn rivalled, or outran Walpole in his admiration of Madame de Sévigné, and paid a visit to her residence, *Les Rochers* (excellently described, as at present existing, in Lady Morgan's " Book of the Boudoir ; "). but we find no other proof of direct literary intentions on his part; and there is consequently no ground for disputing the applicability of the remark with which Mr. Jesse introduces the topic of his wit : —

" Perhaps no individual has ever acquired so general a reputation for mere wit as George Selwyn. Villiers, Duke of Buckingham, Lords Dorset, Rochester, Chesterfield, and Hervey, Sir Charles Hanbury Williams, Bubb Doddington, Sheridan, and (perhaps the most brilliant luminary in this galaxy of wit) the late Theodore Hook, were men who had, one and all, distinguished themselves in following the paths of literature, while more than one of them had rendered himself eminent in the senate. Thus the character which each maintained for wit was supported by the adventitious aid of a reputation for literary or oratorical talents, while the fame of George Selwyn stands exclusively on his character for social pleasantry and conversational wit."

Not quite, we must observe. It stood also on his three seats in Parliament, and his family connections. These, at the very outset, procured him that vantage-ground to which Sheridan and Hook were obliged to win their way at the risk of fretting a thousand vanities. This may not apply to the rest on Mr. Jesse's list; but then it is a very imperfect one, and

admits of large additions — as (omitting all living examples) Foote, Wilkes, Jekyll, Curran, Colman.

Dr. Johnson disliked Foote; but when one of the
company, at a dinner party at Dilly's, called him a
merry-andrew, a buffoon, the sage at once declared
that he had wit, and added, " The first time I was
in company with Foote was at Fitzherbert's. Having no good opinion of the fellow, I was resolved
not to be pleased; and it is very difficult to please
a man against his will. I went on taking my dinner pretty sullenly, affecting not to mind him. But
the dog was so very comical, that I was obliged to
lay down my knife and fork, throw myself back on
my chair, and fairly laugh it out. No, sir, he was
irresistible." It was said to be impossible to take
Foote unawares, or put him out. As he was telling a story at a fine dinner party, a gentleman, to
try him, pulled him by the coat-tail, and told him
that his handkerchief was hanging out. " Thank you,
sir," said Foote, replacing it, " you know the company better than I do," and went on with his story.

Wilkes's fame may be rested on his reply to Lord
Sandwich, and his fling at Thurlow. Jekyll needs
no trumpeter. Lord Byron says of Colman, " If
I had to choose, and could not have both at a time,
I would say, ' Let me begin the evening with Sheridan, and finish it with Colman.' " Of Curran he
says, " I have met him at Holland House; he beats
everybody — his imagination is beyond human, and
his humor (it is difficult to define what is wit) perfect. Then he has fifty faces, and twice as many
voices, when he mimics." This, we may add, was

Hook's great charm. His best stories were dramatic representations *à la Mathews*, little inferior to that fine observer's " At Homes."

Why, again, since Mr. Jesse has gone back so far, did he not go back a little farther, and mention the old Earl of Norwich — a singular illustration of the fickleness of taste, and the truth of the maxim, " A jest's prosperity lies in the ear of him who hears it." He was the acknowledged wit of Charles the First's court, but was voted a dead bore when he attempted to resume his wonted place at Whitehall, after the Restoration.

It should be remembered, moreover — to be placed on the opposite column of the account — that high reputation in one line may sometimes prevent a man from acquiring much in another; not merely because of the prevalent dislike to pluralities, but because the less is merged in the greater. Thus it was admirably said of Sir James Mackintosh, by the Rev. Sydney Smith, " that he had not only humor, but wit also; at least, new and sudden relations of ideas flashed across his mind in reasoning, and produced the same effect as wit, *and would have been called wit, if a sense of their utility and importance had not often overpowered the admiration of novelty.*" Wilberforce, speaking of Pitt, said, " He was the wittiest man I ever knew, and (what was quite peculiar to himself) had at all times his wit under entire control. Others appeared struck by the unwonted association of brilliant images, but every possible combination of ideas seemed always present to his mind, and he could at once produce whatever he desired. I was one of those who met to spend an evening in memory of Shakespeare, at the Boar's Head, Eastcheap. Many professed wits were present, but Pitt was the most amusing of the party, and the readiest and most apt in the required allusions."

In addition to Selwyn's other places, the voice of his contemporaries conferred on him that of receiver general of waif and stray jokes — a sufficient proof that he had plenty of his own; for as D'Alembert sarcastically observed to the Abbé Voisenon, who complained that he was unduly charged with the absurd sayings of others "*Monsieur l'Abbé, on ne prête qu'aux riches.*" Selwyn's *droits*, in respect of his anomalous office, were not limited to the clubs. Lord Holland writes in 1770, "As the newspapers impute so much wit to you, I hope they give you the invention of that pretty motto they have put upon Lord Carlisle's cap." Lord Carlisle, in 1776 — "What the witty Mr. G. S. says in the newspapers is admirable about the red-hot poker, though I like *Diis placuit* better." Lord March, in 1767 — "The king talked of you at his dressing, and told me something that you had said of the Macaronis that he thought very good." It was Mr. Jesse's duty as editor to find out what these good things were; but he leaves us in entire ignorance regarding them. At the same time, we must do him the justice to say, that he has brought together quite enough to support Selwyn's reputation, and render superfluous the generally just remark with which he prefaces them. "No task can be more disappointing in its result than that of collecting the scattered *bon-mots* of a man

of professed wit, with a view to prove that his reputation is well deserved. Many of his best sayings
have, probably, been lost to us; others, perhaps,
have suffered in the narrative; and, moreover, the
charm of manner, which must greatly have enhanced
their value at the moment they were uttered, can
now, of course, only be taken on credit."

According to Walpole, it was Selwyn's habit to
turn up the whites of his eyes, and assume an expression of demureness, when giving utterance to
a droll thought; and Wraxall says, that the effect
of his witticisms was greatly enhanced by his listless,
drowsy manner. Nor is this all. What makes a
man like Selwyn the delight of his contemporaries,
is that lightness, richness, and elasticity of mind,
which invests the commonest incidents with amusing or inspiriting associations, lights intuitively on
the most attractive topics, grasps them one moment,
lets them go the next, and, in a word, never suffers
companionship to become tiresome, or conversation
to grow dull. He may do this without uttering anything that will be generally recognized as wit.

We shall here quote some of the best of Selwyn's
witticisms and pleasantries: they occupy little room,
and there is nothing more provoking than to be told
of "the well-known anecdote" which one does *not*
know.

When a subscription was proposed for Fox, and
some one was observing that it would require some
delicacy, and wondering how Fox would take it, —
"Take it? Why, *quarterly*, to be sure."

When one of the Foley family crossed the Channel to avoid his creditors — "It is a *pass over* that will not be much relished by the Jews."

When Fox was boasting of having prevailed on the French court to give up the gum trade — " As you have permitted the French to draw your *teeth*, they would be fools, indeed, to quarrel with you about your *gums.*"

When Walpole, in allusion to the sameness of the system of politics continued in the reign of George the Third, observed, " But there is nothing new under the sun." " No," said Selwyn, " nor under the *grandson.*" One night, at White's, observing the postmaster-general, Sir Everard Fawkener, losing a large sum of money at piquet, Selwyn, pointing to the successful player, remarked, "See how he is robbing the mail!"

On another occasion, in 1756, observing Mr. Ponsonby, the Speaker of the Irish House of Commons, tossing about bank bills at a hazard table at Newmarket — " Look how easily the speaker passes the *money bills.*"

The beautiful Lady Coventry was exhibiting to him a splendid new dress, covered with large silver spangles, the size of a shilling, and inquired of him whether he admired her taste, " Why," he said, " you will be *change for a guinea.*"

This bears a strong resemblance to one of Lord Mansfield's judicial pleasantries. Serjeant Davy was cross-examining a Jew at great length, in order to prove his insufficiency as bail. The sum was small, and the Jew was dressed in a suit of clothes bedizened with silver lace. Lord Mansfield at length interfered

27

— " Come, come, brother Davy, don't you see the
man would burn for the money? "

At the sale of the effects of the minister, Mr. Pelham, Selwyn, pointing to a silver dinner-service, observed, " Lord, how many toads have been eaten off
these plates ! "

A namesake of Charles Fox having been hung at
Tyburn, Fox inquired of Selwyn whether he had attended the execution — " No, I make a point of never
frequenting *rehearsals.*"

A fellow-passenger in a coach, imagining from his
appearance that he was suffering from illness, kept
wearying him with good-natured inquiries as to the
state of his health. At length, to the repeated question of " How are you now, sir ? " Selwyn replied,
" Very well, I thank you ; and I mean to continue so
for the rest of the journey."

He was one day walking with Lord Pembroke,
when they were besieged by a number of young chimney-sweepers, who kept plaguing them for money.
At length Selwyn made them a low bow. "I have
often," he said, " heard of the sovereignty of the people ; I suppose your Highnesses are in court mourning."

" On Sunday last," says Walpole, "George Selwyn was
strolling home to dinner at half an hour after four. He saw
my Lady Townshend's coach stop at Caraccioli's chapel.
He watched, saw her go in; her footman laughed; he followed. She went up to the altar, a woman brought her a
cushion; she knelt, crossed herself, and prayed. He stole
up and knelt by her. Conceive her face, if you can, when
she turned and found him close to her. In his demure
voice he said, ' Pray, madam, how long has your ladyship
left the pale of our church?' She looked furious, and made
no answer. Next day he went to her, and she turned it off

upon curiosity; but is anything more natural? No, she certainly means to go armed with every viaticum; the Church
of England in one hand, Methodism in the other, and the
Host in her mouth."

Wraxall stands godfather to the next: —

"The late Duke of Queensberry, who lived in the most
intimate friendship with him, told me that Selwyn was present at a public dinner with the mayor and corporation of
Gloucester, in the year 1758, when the intelligence arrived
of our expedition having failed before Rochfort. The may-
or, turning to Selwyn, 'You, sir,' said he, 'who are in the
ministerial secrets, can, no doubt, inform us of the cause of
this misfortune.' Selwyn, though utterly ignorant on the
subject, yet unable to resist the occasion of amusing himself at the inquirer's expense — 'I will tell you, in confidence, the reason, Mr. Mayor,' answered he; 'the fact is, that
the scaling-ladders prepared for the occasion were found, on
trial, to be too short.' This solution, which suggested itself
to him at the moment, was considered by the mayor to be
perfectly explanatory of the failure, and as such he com-
municated it to all his friends — not being aware, though
Selwyn was, that Rochfort lies on the River Charente, some
leagues from the sea-shore, and that our troops had never
even effected a landing on the French coast."

Mr. Jesse has omitted the capital reply to the man,
who, being cut by Selwyn in London, came up and
reminded him that they had been acquainted at Bath.
"I remember it very well; and when we next meet
at Bath, I shall be happy to meet you again."
Once, and once only, was he guilty of verse —

On a Pair of Shoes found in a Lady's Bed.
"Well may suspicion shake its head,
    Well may Clarinda's spouse be jealous,
When the dear wanton takes to bed
    Her very shoes because they're fellows."

Selwyn died at his house in Cleaveland Row, Jan-
uary 25, 1791. He had been for many years a severe
sufferer from gout and dropsy; and Wilberforce de-

scribes him as looking latterly like the wax figure of a corpse. He continued to haunt the clubs till within a short period before his death ; but Mr. Jesse assures us that he died penitent, and that the Bible was frequently read to him at his own request during his last illness. By his will he gave thirty-three thousand pounds to Maria Fagniani ; one hundred pounds each to his two nephews ; his wardrobe and thirty pounds a year to his valet ; and the residue of his property to the Duke of Queensberry, with the exception of Ludgershall, which was entailed on the Townshend family. Mr. Jesse quotes some lines from a poetical tribute published soon after his death, in which the Graces are invoked to fulfil several appropriate duties : —

> " And fondly dictate to a faithful Muse
> The prime distinction of the friend they lose.
> 'Twas social wit, which, never kindling strife,
> Blazed in the small, sweet courtesies of life."

Had we been at the writer's elbow, we should have suggested *shone* or *glowed* in preference to *blazed*.

Walpole, writing to Miss Berry, on the day of Selwyn's death, says, " I am on the point of losing, or have lost, my oldest acquaintance and friend, George Selwyn, who was yesterday at the extremity. These misfortunes, though they can be so but for a short time, are very sensible to the old : but him I really loved, not only for his infinite wit, but for a thousand good qualities."

Again : "Poor Selwyn is gone, to my sorrow : and no wonder Ucalegon feels it ! "

The heartlessness of the French set to which Selwyn and Walpole belonged is beyond a question. Madame du Defland's colloquy with one lover, as to the cause of their fifty years' unbroken harmony, and her behavior on the death of another, are not invented pleasantries, but melancholy facts. Yet either we were wrong in supposing that the malady was infectious, and Miss Berry was right in her generous and able vindication of her friend, or Selwyn possessed the peculiar talismanic power of kindling and fixing the affections of his associates; for not only does Walpole invariably mention him when living, and mourn over him when dead, in terms of heartfelt sincerity, but the same influence appears to have operated on one whom (possibly with equal injustice) we should have suspected of being, in his own despite, a little hardened by a long course of selfish indulgences — Lord March. Here are a few, and but a few, of the proofs : —

"As to your banker," says his lordship, " I will call there to-morrow; make yourself easy about that, for I have three thousand pounds now at Coutts'. There will be no bankruptcy without we are both ruined at the same time. How can you think, my dear George, — and I hope you do not think, — that anybody, or anything, can make a *tracasserie* between you and me ! I take it ill that you even talk of it, which you do in the letter I had by Ligonier. I must be the poorest creature upon earth,— after having known you so long, and always as the best and sincerest friend that any one ever had,— if any one alive can make any impression upon me when you are concerned. I told you, in a letter some time ago, that I depended more upon the continuance of our friendship than anything else in the world, which I certainly do, because I have so many reasons to know you, and I am sure I know myself."

This speaks well for both head and heart: and how much unhappiness would be prevented by the universal adoption of the principle — never to listen to, much less believe, the alleged unkindness of a friend. All of us have our dissatisfied, complaining, uncongenial moments, when we may let drop words utterly at variance with the habitual suggestions of our hearts. These are repeated from design or carelessness; then come complaints and explanations; confidence is destroyed; " the credulous hope of mutual minds is over ;" and thus ends at once the solace of a life.

Lord March's letters are, on the whole, the most valuable in the collection — most characteristic of the writer, and most redolent of the times. This unfold-ing of his private relations and inmost feelings is highly favorable to him. As we see him now, he is the very impersonation of his class — shrewd, sensi-ble, observing, generous, and affectionate, amid all his profligacy ; with talents uncultivated, because cul-tivation was not the passion of that age, but amply sufficient to make him a president of the council or first lord of the admiralty in this. His letters are dashed off in clear, manly, unaffected language, on the spur of the occasion ; and though they are ac-tually better written than those of many of his noble contemporaries who pretended to literature, it is ob-vious that the last thing he ever thought of was the style. Walpole's are epistolary compositions ; Lord March's are letters in the ordinary acceptation of the term. In their pregnant brevity, they often resemble Swift's hasty dottings down of public events, or pri-vate chit-chat in the journal to Stella.

"November, 1766.

"MY DEAR GEORGE: I intended to have written to you last Tuesday, but we sat so late at the House of Lords that I had no time. It was a dull debate, though it lasted a great while. Lord Chatham spoke very well, and with a great deal of temper, and great civility towards the Duke of Bedford; who spoke and approved of the measure at the time of laying the embargo, because of the necessity; but complained of Parliament not being called sooner, because what had been done was illegal, and only to be justified from necessity, which was the turn of the whole debate. Lord Mansfield trimmed in his usual manner, and avoided declaring his opinion, though he argued for the illegality. Lord Camden attacked him very close upon not speaking out his opinion, and declared strongly for the legality. Upon the whole, I think we shall have very little to do in Parliament, and your attendance will be very little wanted."

This was Lord Chatham's first appearance in the House of Lords. In letters dated the same month we find —

"Monday, 19th November, 1766.

"MY DEAR GEORGE: For fear that I should not have any other moment to write you, I write this in the king's rooms. I was obliged to dress early to come here, it being the princess's birthday. I dine at Lord Hertford's, which, with the ball at night, will take up the whole day; you know that he is chamberlain. The Duke of Bedford comes to-day, and, on Wednesday, I suppose they will kiss hands; but nothing is known. Everybody agrees that this resignation of the Cavendishes is, of all the resignations, the most foolish; and I hear they begin already to repent of it. They make a fine opportunity for Chatham to strengthen his administration. They want T. Pelham to resign; Ashburnham certainly will now. *The only people that do well are those that never resign;* which Lord Hertford seems to have found out long ago. Saunders and Keppel resign to-morrow."

"November, 1766.

"MY DEAR GEORGE: Jack Shelly has kissed hands for Lord Edgecombe's place. He was offered to be of the bedchamber, which he has refused, and wants to have the post-office, which they won't give him. *I find it is imagined that we shall be obliged to send troops into North America to bring them to a proper obedience.* It is whispered about that the

Cavendishes and Rockingham's friends will take the first
opportunity they can to be hostile to government; and likewise, that Norton and Wedderburne will certainly oppose:
if these things are so, we may perhaps hàve some more convulsions in the state."

Such letters are excellent correctives of history;
but we are not writing history just now, and must
turn to those which throw light on manners: —

"HINCHINBROOKE, Thursday (1770).

"MY DEAR GEORGE: Our party at Wakefield went off
very well. We had hunting, racing, whist, and quinze.
My horse won, as I expected, but the odds were upon him,
so that I betted very little.

"After hunting on Monday I went to Ossory's, where I
lay in my way here. He came with me, and went back yesterday. I imagine he would have liked to have staid if
Lady Ossory had not been alone. They live but a dull life,
and there must be a great deal of love on both sides not to
tire. I almost promised to go back for Bedford races, but
believe I shall not. I go to Newmarket to-night, and to
London to-morrow. Sandwich's house is full of people, and
all sorts of things going forward. Miss Ray does the honors
perfectly well. While I am writing they are all upon the
grass plot at a foot-race."

To make this intelligible, we must go behind the
scenes. Wakefield Lodge was the seat of the minister, Duke of Grafton. Lady Ossory was his *ci-de-
vant* duchess. She had divorced him on account of
his intimacy with Nancy Parsons, described by Walpole as " one of the commonest creatures in London;
once much liked, but out of date. He is certainly
grown immensely attached to her; so much so, that
it has put an end to all his decorum." The culpable
excesses into which the duke was hurried by his passion are stigmatized by Junius: " It is not the private indulgence, but the public insult, of which I
complain. The name of Miss Parsons would hardly

have been known, if the first lord of the treasury had not led her in triumph through the opera-house, even in the presence of the queen." Hinchinbrooke, from which the letter is dated, was the seat of Lord Sandwich, another cabinet minister. Miss Ray, who did the honors so well, was his mistress — shot at Covent Garden in 1779. The story is told by Dr. Warner in a paragraph which may serve as a pattern of good condensation : —

"The history of Hackman, Miss Ray's murderer, is this He was recruiting at Huntingdon; appeared at the ball; was asked by Lord Sandwich to Hinchinbrooke; was introduced to Miss Ray; became violently enamoured of her; made proposals, and was sent into Ireland, where his regiment was. He sold out; came back on purpose to be near the object of his affection; took orders, but could not bend the inflexible fair in a black coat more than in a red. He could not live without her. He meant only to kill himself, and that in her presence; but seeing her coquet it at the play with a young Irish Templar, Macnamara, he determined suddenly to despatch her too. He is to be tried on Friday, and hanged on Monday."

The Morning Post, for April 9, 1799, has this announcement: "When the news of the above misfortune was carried to the admiralty, it was received by her noble admirer with the utmost concern. He wept exceedingly, and lamented, with every other token of grief, the interruption of a connection which had lasted for seventeen years, with great and uninterrupted felicity on both sides."

The catching character of notorious insanity has often been remarked. While the Hackman affair was the popular topic, it seems that no woman, young or old, ugly or pretty, could venture forth without alarm. Lady Ossory writes, —

"This Asiatic weather has certainly affected our cold constitutions. The Duchess of B—— is afraid of being shot wherever she goes. A man has followed Miss Clavering *on foot* from the East Indies; is quite mad; and scenes are daily expected even in the drawing-room. Another man has sworn to shoot a Miss Something, *n'importe*, if she did not run away with him from the opera.

"Sir Joshua Reynolds has a niece who is troubled with one of these passionate admirers, to whom she has refused her hand and her door. He came, a few days since, to Sir Joshua's, asked if she was at home, and on being answered in the negative, he desired the footman to tell her to take care, for he was determined to ravish her (pardon the word) whenever he met her. Keep our little friend (Mie Mie) at Paris whilst this mania lasts, for no age will be spared to be in fashion, and I am sure Mie Mie is quite as much in danger as the person I quoted in my first page."

Before quoting those letters of Lord March which refer to topics of a strictly personal character, we will mention the few authentic particulars that have been recorded of him.

He was born in 1725, succeeded his father in the earldom of March in 1731, his mother in the earldom of Ruglen in 1748, and his cousin in the dukedom of Queensberry in 1778, being then in his fifty-third year. Few men of his day acquired greater notoriety, or were more an object of inquiry and speculation; yet he took little part in political events, except so far as his own interests were affected by them, and it would have been better for his reputation had he taken none. When the king's malady grew serious, in 1788, he gave in his allegiance to Fox, and, on the recovery of his royal master, was unceremoniously dismissed from his situation of lord of the bedchamber, which he had held for twenty-eight years, notwithstanding the known profligacy of his life. Wraxall says he took a journey to Windsor to learn the

exact condition of the king, but was misled by Dr.
Warren. The mistake mattered little. His business
was pleasure, his passions were women and the turf;
and he contrived to gratify both, without impairing
either his fortune or his constitution. As regards the
turf, he was thoroughly versed in all its mysteries,
and seldom indulged in any sort of gaming uncon-
nected with it, or relating to matters where any
undue advantage could be taken of him. On the
contrary, he was generally on the lookout for oppor-
tunities of turning his own shrewdness and coolness
to account. A curious instance is related in Edgeworth's memoirs.

Lord March had noticed a coachmaker's journeyman running with a wheel, and on minuting him by
a stop watch, found that he actually ran a considerable distance faster with it than most men could run
unencumbered. A waiter in Betty's fruit shop was
famous for speed. Lord March adroitly introduced
the topic, and maintaining what appeared a paradox,
easily got bets to a large amount, that the waiter
would run faster for a mile than any one could run
with the hind-wheel of his lordship's carriage, then
standing at the door. But he committed a trifling over-
sight. The wheel was lower than the wheel the man
was used to run with; and the biter would have been
bit, had not Sir Francis Delaval suggested an expedient. The night before the match, planks were obtained from the Board of Works, and a raised groove,
for the wheel to run in, was constructed across the
course. The journeyman won, and the Jockey Club
decided in Lord March's favor. Another of his bets

came before the court of King's Bench. He had laid
a wager of five hundred guineas with young Mr.
Pigot, that old Mr. Pigot (the father) would die before Sir William Codrington. Old Mr. Pigot died
the same morning before the making of the wager,
but neither of the parties were acquainted with the
fact. The court held that the dutiful and hopeful
heir must pay. A startling example of this style of
bet is mentioned by Walpole. " I, t'other night at
White's, found a very remarkable entry in our very
remarkable wager-book. Lord ⸺ bets Sir ⸺
twenty guineas that Nash outlives Cibber. *How
odd that these two old creatures should live to see
both their wagerers put an end to their own lives!* "
Lord March's rate of betting was never very high.
The largest sum he appears to have won or lost at
any race or meeting, during the period over which
this correspondence extends, was four thousand one
hundred pounds, and this is mentioned as a rare occurrence.

He also managed his intercourse with the fair sex
in such a manner as to prevent them from interfering
with his peace, or even his caprices ; and few things
are more amusing than his mode of keeping his occasional *liaisons* from clashing with his permanent
ones — for we are obliged to speak of both classes in
the plural number. His parting with one of his favorites is peculiarly touching : —

" I am just preparing to conduct the poor little Tondino to
Dover. My heart is so full that I can neither think, speak,
nor write. How I shall be able to part with her, or bear to
come back to this house, I do not know. The sound of her
voice fills my eyes with fresh tears. My dear George, *Fai*

le cœur si serrè que je ne suis bon à présent qu' à pleurer.
Take all the care you can of her. *Je la recommende à vous,*
my best and only real friend."

In return for the care Selwyn was to take of the
Tondino, Lord March, it seems, was to keep an eye
to Raton.

"I wrote to you last night, but I quite forgot Raton. I
have not had him to see me to-day, having been the whole
morning in the city with Lady H.; but I have sent to your
maid, and she says that her little king is perfectly well and
in great spirits."

Besides the Tondino, Selwyn had the principal
care of the Rena, a beautiful Italian, who stood in
nearly the same relation to Lord March as Madame
de Pompadour to Louis the Fifteenth. That sagacious
favorite, it will be remembered, troubled herself very
little about the *Parc aux Cerfs* so long as she retained the chief place in his Majesty's confidence.
Queen Caroline is said to have preserved her influence over George the Second by the same policy.
The Rena's prudence was put to a severe trial by the
arrival of Signora Zamperini, a noted dancer and
singer, in 1766. His lordship writes to Selwyn in
Paris, —

"I wish I had set out immediately after Newmarket,
which I believe I should have done, if I had not taken a
violent fancy for one of the opera girls. This passion is a
little abated, and I hope it will be quite so before you and
the Rena come over, else I fear it will interrupt our society.
But whatever is the case, as I have a real friendship and affection for the Rena. I shall show her every mark of regard
and consideration, and be vastly happy to see her. I consider her as a friend, and certainly as one that I love very
much; and as such, I hope she will have some indulgence
for my follies."

A few days afterwards, —

"The Rena must be mad if she takes anything of this sort in a serious way. If she does, there is an end of our society. If she does not, we shall go on as we did. I am sure I have all the regard in the world for her, for I love her vastly, and I shall certainly contrive to make her as easy and as happy as I can. I like this little girl, *but how long this liking will last I cannot tell;* it may increase, or be quite at an end, before you arrive."

His lordship had not attained to equal proficiency with Madame de Girardin's hero : " Albert ne viendra pas — il est amoureux pour une quinzaine, il me l'a dit, et il est toujours à la minute dans ces choses-là." In a subsequent letter we find all three (the Tondino, the Rena, and the Zamperini) mixed up together.

"You see what a situation I am in with my little *Buffa*. She is the prettiest creature that ever was seen ; in short, I like her vastly, and she likes me, *because I give her money.*

"I have had a letter from the Tondino to-day. She tells me that she never passed her time so well at Paris as she does now. ' *Monsieur du Barri est un homme charmante, et nous donne des bals avec des Princesses.*' Pray, my dear George, find out something that will be agreeable to the little Teresina. *Consult the Rena about it.*

"I shall write two or three words to the Rena by this post. I told her, in my last letter, that I was supposed to be very much in love with the Zamperini, which certainly would not prevent me from being very happy to see her. I have been too long accustomed to live with her not to like her, or to be able to forget her, and there is nothing that would give me more pain than not to be able to live with her upon a footing of great intimacy and friendship; *but I am always afraid of every event where women are concerned — they are all so exceedingly wrong-headed.*"

It might be deemed useless, if not impertinent, to keep on repeating that obviously wrong things are wrong; but in connection with the next extract, the

reader should bear in mind that, at the time in question, and for twelve years afterwards, the writer was
a lord of the bedchamber in the decorous court of
George the Third and Queen Charlotte.

" I was prevented from writing to you last Friday, by being at Newmarket with my little girl. I had the whole
family and Cocchi. The beauty went with me in my chaise,
and the rest in the old landau."

The family consisted of father, mother, and sister.
" As March finds a difficulty (says Williams) in separating her from that rascally garlic tribe, whose very
existence depends on her beauty, I do not think he
means to make her what our friend the countess (the
Rena) was." In another place — " March goes on
but heavily with his poor child (she was only fifteen).
He looks miserable, and yet he takes her off in her
opera dress every night in his chariot."

Numerous allusions, in these volumes, show that
Lord March was not devoid of taste for female society
of a better order. He is repeatedly spoken of as about
to marry this or that lady of quality; and Wraxall
says that he cherished an ardent passion for Miss
Pelham, the daughter of the minister, who persevered
in refusing his consent to their union, on account
of the dissipated habits of the peer. He died unmarried, and continued his libertine habits till death.
During the first ten years of the present century, he
might constantly be seen in the bow-window of his
house in Piccadilly (now divided into two houses
occupied by Lord Cadogan and Lord Roseberry),
examining the street passengers through an eye-glass
with his remaining eye (it was currently stated that

the other was of glass), and when a female pedestrian struck his fancy, an emissary was instantly despatched after her. That no time might be lost, a pony was always kept saddled for the purpose. " It is a fact," says Wraxall, " that he performed in his own drawing-room the scene of Paris and the goddesses. This classic exhibition took place in his house opposite the Green Park." We do not believe that any exhibition took place at all — founding our scepticism more on the folly than the vice ; yet it is melancholy to think to what human nature may be degraded by sensuality.

A striking illustration of his shrewdness was given by Lord Brougham, in his evidence before the Lords' Committee on Lord Campbell's libel bill : —

" The late Duke of Queensberry was a great alarmist in 1792, like many other very noble, very rich, and very honorable men. He thought there was an end of all things, and he used to be abusing principally the seditious writings of the day, giving them and their authors ill names in great abundance and variety, as infamous, detestable, abominable — when one day some toad-eater, who attended his person, added, ' Ay, indeed, and full of such falsehoods.' ' No,' said the duke, ' not falsehoods — they are all so true; that is what makes them so abominable and so dangerous.' If his grace had felt all that was said on the corruptions of Parliament and office to be groundless, he would have let them write on in the same strain to the end of time."

A characteristic trait has been preserved by Mr. Wilberforce : —

" I always observe that the owners of your grand houses have some snug corner in which they are glad to shelter themselves from their own magnificence.* I remember dining, when I was a young man, with the Duke of Queens-

* "And thus the most luxurious court in Europe, after all its boasted refinements, was glad to return at last, by this singular contrivance (the *table volante* at Choisy), s the quiet and privacy of humble life." — *Rogers's Poems, Note.*

berry, at his Richmond villa. The party was very small and select — Pitt, Lord and Lady Chatham, the Duchess of Gordon, and George Selwyn (who lived for society, and continued in it till he really looked like the waxwork figure of a corpse) were amongst the guests. We dined early, that some of our party might be ready to attend the opera. The dinner was sumptuous, the views from the villa quite enchanting, and the Thames in all its glory; but the duke looked on with indifference. ' What is there,' he said, ' to make so much of in the Thames? I am quite tired of it — there it goes, flow, flow, flow, always the same.' "

This is precisely what we should have expected from the duke ; and no one was better qualified than Mr. Wilberforce to explain why the glorious scene before them was a sealed book to the worn voluptuary — why his spirit's eye was blind to it — why every simple, innocent, unforced gratification was denied to him — and why the full enjoyment of natural beauty and sublimity is reserved for men of purer lives and higher minds than his.

The duke's notions of comfort, on which his opinion was worth having, were expressed in a letter to Selwyn : " I wish you were here (the place is not stated). It is just the house you would wish to be in. There is an excellent library, *a good parson*, the best English and French cookery you ever tasted, strong coffee, and half-crown whist."

It has been stated that he paid his physicians on the plan adopted by the Chinese emperors — so much per week for keeping him alive. If so, he cheated them ; for the immediate cause of his death was imprudence in eating fruit. He died in 1810, firm and self-possessed. His death-bed was literally covered with unopened billets (more than seventy) from women of all classes, which he ordered to be laid on the

28

counterpane as they were brought. His personal
property exceeded a million, and his will, with its
twenty-five codicils, was a curious document. He
left one hundred and fifty thousand pounds and three
houses to Mie Mie, and made her husband (the late
Marquis of Hertford, a congenial spirit) his residuary
legatee.

Selwyn's most immediate friends and frequent correspondents, after the duke, were George James (alias
Gilly) Williams and Lord Carlisle.

Of Williams little is known. He was the son of
Peere Williams, the compiler of three volumes of
chancery cases, highly esteemed by equity lawyers.
He was connected by marriage with Lord North,
and in 1774 was appointed receiver-general of ex-
cise. Selwyn, Edgecumbe, Walpole, and Williams,
used to meet at stated periods at Strawberry Hill,
and form what Walpole called his out-of-town party.
Gilly's letters convey a highly favorable impression
of his social pleasantry; and it seems that he soon
acquired some reputation as a wit. "I have desired
Lord R. Bertie," he writes in 1751, "to propose me at
White's. Don't let any member shake his head at
me for a wit; for, God knows, he may as well reject
me for being a giant."

Frederick, fifth earl of Carlisle, was a remarkable
man in many ways. He filled some important public
situations with credit; and on his being appointed
lord-lieutenant of Ireland, his intimate friend, Storer,
writes, "I wish he was secretary of state. It is a
joke to think it too high a step. I am of the old
king's opinion, *that a man in this country is fit for*

any place he can get, and I am sure Carlisle will be fit for any place he will take."

In literature he distinguished himself as a poet; but, unluckily, he is principally known in that capacity through Lord Byron, who, in his English Bards and Scoth Reviewers, levels twelve unjust and acrimonious lines at him. In the first sketch of the poem these twelve lines were wanting, and their place was occupied by two —

> " On one alone Apollo deigns to smile,
> And crowns a new Roscommon in Carlisle."

Lord Carlisle had offended his young relation, between the writing and the printing of the poem, by refusing to introduce him on his taking his seat in the House of Lords. Lord Byron afterwards deeply regretted the injury. There is a beautiful atonement in the third canto of Childe Harold; and in writing, in 1814, to Mr. Rogers, he thus expresses himself : " Is there any chance or possibility of making it up with Lord Carlisle, as I feel disposed to do anything, reasonable or unreasonable, to effect it? "

In private life and early youth, Lord Carlisle, endowed with warm feelings, a lively fancy, and an excitable disposition, was peculiarly liable to be led astray by the temptations which assail young men of rank. In 1769, being then in his twenty-first year, he went abroad, desperately in love with some wedded fair one. She forms the burden of many a paragraph in his letters to Selwyn, who, though nearly thirty years older, entered warmly into all his feelings.

" I thought I had got the better of that extravagant passion, but I find I am relapsed again. I tremble at the consequences of the meeting. and yet I have not the courage, even in thought. to oppose its temptations. I shall exert all the firmness I am capable of, which, God knows, is very little, upon that occasion. If I am received with coolness, I shall feel it severely. I shall be miserable if I am made too welcome. Good God, what happiness would I not exchange, to be able to live with her without loving her more than friendship will allow! Is my picture hung up, or is it in the passage with its face turned to the walls?"

From the allusion to the picture, and other indications, it is clear that the mysterious lady (who has given rise to much surmise) was the beautifnl Lady Sarah Bunbury (*née* Lennox), whom it is said his Majesty George the Third would have married, had he been allowed. His Majesty gave up his own wishes for the good of the country, but the impression remained. Mrs. Pope, the actress, was very like Lady Sarah. On one occasion, at the theatre, many years after his marriage, the king turned round to the queen in a fit of melancholy abstraction, and said, pointing to Mrs. Pope, " She is like Lady Sarah still."

Lord Carlisle got the better of this passion, and married at twenty-two. It would have been well for his peace of mind had he been equally successful in getting the. better of a still more fatal one for play. Letter after letter is filled with good resolutions, but the fascination was too strong. The blow came at last.

" July, 1776.

"MY DEAR GEORGE: I have undone myself, and it is to no purpose to conceal from you my abominable madness and folly, though perhaps the particulars may not be known to the rest of the world. I never lost so much in five times as I have done to-night, and am in debt to the house for the whole. You may be sure I do not tell you this with an idea that you can be of the least assistance to me; it is a great deal more than your abilities are equal to. Let me see you, though I shall be ashamed to look at you after your goodness to me."

This letter is indorsed by Selwyn, "After the loss of the ten thousand pounds;" which, following on other losses, appears to have sunk the earl to the lowest depths of despondency.

> "*I do protest to you, that I am so tired of my present manner of passing my time,—however I may be kept in countenance by the number of those in my own rank and superior fortune,— that I never reflect on it without shame.* If they will employ me in any part of the world, I will accept the employment; let it tear me, as it will, from everything dear to me in this country. . . . . .
>
> "If any of our expectations should be gratified in the winter, I cannot expect anything sufficient to balance the expenses of living in London. If I accept anything, I must attend Parliament—I must live in London. If I am not treated with consideration, I can live here, if that can be called living which is wasting the best years of my life in obscurity; without society to dispel the gloom of a northern climate; left to myself to brood over my follies and indiscretions; to see my children deprived of education by those follies and indiscretions; to be forgotten; to lose my temper; to be neglected; to become cross and morose to those whom I have most reason to love! *Except that the welfare and interest of others depend upon my existence, I should not wish that existence to be of long duration.*"

So thought and felt a man apparently possessed of every blessing — youth, health, talent, birth, fortune, connection, consideration, and domestic ties of the most endearing kind —

> "Medio de fonte leporum
> Surgit amari aliquid quod in ipsis floribus angat."

The very accident (miscalled advantage) of his position commends the poisoned chalice to his lips, and the Lord of Castle Howard longs for death at twenty-seven! But a truce to reflection till we have introduced another, and a more memorable subject for it. Lord Carlisle's embarrassments were inextricably mixed up with those of Charles James Fox; and it can therefore hardly be deemed a digression to turn at once to the passages in these volumes which relate to him. The few letters of his own that occur in them are principally remarkable for ease and simplicity. For example,—

"PARIS, November, 1770.

"Quantities of cousins visit us; amongst the rest the Duke of Berwick. What an animal it is! I supped last night with Lauzun, Fitz-James, and some others, at what they call a *Clob à l'Anglaise.* It was in a *petite maison* of Lauzun's. There was Madame Briseau, and two other women. The supper was execrably bad. However, the champagne and tokay were excellent; notwithstanding which the fools made *du pouche* with bad rum. This club is to meet every Saturday, either here or at Versailles: I am glad to see that we cannot be foolisher in point of imitation than they are."

Principally, through Selwyn's introduction, Fox was on a familiar footing with Madame du Deffand and her set.

"Madame Geoffrin *m'a chanté la palinodie.* I dine there to-day; she inquires after you very much. I have supped at Madame du Deffand's, who asked me if I was *déjà sous la tutèle de M. Selvin?* I boasted that I was."

In August 23, 1771, he writes what is most worthy of notice, as follows : —

"I am reading Clarendon, but scarcely get on faster than you did with your Charles the Fifth. I think the style bad, and that he has a good deal of the old woman in his way of thinking, *but hates the opposite party so much that it gives one a kind of partiality for him.*"

His marvellous powers as a debater were remarked very soon after his first entrance into Parliament. In March, 1770, his delighted father writes to Selwyn,—

"You know by this time that your panegyric upon Charles came about an hour after I had wrote mine to you of the 9th. He writes word that upon February the 12th he spoke very ill. I do not mind that, and when he speaks so well, as to be, as Lady Mary says, the wonder of the age, it does not give me so much pleasure as what you very justly, I think, tell me *de son cœur.* And yet that may not signify. I have been honest and good-natured, nor can I repent of it: though convinced now that honesty is not the best policy, and that good-nature does not meet with the return it ought to do."

It appears from a letter addressed by Lord Carlisle to Lady Holland (Fox's mother), in 1773, that he had become security for Fox to the amount of fifteen or sixteen thousand pounds; and a letter to Selwyn, in 1777, puts the ruinous character of their gambling transactions in the strongest light. Lord Ilchester (Fox's cousin) had lost thirteen thousand pounds at one sitting to Lord Carlisle, who offered to take three thousand pounds down. Nothing was paid; but ten years afterwards, when Lord Carlisle pressed for his money, he complains that an attempt was made to construe the offer into a remission of ten thousand pounds : —

"The only way, in honor, that Lord I. could have accepted my offer, would have been by taking some steps to pay the three thousand pounds. I remained in a state of uncertainty, I think, for nearly three years; but his taking no notice of it during that time convinced me that he had no intention of availing himself of it. Charles Fox was also at a much earlier period clear that he never meant to accept it. There is also great justice in the behavior of the family in passing by the instantaneous payment of, I believe, five thousand pounds to Charles, won at the same sitting, without any observations. *At one period of the play, I remember, there was a balance in favor of one of those gentlemen. but of which I protest I do not remember, of about fifty thousand."*

At the time in question, Fox was hardly eighteen. The following letter from Lord Carlisle, written in 1771, contains some highly interesting information respecting the youthful habits, and already vast intellectual pre-eminence of this memorable statesman : —

"It gives me great pain to hear that Charles begins to be unreasonably impatient at losing. I fear it is the prologue to much fretfulness of temper; for disappointment in raising money, and any serious reflections upon his situation, will (in spite of his affected spirits and dissipation, which sit very well upon Richard) occasion him many disagreeable moments. They will be the more painful when he reflects that he is not following the natural bent of his genius; for that would lead him to all serious inquiry and laudable pursuits, which he has in some measure neglected, to hear Lord Bolingbroke's applause, and now is obliged to have recourse to it and play, to hinder him from thinking how he has perverted the ends for which he was born. *I believe there never was a person yet created who had the faculty of reasoning like him. His judgments are never wrong; his decision is formed quicker than any man's I ever conversed with; and he never seems to mistake but in his own affairs.*"

Lord Carlisle's fears proved groundless in one respect. Fox's sweetness of temper remained with him to the last; but it is most painful to think how much mankind has lost through his recklessness. There is no saying what might not have been effected by such a man, had he simply followed the example of his great rival in one respect. "We played a good deal at Goosetree's," says Wilberforce, "and I well remember the intense earnestness which Pitt displayed when joining in these games of chance. He perceived their increasing fascination, and soon after abandoned it forever." Wilberforce's own cure is thus recorded by his biographers, on the authority of his private journal : "'We can have no play to-night,' complained some of the party at the club, 'for St. Andrew is not here to keep bank.' 'Wilberforce,' said Mr. Bankes, who never joined himself, 'if you will keep it I will give you a guinea.' The playful challenge was accepted, but as the game grew deep, he rose the winner of six hundred pounds. Much of this was lost by those who were only heirs to future fortunes, and could not therefore meet such a call without inconvenience. The pain he felt at their annoyance cured him of a taste which seemed but too likely to become predominant."

Goosetree's being then almost exclusively composed of incipient orators and embryo statesmen, the call for a gaming-table there may be regarded as a decisive proof of the universal prevalence of the vice. But most of these were the friends and followers of Pitt; and when his star gained the ascendant, idleness was no longer the order of the day among politicians, and rising young men gave up faro and hazard for Blackstone and Adam Smith. We know of no candidate for high office, entering public life after 1784, who did not affect prudence and propriety; and probably we shall never again see a parliamentary leader aspire, like Bolingbroke,

"To shine a Tully and a Wilmot too."

Gaming, however, continued a blot on our manners and morals for many years afterwards; and it may not be uninstructive to trace its progress and decline. During the whole of the last century, gaming of some sort was an ordinary amusement for both sexes in the best society.* Till near the commencement of the present, the favorite game was faro; and as it was a decided advantage to hold the bank, masters and mis-

---

* In General Burgoyne's play of The Heiress, Mrs. Blandish exclaims "Time thrown away in the country l as if women of fashion left London to turn freckled shepherdesses. No, no ; cards, cards and backgammon, are the delights of rural life : and, slightly as you may think of my skill, at the year's end I am no inconsiderable sharer in the pin-money of my society."

tresses of noble houses, less scrupulous than Wilberforce, frequently volunteered to fleece and amuse their
company.   But scandal having made busy with the
names of some of them, it became usual to hire a
professed gamester at five or ten guineas a night to
set up a table for the evening, as we should hire La-
blache for a concert, or Weippart for a ball.   Faro
gradually dropped out of fashion; macao took its
place; hazard was never wanting, and whist began
to be played for stakes which would have satisfied
Fox himself, who, though it was calculated that he
might have netted four or five thousand a year by
games of skill, complained that they afforded no excitement.

Watier's club, in Piccadilly, was the resort of the
macao players.   It was kept by an old *maître d'hôtel*
of George the Fourth, a character in his way, who
took a just pride in the cookery and wines of his establishment.   All the brilliant stars of fashion (and
fashion was power then) frequented it, with Brummell for their sun.   " Poor Brummell dead, in misery
and idiocy, at Caen ! and I remember him in all his
glory, cutting his jokes after the opera at White's, in
a black velvet great-coat, and a cocked hat on his
well-powdered head." *   Nearly the same turn of reflection is suggested as we run over the names of his
associates.   Almost all of them were ruined ; three
out of four irretrievably.   Indeed, it was the forced
expatriation of its supporters that caused the club to
be broken up.   During the same period (from 1810

---

* Private MS.

to 1815 or thereabouts) there was a great deal of high play at White's and Brookes', particularly whist. At Brookes' figured some remarkable characters — as Tippoo Smith, by common consent the best whist-player of his day; and an old gentleman nicknamed Neptune, from his having once flung himself into the sea in a fit of despair at being, as he thought, ruined. He was fished out in time, found he was not ruined, and played on during the remainder of his life.

The most distinguished player at White's was the nobleman who was presented at the salon in Paris as *Le Wellington des Joueurs;* and he richly mer-ited the name, if skill, temper, and the most daring courage, are titles to it. The greatest genius, how-ever, is not infallible. He once lost three thousand four hundred pounds at whist by not remembering that the seven of hearts was in. He played at haz-ard for the highest stakes that any one could be got to play with him, and at one time was supposed to have won nearly a hundred thousand pounds; but it all went, along with a great deal more, at Crockford's.

There was also a great deal of play at Graham's, the Union, the Cocoa-Tree, and other clubs of the second order in point of fashion. Here large sums were hazarded with equal rashness, and remarkable characters started up. Among the most conspicuous was the late Colonel Aubrey, who literally passed his life at play. He did nothing else, morning, noon, and night; and it was computed that he had paid more than sixty thousand pounds for card-money. He was a very fine player at all games, and a shrewd, clever man. He had been twice to India, and made two fortunes. It was said that he lost the first on his way home, transferred himself from one ship to another without landing, went back, and made the second. His life was a continual alternation between poverty and wealth ; and he used to say, the greatest pleasure in life is winning at cards — the next greatest, losing.

For several years deep play went on at all these clubs, — fluctuating both as to locality and amount, — till by degrees it began to flag. It had got to a low ebb when Mr. Crockford came to London, and laid the foundation of the most colossal fortune that was ever made by play. He began by taking Watier's old club-house, in partnership with a man named Taylor. They set up a hazard-bank, and won a great deal of money, but quarrelled, and separated at the end of the first year. Taylor continued where he was, had a bad year, and broke. Crockford removed to St. James' Street, had a good year, and instantly set about building the magnificent club-house which bears his name. It rose like a creation of Aladdin's lamp ; and the genii themselves could hardly have surpassed the beauty of the internal decorations, or furnished a more accomplished *maître d'hôtel* than Ude. To make the company as select as possible, the establishment was regularly organized as a club, and the election of members vested in a committee. " Crockford's " became the rage, and the votaries of fashion, whether they liked play or not, hastened to enroll themselves. The Duke of Wellington was an original member, though (unlike Blucher, who repeatedly lost everything he had at play) the great captain was never known to play deep at any game but war or politics. Card-tables were regularly placed, and whist was played occasionally ; but the aim, end, and final cause of the whole was the hazard-bank, at which the proprietor took his nightly stand, prepared for all comers. There was a recognized limit, at which (after losing a certain sum) he might declare the bank broke for the night ; but he knew his business too well to stop.

The speculation, it is hardly necessary to add, was eminently successful. During several years, everything that anybody had to lose and cared to risk, was swallowed up. *Le Wellington des Joueurs* lost twenty-three thousand pounds at a sitting, beginning at twelve at night, and ending at seven the following evening. He and three other noblemen could not have lost less, sooner or later, than a hundred thousand pounds apiece. Others lost in proportion (or out of proportion) to their means ; but we leave it to less occupied moralists and better calculators to say how many ruined families went to make Mr. Crockford a *millionnaire* — for a *millionnaire* he was and is, in the English sense of the term, after making the largest possible allowance for bad debts. A vast sum, perhaps half a million, is due to him ; but as he won all his debtors were able to raise, and easy credit was the most fatal of his lures,* we cannot make up our minds to con-

---

* Brookes was equally accommodating : —

"From liberal Brookes, whose speculative skill
Is hasty credit and a distant bill :
Who, nursed in clubs, disdains a vulgar trade,
Exults to trust and blushes to be paid."

Verses, *From the Hon. Charles James Fox, partridge-shooting, to the Hon. John Townshend, cruising ;* by Tickell, whom Mr. Jesse praises for his *poem* of "Anticipation."

dole with him on that amount, frightful though it be. He retired, three or four years ago, much as an Indian chief retires from a hunting-country when there is not game enough left for his tribe; and the club is said to be now tottering to its fall.

Some good was certainly produced by it. In the first place, private gambling (between gentleman and gentleman) with its degrading incidents, illustrated by the foregoing letters, is at an end. In the second place, this very circumstance brings the worst part of the practice within the reach of the law. Public gambling, which only exists by and through what are popularly termed "hells," may be easily suppressed. There are at present more than twenty of these establishments in Pall Mall, Piccadilly, and St. James', called into existence by Mr. Crockford's success. Why does not the police interfere? If the police cannot, why does not the legislature? Not an hour should be lost in putting down this monstrous evil. We claim to be superior in morals and public order to the French; yet all the public gaming-tables of Paris were suppressed four or five years ago, and (what is more) suppressed without difficulty, the moment the police set to work in good earnest.*

Space permitting, we should be glad to make a few extracts from the numerous letters, in this collection, of the Rev. Dr. Warner, who has described many objects of interest, and hit off some curious traits of character, in a gay, vivacious style, which would be

---

* Since this was written, a few of the most notorious London establishments have been suppressed.

much more pleasing had there been less effort to make it so. He apparently took for his model the well-known letter of Madame de Sévigné, announcing the marriage of " la grande Mademoiselle," in which the main object seems to be to keep beating about the bush as long as possible. But the reverend doctor is inexcusably coarse and loose, and has often tempted us to exclaim, like Dr. Johnson when some clergy. men were endeavoring to· show off in his company by assuming the lax jollity of men of the world, " This merriment of parsons is mighty offensive." Independently of the indecorous tone, there are several expressions and allusions in Dr. Warner's letters, and two or three in Gilly Williams's and Lord Carlisle's, which offend, not merely against good taste, but common decency; and Mr. Jesse has exposed himself to much censure by printing them.

We are also obliged to omit many passages from the letters of Lord Holland, Miss Townshend, Mr. Storer, the Dowager Lady Carlisle, and Lady Sarah Bunbury, which we had marked for insertion; as well as an entire letter of Horace Walpole's (vol. i., p. 4), which maintains his superiority as a writer of epistolary compositions.

In conclusion, we are happy to say that the comparison, suggested by these volumes, between the manners and morals of the last century and our own, is highly satisfactory. Intellectual tastes have nearly superseded the necessity, formerly felt by the unoccupied classes, of resorting to coarse indulgences or strong excitements; and respect for public opinion induces those among them who continue unreclaimed, to conceal their transgressions from the world. It is also worthy of note, that the few persons of noble birth or high connection who have recently attracted attention by their laxity, are professed votaries of (what they call) pleasure, and are no longer encouraged by the example, or elevated by the companionship, of men distinguished in the senate, the cabinet, or the court. No prime minister escorts a woman of the town through the crush-room of the opera; no first lord of the admiralty permits his mistress to do the honors of his house, or weeps over her in the columns of the Morning Post; no lord of the bedchamber starts for Newmarket with a *danseuse* in his carriage, and her whole family in his train; our parliamentary leaders do not dissipate their best energies at the gaming-table; our privy councillors do not attend cock-fights; and among the many calumnies levelled at our public men, not one has been accused (as General Burgoyne was by Junius) of lying in wait for inexperienced lads to plunder at play.

Though the signs are less marked, the improvement in the female sex is not less certain; for it may safely be taken for granted, that the practice of gambling was fraught with the worst consequences to the finest feelings and best qualities of the sex. The chief danger is hinted at in The Provoked Husband.

"*Lord Townley.* 'Tis not your ill hours that always disturb me, but as often the ill company that occasion those hours.

"*Lady Townley.* Sure I don't understand you now, my lord. What ill company do I keep?"

"*Lord Townley*. Why, at best, women that lose their money, and men that win it; *or perhaps men that are voluntarily bubbles at one game, in hopes a lady will give them fair play at another.*"

The facts confirm the theory. Walpole's Letters, and the volumes before us, teem with allusions to proved or understood cases of matrimonial infidelity; and the manner in which notorious irregularities were brazened out, shows that the offenders did not always encounter the universal reprobation of society. Miss Berry, speaking, in her very instructive book, of the Duchess of Norfolk's divorce in 1697, observes, —

"Many circumstances of this lady's case show how much the ordinary habits of life were overstepped, and what precautions were thought necessary previous to such misconduct. A house taken at Lambeth, then a small and little frequented village, whose nearest communication with Westminster was by a horse-ferry, — this house, hired and resorted to under feigned names, and occupied by foreign servants, who, it was supposed, could not identify the lady, are not measures taken in a country where the crime they were meant to conceal was frequent." — *England and France*, vol. i., p. 297.

This test would be fatal to the female nobility of England half a century later; for many of them took no pains whatever to conceal their immoralities. We are obliged, from obvious motives, to refrain from mentioning some conclusive instances; but it is notorious that Lady Vane gave Smollett the materials for the Memoirs of a Lady of Quality (herself) published in Peregrine Pickle; that Lady Townshend sat (perhaps not so willingly) for the portrait of Lady Bellaston in Tom Jones; and we can hardly do wrong in copying a note, which Lord Dover has annexed to

29

the name of a Miss Edwards, in his edition of Walpole's Letters: "Miss Edwards, an unmarried lady of great fortune, who (1742) openly kept Lord A. Hamilton."

Gilly Williams mentions a caprice of a more respectable kind, which was far from uncommon at the period: —

"Lord Rockingham's youngest sister has just married her footman, John Sturgeon. Surely he is the very first of that name that ever had a Right Honorable annexed to it. I made the Duchess of Bedford laugh yesterday with the story of Lord March's handsome Jack wanting to go to live with Lady Harrington."

.   .   .   .

"The girls talk of nothing but the match between Lord Rockingham's sister and her footman. Never so much —— and discretion met together; for she has entailed her fortune with as much circumspection as Lord Mansfield could have done, and has not left one cranny of the law unstopped. They used to pass many hours together, which she called teaching John the mathematics."

Unless John was a very unapt scholar, he must soon have become as worthy an object of a lady's favor, so far as mental culture was concerned, as Sir John Germaine; who, after occasioning the Duchess of Norfolk's divorce, married a noble heiress, Lady Betty Berkeley, and lived till the middle of the last century. Miss Berry tells us that he actually left a legacy to Sir Matthew Decker, under a belief that he was the author of the Gospel of St. Matthew!

It has been thought by some that we have lost in grace what we have gained in decency, and that society is no longer so gay, easy, accomplished, or even lettered, as it used to be. Miss Berry, though she commends the fashion which encouraged occupation and mental acquirements, cannot refrain from a sly sarcasm at the "new prodigies, who were already great orators at Eton, and profound politicians before they left Christ-church or Trinity," — the gentlemen to whom " it was easier to be foolishly bustling than seriously employed;" and Mr. Moore maintains a yet more startling doctrine : " Without any disparagement of the many and useful talents which are at present nowhere more conspicuous than in the upper ranks of society, it may be owned, that for wit, social powers, and literary accomplishments, the political men of the period under consideration (1780) formed such an assemblage as it would be flattery to say that our times can parallel. The natural tendency of the French revolution was to produce in the higher classes of England an increased reserve of manner, and of course a proportionate restraint on all within their circle, which have been fatal to conviviality and humor, and not very propitious to wit — subduing both manners and conversation to a sort of polished level, to rise above which is often thought almost as vulgar as to sink below it. Of the greater ease of manners that existed some forty or fifty years ago, one trifling, but not the less significant, indication was the habit, then prevalent among men of high station, of calling each other by such familiar names as Dick, Jack, Tom, &c., &c. — a mode of address that brings with it in its very sound the notion of conviviality and playfulness, and, however unrefined, implies at least that ease and *sea-room* in which wit spreads its canvas most fearlessly." — *Life of Sheridan.*

We differ, with unfeigned reluctance, from Mr.

Moore ; but he is surely mistaken in supposing that the higher classes of England have contracted an increased reserve of manner in consequence of the French revolution, or shown more anxiety on that account to intrench themselves within the privileges of their rank. On the contrary, the tendency of that event, and our own reform bill, was and is to make them more anxious to identify themselves in feeling and interest with the people. If they have ceased to be familiar, it is because they have ceased to be exclusive ; restraint is necessary, because society is mixed ; and there is no reason why men of rank should change their mode of address to men of rank, except that they live less with one another, and more with the world at large. The very peculiarity in question was observed by Mrs. Trollope in the most exclusive coterie in Europe, the *crème de la crème* of Vienna. "All the ladies address each other by their Christian names, and you may pass evening after evening, surrounded by princesses and countesses, without ever hearing any other appellations than Therese, Flora, Laura, or Pepè."

This may be very agreeable for the privileged few, and we readily admit that intimacy is a great promoter of humor. Few of Selwyn's bon-mots could have been hazarded at a mixed party. But we are as far as ever from admitting Mr. Moore's proposition in the main. It is not flattery, but sober truth, to say that our public men have contracted no reserve beyond that which the voluntary enlargement of their circle has entailed upon them. It would be difficult to contend that they have impaired their social powers by mixing with eminent authors, men of science, and artists, whatever influence these may have exercised upon their wit or humor; and, even as regards wit or humor, it would simply be necessary to run over a few known names to vindicate our equality in both. Modern conversation is rich with the product of every soil, the spoils of every clime; and it would be a grave error to suppose that those who contribute most to it seldom meet in intimacy. They meet very often, but they belong to several coequal and intersecting circles, instead of keeping to one, and making that the sole object of interest.

There are signs, moreover, that he who runs may read. It is clear that they talk politics as much as we do; perhaps more, since their eagerness was so manifest to a French woman. " Madame de Bouf-flers (writes Williams in 1763) is out of patience with our politics, and our ridiculous abuse of every person who either governs or is likely to govern us." This was a serious drawback, but not the most serious. Selwyn's principal correspondents were not dandies and fine ladies, but the most cultivated men and women of the highest class; including several on whom Mr. Moore would rely, if we came to a di-vision on the question. The masterpieces of English light literature, and several other standard works, ap-peared during their correspondence. Yet neither Field-ing, Richardson, Smollett, Gray, Goldsmith, Hume, Robertson, Johnson, Gibbon, or even Burke, elicits a remark. There is one allusion to Garrick (by Rigby); one to Reynolds (by Lord Carlisle); and one to Gainsborough (by Gilly Williams), as " the painter

by whom, if you remember, we once saw the caricature of old Winchelsea."

There was no want of classical acquirement, it is
true ; many wrote graceful verses ; and Fox and Walpole had a taste for contemporary literature ; but Fox
kept it to himself for lack of sympathy, and Walpole
was ashamed of it.   By literature, however, must be
understood merely the Belles Lettres ; for Fox confessed, late in life, that he had never been able to get
through the Wealth of Nations.

Familiarity, again, is a great charm, but the habits
which are the conditions of its existence, beget monotony.   In Charles the Second's reign, when it was
the fashion to go to sea and fight the Dutch, instead
of taking lodgings at Melton or attending Battues,
Sheffield, Duke of Buckingham, tells us in his Memoirs, that a party of gay, witty, lettered profligates
were becalmed on board the Duke of York's ship,
and got so tired of one another, that the first care each
took on landing was to ascertain where the rest were
going, in order to get away from them.   We are not
aware whether the *habitués* of White's or Brookes',
seventy or eighty years ago, were ever brought to
such a pass ; but we know (and there is no getting
over this) that they habitually resorted to the gaming-
table, —

> "Unknown to such, when sensual pleasures cloy,
> To fill the languid pause with finer joy."

With rare exceptions, the most accomplished persons, about to risk more than they can afford to lose,
will be found both ill disposed and ill qualified for
the easy, equable enjoyment of conversation ; though

(with the aid of wine) they may have their occasional bursts of sparkling pleasantry.

To sum up all — there is a halo floating over certain periods; dazzling associations may cluster round a name: " 'tis distance lends enchantment to the view;" and living witnesses, who have known both generations, will always, by a law of our nature, award the palm to the companions of their youth. But it will require stronger arguments than have been adduced yet to convince us that the social powers of any class have fallen off, whilst morality, taste, knowledge, general freedom of intercourse, and liberality of opinion, have been advancing; or that the mind necessarily loses any portion of its playfulness, when it quits the enervating atmosphere of idleness and dissipation for the purer air and brighter skies of art, literature, and philosophy.